This Book Belongs to

Nicola Wood

Age 9

18 Blofield Road

Brundall NORWICH

NORFOLK NR135NN

The Catholic Children's Bible

Passages selected by
David L. Edwards
from
Good News Bible in Today's English Version

Illustrated by Guido Bertello

Collins
London and Glasgow

First published in this edition 1979
Second Impression 1981
Old Testament section of this volume
first published as Good News Bible 1976
New Testament section of this volume originally
published as "Today's Story of Jesus" 1976 from
Good News for Modern Man in Fontana Books 1968
Published by William Collins Sons and Company Limited Glasgow and London
© Text 1966, 1971, 1976 American Bible Society, New York
© Illustrations 1976 and 1978 William Collins Sons and Company Limited
Nihil obstat: R. J. Cuming, D.D., *censor deputatus*
Imprimatur: David Norris, V.G.
Westminster, 5th March, 1979
The Good News Bible is published in the United Kingdom
and Commonwealth by Collins
Phototypeset in Great Britain by
Filmtype Services Limited, Scarborough
Printed in Great Britain

ISBN 0 00 107185 8

Preface

When Jesus was a boy at Nazareth, he went to the school attached to the synagogue. We know this because it was a rule that every Jewish community over a certain size should have a school. We also know what text-books were used by Jesus and his fellow pupils. It was the rule that every young Jew should be taught these books thoroughly — and the gospels show us that Jesus of Nazareth, when he grew up to be a great teacher, very often quoted from these books. As he hung on the cross dying, he was still quoting from them. You hold these books in your hands now.

Or at least, you hold a selection of the most important passages in them. For these books are many, and together they make up quite a big library. Selections have been made from them ever since they were first written. And one reason why it is necessary to make a selection for young Christian readers today is that other books are written as a result of what Jesus himself did. These new books about Jesus and his followers are called The New Agreement or The New Testament. They were added to The Old Testament. Together they make up the Christians' Bible (which means "Books") or the Holy Scriptures (which means "Writing"). A selection has to be made from these new books, too, if you are to have a Children's Bible which you will find easy to read and to remember.

This Bible tells how God showed himself. God is never described completely, because he is never seen completely. Always mystery surrounds him. But you can tell that he is there. At the dawn of history Abraham, Isaac, Jacob and Joseph feel him to be there. Moses and the Israelites follow God's guidance out of slavery in Egypt, into the Promised Land — Canaan or Palestine (called Israel today). In this land great leaders are given to them. They follow kings such as David, and prophets (or spokesmen for God) such as Elijah. But always their real leader is God. They find this out in war and peace. They suffer great defeats, but they still hear God's great promises. And eventually the promises come true when Jesus is born. In what Jesus teaches, God speaks in a way people can understand. In what Jesus does, God expresses himself through a man we can know and love. In what Jesus is, God's light shines in our darkness. And the Christian Church goes boldly into the world with this good news.

There is no single book which tells the whole history in preparation for the coming of Jesus. Indeed, there is no one book which gives all the message of Jesus and which includes all the history of the Church. The Old Testament as we have it was written at various times over a thousand years, and the New Testament includes four "gospels" or accounts of the work of Jesus plus many letters by Paul and other Christians. Many people guided by God and grateful for what they saw of God, made the complete Bible.

But what I have attempted to do here, by collecting many stories in this way, is to help you understand the one essential story which runs through the whole long drama. The story begins with Abraham looking forward. (The stories about the creation of the world, and about Adam and Eve, and about Noah and the flood, were told by the Jews when they had already learned much and suffered much; so you will not find them at the beginning of this book.) The story which gives a unity to the Bible has Jesus at its centre — and it ends with Paul looking back. It is the greatest story ever told, and it is the most important story you will ever hear. It is the story of your God.

I do not want to try to tell the stories of the Bible again in my own words. Why should I try, when they are already told so well in the Bible — sometimes in such a vivid way that you feel you are there to watch the action; sometimes in a way which shows that many people have already told and retold them with love. And I do not want to explain everything in these stories. Why should I attempt to make all the ideas seem simple, or all the words easy? I give a few hints in my brief comments which link the bits of the Bible, but I am sure that we all grew by wrestling with the difficulties in the Bible. I am also sure that no one understands the Bible completely.

The only merit in modern writers' attempts to retell the biblical stories has been, I think, that the modern writers have used modern language. But what we really need is a modern Bible! Fortunately the Good News Bible, published in 1976, lives up to its claim to be "Today's English Version" and that is the translation of the ancient Scriptures that I have used here. I am very grateful for the privilege of being allowed to use such an excellent translation of the original Hebrew and Greek language, and I am sure that you, too, will admire and enjoy it. If you want to know what I think about some of the historical questions, my books *A Key to the Old Testament* and *Jesus for Modern Man* may interest you.

I am also very grateful to the Italian artist, Guido Bertello, whose illustrations show that he, too, loves the Bible.

DAVID L. EDWARDS

Contents

The Old Testament

1 The Dawn of History 17
The Father of Nations; *God's Call to Abraham; Abraham Asks God to Forgive; Abraham and His Son Isaac; Finding a Wife for Isaac;* **The Rival Brothers;** *Esau and Jacob; Jacob Cheats Esau Again; Jacob's Dream of the Stairway to God; Jacob Wrestles with God;* **The Israelites Go to Egypt;** *Joseph Is Taken to Egypt; His Whole Family Joins Joseph; The Israelites Become Slaves;*

2 The Great Escape 35
The Great Leader; *The Birth of Moses; God Calls Moses; Moses and Aaron before the King of Egypt;* **The Israelites leave Egypt;** *Passover; Exodus; Crossing the Sea; The Song of Moses;* **The Long Journey;** *Food in the Desert; Water in the Desert; At Mount Sinai; Moses on Mount Sinai; The Holy God; The Ten Commandments; Love Your Neighbour; The Gold Bull; Moses Complains to God; The Death of Moses; The Story of the Far-seeing Donkey; Balaam and his Donkey; Balaam's Blessing on Israel;*

3 Men of Courage 57
The Promised Land; *Joshua Is Told to be Confident; The Fall of Jericho; Joshua Speaks to the People; Gideon's Three Hundred;* **Samson the Strong Man;** *Samson and Delilah; The Death of Samson;* **A Great Prophet;** *The Birth of Samuel; The Lord Appears to Samuel; Saul Is Acclaimed as King;* **The Young David;** *Ruth Comes to Bethlehem; Ruth Works in the Field of Boaz; Boaz Marries Ruth; David Is Anointed King; Goliath Challenges the Israelites; David in Saul's Camp; David Defeats Goliath; David Is Presented to Saul; Saul Becomes Jealous of David;* **David at the Court of King Saul;** *The Friendship of David and Jonathan; Jonathan Warns David to Escape; The Death of Saul and His Sons; David's Lament for Saul and Jonathan;*

4 War and Peace 85
David the King; *David's Sin; David Is Told of His Sin; David's Son Absalom Rebels; The Death of Absalom; David Is Told of Absalom's Death;* **The Wise King;** *Solomon Is Anointed King; Solomon Prays for Wisdom; Peace under Solomon; The Visit of the Queen of Sheba; Solomon Builds the Temple;* **Songs of Love for the Temple;** *In Praise of Jerusalem; Longing for God's House;* **Good House Keeping in Ancient Times;** **They Spoke for God;** *Elijah and the Prophets of Baal; Elijah on Mount Sinai; The Call of Elisha; Ahab Is Told of His Sin; Elijah Is Taken Up to Heaven; Naaman Is Cured; A Prophet Is Called by God;* **The Prophets Speak;** *God the Judge; What God Wants; God the Father;* **Peace for Jerusalem;** *God Calls Isaiah; The Assyrians Come; Isaiah's Message to the King; The Peaceful Kingdom; The Nations Learn Peace; Peace at the End of War;* **The Law of God;** *The Book of the Law Is Found; Josiah Does Away with Pagan Worship; The Great Commandment;* **The Fall of the City;** *God Calls Jeremiah to be a Prophet; God's New Agreement; Jerusalem Is Captured; A Song of the Exiles;*

5 The Great Promise 125
A Prophet in Exile; *Ezekiel Sees the Glory of God; God Calls Ezekiel to Be a Prophet; The Good Shepherd; The Valley of Dry Bones;* **God Is with His People;** *Words of Hope; God's Suffering Servant;* **Daniel Sees the Triumph of God;** *Victory Is Coming; In the Furnace; The Writing on the Wall; Daniel Explains the Writing; Daniel in the Den of Lions;* **Jonah Is Sent to the Great City;** *Jonah Disobeys the Lord; Jonah Obeys the Lord; Jonah's Anger and God's Mercy;* **Three Songs about God;** *God our Hope; God our Shepherd; God our Refuge; Your King Is Coming;*

6 This Is God's World 145
God's Good Creation; *In the Beginning; In Praise of the Creator;* **God Created Them All;** *Underneath the Earth; Horses; Crocodiles;* **Mankind Goes Wrong;** *Adam and Eve; The Disobedience of Mankind; The First Hatred; The First Murder; The Great Tower of Pride;* **Noah and the Flood;** *God Calls Noah; The Flood Ends with God's Promise; God's Promise to Everyone; The Great Promise Comes True.*

The New Testament

1 When Jesus Was Young 169
The First Christmas: *The Birth of Jesus Announced; Mary Visits Elizabeth; Mary's Song of Praise; The Birth of Jesus; The Shepherds and the Angels; Jesus is Named;* **Jesus is Presented in the Temple; The Wise Men in Matthew's Gospel;** *Visitors from the East; The Escape to Egypt; The Killing of the Children; The Return from Egypt;* **The Boy Jesus in the Temple; John the Baptist, God's Messenger;** *The Birth of John the Baptist; Zechariah's Prophecy; The Preaching of John the Baptist;*

2 How Jesus Lived 183
Jesus is Baptized and Tempted; *The Baptism of Jesus; The Temptation of Jesus;* **Jesus Begins his Work;** *Jesus Calls Four Fishermen; A Man with an Evil Spirit; Jesus Heals Many People; Jesus Preaches in Galilee; Jesus Makes a Leper Clean; Jesus Heals a Paralysed Man; Jesus calls Matthew; The Question about Fasting; Jesus Has Pity for the People;* **The New Family Chosen by Jesus;** *A Crowd by the Lake; Jesus Chooses the Twelve Apostles; Jesus' Mother and Brothers; Jesus Rejected at Nazareth;* **The Good News is Spread by Word and Deed;** *Jesus Heals a Roman Officer's Servant; Jesus Raises a Widow's Son; The Messengers from John the Baptist; J sus at the Home of Simon the Pharisee; Women who Accompanied Jesus; Jesus Heals a Boy with an Evil Spirit; Jesus Calms a Storm; Jesus Heals a Man with Evil Spirits; Jairus' Daughter and the Woman who Touched Jesus' Cloak; Jesus Sends the Apostles to Heal and Preach; Jesus Feeds the Five Thousand; Jesus Walks on the Water; Jesus Heals the Sick in Gennesaret; A Woman's Faith; Jesus Heals a Deaf and Dumb Man;*

3 Stories Told by Jesus 207
Stories about God's Love: The Lost Sheep; *The Parable of the Lost Coin; The Parable of the Lost Son; The Parable of the Workers in the Vineyard; The Parable of the Hidden Treasure; The Parable of the Pearl; The Parable of the Net; The Parable of the Storage Room;* **Stories about God's Patience: The Growing Seed;** *The Parable of the Sower; The Parable of the Weeds; The Parable of the Mustard Seed; The Parable of the Yeast; The Lesson of the Fig Tree; The Parable of the Unfruitful Fig Tree; The Parable of the Great Feast;* **Stories about our Danger: the Ten Girls;** *The Parable of the Three Servants; Watchful Servants; The Faithful or the Unfaithful Servant; The Parable of the Rich Fool; The Rich Man and Lazarus; The Parable of the Tenants in the Vineyard; The Parable of the Unforgiving Servant; The Parable of the Two Sons; The Return of the Evil Spirit;* **Stories about our Duty;** *The Parable of the Widow and the Judge; The Parable of the Friend at Midnight; The Parable of the Pharisee and the Tax Collector; The Parable of the Good Samaritan; The Final Judgment;*

4 Jesus Teaches 223
The Sermon on the Mount; *True Happiness; Salt and Light; Teaching about the Law; Teaching about Anger; Teaching about Adultery; Teaching about Divorce; Teaching about Vows; Teaching*

about Revenge; Love for Enemies; Teaching about Charity; Teaching about Prayer; Teaching about Forgiveness; Teaching about Fasting; Riches in Heaven; The Light of the Body; God and Possessions; Judging Others; Ask, Seek, Knock; The Narrow Gate; A Tree and its Fruit; I Never Knew You; The Two House Builders; The Authority of Jesus; **Some Other Teaching Given by Jesus;** Whom to Fear; Who Belongs; Not Peace, but a Sword; Come to Me and Rest: The Question about Paying Taxes; The Question about Rising from Death; The Great Commandment; **Jesus Warns against Hypocrisy;** Jesus Warns against the Teachers of the Law and the Pharisees; Jesus Condemns their Hypocrisy; The Things that Make a Person Unclean;

5 The Road to the Cross 237

John the Baptist is Killed; **Jesus Sees that he Must Die;** Peter's Declaration about Jesus; Jesus Speaks about his Suffering and Death; The Transfiguration; **Jesus Teaches Humility;** Who Is the Greatest?; Who Is not against Us Is for Us; Jesus Blesses Little Children; The Rich Man; A Samaritan Village Refuses to Receive Jesus; The Would-be Followers of Jesus; Jesus Sends out the Seventy-two; The Unbelieving Towns; The Return of the Seventy-two; Jesus Heals a Sick Man; Humility and Hospitality; Jesus Visits Martha and Mary; The Request of James and John; Jesus' Love for Jerusalem; **Jesus Enters Jerusalem;** Jesus Heals a Blind Beggar; Jesus and Zacchaeus; The Triumphant Entry into Jerusalem; Jesus Goes to the Temple; The Question about Jesus' Authority; The Widow's Offering; Jesus Speaks of the Destruction of the Temple; Troubles and Persecutions;

6 How Jesus Died 257

The Plot against Jesus; Jesus anointed at Bethany; Judas Agrees to Betray Jesus; Jesus Eats the Passover Meal with his Disciples; The Lord's Supper; Jesus Predicts Peter's Denial; Jesus Prays in Gethsemane; The Arrest of Jesus; Jesus before the Council; Peter Denies Jesus; Jesus before Pilate; Jesus Sentenced to Death; The Soldiers Make Fun of Jesus; Jesus Nailed to the Cross; The Death of Jesus; The Burial of Jesus;

7 The Victory of Jesus 271

The Empty Tomb; Jesus Appears to Mary Magdalene; The Walk to Emmaus; Jesus Appears to his Disciples; Jesus and Thomas; Jesus appears to Seven Disciples; Jesus and Peter; Jesus and the Other Disciple; Jesus Appears to his Disciples; **Stephen and Paul see Jesus in his Glory;** The Arrest of Stephen; The Stoning of Stephen; Saul Persecutes the Church; The Conversion of Saul; Saul Preaches in Damascus; **The Victory through our Lord Jesus Christ;** Paul, previously Saul the enemy of the Church, writes to the Corinthians; The Resurrection of Christ; The Resurrection Body; **The New Life is Stronger than Death;** Paul Writes to the Romans; Life in the Spirit; The Future Glory; God's Love in Christ Jesus; **Jesus is Lord;** John the Divine writes to Christians in Asia from the prison on the *island of Patmos; A Vision of Christ; The New Heaven and the New Earth; The New Jerusalem;* **Two Early Christian Hymns**; *quoted by Paul to the Philippians; and to Timothy;*

8 We Saw his Glory 290

The Light Shines; *The Word of Life; The Wedding at Cana; Jesus and Nicodemus; Jesus and the Woman of Samaria; Jesus Heals an Official's Son; Jesus the Bread of Life; Jesus Forgives a Woman in Jerusalem; Jesus the Resurrection and the Life; Jesus the Light of the World; Jesus Heals a Man Born Blind; The Parable of the Sheepfold; Jesus the Good Shepherd; Jesus Washes his Disciples' Feet;* **Jesus Speaks to his Friends at the Last Supper**; *Jesus the Way to the Father; The Promise of the Holy Spirit; Jesus the Real Vine; The World's Hatred; The Work of the Holy Spirit; Sadness and Gladness; Victory over the World; Jesus Prays for his Friends before his Death; Conclusion;*

9 How to Follow Jesus 309

Why the Apostles Acted; *Luke writes; Jesus Is Taken up to Heaven; The Coming of the Holy Spirit; Peter's Message; Life among the Believers;* **John Writes about God's Love**; *Children of God; God Is Love;* **A Prayer in the Letter to the Ephesians; Unity and Love: Paul Writes to the Corinthians**; *One Body with Many Parts; Love; Paul's Prayer;* **The Christian Life in Paul's Letters**; *Father, my Father!; The Spirit and Human Nature; The Power of the Gospel; The Whole Armour of God; To Live Is Christ; Christian Joy and Peace; Running towards the Goal; Paul's Farewell.*

The Old Testament

1
The Dawn of History

As the history of Ancient Israel dawns, the men and women who move about are shadowy. The stories told about them were already old three thousand years ago, but they are not so old as the people themselves — Abraham, Isaac, Jacob, Joseph and their families. The first story tells how Abraham left the city of Haran by the great River Euphrates and moved with all his family to the land of Canaan, or Palestine, which God promised to give to him and to his descendants. He put his trust in God.

The Father of Nations

God's Call to Abraham

The Lord said to Abraham, "Leave your native land, your relatives, and your father's home, and go to a country that I am going to show you. I will give you many descendants, and they will become a great nation. I will bless you and make your name famous, so that you will be a blessing.
 I will bless those who bless you,
 But I will curse those who curse you.
 And through you I will bless all the nations."
When Abraham was seventy-five years old, he started out from Haran, as the Lord had told him to do. Abraham took his wife Sarai, his nephew Lot, and all the wealth and all the slaves they had acquired in Haran, and they started out for the land of Canaan.
When they arrived in Canaan, Abraham travelled through the land until he came to the sacred tree of Moreh, the holy place at Shechem. (At that time the Canaanites were still living in the land.) The Lord appeared to Abraham and said to him, "This is the country that I am going to give to your descendants." Then Abraham built an altar there to the Lord, who had appeared to him.
Abraham put his trust in the Lord, and because of this the Lord was pleased with him and accepted him.

Abraham Asks God to Forgive

A delightful story shows Abraham praying to God for two wicked cities, and suggesting that these cities may not be completely wicked. But the story ends sadly.

The Lord said to Abraham, "There are terrible accusations against Sodom and Gomorrah, and their sin is very great. I must go down to find out whether or not the accusations which I have heard are true."

Abraham approached the Lord and asked, "Are you really going to destroy the innocent with the guilty? If there are fifty innocent people in the city, will you destroy the whole city? Won't you spare it in order to save the fifty? Surely you won't kill the innocent with the guilty. That's impossible! You can't do that. If you did, the innocent would be punished along with the guilty. That is impossible. The judge of all the earth has to act justly."

The Lord answered, "If I find fifty innocent people in Sodom, I will spare the whole city for their sake."

Abraham spoke again: "Please forgive my boldness in continuing to speak to you, Lord. I am only a man and have no right to say anything. But perhaps there will be only forty-five innocent people instead of fifty. Will you destroy the whole city because there are five too few?"

Abraham is even willing to kill his son (text on page 20)

The Lord answered, "I will not destroy the city if I find forty-five innocent people."

Abraham spoke again: "Perhaps there will be only forty."

He replied, "I will not destroy it if there are forty."

Abraham said, "Please don't be angry, Lord, but I must speak again. What if there are only thirty?"

He said, "I will not do it if I find thirty."

Abraham said, "Please forgive my boldness in continuing to speak to you, Lord. Suppose that only twenty are found?"

He said, "I will not destroy the city if I find twenty."

Abraham said, "Please don't be angry, Lord, and I will speak just once more. What if only ten are found?"

He said, "I will not destroy it if there are ten." After he had finished speaking with Abraham, the Lord went away, and Abraham returned home.

Early the next morning Abraham hurried to the place where he had stood in the presence of the Lord. He looked down at Sodom and Gomorrah and the whole valley and saw smoke rising from the land, like smoke from a huge furnace.

Abraham and His Son Isaac

Abraham is even willing to kill his only son, Isaac, when he believes that this is God's will. But God stops him.

Some time later God tested Abraham; he called to him, "Abraham!" And Abraham answered, "Yes, here I am!"

"Take your son," God said, "your only son, Isaac, whom you love so much, and go to the land of Moriah. There on a mountain that I will show you, offer him as a sacrifice to me."

Early the next morning Abraham cut some wood for the sacrifice, loaded his donkey, and took Isaac and two servants with him. They started out for the place that God had told him about. On the third day Abraham saw the place in the distance. Then he said to the servants, "Stay here with the donkey. The boy and I will go over there and worship, and then we will come back to you."

Abraham made Isaac carry the wood for the sacrifice, and he himself carried a knife and live coals for starting the fire. As they walked along together, Isaac said, "Father!"

He answered, "Yes, my son?"

Isaac asked, "I see that you have the coals and the wood, but where is the lamb for the sacrifice?"

Abraham answered, "God himself will provide one." And the two of them walked on together.

When they came to the place which God had told him about, Abraham built an altar and arranged the wood on it. He bound his son and placed him on the altar, on top of the wood. Then he picked up the knife to kill him. But the angel of the Lord called to him from heaven, "Abraham, Abraham!"

He answered, "Yes, here I am."

"Don't hurt the boy or do anything to him," he said. "Now I know that you fear God, because you have not kept back your only son from him."

Abraham looked round and saw a ram caught in a bush by its horns. He went and got it and offered it as a burnt-offering instead of his son. Abraham named that place "The Lord Provides." And even today people say, "On the Lord's mountain he provides."

The angel of the Lord called to Abraham from heaven a second time, "I make a vow by my own name – the Lord is speaking – that I will richly bless you. Because you did this and did not keep back your only son from me, I promise that I will give you as many descendants as there are stars in the sky or grains of sand along the seashore. Your descendants will conquer their enemies. All the nations will ask me to bless them as I have blessed your descendants – all because you obeyed my command."

Finding a Wife for Isaac

Abraham's son Isaac is now old enough to marry. So a servant is sent back to the place where Abraham had first lived, to find a wife for Isaac. Abraham was now very old, and the Lord had blessed him in everything he did. He said to his oldest servant, who was in charge of all that he had, "I want you to make a vow in the name of the Lord, the God of heaven and earth, that you will not choose a wife for my son from the people here in Canaan. You must go back to the country where I was born and get a wife for my son Isaac from among my relatives."

But the servant asked, "What if the girl will not leave home to come with me to this land? Shall I send your son back to the land you came from?"

Abraham answered, "Take care that you don't send my son back there! The Lord, the God of heaven, brought me from the home of my father and from the land of my relatives, and he solemnly promised me that he would give this land to my descendants. He will send his angel before you, so that you can get a wife there for my son. If the girl is not willing to come with you, you will be free from this promise. But you must not under any circumstances take my son back there." So the servant put his hand between the thighs of Abraham, his master, and made a vow to do what Abraham had asked.

The servant, who was in charge of Abraham's property, took ten of his master's camels and went to the city where Abraham's brother Nahor had lived in northern Mesopotamia. When he arrived, he made the camels kneel down at the well outside the city. It was late afternoon, the time when women came out to get water. He prayed, "Lord, God of my master Abraham, give me success today and keep your promise to my master. Here I am at the well where the young women of the city will be coming to get water. I will say to one of them, 'Please, lower your jar and let me have a drink.' If she says, 'Drink, and I will also bring water for your camels,' may she be the one that you have chosen for your servant Isaac. If this happens, I will know that you have kept your promise to my master."

Before he had finished praying, Rebecca arrived with a water-jar on her shoulder. She was the daughter of Bethuel, who was the son of Abraham's brother Nahor and his wife Milcah. She was a very beautiful young girl and still a virgin. She went down to the well, filled her jar, and came back. The servant ran to meet her and said, "Please give me a drink of water from your jar."

She said, "Drink, sir," and quickly lowered her jar from her shoulder and held it while he drank. When he had finished, she said, "I will also bring water for your camels and let them have all they want." She quickly emptied her jar into the animals' drinking-trough and ran to the well to get more water, until she had watered all his camels. The man kept watching her in silence, to see if the Lord had given him success.

When she had finished, the man took an expensive gold ring and put it in her nose and put two large gold bracelets on her arms. He said, "Please tell me who your father is. Is there room in his house for my men and me to spend the night?"

"My father is Bethuel son of Nahor and Milcah," she answered. "There is plenty of straw and fodder at our house, and there is a place for you to stay."

Then the man knelt down and worshipped the Lord. He said, "Praise the Lord, the God of my master Abraham, who has faithfully kept his promise to my master. The Lord has led me straight to my master's relatives."

The girl ran to her mother's house and told the whole story.

The Rival Brothers

Esau and Jacob

> *Isaac marries Rebecca, and they have twins: Esau (or "Hairy") and Jacob (or "Heel"). According to the custom of the time, Esau has the more privileges because he counts as the elder brother. But Esau sells the elder brother's rights to Jacob.*

The time came for Rebecca to give birth, and she had twin sons. The first one was reddish, and his skin was like a hairy robe, so he was named Esau. The second one was born holding on tightly to the heel of Esau, so he was named Jacob. Isaac was sixty years old when they were born.

The boys grew up, and Esau became a skilled hunter, a man who loved the outdoor life, but Jacob was a quiet man who stayed at home. Isaac preferred Esau, because he enjoyed eating the animals Esau killed, but Rebecca preferred Jacob.

One day while Jacob was cooking some bean soup. Esau came in

from hunting. He was hungry and said to Jacob, "I'm starving; give me some of that red stuff." (That is why he was called Edom.)

Jacob answered, "I will give it to you if you give me your rights as the first-born son."

Esau said, "All right! I am about to die; what good will my rights do me then?"

Jacob answered, "First make a vow that you will give me your rights."

Esau made the vow and gave his rights to Jacob. Then Jacob gave him some bread and some of the soup. He ate and drank and then got up and left. That was all Esau cared about his rights as the first-born son.

25

Jacob Cheats Esau Again

This is another story about the rival brothers. Their father Isaac is about to die. Who will get his blessing?

Isaac was now old and had become blind. He sent for his elder son Esau and said to him, "My son!"

"Yes," he answered.

Isaac said, "You see that I am old and may die soon. Take your bow and arrows, go out into the country, and kill an animal for me. Cook me some of that tasty food that I like, and bring it to me. After I have eaten it, I will give you my final blessing before I die."

While Isaac was talking to Esau, Rebecca was listening. So when Esau went out to hunt, she said to Jacob, "I have just heard your father say to Esau, 'Bring me an animal and cook it for me. After I have eaten it, I will give you my blessing in the presence of the Lord before I die.' Now, my son," Rebecca continued, "listen to me and do what I say. Go to the flock and pick out two fat young goats, so that I can cook them and make some of that food your father likes so much. You can take it to him to eat, and he will give you his blessing before he dies."

But Jacob said to his mother, "You know that Esau is a hairy man, but I have smooth skin. Perhaps my father will touch me and find out that I am deceiving him; in this way I will bring a curse on myself instead of a blessing."

His mother answered, "Let any curse against you fall on me, my son; just do as I say, and go and get the goats for me." So he went to get them and brought them to her, and she cooked the kind of food that his father liked. Then she took Esau's best clothes, which she kept in the house, and put them on Jacob. She put the skins of the goats on his arms and on the hairless part of his neck. She handed him the tasty food, together with the bread she had baked.

Then Jacob went to his father and said, "Father!"

"Yes," he answered. "Which of my sons are you?"

Jacob answered, "I am your elder son Esau; I have done as you told me. Please sit up and eat some of the meat that I have brought you, so that you can give me your blessing."

Isaac said, "How did you find it so quickly, my son?"

Jacob answered, "The Lord your God helped me to find it."

Isaac said to Jacob, "Please come closer so that I can touch you. Are you really Esau?" Jacob moved closer to his father, who felt him and said, "Your voice sounds like Jacob's voice, but your arms feel like Esau's arms." He did not recognize Jacob, because his arms were hairy like Esau's. He was about to give him his blessing, but asked again, "Are you really Esau?"

"I am," he answered.

Isaac said, "Bring me some of the meat. After I have eaten it, I will give you my blessing." Jacob brought it to him, and he also brought him some wine to drink. Then his father said to him, "Come closer and kiss me, my son." As he came up to kiss him, Isaac smelt his clothes — so he gave him his blessing. He said, "The pleasant smell of my son is like the smell of a field which the Lord has blessed. May God give you dew from heaven and make your fields fertile! May he give you plenty of corn and wine! May nations be your servants, and may peoples bow down before you. May you rule over all your relatives, and may your mother's descendants bow down before you. May those who curse you be cursed, and may those who bless you be blessed."

Isaac finished giving his blessing, and as soon as Jacob left, his brother Esau came in from hunting. He also cooked some tasty food and took it to his father. He said, "Please, father, sit up and eat some of the meat that I have brought you, so that you can give me your blessing."

"Who are you?" Isaac asked.

"Your elder son Esau," he answered.

Isaac began to tremble and shake all over, and he asked, "Who was it, then, who killed an animal and brought it to me? I ate it just before you came. I gave him my final blessing, and so it is his for ever."

When Esau heard this, he cried out loudly and bitterly and said, "Give me your blessing also, father!"

Isaac answered, "Your brother came and deceived me. He has taken away your blessing."

Esau said, "This is the second time that he has cheated me. No wonder his name is Jacob. He took my rights as the first-born son, and now he has taken away my blessing. Haven't you saved a blessing for me?"

Isaac answered, "I have already made him master over you, and I have made all his relatives his slaves. I have given him corn and wine. Now there is nothing that I can do for you, my son!"

Esau continued to plead with his father: "Have you only one blessing, father? Bless me too, father!" He began to cry.

Then Isaac said to him,
"No dew from heaven for you,
No fertile fields for you.
You will live by your sword,
But be your brother's slave.
Yet when you rebel,
You will break away from his control."

Jacob's Dream of the Stairway to God

So Jacob was a cheat. But he had a dream!

At sunset Jacob came to a holy place and camped there. He lay down to

sleep, resting his head on a stone. He dreamt that he saw a stairway reaching from earth to heaven, with angels going up and coming down on it. And there was the Lord standing beside him. "I am the Lord, the God of Abraham and Isaac," he said. "I will give to you and to your descendants this land on which you are lying. They will be as numerous as the specks of dust on the earth. They will extend their territory in all directions, and through you and your descendants I will bless all the nations. Remember, I will be with you and protect you wherever you go, and I will bring you back to this land. I will not leave you until I have done all that I have promised you."

Jacob woke up and said, "The Lord is here! He is in this place, and I didn't know it!" He was afraid and said, "What a terrifying place this is! It must be the house of God; it must be the gate that opens into heaven."

Jacob Wrestles with God

Jacob's other name, Israel, means: "He struggles with God".
A man came and wrestled with Jacob until just before daybreak. When the man saw that he was not winning the struggle, he struck Jacob on the hip, and it was thrown out of joint. The man said, "Let me go; daylight is coming."

"I won't, unless you bless me," Jacob answered.

"What is your name?" the man asked.

"Jacob," he answered.

The man said, "Your name will no longer be Jacob. You have struggled with God and with men, and you have won; so your name will be Israel."

Jacob said, "Now tell me your name."

But he answered, "Why do you want to know my name?" Then he blessed Jacob.

Jacob said, "I have seen God face to face, and I am still alive." The sun rose as Jacob was leaving Peniel, and he was limping because of his hip.

The Israelites Go to Egypt

Joseph Is Taken to Egypt

The children of Jacob or Israel begin to enter Egypt.
Jacob continued to live in the land of Canaan, where his father had lived, and this is the story of Jacob's family.

Joseph, a young man of seventeen, took care of the sheep and goats with his brothers. He brought bad reports to his father about what his brothers were doing.

Jacob loved Joseph more than all his other sons, because he had been born to him when he was old. He made a long robe with full sleeves for him. When his brothers saw that their father loved Joseph more than he loved them, they hated their brother so much that they would not speak to him in a friendly manner.

One night Joseph had a dream, and when he told his brothers about it, they hated him even more. He said, "Listen to the dream I had. We were all in the field tying up sheaves of wheat, when my sheaf got up and stood up straight. Yours formed a circle round mine and bowed down to it."

"Do you think you are going to be a king and rule over us?" his brothers asked. So they hated him even more because of his dreams and because of what he said about them.

Then Joseph had another dream and said to his brothers, "I had another dream, in which I saw the sun, the moon, and eleven stars bowing down to me."

He also told the dream to his father, and his father scolded him: "What kind of a dream is that? Do you think that your mother, your brothers, and I are going to come and bow down to you?" Joseph's brothers were jealous of him, but his father kept thinking about the whole matter.

One day when Joseph's brothers had gone to Shechem to take care of their father's flock, Jacob said to Joseph, "I want you to go to Shechem, where your brothers are taking care of the flock."

Joseph answered, "I am ready."

His father said, "Go and see if your brothers are safe and if the flock is all right; then come back and tell me." So his father sent him on his way. Joseph went after his brothers and found them at Dothan.

They saw him in the distance, and before he reached them, they plotted against him and decided to kill him. They said to one another, "Here comes that dreamer. Come on now, let's kill him and throw his body into one of the dry wells. We can say that a wild animal killed him. Then we will see what becomes of his dreams."

Reuben heard them and tried to save Joseph. "Let's not kill him," he said. "Just throw him into this well in the wilderness, but don't hurt him." He said this, planning to save him from them and send him back to his father. When Joseph came up to his brothers, they ripped off his long robe with full sleeves. Then they took him and threw him into the well, which was dry.

While they were eating, they suddenly saw a group of Ishmaelites travelling from Gilead to Egypt. Their camels were loaded with spices and resins. Judah said to his brothers, "What will we gain by killing our brother and covering up the murder? Let's sell him to these Ishmaelites. Then we won't have to hurt him; after all, he is our brother, our own flesh and blood." His brothers agreed, and when some Midianite traders came by, the brothers pulled Joseph out of the well and sold him for

twenty pieces of silver to the Ishmaelites, who took him to Egypt.

When Reuben came back to the well and found that Joseph was not there, he tore his clothes in sorrow. He returned to his brothers and said, "The boy is not there! What am I going to do?"

Then they killed a goat and dipped Joseph's robe in its blood. They took the robe to their father and said, "We found this. Does it belong to your son?"

He recognized it and said, "Yes, it is his! Some wild animal has killed him. My son Joseph has been torn to pieces!" Jacob tore his clothes in sorrow and put on sackcloth. He mourned for his son a long time. All his sons and daughters came to comfort him, but he refused to be comforted and said, "I will go down to the world of the dead still mourning for my son." So he continued to mourn for his son Joseph.

His Whole Family Joins Joseph

Years later Joseph has become the ruler of Egypt under the king. In the king's palace he meets his brothers. They have come to buy corn during a famine. But at first his brothers do not know who he is.

Joseph was no longer able to control his feelings in front of his servants, so he ordered them all to leave the room. No one else was with him when Joseph told his brothers who he was. He cried with such loud sobs that the Egyptians heard it, and the news was taken to the king's palace. Joseph said to his brothers, "I am Joseph. Is my father still alive?" But when his brothers heard this, they were so terrified that they could not answer. Then Joseph said to them, "Please come closer." They did, and he said, "I am your brother Joseph, whom you sold into Egypt. Now do not be upset or blame yourselves because you sold me here. It was really God who sent me ahead of you to save people's lives. This is only the second year of famine in the land; there will be five more years in which there will be neither ploughing nor reaping. God sent me ahead of you to rescue you in this amazing way and to make sure that you and your descendants survive. So it was not really you who sent me here, but God. He has made me the king's highest official. I am in charge of his whole country; I am the ruler of all Egypt.

"Now hurry back to my father and tell him that this is what his son Joseph says: 'God has made me ruler of all Egypt; come to me without delay. You can live where you can be near me — you, your children, your grandchildren, your sheep, your goats, your cattle, and everything else that you have. I can take care of you. There will still be five years of famine; and I do not want you, your family, and your livestock to starve.' "

Joseph continued, "Now all of you, and you too, Benjamin, can see that I am really Joseph. Tell my father how powerful I am here in Egypt and tell him about everything that you have seen. Then hurry and bring him here."

He threw his arms round his brother Benjamin and began to cry; Benjamin also cried as he hugged him. Then, still weeping, he embraced each of his brothers and kissed them. After that, his brothers began to talk with him.

They left Egypt and went back home to their father Jacob in Canaan. "Joseph is still alive!" they told him. "He is the ruler of all Egypt!" Jacob was stunned and could not believe them.

But when they told him all that Joseph had said to them, and when he saw the wagons which Joseph had sent to take him to Egypt, he recovered from the shock. "My son Joseph is still alive!" he said. "This is all I could ask for! I must go and see him before I die."

The Israelites Become Slaves

The time comes when Jacob and Joseph are dead. Then the Israelites are treated cruelly in Egypt.

The sons of Jacob who went to Egypt with him, each with his family, were Reuben, Simeon, Levi, Judah, Issachar, Zebulun, Benjamin, Dan, Naphtali, Gad, and Asher. The total number of these people directly descended from Jacob was seventy. His son Joseph was already in Egypt. In the course of time Joseph, his brothers, and all the rest of that generation died, but their descendants, the Israelites, had many children and became so numerous and strong that Egypt was filled with them.

Then, a new king, who knew nothing about Joseph, came to power in Egypt. He said to his people, "These Israelites are so numerous and strong that they are a threat to us. In case of war they might join our enemies in order to fight against us, and might escape from the country. We must find some way to keep them from becoming even more numerous." So the Egyptians put slave-drivers over them to crush their spirits with hard labour. The Israelites built the cities of Pithom and Rameses to serve as supply centres for the king. But the more the Egyptians oppressed the Israelites, the more they increased in number and the further they spread through the land. The Egyptians came to fear the Israelites and made their lives miserable by forcing them into cruel slavery. They made them work on their building projects and in their fields, and they had no mercy on them.

2
The Great Escape

This is the story of how the people of Israel, or "the Hebrews", escaped from slavery in Egypt. Their leader was Moses. This was an Egyptian name, and it is said that Moses was brought up at the Egyptian royal court. But more important is the story that, while working as a humble shepherd, he met God. This took place about 1,250 years before the birth of Christ.

The Great Leader

The Birth of Moses

During this time a man from the tribe of Levi married a woman of his own tribe, and she bore him a son. When she saw what a fine baby he was, she hid him for three months. But when she could not hide him any longer, she took a basket made of reeds and covered it with tar to make it watertight. She put the baby in it and then placed it in the tall grass at the edge of the river. The baby's sister stood some distance away to see what would happen to him.

The king's daughter came down to the river to bathe, while her servants walked along the bank. Suddenly she noticed the basket in the tall grass and sent a slave-girl to get it. The princess opened it and saw a baby boy. He was crying, and she felt sorry for him. "This is one of the Hebrew babies," she said.

Then the baby's sister asked her, "Shall I go and call a Hebrew woman to act as a wet-nurse?"

"Please do," she answered. So the girl went and brought the baby's own mother. The princess told the woman, "Take this baby and nurse him for me, and I will pay you." So she took the baby and nursed him. Later, when the child was old enough, she took him to the king's daughter, who adopted him as her own son. She said to herself, "I pulled him out of the water, and so I name him Moses."

God Calls Moses

One day while Moses was taking care of the sheep and goats of his father-in-law Jethro, the priest of Midian, he led the flock across the desert and came to Sinai, the holy mountain. There the angel of the Lord appeared to him as a flame coming from the middle of a bush. Moses saw that the bush was on fire but that it was not burning up.

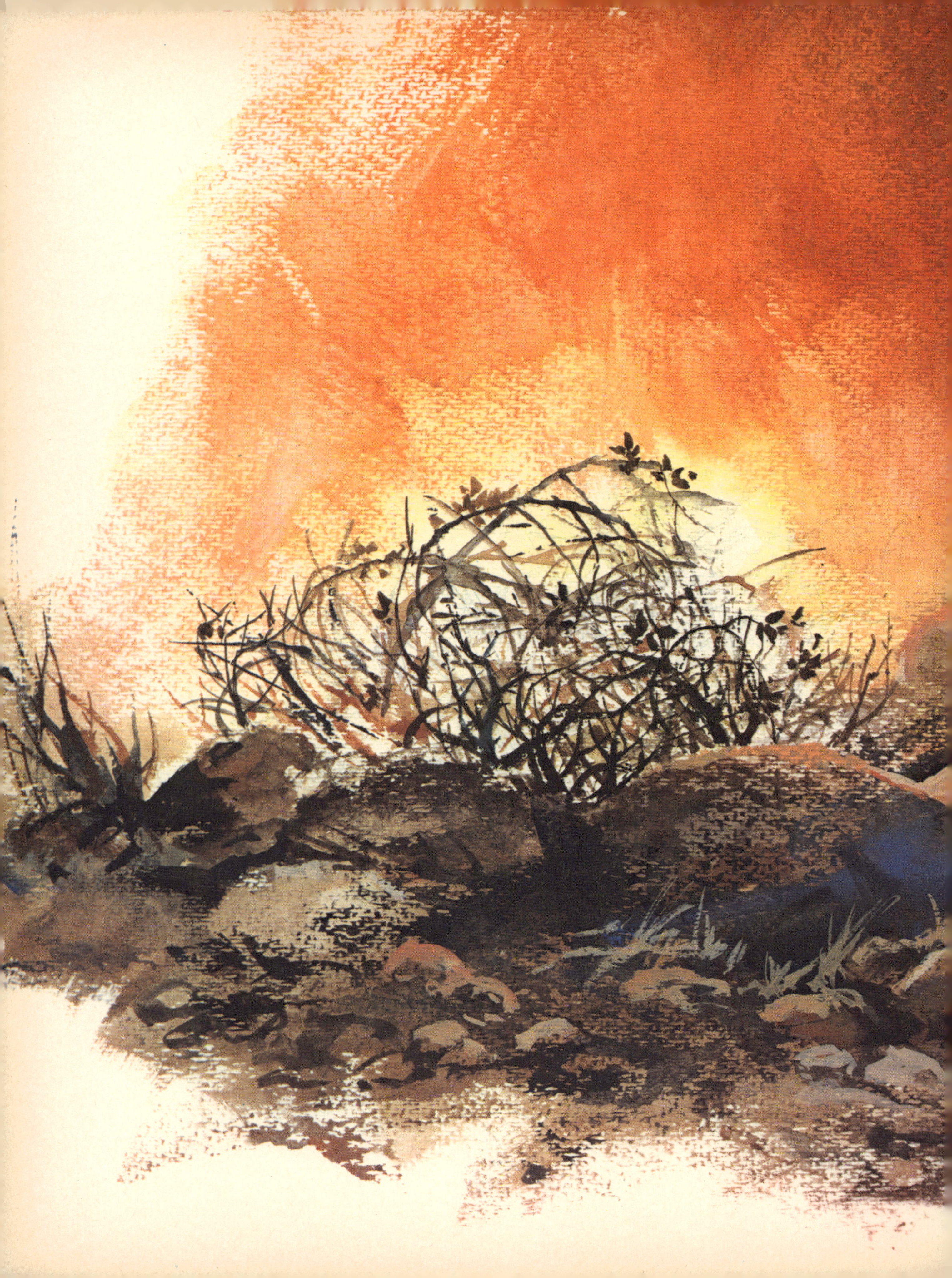

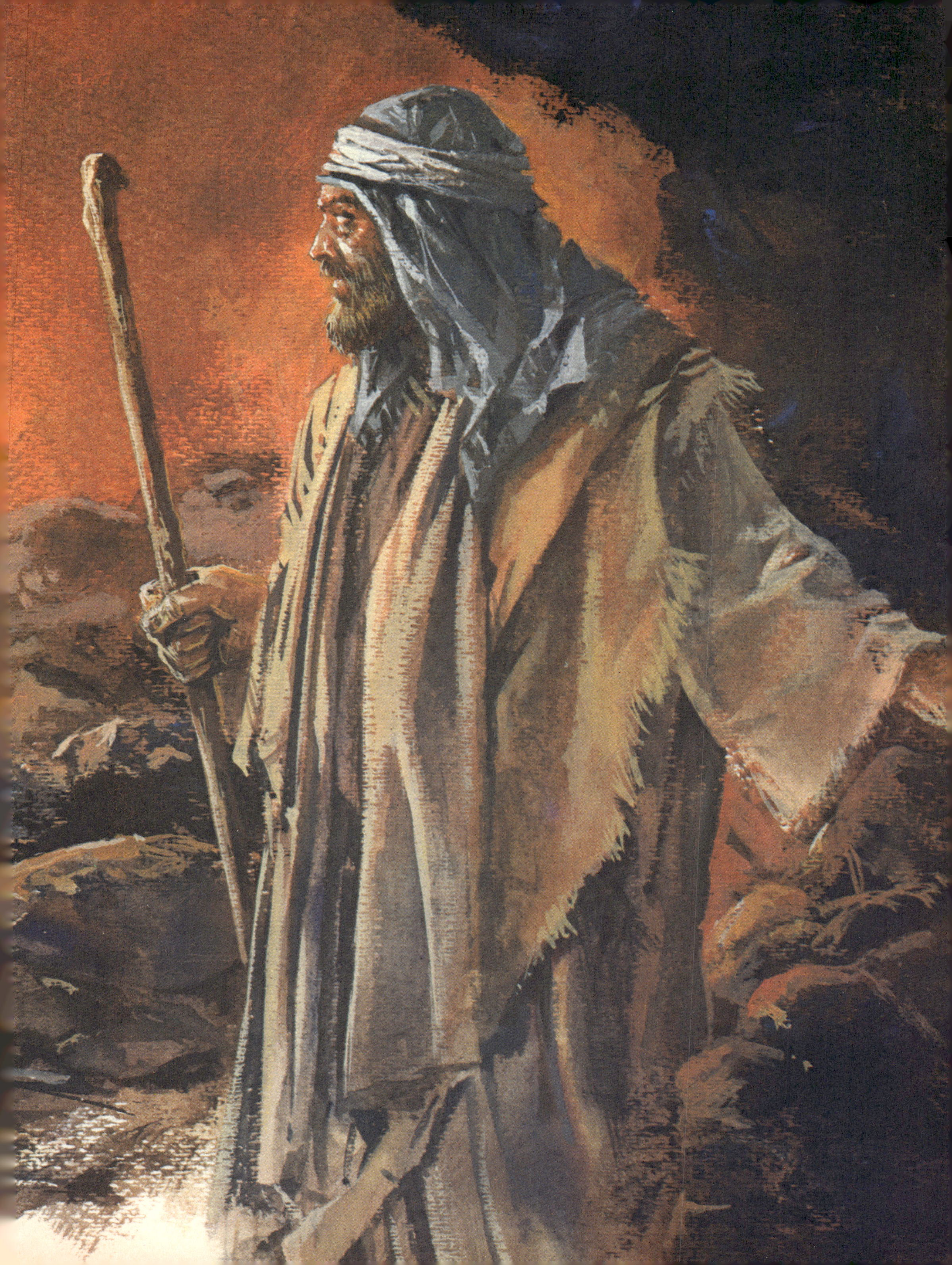

"This is strange," he thought. "Why isn't the bush burning up? I will go closer and see."

When the Lord saw that Moses was coming closer, he called to him from the middle of the bush and said, "Moses! Moses!"

He answered, "Yes, here I am."

God said, "Do not come any closer. Take off your sandals, because you are standing on holy ground. I am the God of your ancestors, the God of Abraham, Isaac, and Jacob." So Moses covered his face, because he was afraid to look at God.

Then the Lord said, "I have seen how cruelly my people are being treated in Egypt; I have heard them cry out to be rescued from their slave-drivers. I know all about their sufferings, and so I have come down to rescue them from the Egyptians and to bring them out of Egypt to a spacious land, one which is rich and fertile and in which the Canaanites, the Hittites, the Amorites, the Perizzites, the Hivites, and the Jebusites now live. I have indeed heard the cry of my people, and I see how the Egyptians are oppressing them. Now I am sending you to the king of Egypt so that you can lead my people out of his country."

But Moses said to God, "I am nobody. How can I go to the king and bring the Israelites out of Egypt?"

God answered, "I will be with you, and when you bring the people out of Egypt, you will worship me on this mountain. That will be the proof that I have sent you."

But Moses replied, "When I go to the Israelites and say to them, 'The God of your ancestors sent me to you,' they will ask me, 'What is his name?' So what can I tell them?"

God said, "I am who I am. This is what you must say to them: 'The one who is called I AM has sent me to you.' Tell the Israelites that I, the Lord, the God of their ancestors, the God of Abraham, Isaac, and Jacob, have sent you to them. This is my name for ever; this is what all future generations are to call me. Go and gather the leaders of Israel together and tell them that I, the Lord, the God of their ancestors, the God of Abraham, Isaac, and Jacob, appeared to you. Tell them that I have come to them and have seen what the Egyptians are doing to them. I have decided that I will bring them out of Egypt, where they are being treated cruelly, and will take them to a rich and fertile land."

But Moses said, "No, Lord, don't send me. I have never been a good speaker, and I haven't become one since you began to speak to me. I am a poor speaker, slow and hesitant."

The Lord said to him, "Who gives man his mouth? Who makes him deaf or dumb? Who gives him sight or makes him blind? It is I, the Lord. Now, go! I will help you to speak, and I will tell you what to say."

But Moses answered, "No, Lord, please send someone else."

At this the Lord became angry with Moses and said, "What about your brother Aaron, the Levite? I know that he can speak well. In fact, he is now coming to meet you and will be glad to see you. You can speak to him and tell him what to say. I will help both of you to speak, and I will tell you both what to do. He will be your spokesman and speak to the people for you. Then you will be like God, telling him what to say."

Moses and Aaron before the King of Egypt

Then Moses and Aaron went to the king of Egypt and said, "The Lord, the God of Israel, says, 'Let my people go, so that they can hold a festival in the desert to honour me.'"

"Who is the Lord?" the king demanded. "Why should I listen to him and let Israel go? I do not know the Lord; and I will not let Israel go."

Moses and Aaron replied, "The God of the Hebrews has revealed himself to us. Allow us to travel for three days into the desert to offer sacrifices to the Lord our God. If we don't do so, he will kill us with disease or by war."

The king said to Moses and Aaron, "What do you mean by making the people neglect their work? Get those slaves back to work! You people have become more numerous than the Egyptians. And now you want to stop working!"

That same day the king commanded the Egyptian slave-drivers and the Israelite foremen: "Stop giving the people straw for making bricks. Make them go and find it for themselves. But still require them to make the same number of bricks as before, not one brick less. They haven't enough work to do, and that is why they keep asking me to let them go and offer sacrifices to their God! Make these men work harder and keep them busy, so that they won't have time to listen to a pack of lies."

The Israelites Leave Egypt

Many stories are told about the plagues which Egypt suffered while the Israelites remained in slavery there. Then comes the great story of the night which Jews have always remembered and celebrated in the Feast called "Passover". It is the night of the great escape, called "Exodus".

Passover

The Lord spoke to Moses and Aaron in Egypt: "This month is to be the first month of the year for you. Give these instructions to the whole community of Israel: On the tenth day of this month each man must choose either a lamb or a young goat for his household. If his family is too small to eat a whole animal, he and his next-door neighbour may share an animal, in proportion to the number of people and the amount that each person can eat. You may choose either a sheep or a goat, but

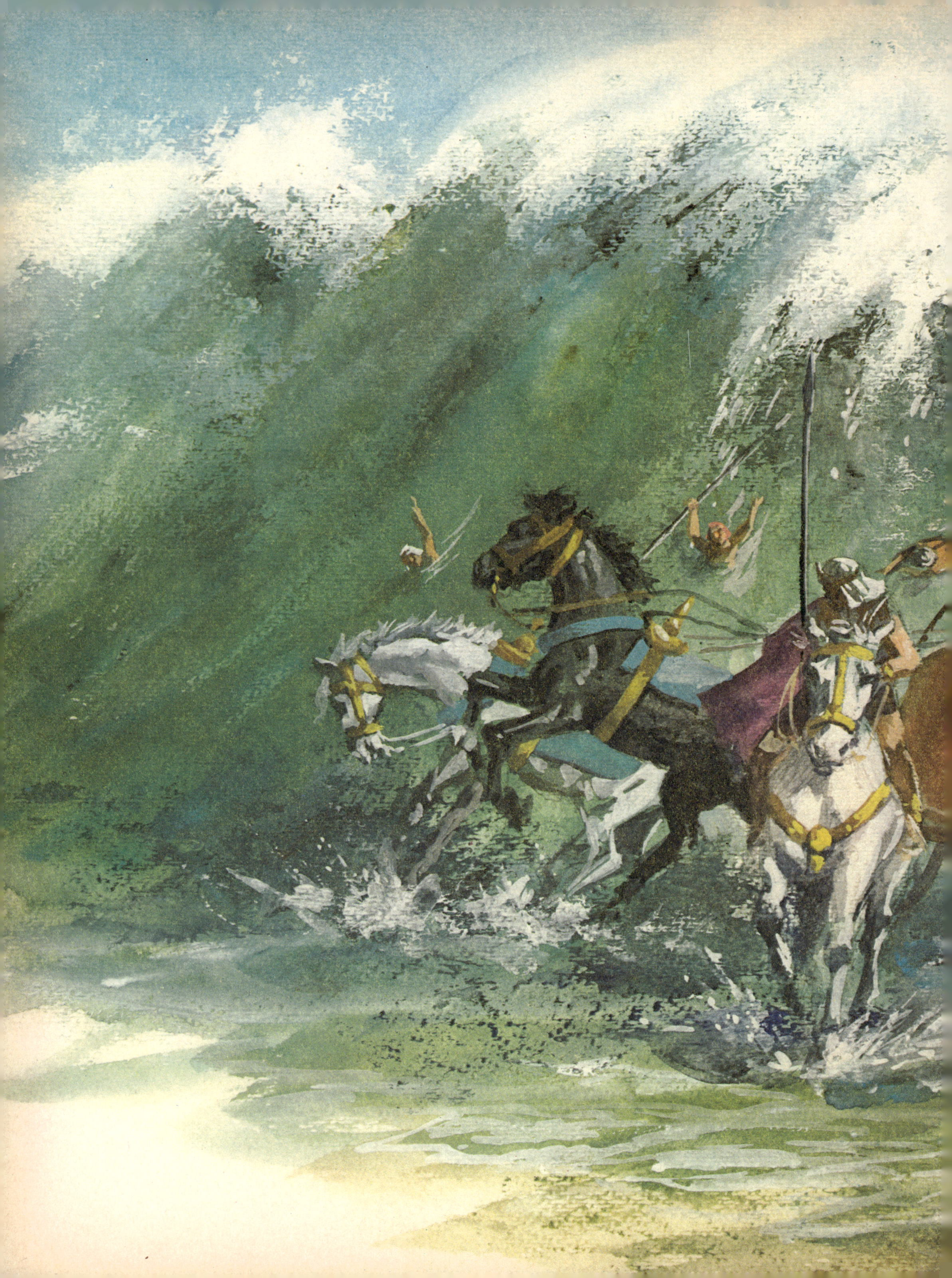

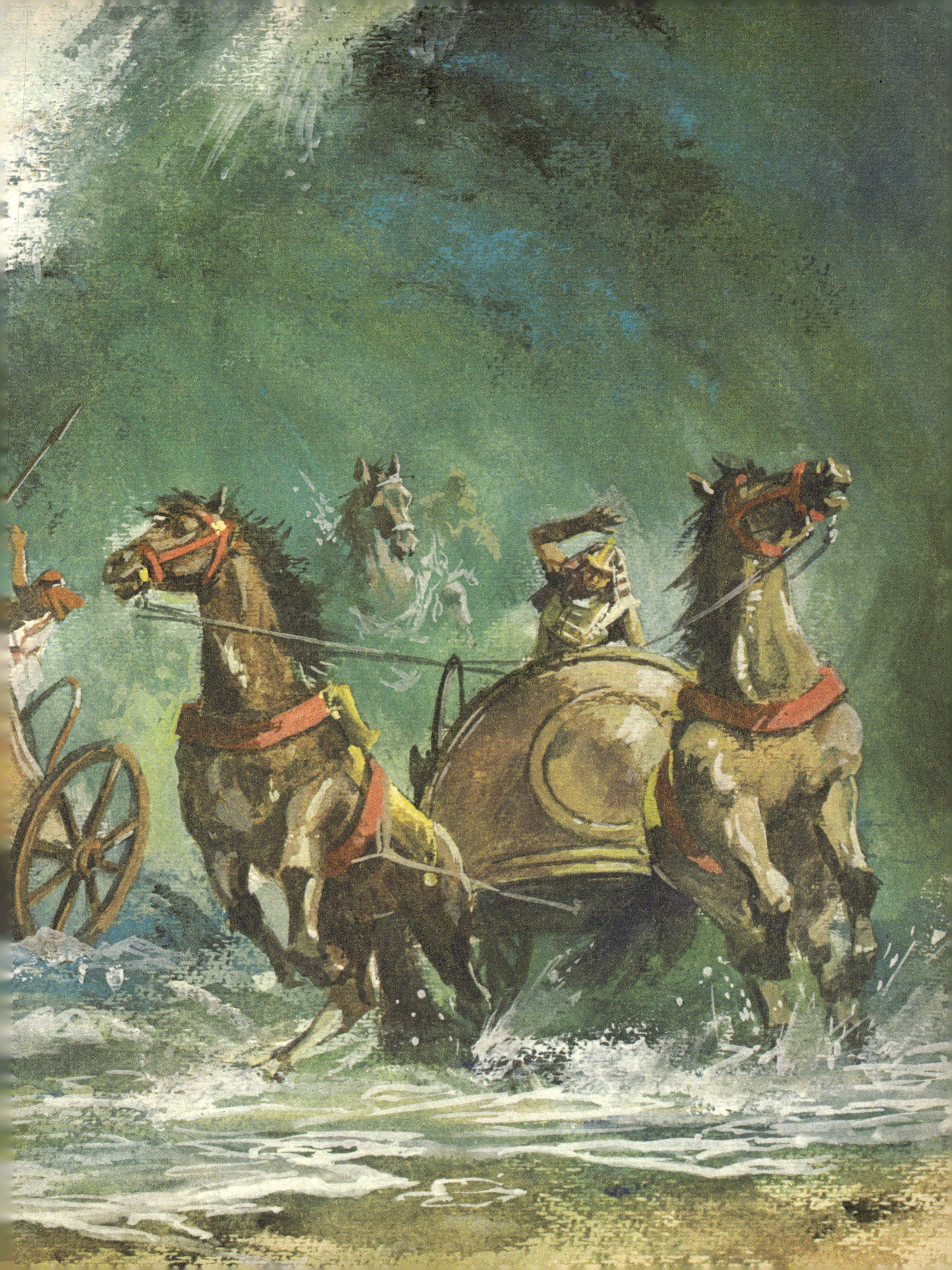

it must be a one-year-old male without any defects. Then, on the evening of the fourteenth day of the month, the whole community of Israel will kill the animals. The people are to take some of the blood and put it on the door-posts and above the doors of the houses in which the animals are to be eaten. That night the meat is to be roasted, and eaten with bitter herbs and with bread made without yeast. Do not eat any of it raw or boiled, but eat it roasted whole, including the head, the legs, and the internal organs. You must not leave any of it until morning; if any is left over, it must be burnt. You are to eat it quickly, for you are to be dressed for travel, with your sandals on your feet and your stick in your hand. It is the Passover Festival to honour me, the Lord.

"On that night I will go through the land of Egypt, killing every first-born male, both human and animal, and punishing all the gods of Egypt. I am the Lord. The blood on the door-posts will be a sign to mark the houses in which you live. When I see the blood, I will pass over you and will not harm you when I punish the Egyptians. You must celebrate this day as a religious festival to remind you of what I, the Lord, have done. Celebrate it for all time to come."

Exodus

The Israelites set out on foot from Rameses for Sukkoth. There were about six hundred thousand men, not counting women and children. A large number of other people and many sheep, goats, and cattle also went with them. They baked unleavened bread from the dough that they had brought out of Egypt, for they had been driven out of Egypt so suddenly that they did not have time to get their food ready or to prepare leavened dough.

The Israelites had lived in Egypt for 430 years. On the day the 430 years ended, all the tribes of the Lord's people left Egypt. It was a night when the Lord kept watch to bring them out of Egypt; this same night is dedicated to the Lord for all time to come as a night when the Israelites must keep watch.

Crossing the Sea

The Egyptians chase after the Israelites with chariots. But as they are crossing a marsh the wind changes and the marsh becomes a sea of water. The chariots are bogged down. The Israelites are safe.
When the king of Egypt was told that the people had escaped, he and his officials changed their minds and said, "What have we done? We have let the Israelites escape, and we have lost them as our slaves!" The king got his war chariot and his army ready. He set out with all his chariots, including the six hundred finest, commanded by their officers. The Lord made the king stubborn, and he pursued the Israelites, who were leaving

triumphantly. The Egyptian army, with all the horses, chariots, and drivers, pursued them and caught up with them where they were camped by the Red Sea.

When the Israelites saw the king and his army marching against them, they were terrified and cried out to the Lord for help. They said to Moses, "Weren't there any graves in Egypt? Did you have to bring us out here in the desert to die? Look what you have done by bringing us out of Egypt! Didn't we tell you before we left that this would happen? We told you to leave us alone and let us go on being slaves of the Egyptians. It would be better to be slaves there than to die here in the desert."

Moses answered, "Don't be afraid! Stand your ground, and you will see what the Lord will do to save you today; you will never see these Egyptians again. The Lord will fight for you, and there is no need for you to do anything."

The Lord said to Moses, "Why are you crying out for help? Tell the people to move forward. Lift up your stick and hold it out over the sea. The water will divide, and the Israelites will be able to walk through the sea on dry ground. I will make the Egyptians so stubborn that they will go in after them, and I will gain honour by my victory over the king, his army, his chariots, and his drivers. When I defeat them, the Egyptians will know that I am the Lord."

The angel of God, who had been in front of the army of Israel, moved and went to the rear. The pillar of cloud also moved until it was between the Egyptians and the Israelites. The cloud made it dark for the Egyptians, but gave light to the people of Israel, and so the armies could not come near each other all night.

Moses held out his hand over the sea, and the Lord drove the sea back with a strong east wind. It blew all night and turned the sea into dry land. The water was divided, and the Israelites went through the sea on dry ground, with walls of water on both sides. The Egyptians pursued them and went after them into the sea with all their horses, chariots, and drivers. Just before dawn the Lord looked down from the pillar of fire and cloud at the Egyptian army and threw them into a panic. He made the wheels of their chariots get stuck, so that they moved with great difficulty. The Egyptians said, "The Lord is fighting for the Israelites against us. Let's get out of here!"

The Lord said to Moses, "Hold out your hand over the sea, and the water will come back over the Egyptians and their chariots and drivers." So Moses held out his hand over the sea, and at daybreak the water returned to its normal level. The Egyptians tried to escape from the water, but the Lord threw them into the sea. The water returned and covered the chariots, the drivers, and all the Egyptian army that had followed the Israelites into the sea; not one of them was left. But the

Israelites walked through the sea on dry ground, with walls of water on both sides.

On that day the Lord saved the people of Israel from the Egyptians, and the Israelites saw them lying dead on the seashore. When the Israelites saw the great power with which the Lord had defeated the Egyptians, they feared the Lord; and they had faith in the Lord and in his servant Moses.

The Song of Moses

Then Moses and the Israelites sang this song to the Lord:
> I will sing to the Lord, because he has won a glorious victory;
>> he has thrown the horses and their riders into the sea.
>
> The Lord is my strong defender;
>> he is the one who has saved me.
>
> He is my God, and I will praise him,
>> my father's God, and I will sing about his greatness.
>
> The Lord is a warrior;
>> the Lord is his name.

The Long Journey

Food in the Desert

The Israelites have to spend many years in the desert between Egypt and the land of Canaan to which they are going. They complain that they will die of hunger and thirst, but they find a strange food and water to drink. Moses said to Aaron, "Tell the whole community to come and stand before the Lord, because he has heard their complaints." As Aaron spoke to the whole community, they turned towards the desert, and suddenly the dazzling light of the Lord appeared in a cloud. The Lord said to Moses, "I have heard the complaints of the Israelites. Tell them that at twilight they will have meat to eat, and in the morning they will have all the bread they want. Then they will know that I, the Lord, am their God."

In the evening a large flock of quails flew in, enough to cover the camp, and in the morning there was dew all round the camp. When the dew evaporated, there was something thin and flaky on the surface of the desert. It was as delicate as frost. When the Israelites saw it, they didn't know what it was and asked each other, "What is it?"

Moses said to them, "This is the food that the Lord has given you to eat. The Lord has commanded that each of you is to gather as much of it as he needs."

Opposite: Moses strikes the rock (text on page 46)

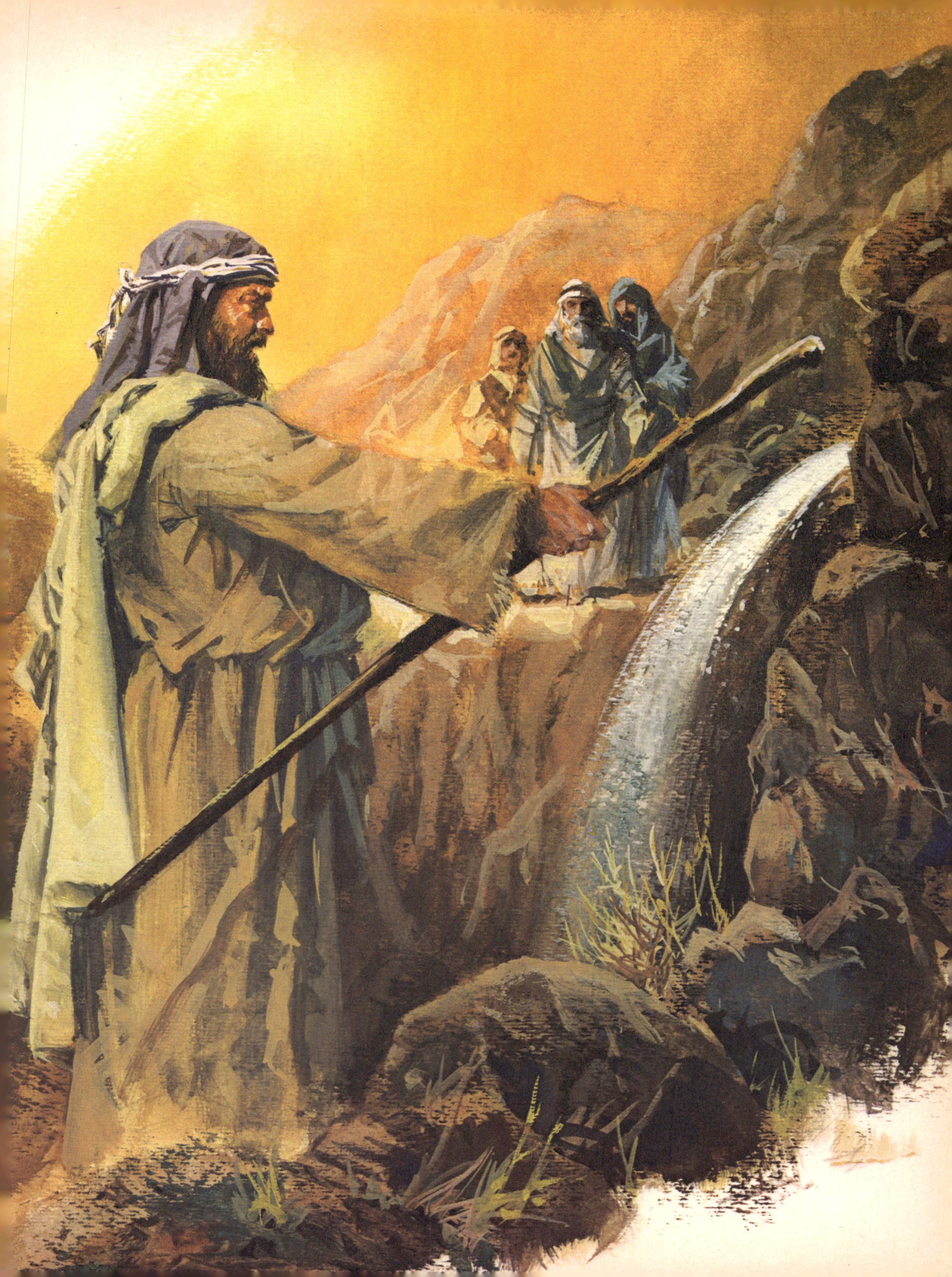

Water in the Desert

The whole Israelite community left the desert of Sin, moving from one place to another at the command of the Lord. They made camp at Rephidim, but there was no water there to drink. They complained to Moses and said, "Give us water to drink."

Moses answered, "Why are you complaining? Why are you putting the Lord to the test?"

But the people were very thirsty and continued to complain to Moses. They said, "Why did you bring us out of Egypt? To kill us and our children and our livestock with thirst?"

Moses prayed earnestly to the Lord and said, "What can I do with these people? They are almost ready to stone me."

The Lord said to Moses, "Take some of the leaders of Israel with you, and go on ahead of the people. I will stand before you on a rock at Mount Sinai. Strike the rock, and water will come out of it for the people to drink." Moses did so in the presence of the leaders of Israel.

At Mount Sinai

At a mountain in the wilderness, the Israelites under Moses make a "covenant" or agreement with the Lord their God; and God gives them his commandments.

They set up camp at the foot of Mount Sinai, and Moses went up the mountain to meet with God.

The Lord called to him from the mountain and told him to say to the Israelites, Jacob's descendants: "You saw what I, the Lord, did to the Egyptians and how I carried you as an eagle carries her young on her wings, and brought you here to me. Now, if you will obey me and keep my covenant, you will be my own people. The whole earth is mine, but you will be my chosen people, a people dedicated to me alone, and you will serve me as priests." So Moses went down and called the leaders of the people together and told them everything that the Lord had commanded him. Then all the people answered together, "We will do everything that the Lord has said," and Moses reported this to the Lord.

Moses on Mount Sinai

The Lord said to Moses, "Come up the mountain to me, and while you are here, I will give you two stone tablets which contain all the laws that I have written for the instruction of the people." Moses and his helper Joshua got ready, and Moses began to go up the holy mountain. Moses said to the leaders, "Wait here in the camp for us until we come back. Aaron and Hur are here with you; and so whoever has a dispute to settle can go to them."

Moses went up Mount Sinai, and a cloud covered it. The dazzling light of the Lord's presence came down on the mountain. To the Israelites the light looked like a fire burning on top of the mountain. The cloud covered the mountain for six days, and on the seventh day the Lord called to Moses from the cloud. Moses went on up the mountain into the cloud. There he stayed for forty days and nights.

The Holy God

The Lord came down in a cloud, stood with him there, and pronounced his holy name, the Lord. The Lord then passed in front of Moses and called out, "I, the Lord, am a God who is full of compassion and pity, who is not easily angered and who shows great love and faithfulness. I keep my promise for thousands of generations and forgive evil and sin; but I will not fail to punish children and grandchildren to the third and fourth generation for the sins of their parents."

Moses quickly bowed down to the ground and worshipped. He said, "Lord, if you really are pleased with me, I ask you to go with us. These people are stubborn, but forgive our evil and our sin, and accept us as your own people."

The Ten Commandments

God spoke, and these were his words: "I am the Lord your God who brought you out of Egypt, where you were slaves.

"Worship no god but me.

"Do not make for yourselves images of anything in heaven or on earth or in the water under the earth. Do not bow down to any idol or worship it, because I am the Lord your God and I tolerate no rivals. I bring punishment on those who hate me and on their descendants down to the third and fourth generation. But I show my love to thousands of generations of those who love me and obey my laws.

"Do not use my name for evil purposes, because I, the Lord your God, will punish anyone who misuses my name.

"Observe the Sabbath and keep it holy. You have six days in which to do your work, but the seventh day is a day of rest dedicated to me. On that day no one is to work — neither you, your children, your slaves, your animals, nor the foreigners who live in your country. In six days I, the Lord, made the earth, the sky, the sea, and everything in them, but on the seventh day I rested. That is why I, the Lord, blessed the Sabbath and made it holy.

"Respect your father and your mother, so that you may live a long time in the land that I am giving you.

"Do not commit murder.

"Do not commit adultery.

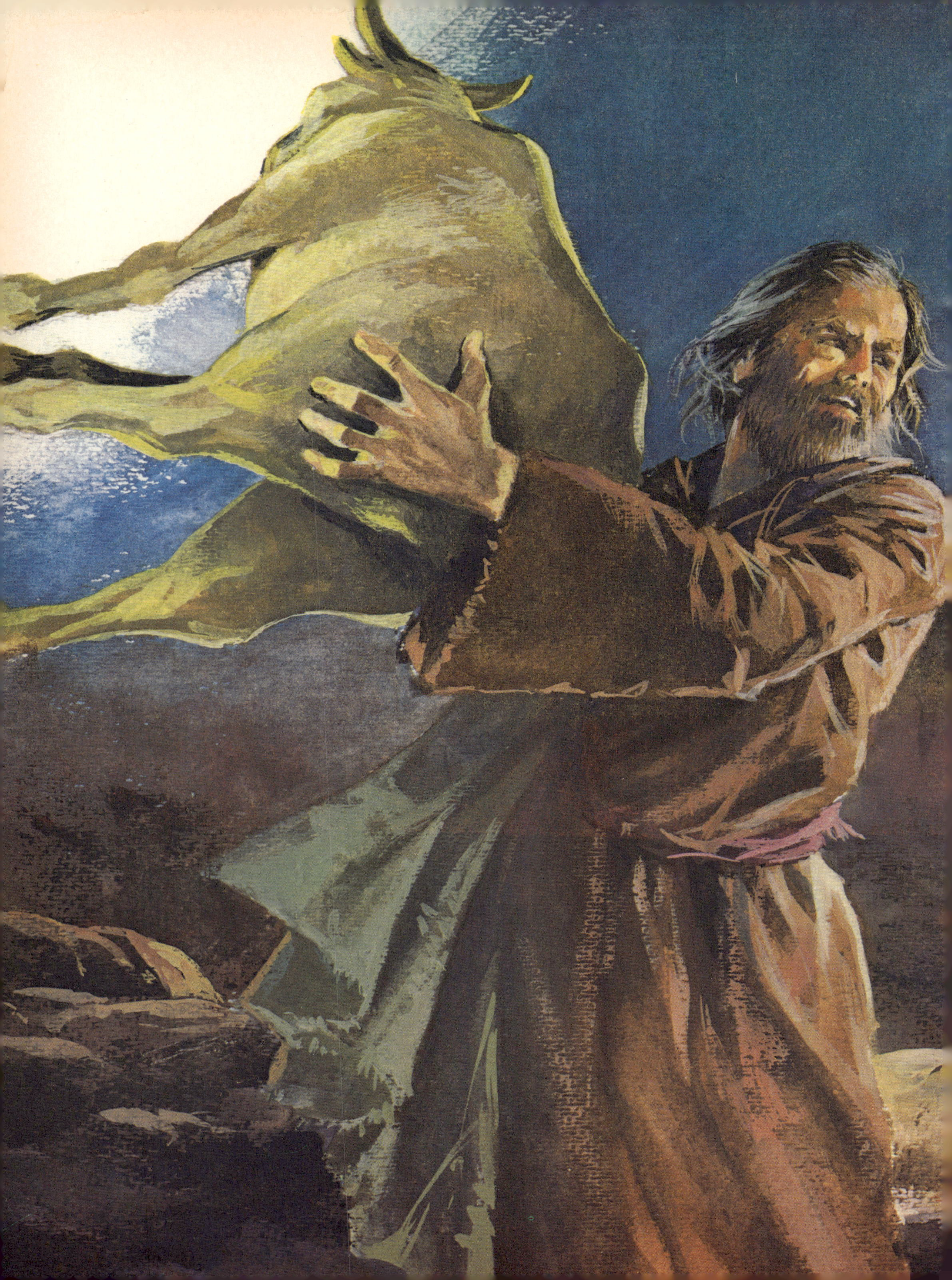

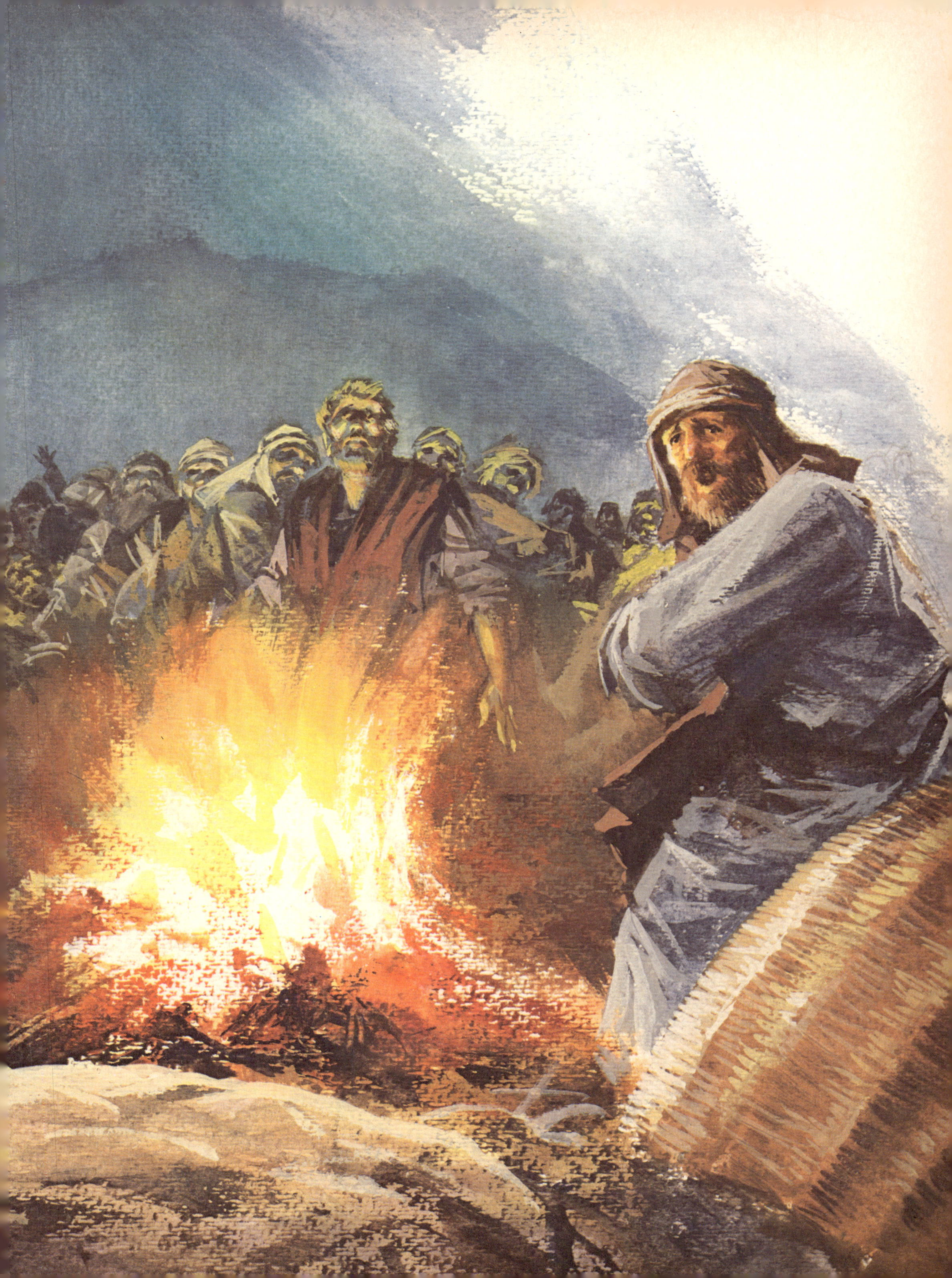

"Do not steal.

"Do not accuse anyone falsely.

"Do not desire another man's house; do not desire his wife, his slaves, his cattle, his donkeys, or anything else that he owns."

Love Your Neighbour

> *Gradually more and more laws were added. But Jesus taught that the greatest laws were the simplest: love God, and love your neighbour. Here the love of the neighbour is commanded.*

The Lord told Moses to say to the community of Israel, "Be holy, because I, the Lord your God, am holy.

"Do not take advantage of anyone or rob him. Do not hold back the wages of someone you have hired, not even for one night. Do not curse a deaf man or put something in front of a blind man so as to make him stumble over it.

"Be honest and just when you make decisions in legal cases; do not show favouritism to the poor or fear the rich. Do not spread lies about anyone, and when someone is on trial for his life, speak out if your testimony can help him.

"Do not bear a grudge against anyone, but settle your differences with him, so that you will not commit a sin because of him. Do not take revenge on anyone or continue to hate him, but love your neighbour as you love yourself."

The Gold Bull

> *The people think that Moses has disappeared. So they make a statue of a bull to worship instead of God.*

When the people saw that Moses had not come down from the mountain but was staying there a long time, they gathered round Aaron and said to him, "We do not know what has happened to this man Moses, who led us out of Egypt; so make us a god to lead us."

Aaron said to them, "Take off the gold earrings which your wives, your sons, and your daughters are wearing, and bring them to me." So all the people took off their gold earrings and brought them to Aaron. He took the earrings, melted them, poured the gold into a mould, and made a gold bull.

The people said, "Israel, this is our god, who led us out of Egypt!"

Then Aaron built an altar in front of the gold bull and announced, "Tomorrow there will be a festival to honour the Lord." Early the next morning they brought some animals to burn as sacrifices and others to eat as fellowship-offerings. The people sat down to a feast, which turned into an orgy of drinking and sex.

The Lord said to Moses, "Go back down at once, because your people, whom you led out of Egypt, have sinned and rejected me. They have already left the way that I commanded them to follow: they have made a bull out of melted gold and have worshipped it and offered sacrifices to it. They are saying that this is their god, who led them out of Egypt. I know how stubborn these people are. Now, don't try to stop me. I am angry with them, and I am going to destroy them. Then I will make you and your descendants into a great nation."

But Moses pleaded with the Lord his God and said, "Lord, why should you be so angry with your people, whom you rescued from Egypt with great might and power? Why should the Egyptians be able to say that you led your people out of Egypt, planning to kill them in the mountains and destroy them completely? Stop being angry; change your mind and do not bring this disaster on your people. Remember your servants Abraham, Isaac, and Jacob. Remember the solemn promise you made to them to give them as many descendants as there are stars in the sky and to give their descendants all that land you promised would be their possession for ever." So the Lord changed his mind and did not bring on his people the disaster he had threatened.

Moses went back down the mountain, carrying the two stone tablets with the commandments written on both sides. God himself had made the tablets and had engraved the commandments on them.

Joshua heard the people shouting and said to Moses, "I hear the sound of battle in the camp."

Moses said, "That doesn't sound like a shout of victory or a cry of defeat; it's the sound of singing."

When Moses came close enough to the camp to see the bull and to see the people dancing, he was furious. There at the foot of the mountain, he threw down the tablets he was carrying and broke them. He took the bull which they had made, melted it, ground it into fine powder, and mixed it with water. Then he made the people of Israel drink it.

Moses Complains to God

> *This story shows what a strain it was for Moses, to lead the people through forty years in the wilderness.*

Moses heard all the people complaining as they stood about in groups at the entrances of their tents. He was distressed because the Lord was angry with them, and he said to the Lord, "Why have you treated me so badly? Why are you displeased with me? Why have you given me the responsibility for all these people? I didn't create them or bring them to birth! Why should you ask me to act like a nurse and carry them in my arms like babies all the way to the land you promised to their ancestors? Where could I get enough meat for all these people? They keep whining and asking for meat. I can't be responsible for all these people by myself;

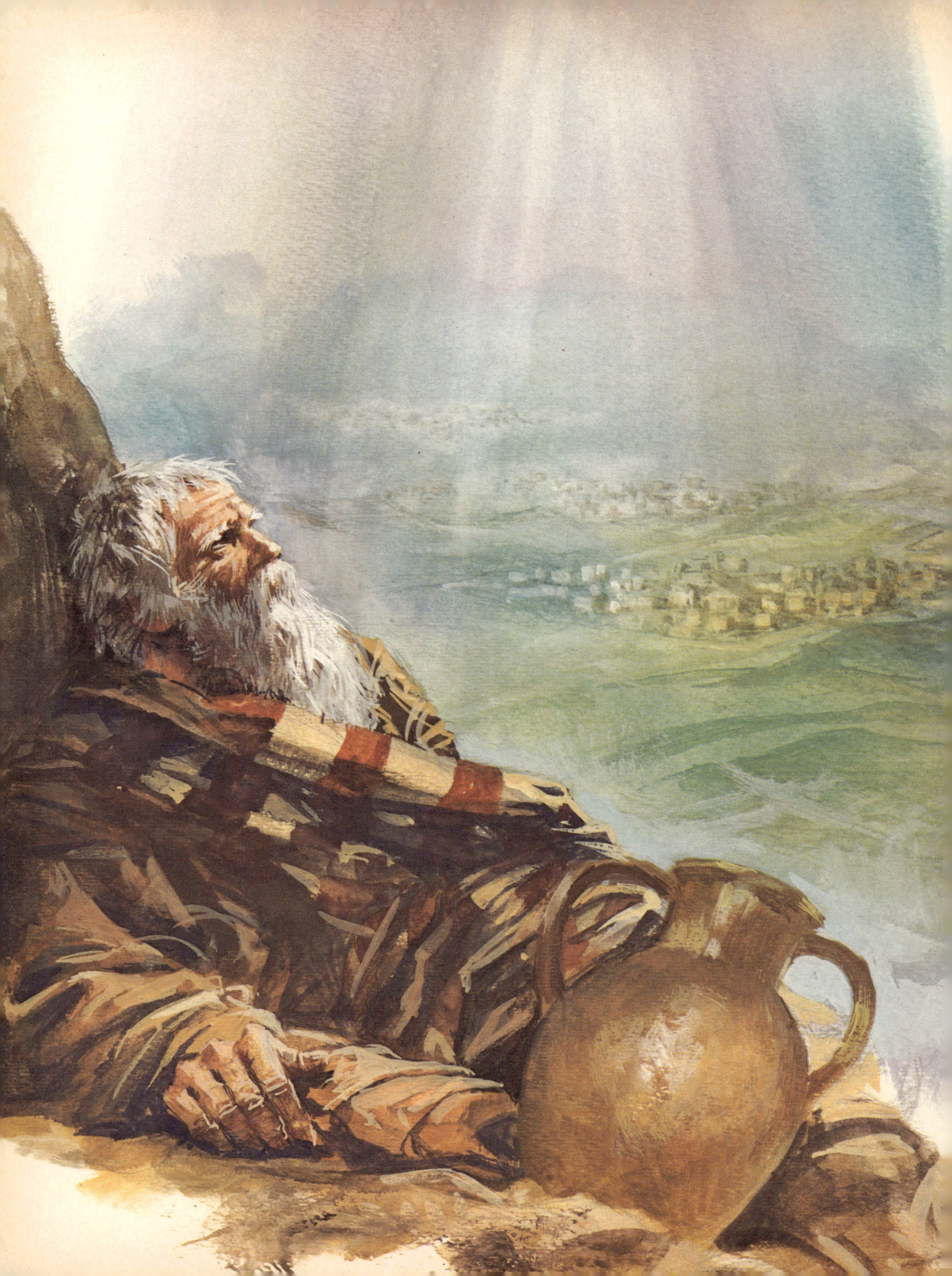

it's too much for me! If you are going to treat me like this, take pity on me and kill me, so that I won't have to endure your cruelty any longer."

The Lord said to Moses, "Assemble seventy respected men who are recognized as leaders of the people, bring them to me at the Tent of my presence, and tell them to stand there beside you. I will come down and speak with you there, and I will take some of the spirit I have given you and give it to them. Then they can help you to bear the responsibility for these people, and you will not have to bear it alone."

The Death of Moses

Before he dies, Moses goes up Mount Pisgah, and from there he sees the promised land of Canaan.

Moses went up from the plains of Moab to Mount Nebo, to the top of Mount Pisgah east of Jericho, and there the Lord showed him the whole land. Then the Lord said to Moses, "This is the land that I promised Abraham, Isaac, and Jacob I would give to their descendants. I have let you see it, but I will not let you go there."

So Moses, the Lord's servant, died there in the land of Moab, as the Lord had said he would. The Lord buried him in a valley in Moab, opposite the town of Bethpeor, but to this day no one knows the exact place of his burial. Moses was a hundred and twenty years old when he died; he was as strong as ever, and his eyesight was still good. The people of Israel mourned for him for thirty days in the plains of Moab.

Joshua son of Nun was filled with wisdom, because Moses had appointed him to be his successor. The people of Israel obeyed Joshua and kept the commands that the Lord had given them through Moses.

There has never been a prophet in Israel like Moses; the Lord spoke with him face to face. No other prophet has ever done miracles and wonders like those that the Lord sent Moses to perform against the king of Egypt, his officials, and the entire country. No other prophet has been able to do the great and terrifying things that Moses did in the sight of all Israel.

The Story of the Far-seeing Donkey

This is one of the stories that the people of Israel told about the time when they were in the land of Moab, on the way to Canaan.

When the king of Moab, Balak son of Zippor, heard what the Israelites had done to the Amorites and how many Israelites there were, he and all his people became terrified. The Moabites said to the leaders of the Midianites, "This horde will soon destroy everything round us, like a bull eating the grass in a pasture." So King Balak sent messengers to summon Balaam son of Beor, who was at Pethor near the River Euphrates in the land of Amaw. They brought him this message from

Balak: "I want you to know that a whole nation has come from Egypt; its people are spreading out everywhere and threatening to take over our land. They outnumber us, so please come and put a curse on them for me. Then perhaps we will be able to defeat them and drive them out of the land. I know that when you pronounce a blessing, people are blessed, and when you pronounce a curse, they are placed under a curse."

So the Moabite and Midianite leaders took with them the payment for the curse, went to Balaam, and gave him Balak's message. Balaam said to them, "Spend the night here, and tomorrow I will report to you whatever the Lord tells me." So the Moabite leaders stayed with Balaam. The next morning Balaam saddled his donkey and went with the Moabite leaders.

Balaam and His Donkey

God was angry that Balaam was going, and as Balaam was riding along on his donkey, accompanied by his two servants, the angel of the Lord stood in the road to bar his way. When the donkey saw the angel standing there holding a sword, it left the road and turned into the fields. Balaam beat the donkey and brought it back on to the road. Then the angel stood where the road narrowed between two vineyards and had a stone wall on each side. When the donkey saw the angel, it moved over against the wall and crushed Balaam's foot against it. Again Balaam beat the donkey. Once more the angel moved ahead; he stood in a narrow place where there was no room at all to pass on either side. This time, when the donkey saw the angel, it lay down. Balaam lost his temper and began to beat the donkey with his stick. Then the Lord gave the donkey the power of speech, and it said to Balaam, "What have I done to you? Why have you beaten me these three times?"

Balaam answered, "Because you have made a fool of me! If I had a sword I would kill you."

The donkey replied, "Am I not the same donkey on which you have ridden all your life? Have I ever treated you like this before?"

"No," he answered.

Then the Lord let Balaam see the angel standing there with his sword; and Balaam threw himself face downwards on the ground. The angel demanded, "Why have you beaten your donkey three times like this? I have come to bar your way, because you should not be making this journey. But your donkey saw me and turned aside three times. If it hadn't, I would have killed you and spared the donkey."

Balaam replied, "I have sinned. I did not know that you were standing in the road to oppose me; but now if you think it is wrong for me to go on, I will return home."

But the angel said, "Go on with these men, but say only what I tell you to say." So Balaam went on with them.

Balaam's Blessing on Israel

By now Balaam knew that the Lord wanted him to bless the people of Israel, so he did not go to look for omens, as he had done before. He turned towards the desert and saw the people of Israel camped tribe by tribe. The spirit of God took control of him, and he uttered this prophecy:

"The message of Balaam son of Beor,
The words of the man who can see clearly,
Who can hear what God is saying.
With staring eyes I see in a trance
A vision from Almighty God.
The tents of Israel are beautiful,
Like long rows of palms
Or gardens beside a river,
Like aloes planted by the Lord
Or cedars beside the water.
They will have abundant rainfall
And plant their seed in well-watered fields."

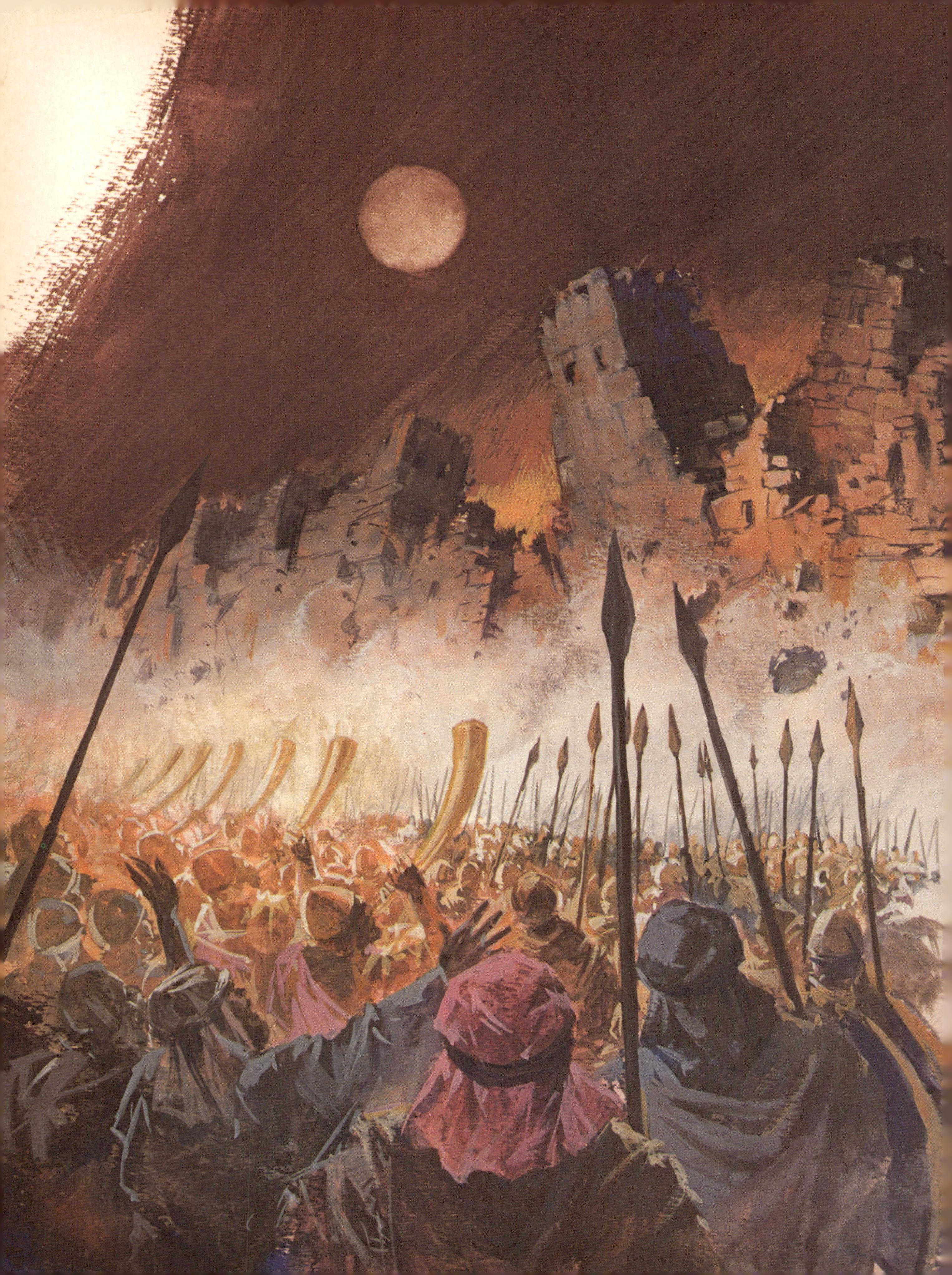

3
Men of Courage

These are some of the stories told about the heroes of Ancient Israel. They were not "saints" as we understand that word, but they were all leaders whose courage came from their faith in God. For example, Joshua needed extraordinary courage to lead the people into the promised land.

The Promised Land

Joshua is Told to be Confident

After the death of the Lord's servant Moses, the Lord spoke to Moses' helper, Joshua son of Nun. He said, "My servant Moses is dead. Get ready now, you and all the people of Israel, and cross the River Jordan into the land that I am giving them. As I told Moses, I have given you and all my people the entire land that you will be marching over. Your borders will reach from the desert in the south to the Lebanon Mountains in the north; from the great River Euphrates in the east, through the Hittite country, to the Mediterranean Sea in the west. Joshua, no one will be able to defeat you as long as you live. I will be with you as I was with Moses. I will always be with you; I will never abandon you. Be determined and confident, for you will be the leader of these people as they occupy this land which I promised their ancestors. Just be determined, be confident; and make sure that you obey the whole Law that my servant Moses gave you. Do not neglect any part of it and you will succeed wherever you go. Be sure that the book of the Law is always read in your worship. Study it day and night, and make sure that you obey everything written in it. Then you will be prosperous and successful. Remember that I have commanded you to be determined and confident! Don't be afraid or discouraged, for I, the Lord your God, am with you wherever you go."

The Fall of Jericho

> *The army that enters the promised land is small. But the cities of Canaan seem to collapse before the courage of Joshua and the Israelites, who carry with them the "Covenant Box" to remind them of God's "Covenant" or agreement to be on their side.*

The gates of Jericho were kept shut and guarded to keep the Israelites out. No one could enter or leave the city. The Lord said to Joshua, "I am putting into your hands Jericho, with its king and all its brave soldiers. You and your soldiers are to march round the city once a day for six days. Seven priests, each carrying a trumpet, are to go in front of the Covenant Box. On the seventh day you and your soldiers are to march round the city seven times while the priests blow the trumpets. Then they are to sound one long note. As soon as you hear it, all the men are to give a loud shout, and the city walls will collapse. Then the whole army will go straight into the city."

Joshua called the priests and said to them, "Take the Covenant Box, and seven of you go in front of it, carrying trumpets." Then he ordered his men to start marching round the city, with an advance guard going on ahead of the Lord's Covenant Box.

Joshua got up early the next morning, and for the second time the priests and soldiers marched round the city in the same order as the day before: first, the advance guard; next, the seven priests blowing the seven trumpets; then, the priests carrying the Lord's Covenant Box; and finally, the rearguard. All this time the trumpets were sounding. On this second day they again marched round the city once and then returned to camp. They did this for six days.

On the seventh day they got up at daybreak and marched seven times round the city in the same way — this was the only day that they marched round it seven times. The seventh time round, when the priests were about to sound the trumpets, Joshua ordered his men to shout, and he said, "The Lord has given you the city!"

So the priests blew the trumpets. As soon as the men heard it, they gave a loud shout, and the walls collapsed. Then all the army went straight up the hill into the city and captured it.

Joshua Speaks to the People

Joshua tells the people they must serve the Lord — not the gods of Mesopotamia where Abraham lived originally; not the gods of Egypt; not the gods of the Amorites who have been living in Canaan.

Joshua said to the people, "Honour the Lord and serve him sincerely and faithfully. Get rid of the gods which your ancestors used to worship in Mesopotamia and in Egypt, and serve only the Lord. If you are not willing to serve him, decide today whom you will serve, the gods your ancestors worshipped in Mesopotamia or the gods of the Amorites, in whose land you are now living. As for my family and me, we will serve the Lord."

The people replied, "We would never leave the Lord to serve other gods! The Lord our God brought our fathers and us out of slavery in Egypt, and we saw the miracles that he performed. He kept us safe wherever we went among all the nations through which we passed. As we advanced into this land, the Lord drove out all the Amorites who lived here. So we also will serve the Lord; he is our God."

Joshua said to the people, "But you may not be able to serve the Lord. He is a holy God and will not forgive your sins. He will tolerate no rivals, and if you leave him to serve foreign gods, he will turn against you and punish you. He will destroy you, even though he was good to you before."

The people said to Joshua, "No! We *will* serve the Lord."

Joshua said to them, "You are your own witnesses to the fact that you have chosen to serve the Lord."

"Yes," they said, "we are witnesses."

"Then get rid of those foreign gods that you have," he demanded, "and pledge your loyalty to the Lord, the God of Israel."

The people then said to Joshua, "We will serve the Lord our God. We will obey his commands."

Gideon's Three Hundred

> *One of the stories told about the conquest of Canaan says that three hundred men were quite enough to terrify the Midianite army.*

The Lord said to Gideon, "The men you have are too many for me to give them victory over the Midianites. They might think that they had won by themselves, and so give me no credit. Announce to the people, 'Anyone who is afraid should go back home, and we will stay here at Mount Gilead.'" So twenty-two thousand went back, but ten thousand stayed.

Then the Lord said to Gideon, "You still have too many men. Take them down to the water, and I will separate them for you there. If I tell you a man should go with you, he will go. If I tell you a man should not go with you, he will not go." Gideon took the men down to the water, and the Lord said to him, "Separate everyone who laps up the water with his tongue like a dog, from everyone who gets down on his knees to drink." There were three hundred men who scooped up water in their hands and lapped it; all the others got down on their knees to drink. The Lord said to Gideon, "I will rescue you and give you victory over the Midianites with the three hundred men who lapped the water. Tell everyone else to go home." So Gideon sent all the Israelites home, except the three hundred, who kept all the supplies and trumpets. The Midianite camp was below them in the valley.

That night the Lord commanded Gideon, "Get up and attack the camp; I am giving you victory over it. But if you are afraid to attack, go down to the camp with your servant Purah. You will hear what they are saying, and then you will have the courage to attack." So Gideon and his servant Purah went down to the edge of the enemy camp. The Midianites, the Amalekites, and the desert tribesmen were spread out in the valley like a swarm of locusts, and they had as many camels as there were grains of sand on the seashore.

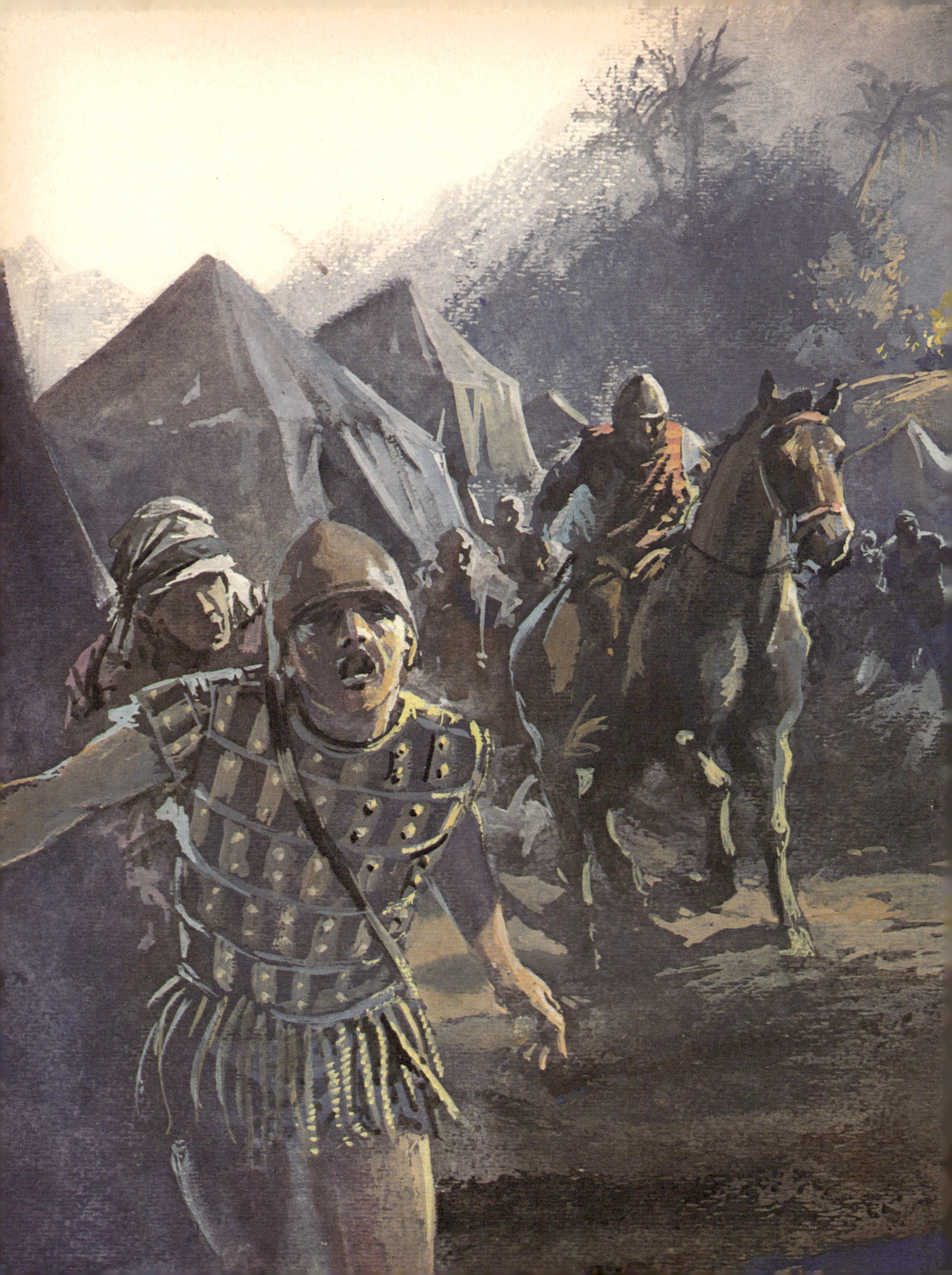

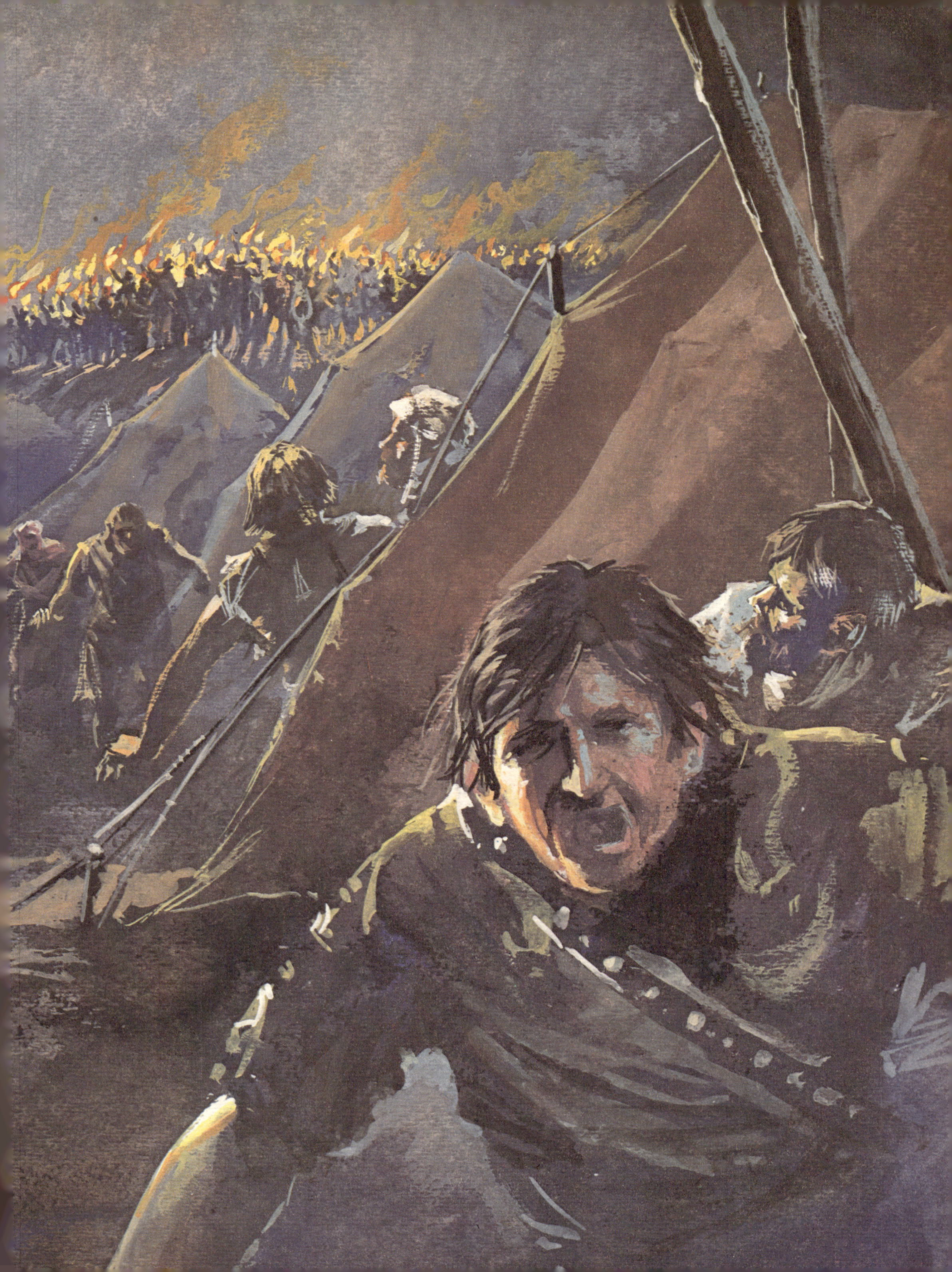

When Gideon arrived, he heard a man telling a friend about a dream. He was saying, "I dreamt that a loaf of barley bread rolled into our camp and hit a tent. The tent collapsed and lay flat on the ground."

His friend replied, "It's the sword of the Israelite, Gideon son of Joash! It can't mean anything else! God has given him victory over Midian and our whole army!"

When Gideon heard about the man's dream and what it meant, he fell to his knees and worshipped God. Then he went back to the Israelite camp and said, "Get up! The Lord is giving you victory over the Midianite army!" He divided his three hundred men into three groups and gave each man a trumpet and a jar with a torch inside it. He told them, "When I get to the edge of the camp, watch me, and do what I do. When my group and I blow our trumpets, then you blow yours all round the camp and shout, 'For the Lord and for Gideon!'"

Gideon and his hundred men came to the edge of the camp a short while before midnight, just after the guard had been changed. Then they blew the trumpets and broke the jars they were holding, and the other two groups did the same. They all held the torches in their left hands, the trumpets in their right, and shouted, "A sword for the Lord and for Gideon!" Every man stood in his place round the camp, and the whole enemy army ran away yelling.

Samson the Strong Man

Many tales are told about the feats of Samson, who led the Israelites against their enemies the Philistines. One story is about how he was tricked by a Philistine agent, the beautiful Delilah.

Samson and Delilah

Samson fell in love with a woman called Delilah. The five Philistine kings went to her and said, "Trick Samson into telling you why he is so strong and how we can overpower him, tie him up, and make him helpless. Each one of us will give you eleven hundred pieces of silver."

So Delilah said to Samson, "Please tell me what makes you so strong. If someone wanted to tie you up and make you helpless, how could he do it?"

Samson answered, "If they tie me up with seven new bowstrings that are not dried out, I'll be as weak as anybody else."

So the Philistine kings brought Delilah seven new bowstrings that were not dried out, and she tied Samson up. She had some men waiting in another room, so she shouted, "Samson! The Philistines are coming!"

But he snapped the bowstrings just as thread breaks when fire touches it. So they still did not know the secret of his strength.

Delilah said to Samson, "Look, you've been making a fool of me and not telling me the truth. Please tell me how someone could tie you up."

He answered, "If they tie me with new ropes that have never been used, I'll be as weak as anybody else."

So Delilah got some new ropes and tied him up. Then she shouted, "Samson! The Philistines are coming!" The men were waiting in another room. But he snapped the ropes off his arms like thread.

Delilah said to Samson, "You're still making a fool of me and not telling me the truth. Tell me how someone could tie you up."

He answered, "If you weave my seven locks of hair into a loom, and make them tight with a peg, I'll be as weak as anybody else."

Delilah then lulled him to sleep, took his seven locks of hair, and wove them into the loom. She made them tight with a peg and shouted, "Samson! The Philistines are coming!" But he woke up and pulled his hair loose from the loom.

So she said to him, "How can you say you love me, when you don't mean it? You've made a fool of me three times, and you still haven't told me what makes you so strong." She kept on asking him, day after day. He got so sick and tired of her nagging him about it that he finally told her the truth. "My hair has never been cut," he said. "I have been dedicated to God as a Nazirite from the time I was born. If my hair were cut, I would lose my strength and be as weak as anybody else."

When Delilah realized that he had told her the truth, she sent a message to the Philistine kings and said, "Come back just once more. He has told me the truth." Then they came and brought the money with them. Delilah lulled Samson to sleep in her lap and then called a man, who cut off Samson's seven locks of hair. Then she began to torment him, for he had lost his strength. Then she shouted, "Samson! The Philistines are coming!" He woke up and thought, "I'll get loose and go free, as always." He did not know that the Lord had left him. The Philistines captured him and put his eyes out. They took him to Gaza, chained him with bronze chains, and put him to work grinding at the mill in the prison. But his hair started growing again.

The Death of Samson

The Philistine kings met together to celebrate and offer a great sacrifice to their god Dagon. They sang, "Our god has given us victory over our enemy Samson!" They were enjoying themselves, so they said, "Call Samson, and let's make him entertain us!" When they brought Samson out of the prison, they made him entertain them and made him stand between the pillars. When the people saw him, they sang praise to their god: "Our god has given us victory over our enemy, who devastated our land and killed so many of us!" Samson said to the boy who was leading him by the hand, "Let me touch the pillars that hold up the building. I want to lean on them." The building was crowded with men and women. All five Philistine kings were there, and there were about three thousand men and women on the roof, watching Samson and making him entertain them.

Then Samson prayed, "Sovereign Lord, please remember me; please, God, give me my strength just once more, so that with this one blow I can get even with the Philistines for putting out my two eyes." So Samson took hold of the two middle pillars holding up the building. Putting one hand on each pillar, he pushed against them and shouted, "Let me die with the Philistines!" He pushed with all his might, and the building fell down on the five kings and everyone else. Samson killed more people at his death than he had killed during his life.

A Great Prophet

The Birth of Samuel

In the temple at Shiloh Hannah prays for a son — who grows up to be Samuel, a great prophet and leader of Israel.

One day, after they had finished their meal in the house of the Lord at Shiloh, Hannah got up. She was deeply distressed, and she cried bitterly as she prayed to the Lord. Meanwhile, Eli the priest was sitting in his place by the door. Hannah made a solemn promise: "Lord Almighty, look at me, your servant! See my trouble and remember me! Don't forget me! If you give me a son, I promise that I will dedicate him to you for his whole life and that he will never have his hair cut."

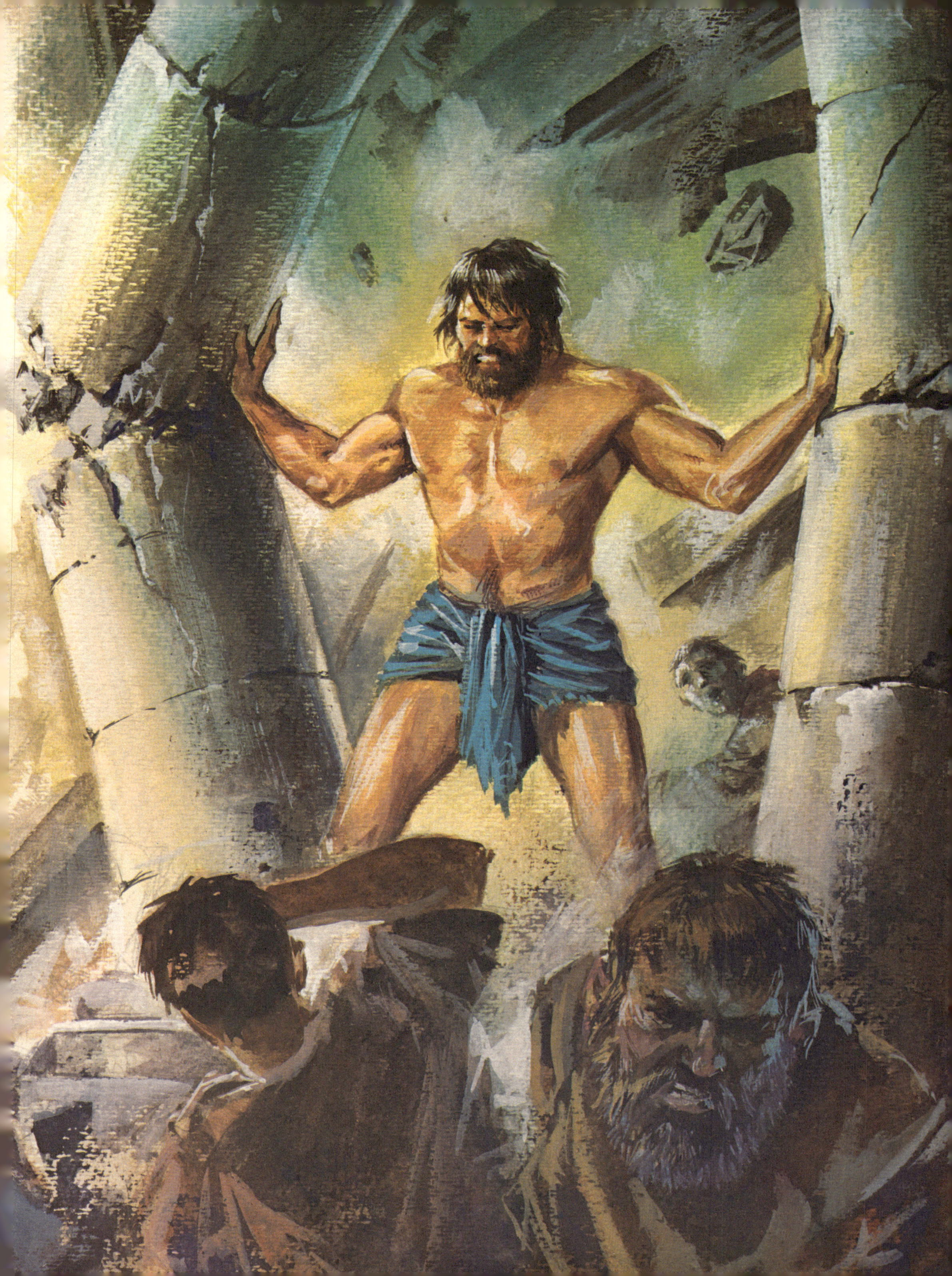

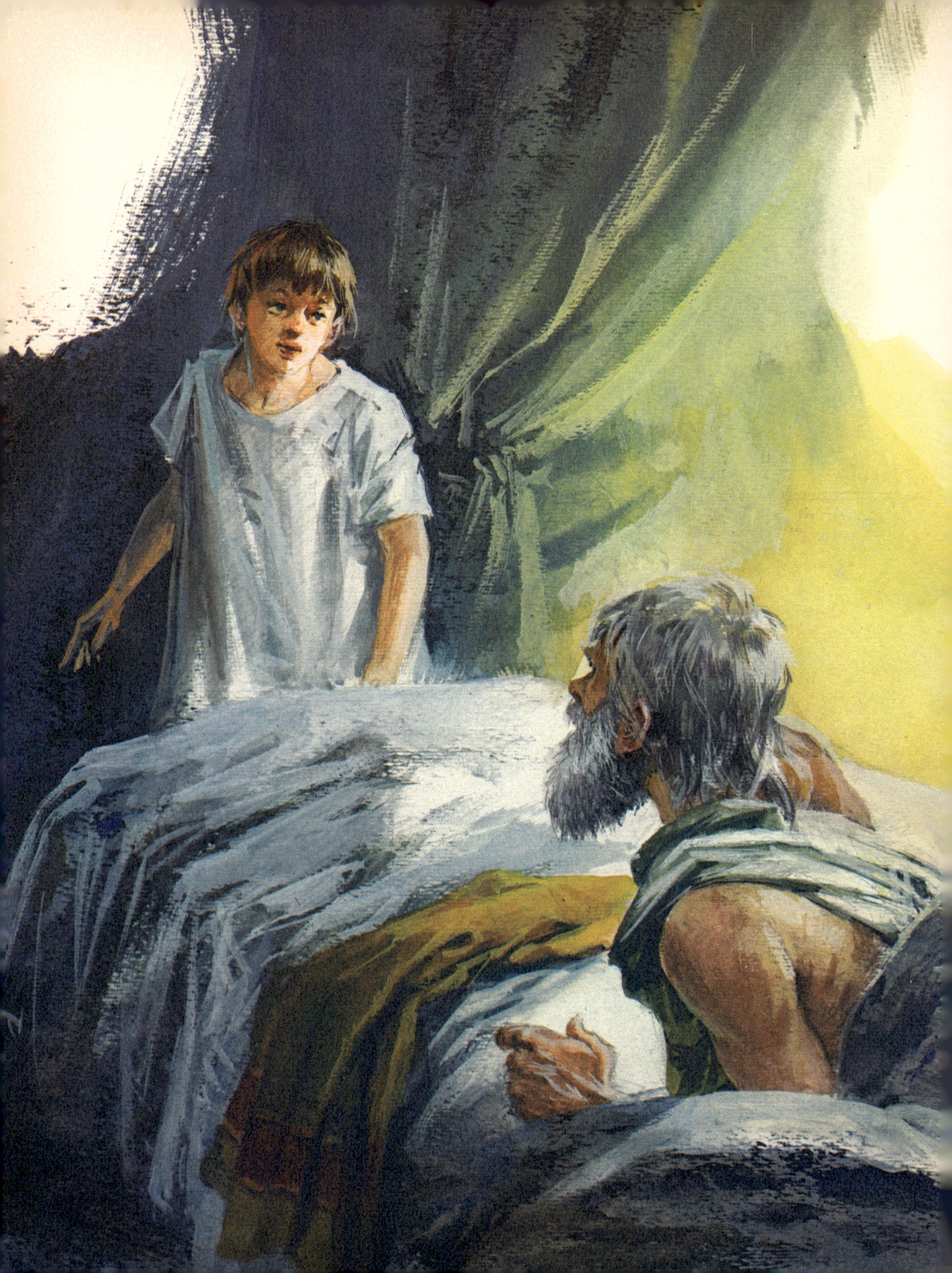

Hannah continued to pray to the Lord for a long time, and Eli watched her lips. She was praying silently; her lips were moving, but she made no sound. So Eli thought that she was drunk, and said to her, "Stop making a drunken show of yourself! Stop your drinking and sober up!"

"No, I'm not drunk, sir," she answered. "I haven't been drinking! I am desperate, and I have been praying, pouring out my troubles to the Lord. Don't think I am a worthless woman. I have been praying like this because I'm so miserable."

"Go in peace," Eli said, "and may the God of Israel give you what you have asked him for."

"May you always think kindly of me," she replied. Then she went away, ate some food, and was no longer sad.

The next morning Elkanah and his family got up early, and after worshipping the Lord, they went back home to Ramah. There Hannah gave birth to a son. She named him Samuel, and explained, "I asked the Lord for him."

Soon she took him back to the temple in Shiloh, where he served the Lord under the priest Eli. Each year his mother would make a little robe and take it to him when she accompanied her husband to offer the yearly sacrifice. Then Eli would bless Elkanah and his wife, and say to Elkanah, "May the Lord give you other children by this woman to take the place of the one you dedicated to him."

After that they would go back home.

The Lord did bless Hannah, and she had three more sons and two daughters. The boy Samuel grew up in the service of the Lord.

The Lord Appears to Samuel

Samuel, while still a boy in the temple at Shiloh, hears what the Lord is going to do to his own teacher, Eli.

When the boy Samuel was serving the Lord under the direction of Eli, there were very few messages from the Lord, and visions from him were quite rare. One night Eli, who was now almost blind, was sleeping in his own room; Samuel was sleeping in the sanctuary, where the sacred Covenant Box was. Before dawn, while the lamp was still burning, the Lord called Samuel. He answered, "Yes, sir!" and ran to Eli and said, "You called me, and here I am."

But Eli answered, "I didn't call you; go back to bed." So Samuel went back to bed.

The Lord called Samuel again. The boy did not know that it was the Lord, because the Lord had never spoken to him before. So he got up, went to Eli, and said, "You called me, and here I am."

But Eli answered, "My son, I didn't call you; go back to bed."

The Lord called Samuel a third time; he got up, went to Eli, and said, "You called me, and here I am."

Then Eli realized that it was the Lord who was calling the boy, so he said to him, "Go back to bed; and if he calls you again, say, 'Speak Lord, your servant is listening.'" So Samuel went back to bed.

The Lord came and stood there, and called as he had before, "Samuel! Samuel!"

Samuel answered, "Speak; your servant is listening."

The Lord said to him, "Some day I am going to do something to the people of Israel that is so terrible that everyone who hears about it will be stunned. On that day I will carry out all my threats against Eli's family, from beginning to end. I have already told him that I am going to punish his family for ever because his sons have spoken evil things against me. Eli knew they were doing this, but he did not stop them. So I solemnly declare to the family of Eli that no sacrifice or offering will ever be able to remove the consequences of this terrible sin."

Samuel stayed in bed until morning; then he got up and opened the doors of the house of the Lord. He was afraid to tell Eli about the vision. Eli called him, "Samuel, my boy!"

"Yes, sir," answered Samuel.

"What did the Lord tell you?" Eli asked. "Don't keep anything from me. God will punish you severely if you don't tell me everything he said." So Samuel told him everything; he did not keep anything back. Eli said, "He is the Lord; he will do whatever seems best to him."

As Samuel grew up, the Lord was with him and made everything that Samuel said come true.

Saul Is Acclaimed as King

Samuel had to admit that the Israelites must have a king like the surrounding nations. The first king is Saul, who turns out to be a disappointment.

Samuel called the people together for a religious gathering at Mizpah and said to them, "The Lord, the God of Israel, says, 'I brought you out of Egypt and rescued you from the Egyptians and all the other peoples who were oppressing you. I am your God, the one who rescues you from all your troubles and difficulties, but today you have rejected me and have asked me to give you a king. Very well, then, gather yourselves before the Lord by tribes and by clans.'"

Then Samuel made each tribe come forward, and the Lord picked the tribe of Benjamin. Then Samuel made the families of the tribe of Benjamin come forward, and the family of Matri was picked out. Then the men of the family of Matri came forward, and Saul son of Kish was picked out. They looked for him, but when they could not find him, they asked the Lord, "Is there still someone else?"

The Lord answered, "Saul is over there, hiding behind the supplies."

So they ran and brought Saul out to the people, and they could see

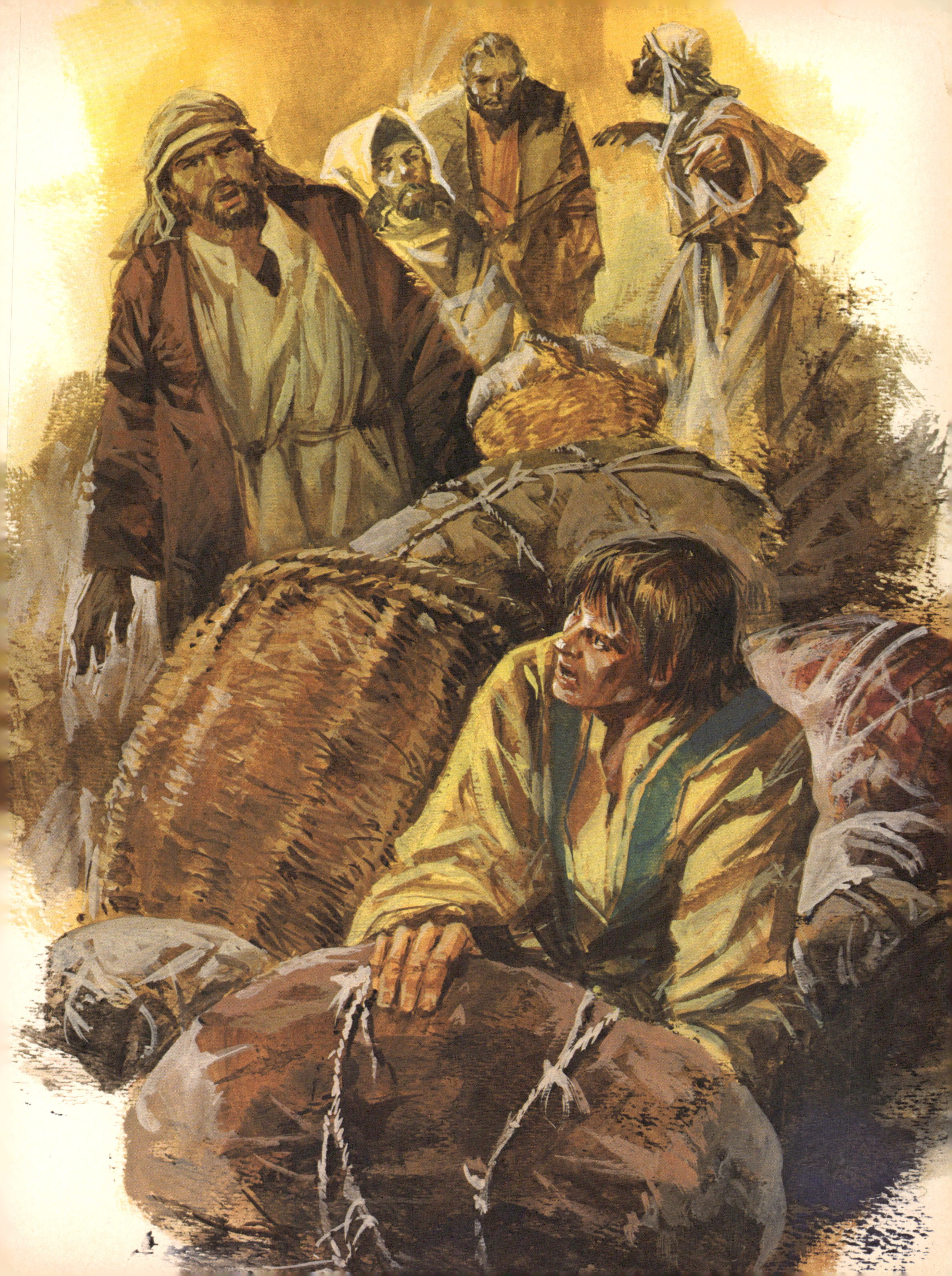

that he was a head taller than anyone else. Samuel said to the people, "Here is the man the Lord has chosen! There is no one else among us like him."

All the people shouted, "Long live the king!"

Samuel explained to the people the rights and duties of a king, and then wrote them in a book, which he deposited in a holy place. Then he sent everyone home.

The Young David

Ruth Comes to Bethlehem

Now our attention moves to David. He was the first great King of the Jews but he was descended from an Arab girl, Ruth. This is the story of how Ruth came to live in Bethlehem. In her own country she had married a Jew, who had died. Her husband's mother, Naomi, was herself a widow. So Ruth decided to go with her back to her home town, Bethlehem, a village near Jerusalem.

Naomi was left all alone, without husband or sons. Some time later Naomi heard that the Lord had blessed his people by giving them a good harvest; so she got ready to leave Moab with her daughters-in-law, Orpah and Ruth. They started out together to go back to Judah, but on the way she said to them, "Go back home and stay with your mothers. May the Lord be as good to you as you have been to me and to those who have died. And may the Lord make it possible for each of you to marry again and have a home."

But Ruth answered, "Don't ask me to leave you! Let me go with you. Wherever you go, I will go; wherever you live, I will live. Your people will be my people, and your God will be my God. Wherever you die, I will die, and that is where I will be buried. May the Lord's worst punishment come upon me if I let anything but death separate me from you!"

When Naomi saw that Ruth was determined to go with her, she said nothing more.

They went on until they came to Bethlehem.

Ruth Works in the Field of Boaz

Naomi had a relative named Boaz, a rich and influential man who belonged to the family of her husband Elimelech. One day Ruth said to Naomi, "Let me go to the fields to gather the corn that the harvest workers leave. I am sure to find someone who will let me work with him."

Naomi answered, "Go ahead, my daughter."

So Ruth went out to the fields and walked behind the workers, picking up the corn which they left. It so happened that she was in a field that belonged to Boaz.

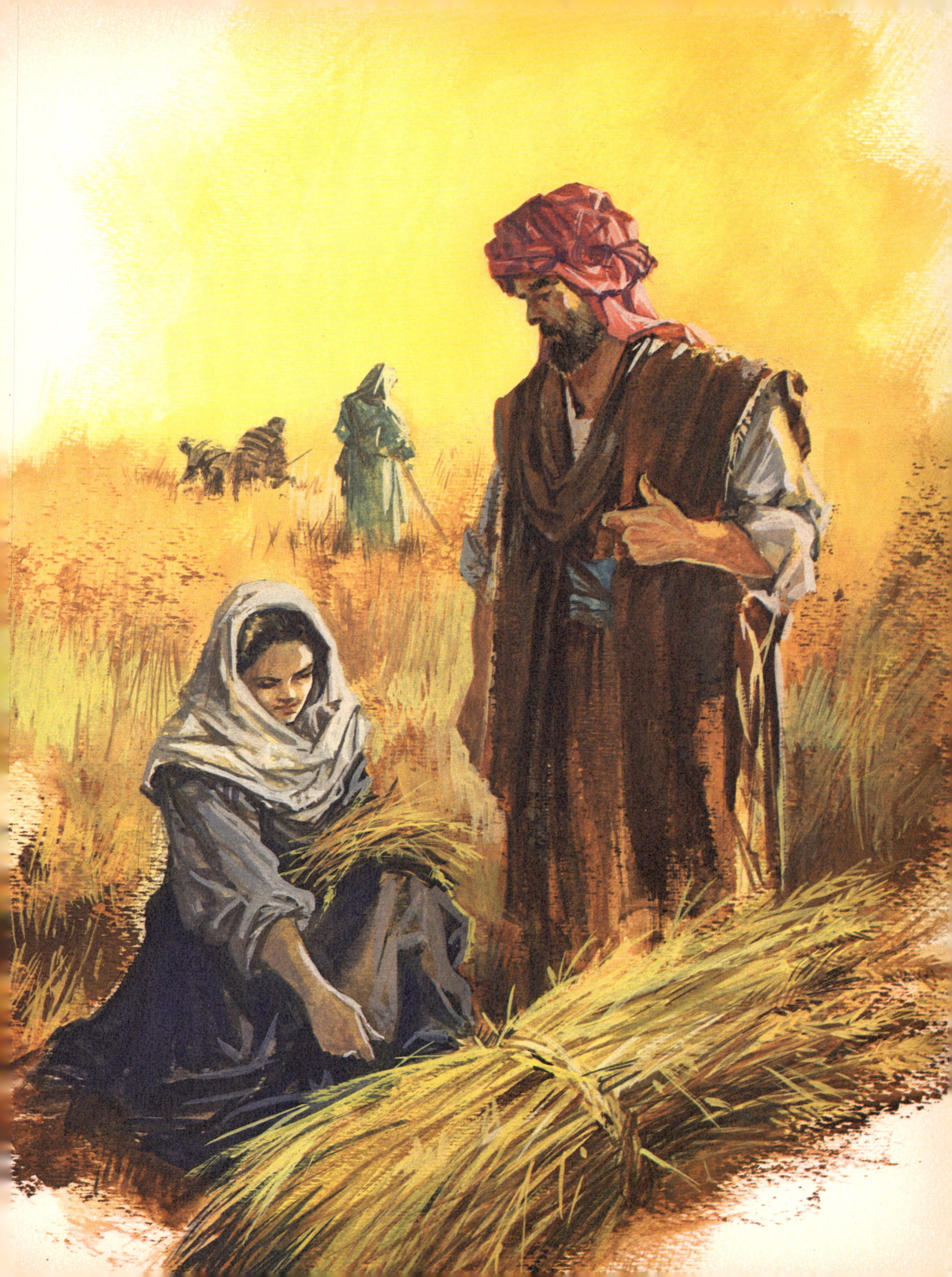

At meal-time Boaz said to Ruth, "Come and have a piece of bread, and dip it in the sauce." So she sat with the workers, and Boaz passed some roasted grain to her. She ate until she was satisfied, and she still had some food left over. After she had left to go on picking up corn, Boaz ordered the workers, "Let her pick it up even where the bundles are lying, and don't say anything to stop her. Besides that, pull out some corn from the bundles and leave it for her to pick up."

Boaz Marries Ruth

So Boaz took Ruth home as his wife. The Lord blessed her, and she became pregnant and had a son. The women said to Naomi, "Praise the Lord! He has given you a grandson today to take care of you. May the boy become famous in Israel! Your daughter-in-law loves you, and has done more for you than seven sons. And now she has given you a grandson, who will bring new life to you and give you security in your old age." Naomi took the child, held him close, and took care of him.

The women of the neighbourhood named the boy Obed. They told everyone, "A son has been born to Naomi!"

Obed became the father of Jesse, who was the father of David.

This is the family line from Perez to David: Perez, Hezron, Ram, Amminadab, Nahshon, Salmon, Boaz, Obed, Jesse, David.

David Is Anointed King

When David the shepherd-boy of Bethlehem is anointed King of the Jews, we remember that Jesus was called the "Anointed King" (in Hebrew "Messiah", in Greek "Christos") and the "Son of David".

The Lord said to Samuel, "How long will you go on grieving over Saul? I have rejected him as king of Israel. But now get some olive-oil and go to Bethlehem, to a man named Jesse, because I have chosen one of his sons to be king."

"How can I do that?" Samuel asked. "If Saul hears about it, he will kill me!"

The Lord answered, "Take a calf with you and say that you are there to offer a sacrifice to the Lord. Invite Jesse to the sacrifice, and I will tell you what to do. You will anoint as king the man I tell you to."

Samuel did what the Lord told him to do and went to Bethlehem, where the city leaders came trembling to meet him and asked, "Is this a peaceful visit, seer?"

"Yes," he answered. "I have come to offer a sacrifice to the Lord. Purify yourselves and come with me." He also told Jesse and his sons to purify themselves, and he invited them to the sacrifice.

When they arrived, Samuel saw Jesse's son Eliab and said to himself,

"This man standing here in the Lord's presence is surely the one he has chosen." But the Lord said to him, "Pay no attention to how tall and handsome he is. I have rejected him, because I do not judge as man judges. Man looks at the outward appearance, but I look at the heart."

Then Jesse called his son Abinadab and brought him to Samuel. But Samuel said, "No, the Lord hasn't chosen him either." Jesse then brought Shammah. "No, the Lord hasn't chosen him either," Samuel said. In this way Jesse brought seven of his sons to Samuel. And Samuel said to him, "No, the Lord hasn't chosen any of these." Then he asked him, "Have you any more sons?"

Jesse answered, "There is still the youngest, but he is out taking care of the sheep."

"Tell him to come here," Samuel said. "We won't offer the sacrifice until he comes." So Jesse sent for him. He was a handsome, healthy young man, and his eyes sparkled. The Lord said to Samuel, "This is the one — anoint him!" Samuel took the olive-oil and anointed David in front of his brothers. Immediately the spirit of the Lord took control of David and was with him from that day on.

Goliath Challenges the Israelites

A giant is frightening until a boy is brave.

The Philistines lined up on one hill and the Israelites on another, with a valley between them.

A man named Goliath, from the city of Gath, came out from the Philistine camp to challenge the Israelites. He was nearly three metres tall and wore bronze armour that weighed about fifty-seven kilogrammes and a bronze helmet. His legs were also protected by bronze armour, and he carried a bronze javelin slung over his shoulder. His spear was as thick as the bar on a weaver's loom, and its iron head weighed about seven kilogrammes. A soldier walked in front of him carrying his shield. Goliath stood and shouted at the Israelites, "What are you doing there, lined up for battle? I am a Philistine, you slaves of Saul! Choose one of your men to fight me. If he wins and kills me, we will be your slaves; but if I win and kill him, you will be our slaves. Here and now I challenge the Israelite army. I dare you to pick someone to fight me!" When Saul and his men heard this, they were terrified.

David in Saul's Camp

David was the son of Jesse, who was an Ephrathite from Bethlehem in Judah. Jesse had eight sons, and at the time Saul was king, he was already a very old man. His three eldest sons had gone with Saul to war. The eldest was Eliab, the next was Abinadab, and the third was Shammah. David was the youngest son, and while the three eldest brothers stayed with Saul, David would leave them and go back to Bethlehem from time to time, to take care of his father's sheep.

Goliath challenged the Israelites every morning and evening for forty days.

One day Jesse said to David, "Take ten kilogrammes of this roasted grain and these ten loaves of bread, and hurry with them to your brothers in the camp. And take these ten cheeses to the commanding officer. Find out how your brothers are getting on and bring back something to show that you saw them and that they are well. King Saul, your brothers, and all the other Israelites are in the Valley of Elah fighting the Philistines."

David got up early the next morning, left someone else in charge of the sheep, took the food, and went as Jesse had told him to. He arrived at the camp just as the Israelites were going out to their battle line, shouting the war-cry. The Philistine and the Israelite armies took up positions for battle, facing each other. David left the food with the officer in charge of the supplies, ran to the battle line, went to his brothers, and asked how they were getting on. As he was talking to them, Goliath came forward and challenged the Israelites as he had done before. And David heard him. When the Israelites saw Goliath, they ran away in terror. "Look at him!" they said to each other. "Listen to his challenge! King Saul has promised to give a big reward to the man who kills him; the king will also give him his daughter to marry and will not require his father's family to pay taxes."

David asked the men who were near him, "What will the man get who kills this Philistine and frees Israel from this disgrace? After all, who is this heathen Philistine to defy the army of the living God?" They told him what would be done for the man who killed Goliath.

Eliab, David's eldest brother, heard David talking to the men. He was angry with David and said, "What are you doing here? Who is taking care of those sheep of yours out there in the wilderness? You cheeky brat, you! You just came to watch the fighting!"

"Now what have I done?" David asked. "Can't I even ask a question?" He turned to another man and asked him the same question, and every time he asked, he got the same answer.

Some men heard what David had said, and they told Saul, who sent for him. David said to Saul, "Your Majesty, no one should be afraid of this Philistine! I will go and fight him."

"No," answered Saul. "How could you fight him? You're just a boy, and he has been a soldier all his life!"

"Your Majesty," David said, "I take care of my father's sheep. Whenever a lion or a bear carries off a lamb, I go after it, attack it, and rescue the lamb. And if the lion or bear turns on me, I grab it by the throat and

Opposite: David kills Goliath (text on page 76)

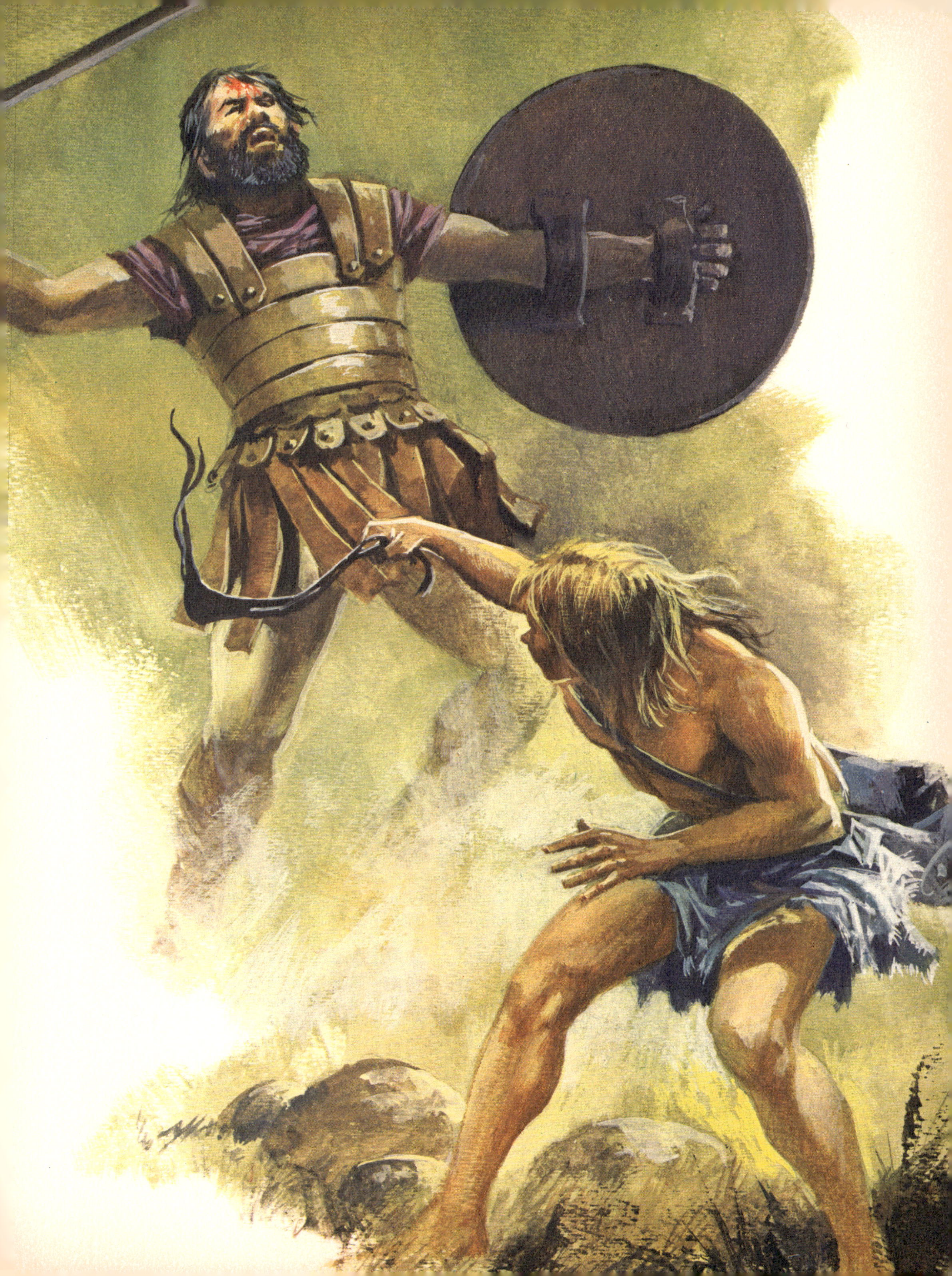

beat it to death. I have killed lions and bears, and I will do the same to this heathen Philistine, who has defied the army of the living God. The Lord has saved me from lions and bears; he will save me from this Philistine."

"All right," Saul answered. "Go, and the Lord be with you." He gave his own armour to David for him to wear: a bronze helmet, which he put on David's head, and a coat of armour. David strapped Saul's sword over the armour and tried to walk, but he couldn't, because he wasn't used to wearing them. "I can't fight with all this," he said to Saul. "I'm not used to it." So he took it all off. He took his shepherd's stick and then picked up five smooth stones from the stream and put them in his bag. With his catapult ready, he went out to meet Goliath.

David Defeats Goliath

The Philistine started walking towards David, with his shield-bearer walking in front of him. He kept coming closer, and when he got a good look at David, he was filled with scorn for him because he was just a nice, good-looking boy. He said to David, "What's that stick for? Do you think I'm a dog?" And he called down curses from his god on David. "Come on," he challenged David, "and I will give your body to the birds and animals to eat."

David answered, "You are coming against me with sword, spear, and javelin, but I come against you in the name of the Lord Almighty, the God of the Israelite armies, which you have defied. This very day the Lord will put you in my power; I will defeat you and cut off your head. And I will give the bodies of the Philistine soldiers to the birds and animals to eat. Then the whole world will know that Israel has a God, and everyone here will see that the Lord does not need swords or spears to save his people. He is victorious in battle, and he will put all of you in our power."

Goliath started walking towards David again, and David ran quickly towards the Philistine battle line to fight him. He put his hand into his bag and took out a stone, which he slung at Goliath. It hit him on the forehead and broke his skull, and Goliath fell face downwards on the ground. And so, without a sword, David defeated and killed Goliath with a catapult and a stone! He ran to him, stood over him, took Goliath's sword out of its sheath, and cut off his head and killed him.

David Is Presented to Saul

When Saul saw David going out to fight Goliath, he asked Abner, the commander of his army, "Abner, whose son is he?"

"I have no idea, Your Majesty," Abner answered.

"Then go and find out," Saul ordered.

So when David returned to camp after killing Goliath, Abner took him to Saul. David was still carrying Goliath's head. Saul asked him, "Young man, whose son are you?"

"I am the son of your servant Jesse from Bethlehem," David answered.

Saul and David finished their conversation. After that, Saul's son Jonathan was deeply attracted to David and came to love him as much as he loved himself. Saul kept David with him from that day on and did not let him go back home. Jonathan swore eternal friendship with David because of his deep affection for him. He took off the robe he was wearing and gave it to David, together with his armour and also his sword, bow, and belt. David was successful in all the missions on which Saul sent him, and so Saul made him an officer in his army. This pleased all of Saul's officers and men.

Saul Becomes Jealous of David

As David was returning after killing Goliath and as the soldiers were coming back home, women from every town in Israel came out to meet King Saul. They were singing joyful songs, dancing, and playing tambourines and lyres. In their celebration the women sang, "Saul has killed thousands, but David tens of thousands." Saul did not like this, and he became very angry. He said, "For David they claim tens of thousands, but only thousands for me. They will be making him king next!" And so he was jealous and suspicious of David from that day on.

The next day an evil spirit from God suddenly took control of Saul, and he raved in his house like a madman. David was playing the harp, as he did every day, and Saul was holding a spear. "I'll pin him to the wall," Saul said to himself, and he threw the spear at him twice; but David dodged each time.

Saul was afraid of David because the Lord was with David but had abandoned him. So Saul sent him away and put him in command of a thousand men. David led his men in battle and was successful in all he did, because the Lord was with him. Saul noticed David's success and became even more afraid of him. But everyone in Israel and Judah loved David because he was such a successful leader.

David at the Court of King Saul

The Friendship of David and Jonathan

> When King Saul grew angry with the young David, David relied on his friend, Saul's son Jonathan. But this story tells how Jonathan had to make his warning to David a secret between them.

David went to Jonathan. "What have I done?" he asked. "What crime have I committed? What wrong have I done to your father to make him want to kill me?"

Jonathan answered, "God forbid that you should die! My father tells me everything he does, important or not, and he would not hide this from me. It isn't true!"

But David answered, "Your father knows very well how much you like me, and he has decided not to let you know what he plans to do, because you would be deeply hurt. I swear to you by the living Lord that I am only a step away from death!"

Jonathan said, "I'll do anything you want."

"Tomorrow is the New Moon Festival," David replied, "and I am supposed to eat with the king. But if it's all right with you, I will go and hide in the fields until the evening of the day after tomorrow. If your father notices that I am not at table, tell him that I begged your permission to hurry home to Bethlehem, since it's the time for the annual sacrifice there for my whole family. If he says, 'All right,' I will be safe; but if he becomes angry, you will know that he is determined to harm me. Please do me this favour, and keep the sacred promise you made to me. But if I'm guilty, kill me yourself! Why take me to your father to be killed?"

"Don't even think such a thing!" Jonathan answered. "If I knew for certain that my father was determined to harm you, wouldn't I tell you?"

David then asked, "Who will let me know if your father answers you angrily?"

"Let's go out to the fields," Jonathan answered. So they went, and Jonathan said to David, "May the Lord God of Israel be our witness! At this time tomorrow and on the following day I will question my father. If his attitude towards you is good, I will send you word. If he intends to harm you, may the Lord strike me dead if I don't let you know about it and get you safely away. May the Lord be with you as he was with my father! And if I remain alive, please keep your sacred promise and be loyal to me; but if I die, show the same kind of loyalty to my family for ever. And when the Lord has completely destroyed all your enemies, may our promise to each other still be unbroken. If it is broken, the Lord will punish you."

Once again Jonathan made David promise to love him, for Jonathan loved David as much as he loved himself. Then Jonathan said to him, "Since tomorrow is the New Moon Festival, your absence will be noticed if you aren't at the meal. The day after tomorrow your absence will be noticed even more; so go to the place where you hid the other time, and hide behind the pile of stones there. I will then shoot three arrows at it, as though it were a target. Then I will tell my servant to go and find them. And if I tell him, 'Look, the arrows are on this side of you; get them,' that means that you are safe and can come out. I swear by the living Lord that you will be in no danger. But if I tell him, 'The arrows are on the other side of you,' then leave, because the Lord is sending you away. As for the promise we have made to each other, the Lord will make sure that we will keep it for ever."

Jonathan Warns David to Escape

So David hid in the fields. At the New Moon Festival, King Saul came to the meal and sat in his usual place by the wall. Abner sat next to him, and Jonathan sat opposite him. David's place was empty, but Saul said nothing that day, because he thought, "Something has happened to him, and he is not ritually pure." On the following day, the day after the New Moon Festival, David's place was still empty, and Saul asked Jonathan, "Why didn't David come to the meal either yesterday or today?"

Jonathan answered, "He begged me to let him go to Bethlehem. 'Please let me go,' he said, 'because our family is celebrating the sacrificial feast in town, and my brother ordered me to be there. So then, if you are my friend, let me go and see my relatives.' That is why he isn't in his place at your table."

Saul was furious with Jonathan and said to him, "You bastard! Now I know you are taking sides with David and are disgracing yourself and that mother of yours! Don't you realize that as long as David is alive, you will never be king of this country? Now go and bring him here — he must die!"

"Why should he die?" Jonathan replied. "What has he done?"

At that, Saul threw his spear at Jonathan to kill him, and Jonathan realized that his father was really determined to kill David. Jonathan got up from the table in a rage and ate nothing that day — the second day of the New Moon Festival. He was deeply distressed about David, because Saul had insulted him. The following morning Jonathan went to the fields to meet David, as they had agreed. He took a young boy with him and said to him, "Run and find the arrows I'm going to shoot." The boy ran, and Jonathan shot an arrow beyond him. When the boy reached the place where the arrow had fallen, Jonathan shouted to him, "The arrow is further on! Don't just stand there! Hurry up!" The boy picked up the arrow and returned to his master, not knowing what it all meant; only Jonathan and David knew. Jonathan gave his weapons to the boy and told him to take them back to the town.

After the boy had left, David got up from behind the pile of stones, fell on his knees and bowed with his face to the ground three times. Both he and Jonathan were crying as they kissed each other; David's grief was even greater than Jonathan's.

Saul and the Ghost of Samuel

The ghost of Samuel foretells Saul's own death.

Now Samuel had died, and all the Israelites had mourned for him and had buried him in his own city of Ramah. Saul had forced all the fortune-tellers and mediums to leave Israel.

The Philistine troops assembled and camped near the town of Shunem; Saul gathered the Israelites and camped at Mount Gilboa. When Saul saw the Philistine army, he was terrified, and so he asked the Lord what to do. But the Lord did not answer him at all. Then Saul ordered his officials, "Find me a woman who is a medium, and I will go and consult her."

"There is one in Endor," they answered.

So Saul disguised himself; he put on different clothes, and after dark he went with two of his men to see the woman. "Consult the spirits for me and tell me what is going to happen," he said to her. "Call up the spirit of the man I name."

The woman answered, "Surely you know what King Saul has done, how he forced the fortune-tellers and mediums to leave Israel. Why, then, are you trying to trap me and get me killed?"

Then Saul made a sacred vow. "By the living Lord I promise that you will not be punished for doing this," he told her.

"Whom shall I call up for you?" the woman asked.

"Samuel," he answered.

When the woman saw Samuel, she screamed and said to Saul, "Why have you tricked me? You are King Saul!"

"Don't be afraid!" the king said to her. "What do you see?"

"I see a spirit coming up from the earth," she answered.

"What does it look like?" he asked.

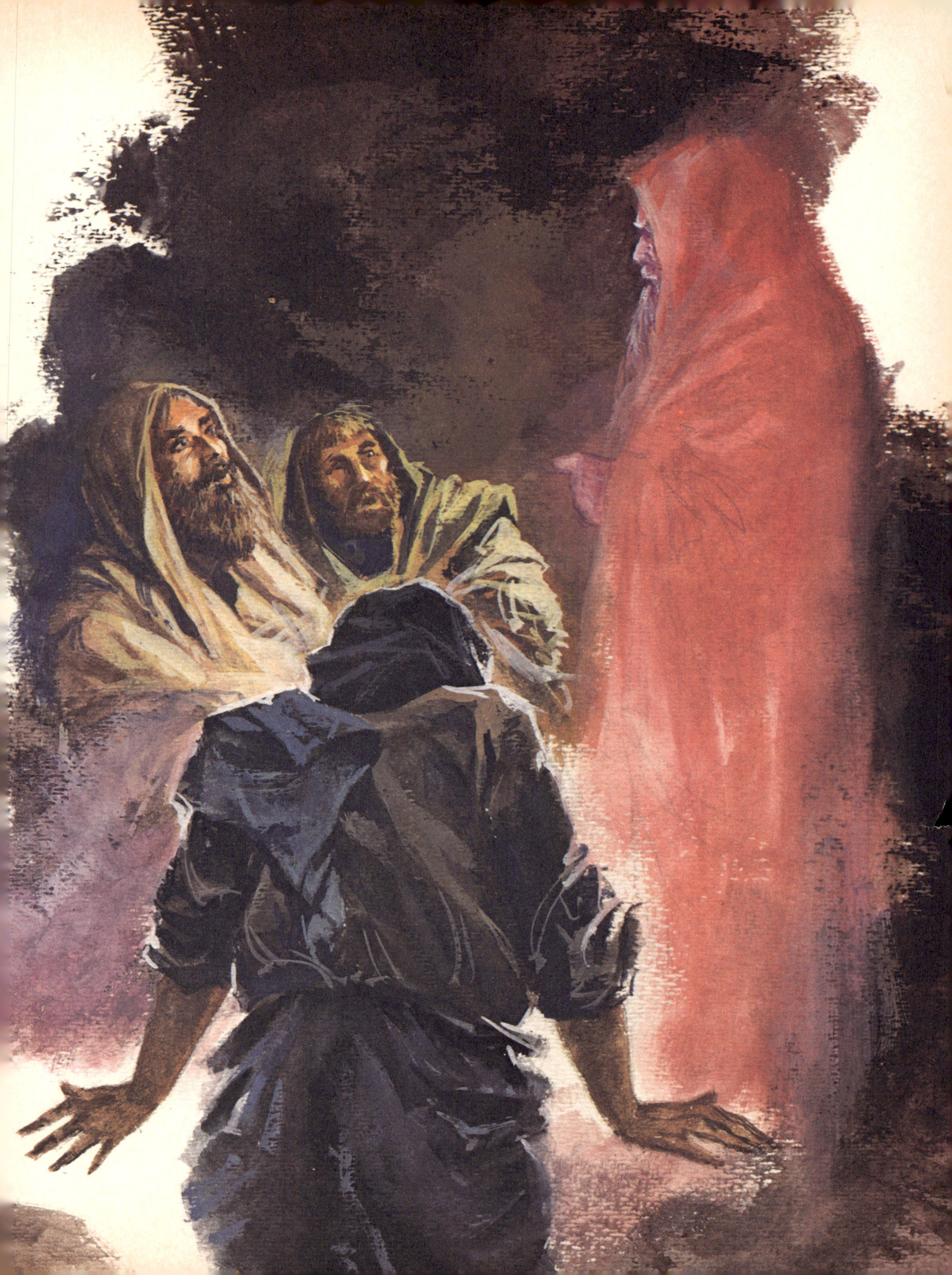

"It's an old man coming up," she answered. "He is wearing a cloak."

Then Saul knew that it was Samuel, and he bowed to the ground in respect.

Samuel said to Saul, "Why have you disturbed me? Why did you make me come back?"

Saul answered, "I am in great trouble! The Philistines are at war with me, and God has abandoned me. He doesn't answer me any more, either by prophets or by dreams. And so I have called you, for you to tell me what I must do."

Samuel said, "Why do you call me when the Lord has abandoned you and become your enemy? The Lord has done to you what he told you through me: he has taken the kingdom away from you and given it to David instead. You disobeyed the Lord's command and did not completely destroy the Amalekites and all they had. That is why the Lord is doing this to you now. He will hand you and Israel over to the Philistines. Tomorrow you and your sons will join me, and the Lord will also hand the army of Israel over to the Philistines."

At once Saul fell down and lay stretched out on the ground, terrified by what Samuel had said. He was weak, because he had not eaten anything all day and all night. The woman went over to him and saw that he was terrified, so she said to him, "Please, sir, I risked my life by doing what you asked. Now please do what I ask. Let me prepare some food for you. You must eat so that you will be strong enough to travel."

Saul refused and said he would not eat anything. But his officers also urged him to eat. He finally gave in, got up from the ground, and sat on the bed. The woman quickly killed a calf which she had been fattening. Then she took some flour, prepared it, and baked some bread without yeast. She set the food before Saul and his officers, and they ate it. And they left that same night.

The Death of Saul and His Sons

The Philistines fought a battle against the Israelites on Mount Gilboa. Many Israelites were killed there, and the rest of them, including King Saul and his sons, fled. But the Philistines caught up with them and killed three of Saul's sons, Jonathan, Abinadab, and Malchishua. The fighting was heavy round Saul, and he himself was hit by enemy arrows and badly wounded. He said to the young man carrying his weapons, "Draw your sword and kill me, so that these godless Philistines won't gloat over me and kill me." But the young man was too terrified to do it. So Saul took his own sword and threw himself on it. The young man saw that Saul was dead, so he too threw himself on his own sword and died with Saul. And that is how Saul, his three sons, and the young man died; all of Saul's men died that day.

David's Lament for Saul and Jonathan

David sang this lament for Saul and his son Jonathan, and ordered it to be taught to the people of Judah.

"On the hills of Israel our leaders are dead!
The bravest of our soldiers have fallen!
Do not announce it in Gath
   or in the streets of Ashkelon.
Do not make the women of Philistia glad;
   do not let the daughters of pagans rejoice.

"May no rain or dew fall on Gilboa's hills;
   may its fields be always barren!
For the shields of the brave lie there in disgrace;
   the shield of Saul is no longer polished with oil.
Jonathan's bow was deadly,
   the sword of Saul was merciless,
   striking down the mighty, killing the enemy.

"Saul and Jonathan, so wonderful and dear;
   together in life, together in death;
   swifter than eagles, stronger than lions.

"Women of Israel, mourn for Saul!
   He clothed you in rich scarlet dresses
   and adorned you with jewels and gold.

"The brave soldiers have fallen,
   they were killed in battle.
   Jonathan lies dead in the hills.

"I grieve for you, my brother Jonathan;
   how dear you were to me!
How wonderful was your love for me,
   better even than the love of women.

"The brave soldiers have fallen,
   their weapons abandoned and useless."

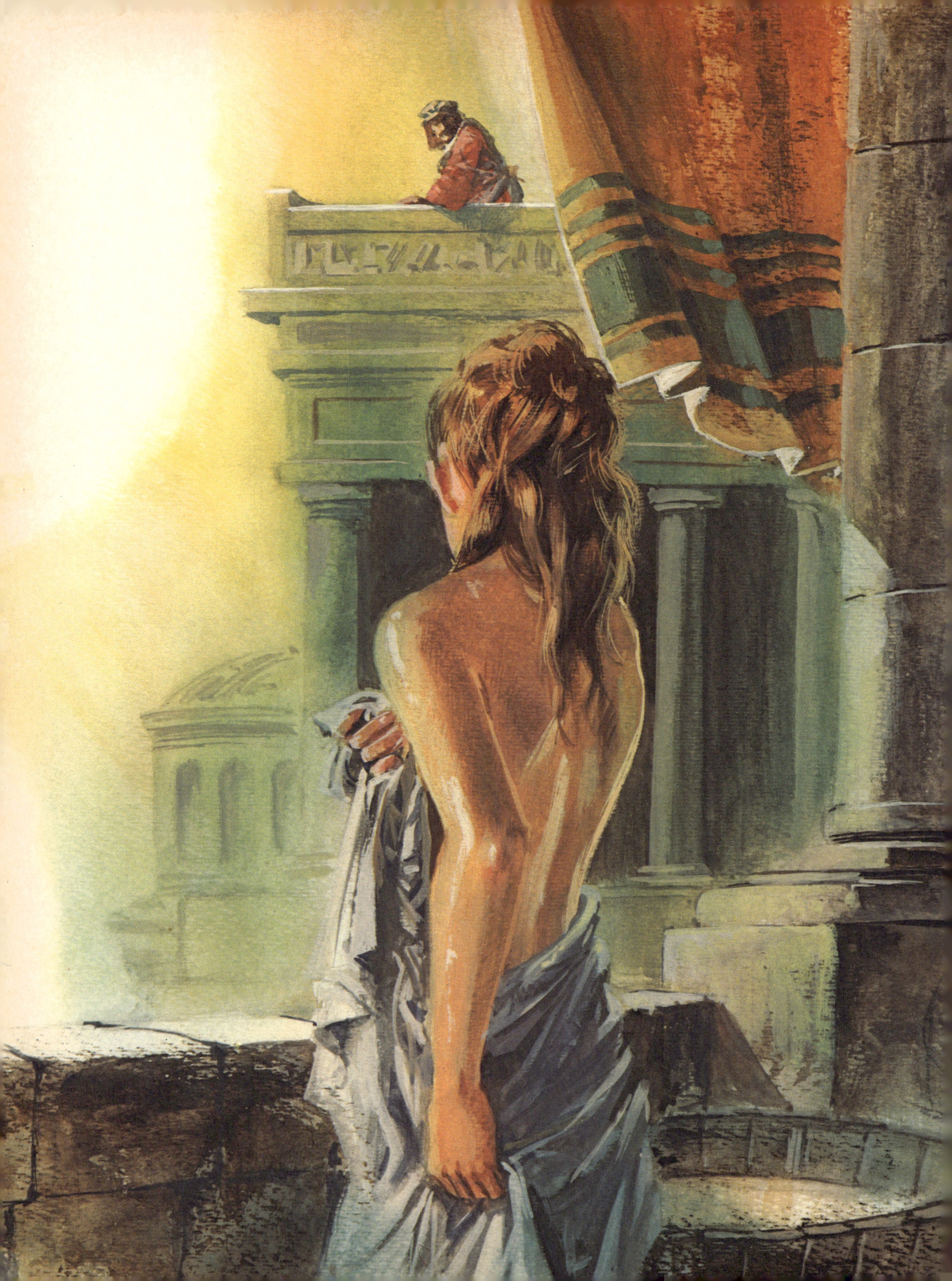

4
War and Peace

In good times or bad the people of Israel still meet their God — and if they refuse to see him, the prophets of the Lord point him out to them.

David the King

David's Sin

>King David falls in love with the beautiful Bathsheba. But she is already married to one of the officers in his army; and tragedy follows.

The following spring, at the time of the year when kings usually go to war, David sent out Joab with his officers and the Israelite army; they defeated the Ammonites and besieged the city of Rabbah. But David himself stayed in Jerusalem.

One day, late in the afternoon, David got up from his nap and went to the palace roof. As he walked about up there, he saw a woman having a bath. She was very beautiful. So he sent a messenger to find out who she was, and learnt that she was Bathsheba, the daughter of Eliam and the wife of Uriah the Hittite. David sent messengers to fetch her; they brought her to him and he made love to her. Then she went back home. Afterwards she discovered that she was pregnant and sent a message to David to tell him.

David then sent a message to Joab: "Send me Uriah the Hittite." So Joab sent him to David. When Uriah arrived, David asked him if Joab and the troops were well, and how the fighting was going. Then he said to Uriah, "Go home and rest a while." Uriah left, and David sent a present to his home. But Uriah did not go home; instead he slept at the palace gate with the king's guards. When David heard that Uriah had not gone home, he asked him, "You have just returned after a long absence; why didn't you go home?"

Uriah answered, "The men of Israel and Judah are away at the war, and the Covenant Box is with them; my commander Joab and his officers are camping out in the open. How could I go home, eat and drink, and sleep with my wife? By all that's sacred, I swear that I could never do such a thing!"

So David said, "Then stay here the rest of the day, and tomorrow I'll send you back." So Uriah stayed in Jerusalem that day and the next. David invited him to supper and made him drunk. But again that night

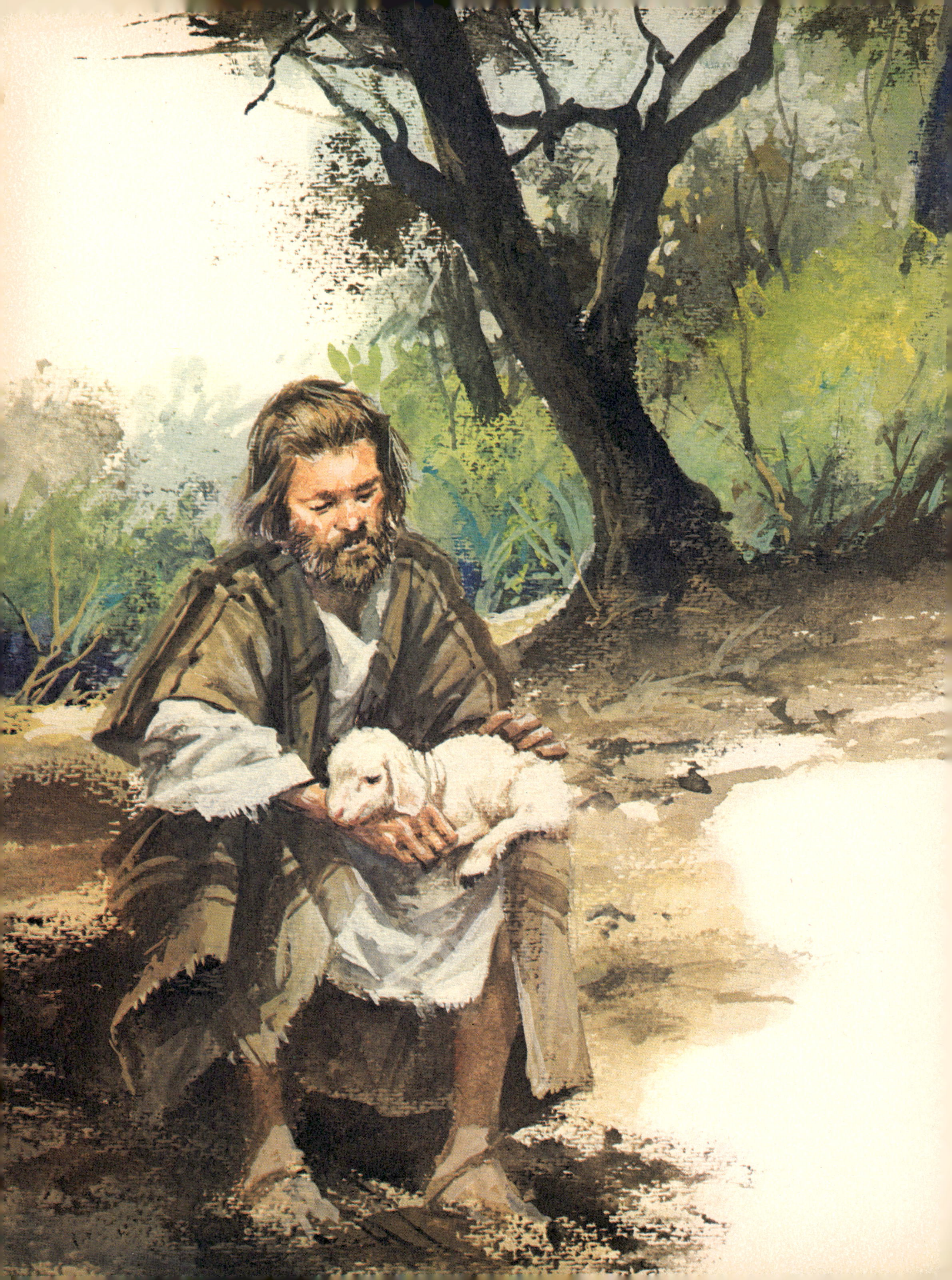

Uriah did not go home; instead he slept on his blanket in the palace guardroom.

The next morning David wrote a letter to Joab and sent it by Uriah. He wrote: 'Put Uriah in the front line, where the fighting is heaviest, then retreat and let him be killed." So while Joab was besieging the city, he sent Uriah to a place where he knew the enemy was strong. The enemy troops came out of the city and fought Joab's forces; some of David's officers were killed, and so was Uriah.

A messenger went to David and told him what Joab had commanded him to say. He said, "Our enemies were stronger than we were and came out of the city to fight us in the open, but we drove them back to the city gate. Then they shot arrows at us from the wall, and some of Your Majesty's officers were killed; your officer Uriah was also killed."

David said to the messenger, "Encourage Joab and tell him not to be upset, since you never can tell who will die in battle. Tell him to launch a stronger attack on the city and capture it."

When Bathsheba heard that her husband had been killed, she mourned for him. When the time of mourning was over, David sent for her to come to the palace; she became his wife and bore him a son. But the Lord was not pleased with what David had done.

David Is Told of His Sin

The Lord sent the prophet Nathan to David. Nathan went to him and said, "There were two men who lived in the same town; one was rich and the other poor. The rich man had many cattle and sheep, while the poor man had only one lamb, which he had bought. He took care of it, and it grew up in his home with his children. He would feed it with some of his own food, let it drink from his cup, and hold it in his lap. The lamb was like a daughter to him. One day a visitor arrived at the rich man's home. The rich man didn't want to kill one of his own animals to prepare a meal for him; instead, he took the poor man's lamb and cooked a meal for his guest."

David was very angry with the rich man and said, "I swear by the living Lord that the man who did this ought to die! For having done such a cruel thing, he must pay back four times as much as he took."

"You are that man," Nathan said to David. "And this is what the Lord God of Israel says: 'I made you king of Israel and rescued you from Saul. I gave you his kingdom and his wives; I made you king over Israel and Judah. If this had not been enough, I would have given you twice as much. Why, then, have you disobeyed my commands? Why did you do this evil thing? You had Uriah killed in battle; you let the Ammonites kill him, and then you took his wife! Now, in every generation some of your descendants will die a violent death because you have

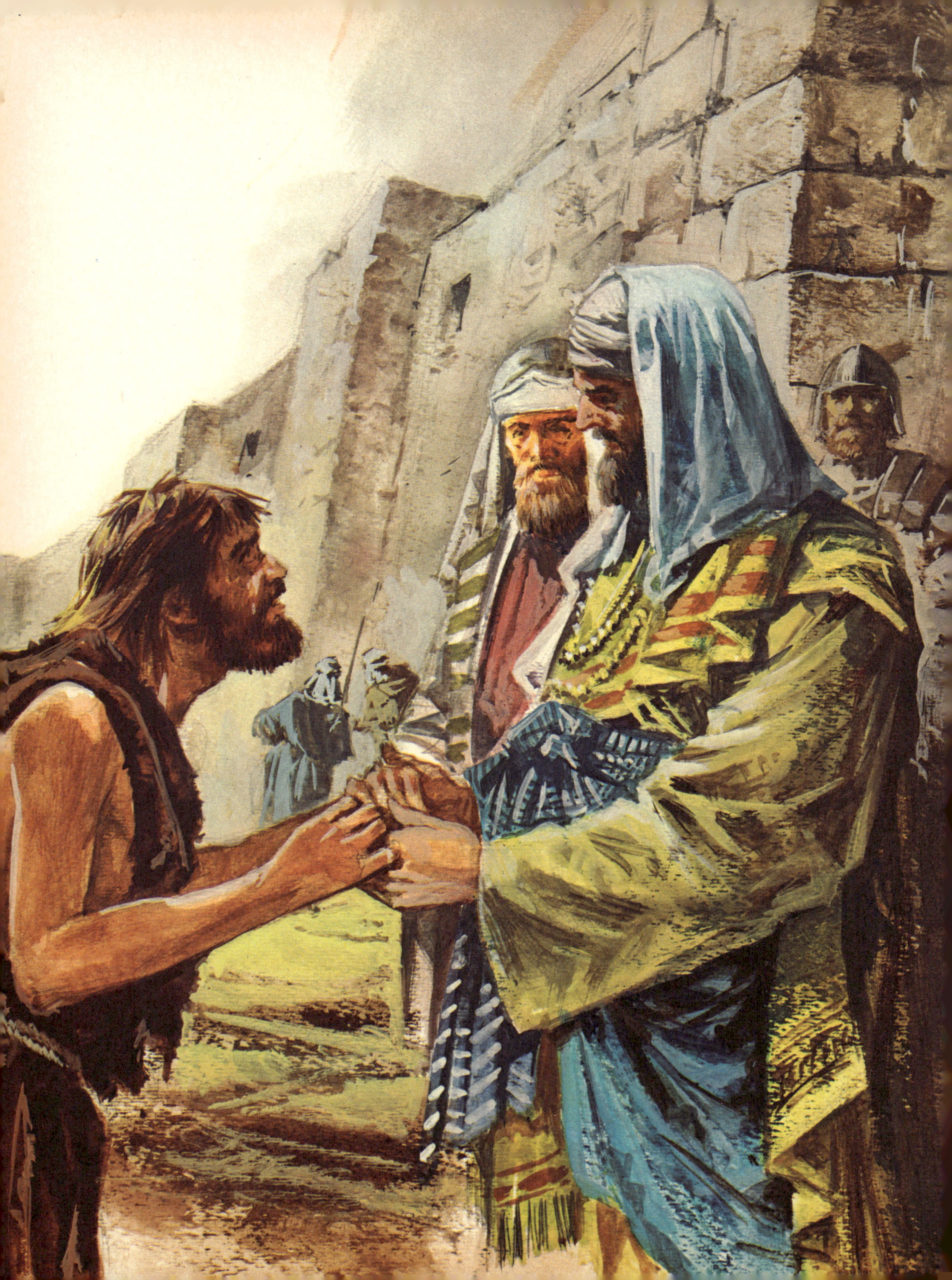

disobeyed me and have taken Uriah's wife. I swear to you that I will cause someone from your own family to bring trouble on you.'"

"I have sinned against the Lord," David said.

Nathan replied, "The Lord forgives you; you will not die. But because you have shown such contempt for the Lord in doing this, your child will die." Then Nathan went home.

David's Son Absalom Rebels

This is the story of how one of David's sons, Absalom, was disloyal to his father.

Absalom provided a chariot and horses for himself, and an escort of fifty men. He would get up early and go and stand by the road at the city gate. Whenever someone came there with a dispute that he wanted the king to settle, Absalom would call him over and ask him where he was from. And after the man had told him what tribe he was from, Absalom would say, "Look, the law is on your side, but there is no representative of the king to hear your case." And he would add, "How I wish I were a judge! Then anyone who had a dispute or a claim could come to me, and I would give him justice." When the man approached Absalom would reach out, take hold of him, and kiss him. Absalom did this with every Israelite who came to the king for justice, and so he won their loyalty.

The plot against the king gained strength, and Absalom's followers grew in number.

A messenger reported to David, "The Israelites are pledging their loyalty to Absalom." So David said to all his officials who were with him in Jerusalem, "We must get away at once if we want to escape from Absalom! Hurry!"

David's army went out into the countryside and fought the Israelites in the forest of Ephraim. The Israelites were defeated by David's men; it was a terrible defeat, with twenty thousand men killed that day. The fighting spread over the countryside, and more men died in the forest than were killed in battle.

The Death of Absalom

Suddenly Absalom met some of David's men. Absalom was riding a mule, and as it went under a large oak-tree, Absalom's head got caught in the branches. The mule ran on and Absalom was left hanging in mid air. One of David's men saw him and reported to Joab, "Sir, I saw Absalom hanging in an oak-tree!"

Joab answered, "If you saw him, why didn't you kill him on the spot? I myself would have given you ten pieces of silver and a belt."

But the man answered, "Even if you gave me a thousand pieces of

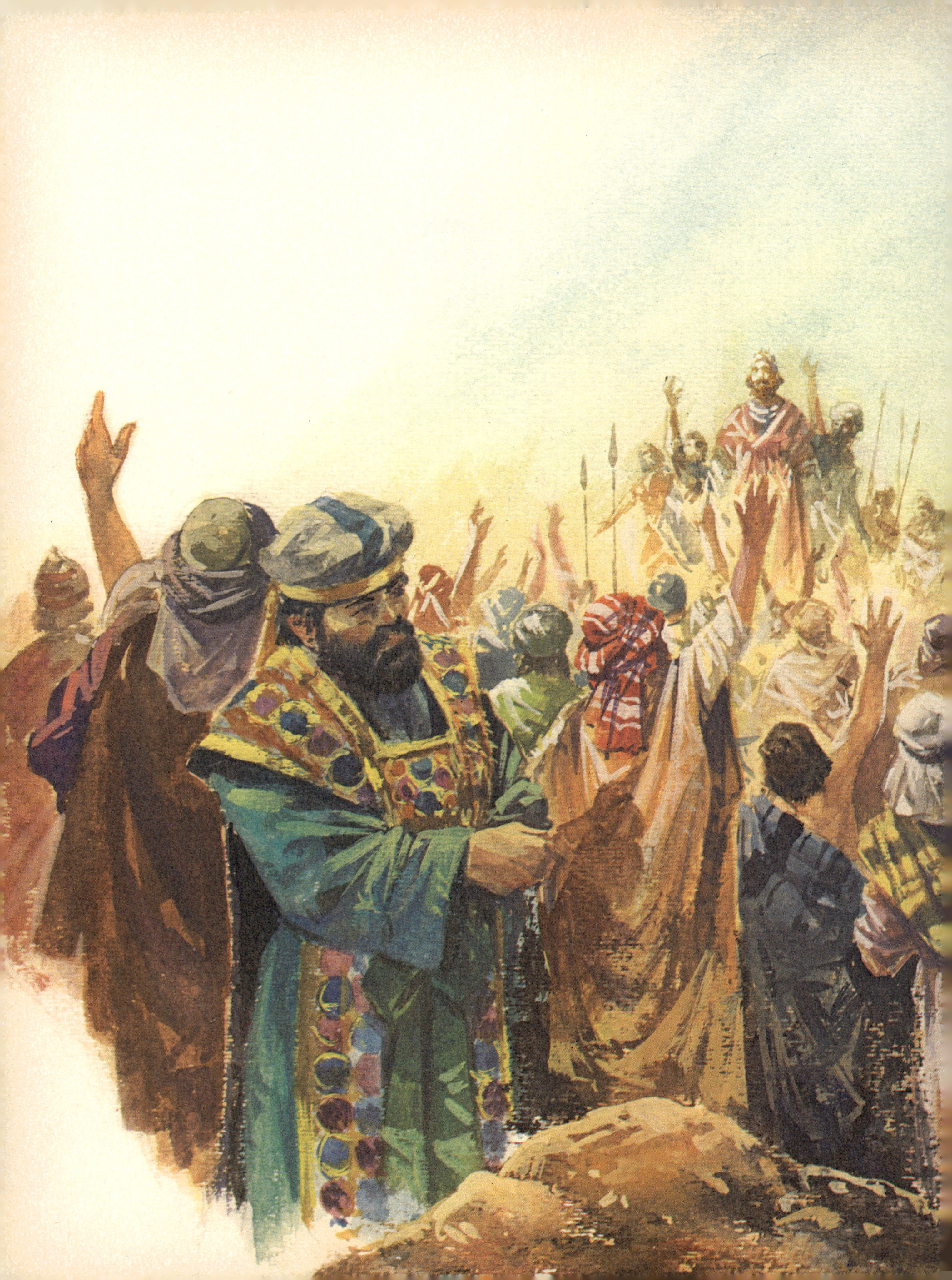

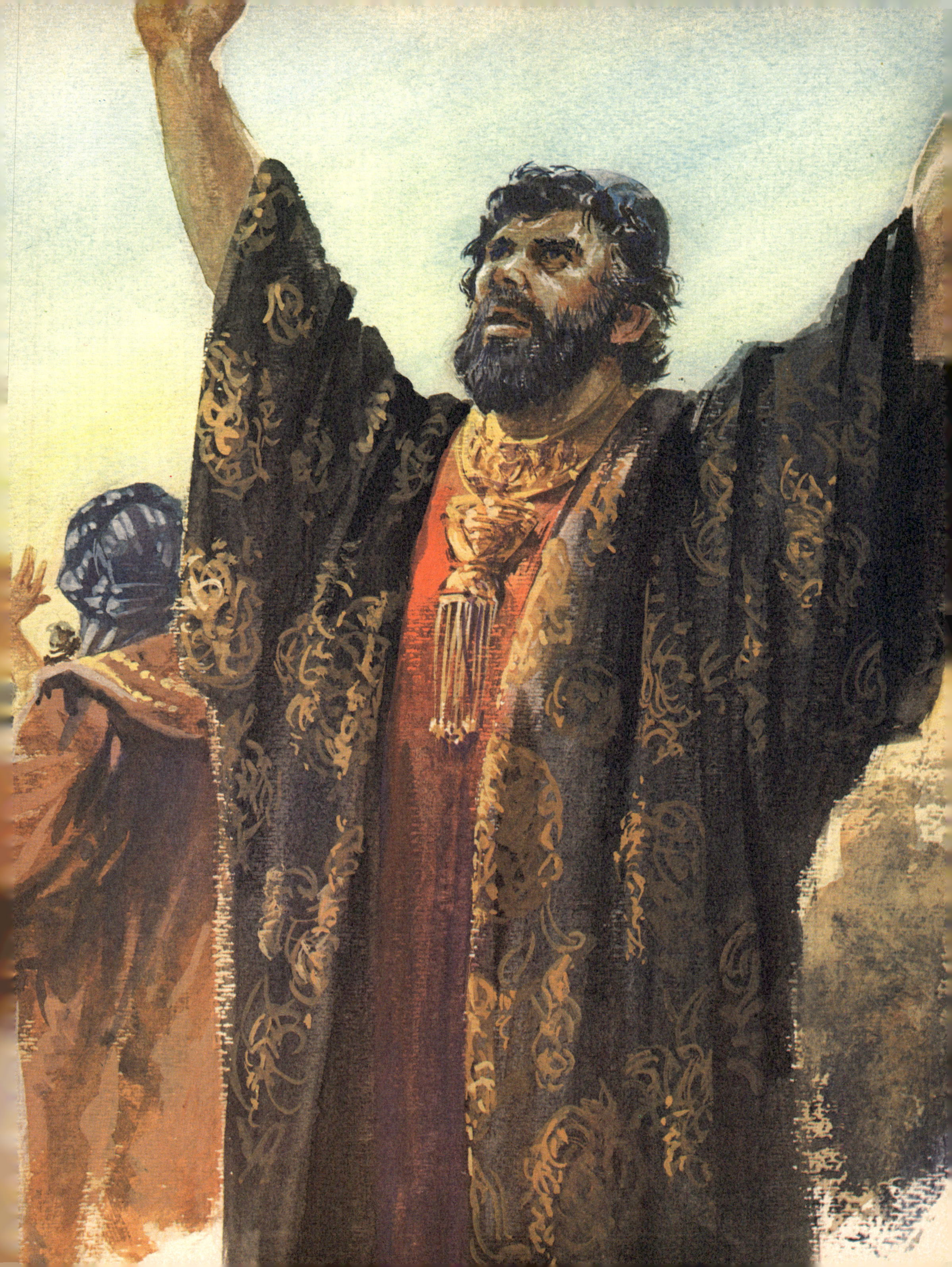

silver, I wouldn't lift a finger against the king's son. We all heard the king command you and Abishai and Ittai, 'For my sake don't harm the young man Absalom.' But if I had disobeyed the king and killed Absalom, the king would have heard about it — he hears about everything — and you would not have defended me."

"I'm not going to waste any more time with you," Joab said. He took three spears and plunged them into Absalom's chest while he was still alive, hanging in the oak-tree. Then ten of Joab's soldiers closed in on Absalom and finished killing him.

Joab ordered the trumpet to be blown to stop the fighting, and his troops came back from pursuing the Israelites. They took Absalom's body, threw it into a deep pit in the forest, and covered it with a huge pile of stones. All the Israelites fled, each man to his own home.

During his lifetime Absalom had built a monument for himself in King's Valley, because he had no son to keep his name alive. So he named it after himself, and to this day it is known as Absalom's Monument.

David Is Told of Absalom's Death

Then Ahimaaz son of Zadok said to Joab, "Let me run to the king with the good news that the Lord has saved him from his enemies."

"No," Joab said, "today you will not take any good news. Some other day you may do so, but not today, for the king's son is dead." Then he said to his Sudanese slave, "Go and tell the king what you have seen." The slave bowed and ran off.

Ahimaaz insisted, "I don't care what happens; please let me take the news also."

"Why do you want to do it, my son?" Joab asked. "You will get no reward for it."

"Whatever happens," Ahimaaz said again, "I want to go."

"Then go," Joab said. So Ahimaaz ran off down the road through the Jordan Valley, and soon he passed the slave.

David was sitting in the space between the inner and outer gates of the city. The watchman went up to the top of the wall and stood on the roof of the gateway; he looked out and saw a man running alone. He called down and told the king, and the king said, "If he is alone, he is bringing good news." The runner came nearer and nearer.

Then the watchman saw another man running alone, and he called down to the gatekeeper, "Look! There's another man running!"

The king answered, "This one also is bringing good news."

The watchman said, "I can see that the first man runs like Ahimaaz."

"He's a good man," the king said, "and he is bringing good news."

Ahimaaz called out a greeting to the king, threw himself down to the ground before him, and said, "Praise the Lord your God, who has given you victory over the men who rebelled against Your Majesty!"

"Is the young man Absalom safe?" the king asked.

Ahimaaz answered, "Sir, when your officer Joab sent me, I saw a great commotion, but I couldn't tell what it was."

"Stand over there," the king said; and he went over and stood there.

Then the Sudanese slave arrived and said to the king, "I have good news for Your Majesty! Today the Lord has given you victory over all who rebelled against you!"

"Is the young man Absalom safe?" the king asked.

The slave answered, "I wish that what has happened to him would happen to all your enemies, sir, and to all who rebel against you."

The king was overcome with grief. He went up to the room over the gateway and wept. As he went, he cried, "O my son! My son Absalom! Absalom, my son! If only I had died in your place, my son! Absalom, my son!"

The Wise King

Solomon Is Anointed King

The next king is David's son, Solomon. In the time when Jesus taught, about a thousand years later, people still remembered King Solomon's glory. Zadok, Nathan, Benaiah, and the royal bodyguard put Solomon on King David's mule, and escorted him to the spring of Gihon. Zadok took the container of olive-oil which he had brought from the Tent of the Lord's presence, and anointed Solomon. They blew the trumpet, and all the people shouted, "Long live King Solomon!" Then they all followed him back, shouting for joy and playing flutes, making enough noise to shake the ground.

Solomon Prays for Wisdom

On one occasion Solomon went to Gibeon to offer sacrifices because that was where the most famous altar was. He had offered hundreds of burnt-offerings there in the past. That night the Lord appeared to him in a dream and asked him, "What would you like me to give you?"

Solomon answered, "You always showed great love for my father David, your servant, and he was good, loyal, and honest in his relations with you. And you have continued to show him your great and constant love by giving him a son who today rules in his place. O Lord God, you have let me succeed my father as king, even though I am very young and don't know how to rule. Here I am among the people you have chosen to be your own, a people who are so many that they cannot be counted. So give me the wisdom I need to rule your people with justice and to know the difference between good and evil. Otherwise, how would I ever be able to rule this great people of yours?"

The Lord was pleased that Solomon had asked for this, and so he said to him, "Because you have asked for the wisdom to rule justly, instead of long life for yourself or riches or the death of your enemies, I will do what you have asked. I will give you more wisdom and understanding than anyone has ever had before or will ever have again. I will also give you what you have not asked for: all your life you will have wealth and honour, more than that of any other king. And if you obey me and keep my laws and commands, as your father David did, I will give you a long life."

Solomon woke up and realized that God had spoken to him in the dream.

Peace under Solomon

The people of Judah and Israel were as numerous as the grains of sand on the seashore; they ate and drank, and were happy. Solomon's kingdom included all the nations from the River Euphrates to Philistia and the Egyptian border. They paid him taxes and were subject to him all his life.

God gave Solomon unusual wisdom and insight, and knowledge too great to be measured. Solomon was wiser than the wise men of the East or the wise men of Egypt. He was the wisest of all men and his fame spread throughout all the neighbouring countries. He composed three thousand proverbs and more than a thousand songs. He spoke of trees and plants, from the Lebanon cedars to the hyssop that grows on walls; he talked about animals, birds, reptiles, and fish. Kings all over the world heard of his wisdom and sent people to listen to him.

The Visit of the Queen of Sheba

The queen of Sheba heard of Solomon's fame, and she travelled to Jerusalem to test him with difficult questions. She brought with her a large group of attendants, as well as camels loaded with spices, jewels, and a large amount of gold. When she and Solomon met, she asked him all the questions that she could think of. He answered them all; there was nothing too difficult for him to explain. The queen of Sheba heard Solomon's wisdom and saw the palace he had built. She saw the food that was served at his table, the living quarters for his officials, the organization of his palace staff and the uniforms they wore, the servants who waited on him at feasts, and the sacrifices he offered in the Temple. It left her breathless and amazed. She said to King Solomon, "What I heard in my own country about you and your wisdom is true! But I couldn't believe it until I had come and seen it all for myself. But I didn't

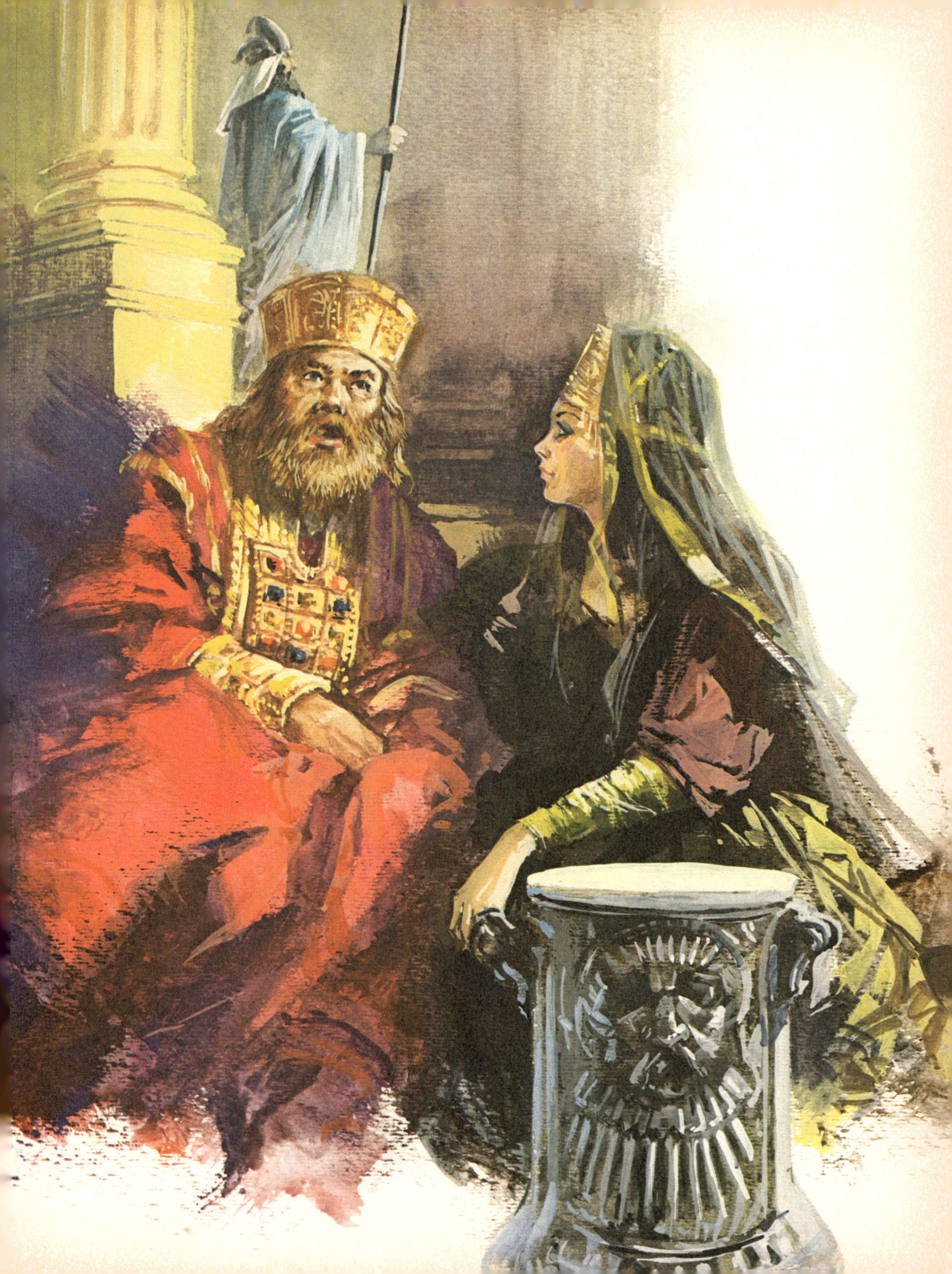

hear even half of it; your wisdom and wealth are much greater than what I was told. How fortunate are your wives! And how fortunate your servants, who are always in your presence and are privileged to hear your wise sayings! Praise the Lord your God! He has shown how pleased he is with you by making you king of Israel. Because his love for Israel is eternal, he has made you their king so that you can maintain law and justice."

Solomon Builds the Temple

> *In alliance with King Hiram of Tyre, Solomon builds the great Temple of the Lord in Jerusalem.*

King Hiram of Tyre had always been a friend of David's, and when he heard that Solomon had succeeded his father David as king he sent ambassadors to him. Solomon sent back this message to Hiram: "You know that because of the constant wars my father David had to fight against the enemy countries all round him, he could not build a temple for the worship of the Lord his God until the Lord had given him victory over all his enemies. But now the Lord my God has given me peace on all my borders. I have no enemies, and there is no danger of attack. The Lord promised my father David, 'Your son, whom I will make king after you, will build a temple for me.' And I have now decided to build that temple for the worship of the Lord my God. So send your men to Lebanon to cut down cedars for me. My men will work with them, and I will pay your men whatever you decide. As you well know, my men don't know how to cut down trees as well as yours do."

Hiram was extremely pleased when he received Solomon's message, and he said, "Praise the Lord today for giving David such a wise son to succeed him as king of that great nation!" Then Hiram sent Solomon the following message: "I have received your message and I am ready to do what you ask. I will provide the cedars and the pine-trees. My men will bring the logs down from Lebanon to the sea, and will tie them together in rafts to float them down the coast to the place you choose. There my men will untie them, and your men will take charge of them. On your part, I would like you to supply the food for my men."

So Hiram supplied Solomon with all the cedar and pine logs that he wanted, and Solomon provided Hiram with two thousand metric tons of wheat and four hundred thousand litres of pure olive-oil every year to feed his men.

Four hundred and eighty years after the people of Israel left Egypt, during the fourth year of Solomon's reign over Israel, in the second month, the month of Ziv, Solomon began work on the Temple.

Songs of Love for the Temple

Psalms 122 and 84 were sung by worshippers as they went on pilgrimages to the Temple in Jerusalem.

In Praise of Jerusalem

> I was glad when they said to me,
>> "Let us go to the Lord's house."
> And now we are here,
>> standing inside the gates of Jerusalem!
> Jerusalem is a city restored
>> in beautiful order and harmony.
> This is where the tribes come,
>> the tribes of Israel,
> to give thanks to the Lord
>> according to his command.
> Here the kings of Israel
>> sat to judge their people.
>
> Pray for the peace of Jerusalem:
>> "May those who love you prosper.
>> May there be peace inside your walls
>> and safety in your palaces."
> For the sake of my relatives and friends
>> I say to Jerusalem, "Peace be with you!"
>
> For the sake of the house of the Lord our God
>> I pray for your prosperity.

Longing for God's House

> How I love your Temple, Almighty God!
>> How I want to be there!
>> I long to be in the Lord's Temple.
> With my whole being I sing for joy
>> to the living God.
> Even the sparrows have built a nest,
>> and the swallows have their own home;
> they keep their young near your altars,
>> Lord Almighty, my king and my God.
> How happy are those who live in your Temple,
>> always singing praise to you.
>
> How happy are those whose strength comes from you,
>> who are eager to make the pilgrimage to Mount Zion.

As they pass through the valley of Baca
   it becomes a place of springs;
   the early rain fills it with pools.
They grow stronger as they go;
   they will see the God of gods on Zion.

Hear my prayer, Lord God Almighty,
   Listen, O God of Jacob!
Bless our king, O God,
   the king you have chosen.

One day spent in your Temple
   is better than a thousand anywhere else;
I would rather stand at the gate of the house of my God
   than live in the homes of the wicked.
The Lord is our protector and glorious king,
   blessing us with kindness and honour.
He does not refuse any good thing
   to those who do what is right.
Almighty God, how happy are those who trust in you!

Good Housekeeping in Ancient Times

From days of peace and prosperity in Ancient Israel, we have this picture of a hard-working housewife.
How hard it is to find a capable wife! She is worth far more than jewels!
Her husband puts his confidence in her, and he will never be poor.
As long as she lives, she does him good and never harm.
She keeps herself busy making wool and linen cloth.
She brings home food from out-of-the-way places, as merchant ships do.
She gets up before daylight to prepare food for her family and to tell her servant-girls what to do.
She looks at land and buys it, and with money she has earned she plants a vineyard.
She is a hard worker, strong and industrious.
She knows the value of everything she makes, and works late into the night.
She spins her own thread and weaves her own cloth.
She is generous to the poor and needy.
She doesn't worry when it snows, because her family has warm clothing.
She makes bedspreads and wears clothes of fine purple linen.
Her husband is well known, one of the leading citizens.
She makes clothes and belts, and sells them to merchants.

She is strong and respected and not afraid of the future.

She speaks with a gentle wisdom.

She is always busy and looks after her family's needs.

Her children show their appreciation, and her husband praises her.

He says, "Many women are good wives, but you are the best of them all."

Charm is deceptive and beauty disappears, but a woman who honours the Lord should be praised.

Give her credit for all she does. She deserves the respect of everyone.

They Spoke for God

Elijah and the Prophets of Baal

> *After Solomon's death his kingdom has split into two: Israel in the north and Judah in the south. Many people now worship the god Baal instead of the Lord, the God of Israel. But when Ahab is king of Israel, Elijah is the prophet who speaks up for the Lord. And a dramatic conflict follows.*

Ahab summoned all the Israelites and the prophets of Baal to meet at Mount Carmel. Elijah went up to the people and said, "How much longer will it take you to make up your minds? If the Lord is God, worship him; but if Baal is God, worship him!" But the people didn't say a word. Then Elijah said, "I am the only prophet of the Lord still left, but there are 450 prophets of Baal. Bring two bulls; let the prophets of Baal take one, kill it, cut it in pieces, and put it on the wood – but don't light the fire. I will do the same with the other bull. Then let the prophets of Baal pray to their god, and I will pray to the Lord, and the one who answers by sending fire – he is God."

The people shouted their approval.

Then Elijah said to the prophets of Baal, "Since there are so many of you, you take a bull and prepare it first. Pray to your god, but don't set fire to the wood."

They took the bull that was brought to them, prepared it, and prayed to Baal until noon. They shouted, "Answer us, Baal!" and kept dancing round the altar they had built. But no answer came.

At noon Elijah started making fun of them: "Pray louder! He is a god! Maybe he is day-dreaming or relieving himself, or perhaps he's gone on a journey! Or maybe he's sleeping, and you've got to wake him up!" So the prophets prayed louder and cut themselves with knives and daggers, according to their ritual, until blood flowed. They kept on ranting and raving until the middle of the afternoon; but no answer came, not a sound was heard.

Then Elijah said to the people, "Come closer to me," and they all gathered round him. He set about repairing the altar of the Lord which had been torn down. He took twelve stones, one for each of the twelve tribes named after the sons of Jacob, the man to whom the Lord had given the name Israel. With these stones he rebuilt the altar for the worship of the Lord. He dug a trench round it, large enough to hold almost fourteen litres of water. Then he placed the wood on the altar, cut the bull in pieces, and laid it on the wood. He said, "Fill four jars with water and pour it on the offering and the wood." They did so, and he said, "Do it again" – and they did. "Do it once more," he said – and they did. The water ran down round the altar and filled the trench.

At the hour of the afternoon sacrifice the prophet Elijah approached the altar and prayed, "O Lord, the God of Abraham, Isaac, and Jacob, prove now that you are the God of Israel and that I am your servant and have done all this at your command. Answer me, Lord, answer me, so that this people will know that you, the Lord, are God, and that you are bringing them back to yourself."

The Lord sent fire down, and it burnt up the sacrifice, the wood, and the stones, scorched the earth and dried up the water in the trench. When the people saw this, they threw themselves on the ground and exclaimed, "The Lord is God; the Lord alone is God!"

Elijah on Mount Sinai

In a moment of despair, Elijah hears the voice of God, quiet but firm.
King Ahab told his wife Jezebel everything that Elijah had done and how he had put all the prophets of Baal to death. She sent a message to Elijah: "May the gods strike me dead if by this time tomorrow I don't do the same thing to you that you did to the prophets." Elijah was afraid, and fled for his life; he took his servant and went to Beersheba in Judah.

Leaving the servant there, Elijah walked a whole day into the wilderness. He stopped and sat down in the shade of a tree and wished he would die. "It's too much, Lord," he prayed. "Take away my life; I might as well be dead!"

He lay down under the tree and fell asleep. Suddenly an angel touched him and said, "Wake up and eat." He looked round, and saw a loaf of bread and a jar of water near his head. He ate and drank, and lay down again. The Lord's angel returned and woke him up a second time, saying, "Get up and eat, or the journey will be too much for you." Elijah got up, ate and drank, and the food gave him enough strength to walk forty days to Sinai, the holy mountain. There he went into a cave to spend the night.

Suddenly the Lord spoke to him, "Elijah, what are you doing here?"

He answered, "Lord God Almighty, I have always served you — you alone. But the people of Israel have broken their covenant with you, torn down your altars, and killed all your prophets. I am the only one left — and they are trying to kill me!"

"Go out and stand before me on top of the mountain," the Lord said to him. Then the Lord passed by and sent a furious wind that split the hills and shattered the rocks — but the Lord was not in the wind. The wind stopped blowing, and then there was an earthquake — but the Lord was not in the earthquake. After the earthquake, there was a fire — but the Lord was not in the fire. And after the fire, there was the soft whisper of a voice.

When Elijah heard it, he covered his face with his cloak and went out and stood at the entrance of the cave. A voice said to him, "Elijah, what are you doing here?"

He answered, "Lord God Almighty, I have always served you — you alone. But the people of Israel have broken their covenant with you, torn down your altars, and killed all your prophets. I am the only one left — and they are trying to kill me."

The Lord said, "Return to the wilderness near Damascus, then enter the city and anoint Hazael as king of Syria; anoint Jehu son of Nimshi as king of Israel, and anoint Elisha son of Shaphat from Abel Meholah to succeed you as prophet. Anyone who escapes being put to death by Hazael will be killed by Jehu, and anyone who escapes Jehu will be killed by Elisha. Yet I will leave seven thousand people alive in Israel — all those who are loyal to me and have not bowed to Baal or kissed his idol."

The Call of Elisha

Elijah left and found Elisha ploughing with a team of oxen; there were eleven teams ahead of him, and he was ploughing with the last one. Elijah took off his cloak and put it on Elisha. Elisha then left his oxen, ran after Elijah, and said, "Let me kiss my father and mother good-bye, and then I will go with you."

Elijah answered, "All right, go back. I'm not stopping you!"

Then Elisha went to his team of oxen, killed them, and cooked the meat, using the yoke as fuel for the fire. He gave the meat to the people, and they ate it. Then he went and followed Elijah as his helper.

Ahab is Told of His Sin

Elijah has to attack King Ahab's greed.

Near King Ahab's palace in Jezreel there was a vineyard owned by a man named Naboth. One day Ahab said to Naboth, "Let me have your vineyard; it is close to my palace, and I want to use the land for a vegetable garden. I will give you a better vineyard for it, or, if you prefer, I will pay you a fair price."

"I inherited this vineyard from my ancestors," Naboth replied. "The Lord forbid that I should let you have it!"

Ahab went home, depressed and angry over what Naboth had said to him. He lay down on his bed, facing the wall, and would not eat. His wife Jezebel went to him and asked, "Why are you so depressed? Why won't you eat?"

He answered, "Because of what Naboth said to me. I offered to buy his vineyard, or, if he preferred, to give him another one for it, but he told me that I couldn't have it!"

"Well, are you the king or aren't you?" Jezebel replied. "Get out of bed, cheer up and eat. I will get you Naboth's vineyard!"

Then she wrote some letters, signed them with Ahab's name, sealed them with his seal, and sent them to the officials and leading citizens of Jezreel. The letters said: "Proclaim a day of fasting, call the people together, and give Naboth the place of honour. Get a couple of scoundrels to accuse him to his face of cursing God and the king. Then take him out of the city and stone him to death."

The officials and leading citizens of Jezreel did what Jezebel had commanded. They proclaimed a day of fasting, called the people together, and gave Naboth the place of honour. The two scoundrels publicly accused him of cursing God and the king, and so he was taken outside the city and stoned to death. The message was sent to Jezebel: "Naboth has been put to death."

As soon as Jezebel received the message, she said to Ahab, "Naboth is dead. Now go and take possession of the vineyard which he refused to sell to you." At once Ahab went to the vineyard to take possession of it.

Then the Lord said to Elijah, the prophet from Tishbe, "Go to King Ahab of Samaria. You will find him in Naboth's vineyard, about to take possession of it. Tell him that I, the Lord, say to him, 'After murdering the man, are you taking over his property as well?' Tell him that this is what I say: 'In the very place that the dogs licked up Naboth's blood they will lick up your blood!'"

When Ahab saw Elijah, he said, "Have you caught up with me, my enemy?"

"Yes, I have," Elijah answered. "You have devoted yourself completely to doing what is wrong in the Lord's sight. So the Lord says to you, 'I will bring disaster on you. I will do away with you and get rid of every male in your family, young and old alike. Your family will become like the family of King Jeroboam son of Nebat and like the family of King Baasha son of Ahijah, because you have stirred up my anger by leading Israel into sin.' And concerning Jezebel, the Lord says that dogs will eat her body in the city of Jezreel. Any of your relatives who die in the city will be eaten by dogs, and any who die in the open country will be eaten by vultures."

Elijah Is Taken Up to Heaven

Elijah was the mighty defender of Israel. No wonder that the story spread that he had been taken home to God in thunder, lightning and a whirlwind!
The time came for the Lord to take Elijah up to heaven in a whirlwind. Elijah and Elisha set out from Gilgal, and on the way Elijah said to Elisha, "Now stay here; the Lord has ordered me to go to Bethel."

But Elisha answered, "I swear by my loyalty to the living Lord and to you that I will not leave you." So they went on to Bethel.

A group of prophets who lived there went to Elisha and asked him, "Do you know that the Lord is going to take your master away from you today?"

"Yes, I know," Elisha answered. "But let's not talk about it."

Then Elijah said to Elisha, "Now stay here; the Lord has ordered me to go to Jericho."

But Elisha answered, "I swear by my loyalty to the living Lord and to you that I will not leave you." So they went on to Jericho.

A group of prophets who lived there went to Elisha and asked him, "Do you know that the Lord is going to take your master away from you today?"

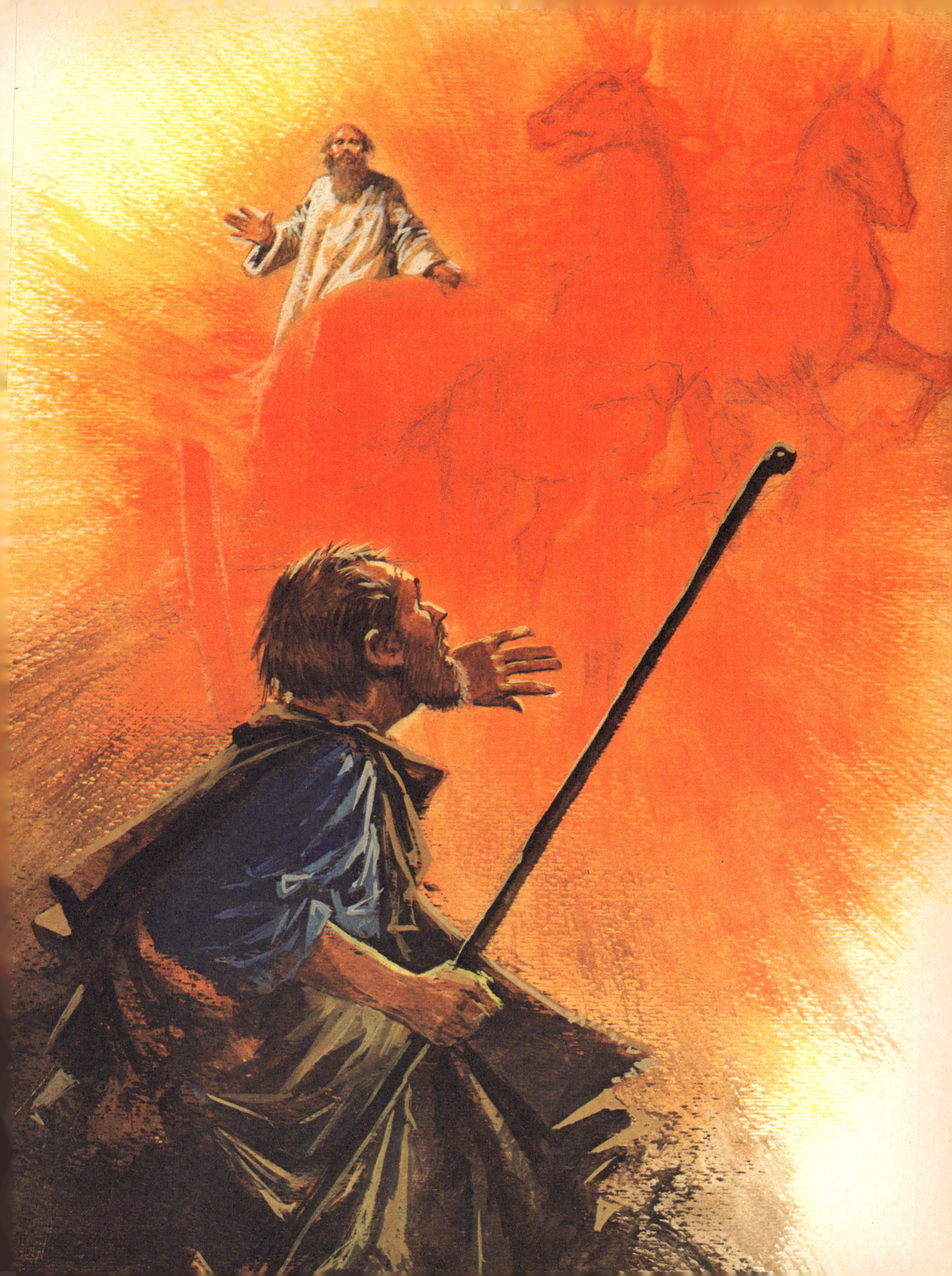

"Yes, I know," Elisha answered. "But let's not talk about it."

Then Elijah said to Elisha, "Now stay here; the Lord has ordered me to go to the River Jordan."

But Elisha answered, "I swear by my loyalty to the living Lord and to you that I will not leave you." So they went on, and fifty of the prophets followed them to the Jordan. Elijah and Elisha stopped by the river, and the fifty prophets stood a short distance away. Then Elijah took off his cloak, rolled it up, and struck the water with it; the water divided, and he and Elisha crossed to the other side on dry ground. There, Elijah said to Elisha, "Tell me what you want me to do for you before I am taken away."

"Let me receive the share of your power that will make me your successor," Elisha answered.

"That is a difficult request to grant," Elijah replied. "But you will receive it if you see me as I am being taken away from you; if you don't see me, you won't receive it."

They kept talking as they walked on; then suddenly a chariot of fire pulled by horses of fire came between them, and Elijah was taken up to heaven by a whirlwind. Elisha saw it and cried out to Elijah, "My father, my father! Mighty defender of Israel! You are gone!" And he never saw Elijah again.

In grief, Elisha tore his cloak in two. Then he picked up Elijah's cloak that had fallen from him, and went back and stood on the bank of the Jordan. He struck the water with Elijah's cloak, and said, "Where is the Lord, the God of Elijah?" Then he struck the water again, and it divided, and he walked over to the other side.

Naaman Is Cured

Elisha heals a foreign general.

Naaman, the commander of the Syrian army, was highly respected and esteemed by the king of Syria, because through Naaman the Lord had given victory to the Syrian forces. He was a great soldier, but he suffered from a dreaded skin-disease. In one of their raids against Israel, the Syrians had carried off a little Israelite girl, who became a servant of Naaman's wife. One day she said to her mistress, "I wish that my master could go to the prophet who lives in Samaria! He would cure him of his disease." When Naaman heard of this, he went to the king and told him what the girl had said. The king said, "Go to the king of Israel and take this letter to him."

So Naaman set out, taking thirty thousand pieces of silver, six thousand pieces of gold, and ten changes of fine clothes. The letter that he took read: "This letter will introduce my officer Naaman. I want you to cure him of his disease."

When the king of Israel read the letter, he tore his clothes in dismay and exclaimed, "How can the king of Syria expect me to cure this man? Does he think that I am God, with the power of life and death? It's plain that he is trying to start a quarrel with me!"

When the prophet Elisha heard what had happened, he sent word to the king: "Why are you so upset? Send the man to me, and I'll show him that there is a prophet in Israel!"

So Naaman went with his horses and chariot, and stopped at the entrance to Elisha's house. Elisha sent a servant out to tell him to go and wash himself seven times in the River Jordan, and he would be completely cured of his disease. But Naaman left in a rage, saying, "I thought that he would at least come out to me, pray to the Lord his God, wave his hand over the diseased spot, and cure me! Besides, aren't the rivers Abana and Pharpar, back in Damascus, better than any river in Israel? I could have washed in them and been cured!"

His servants went up to him and said, "Sir, if the prophet had told you to do something difficult, you would have done it. Now why can't you just wash yourself, as he said, and be cured?" So Naaman went down to the Jordan, dipped himself in it seven times, as Elisha had instructed, and he was completely cured. His flesh became firm and healthy, like that of a child.

A Prophet Is Called by God

> *One of the great men who spoke for God to the people of Israel was Amos, a shepherd. Here he tells one of the king's priests about the time when God called him.*

Amaziah, the priest of Bethel, once sent a report to King Jeroboam of Israel: "Amos is plotting against you among the people. His speeches will destroy the country. This is what he says: 'Jeroboam will die in battle, and the people of Israel will be taken away from their land into exile.'"

Amaziah then said to Amos, "That's enough, prophet! Go on back to Judah and do your preaching there. Let *them* pay you for it. Don't prophesy here at Bethel any more. This is the king's place of worship, the national temple."

Amos answered, "I am not the kind of prophet who prophesies for pay. I am a herdsman, and I take care of fig-trees. But the Lord took me from my work as a shepherd and ordered me to go and prophesy to his people Israel."

The Prophets Speak

God the Judge

> *Amos teaches that God will punish the rich Israelites who are cruel to the poor.*

Listen to this, you that trample on the needy and try to destroy the poor of the country. You say to yourselves, "We can hardly wait for the holy days to be over so that we can sell our corn. When will the Sabbath end, so that we can start selling again? Then we can overcharge, use false measures, and tamper with the scales to cheat our customers. We can sell worthless wheat at a high price. We'll find a poor man who can't pay his debts, not even the price of a pair of sandals, and we'll buy him as a slave."

The Lord, the God of Israel, has sworn, "I will never forget their evil deeds. And so the earth will quake, and everyone in the land will be in distress. The whole country will be shaken; it will rise and fall like the River Nile. The time is coming when I will make the sun go down at noon and the earth grow dark in daytime. I, the Sovereign Lord, have spoken. I will turn your festivals into funerals and change your glad songs into cries of grief. I will make you shave your heads and wear sackcloth, and you will be like parents mourning for their only son. That day will be bitter to the end."

What God Wants

> *The prophet Micah sees that God demands justice, or fairness. The worship in the Temple is far less important.*

What shall I bring to the Lord, the God of heaven, when I come to worship him? Shall I bring the best calves to burn as offerings to him? Will the Lord be pleased if I bring him thousands of sheep or endless streams of olive-oil? Shall I offer him my first-born child to pay for my sins? No, the Lord has told us what is good. What he requires of us is this: to do what is just, to show constant love, and to live in humble fellowship with our God.

The same teaching is found in Psalm 15, one of the hymns sung in the Temple in Jerusalem.

> Lord, who may enter your Temple?
> Who may worship on Zion, your sacred hill?
>
> A person who obeys God in everything
>   and always does what is right,
> whose words are true and sincere,
>   and who does not slander others.
> He does no wrong to his friends
>   and does not spread rumours about his neighbours.
> He despises those whom God rejects,
>   but honours those who obey the Lord.
> He always does what he promises,
>   no matter how much it may cost.
> He makes loans without charging interest
>   and cannot be bribed to testify against the innocent.
>
> Whoever does these things will always be secure.

God the Father

The prophet Hosea sees that God cares for his people.

The Lord says,

> "When Israel was a child, I loved him
>   and called him out of Egypt as my son.
> But the more I called to him,
>   the more he turned away from me.
> My people sacrificed to Baal;
>   they burnt incense to idols.
> Yet I was the one who taught Israel to walk.
> I took my people up in my arms,
>   but they did not acknowledge that I took care of them.
> I drew them to me with affection and love.
>   I picked them up and held them to my cheek;
>   I bent down to them and fed them.

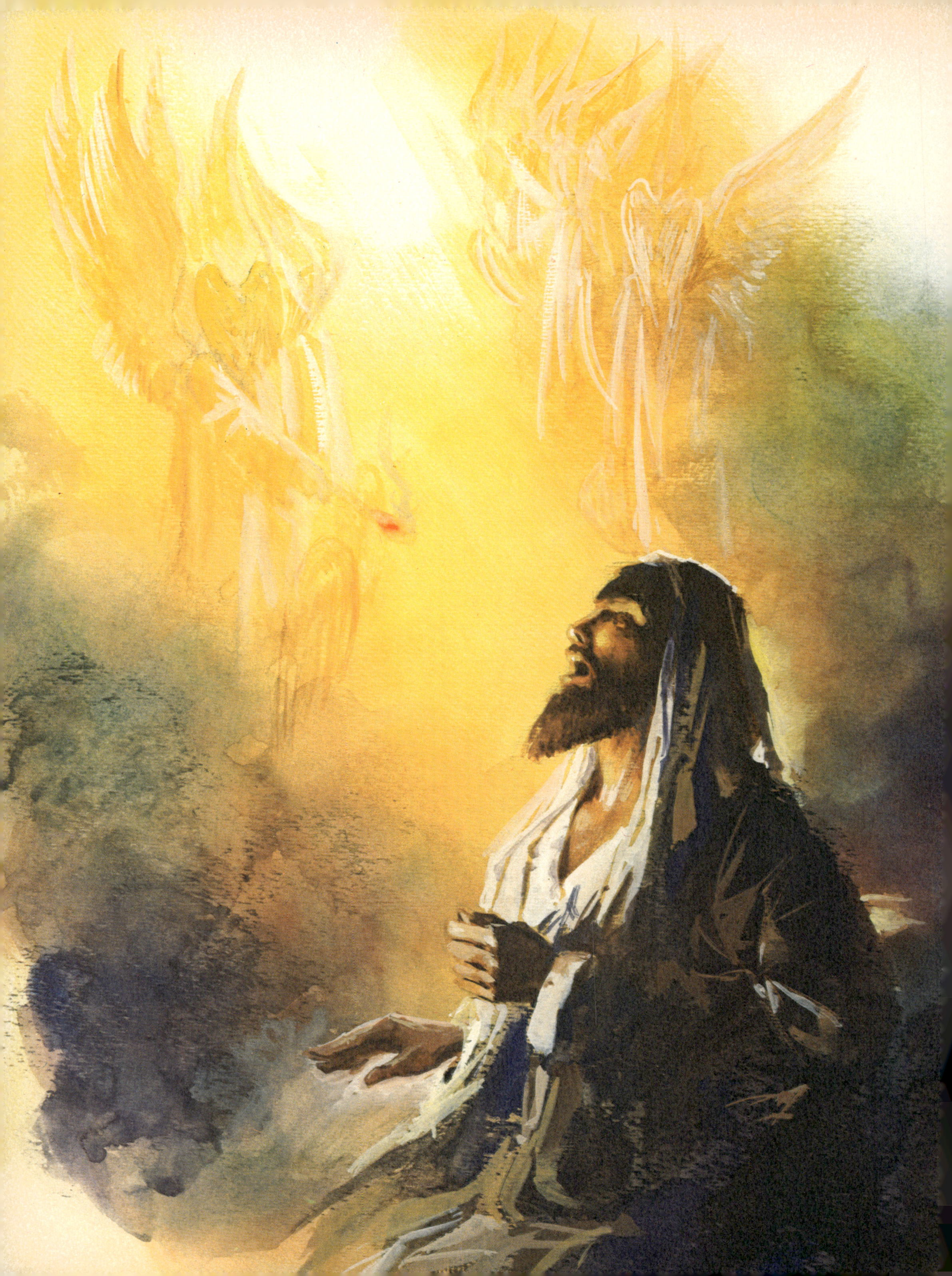

Peace for Jerusalem

God Calls Isaiah

A man meets God in the Temple in Jerusalem.

In the year that King Uzziah died, I saw the Lord. He was sitting on his throne, high and exalted, and his robe filled the whole Temple. Round him flaming creatures were standing, each of which had six wings. Each creature covered its face with two wings, and its body with two, and used the other two for flying. They were calling out to each other:
"Holy, holy, holy!
The Lord Almighty is holy!
His glory fills the world."
The sound of their voices made the foundation of the Temple shake, and the Temple itself was filled with smoke.

I said, "There is no hope for me! I am doomed because every word that passes my lips is sinful, and I live among a people whose every word is sinful. And yet, with my own eyes, I have seen the King, the Lord Almighty!"

Then one of the creatures flew down to me, carrying a burning coal that he had taken from the altar with a pair of tongs. He touched my lips with the burning coal and said, "This has touched your lips, and now your guilt is gone, and your sins are forgiven."

Then I heard the Lord say, "Whom shall I send? Who will be our messenger?"

I answered, "I will go! Send me!"

The Assyrians Come

About seven hundred years before the birth of Christ, the army of the Assyrian emperor has conquered the northern kingdom of Israel and now surrounds Jerusalem, the capital of the southern kingdom of Judah. King Hezekiah receives a letter from the emperor, Sennacherib, and takes it to the Temple.

King Hezekiah took the letter from the messengers and read it. Then he went to the Temple, placed the letter there in the presence of the Lord, and prayed, "O Lord, the God of Israel, seated on your throne above the winged creatures, you alone are God, ruling all the kingdoms of the world. You created the earth and the sky. Now, Lord, look at what is happening to us. Listen to all the things that Sennacherib is saying to insult you, the living God. We all know, Lord, that the emperors of Assyria have destroyed many nations, made their lands desolate, and burnt up their gods – which were no gods at all, only images of wood

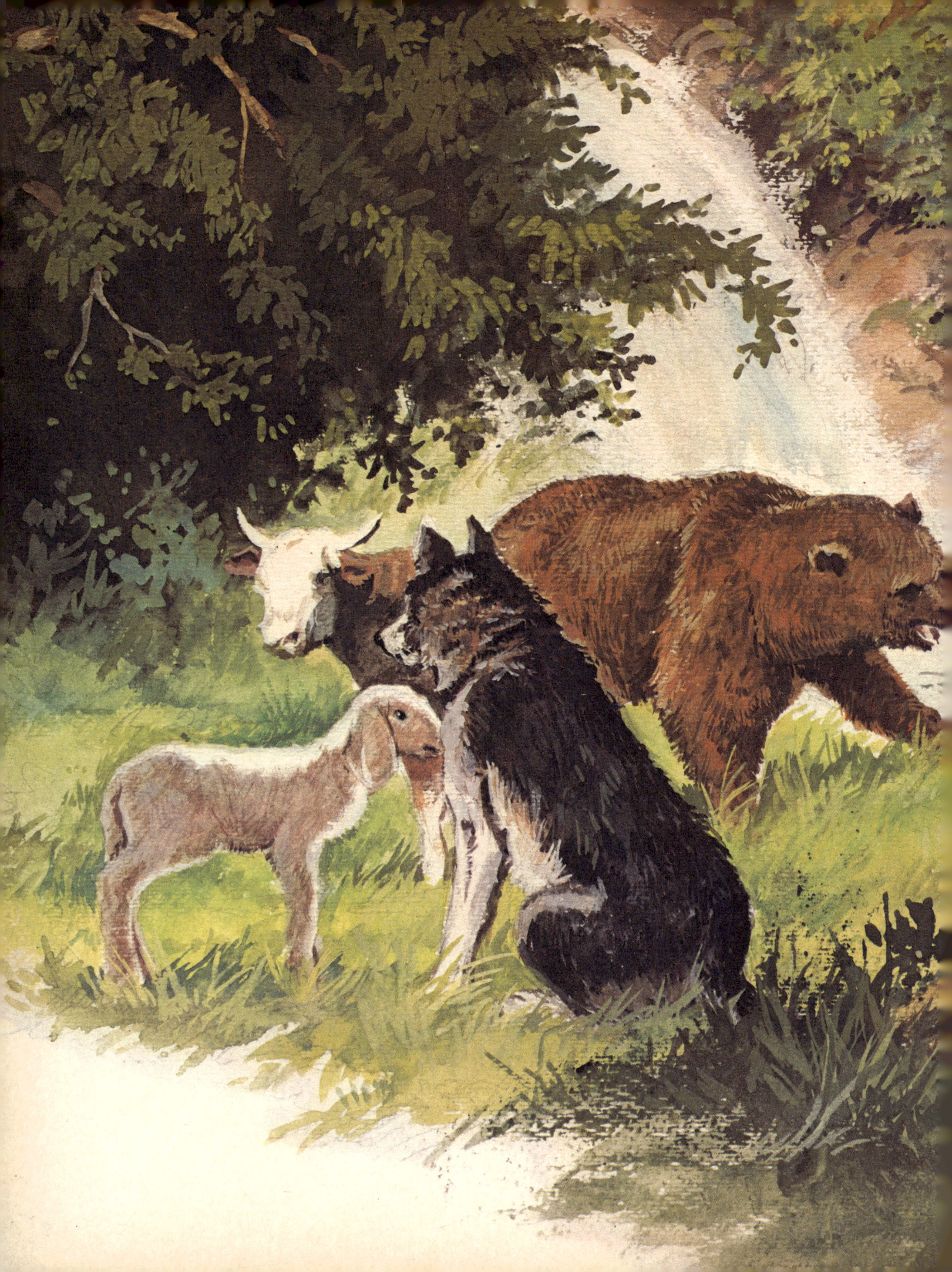

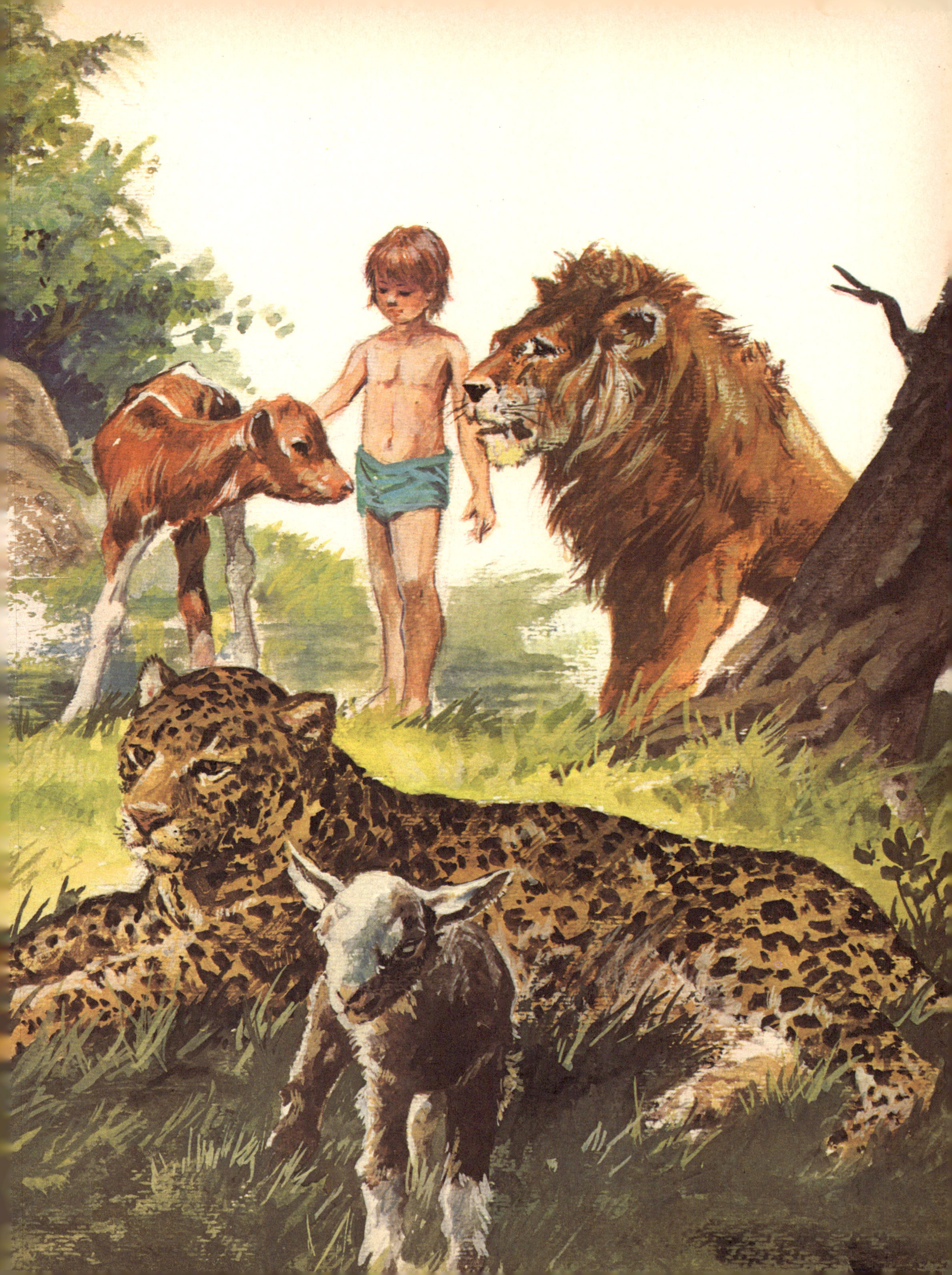

and stone made by human hands. Now, Lord our God, rescue us from the Assyrians, so that all the nations of the world will know that only you, O Lord, are God."

Isaiah's Message to the King

The prophet tells Hezekiah that even the Assyrian army is under God's control.

Then Isaiah sent a message telling King Hezekiah that in answer to the king's prayer the Lord had said, "The city of Jerusalem laughs at you, Sennacherib, and despises you. Whom do you think you have been insulting and ridiculing? You have been disrespectful to me, the holy God of Israel. You sent your messengers to boast to me that with all your chariots you had conquered the highest mountains of Lebanon. You boasted that there you cut down the tallest cedars and the finest cypress-trees and that you reached the deepest parts of the forests. You boasted that you dug wells and drank water in foreign lands and that the feet of your soldiers tramped the River Nile dry.

"Have you never heard that I planned all this long ago? And now I have carried it out. I gave you the power to turn fortified cities into piles of rubble. The people who lived there were powerless; they were frightened and stunned. They were like grass in a field or weeds growing on a roof when the hot east wind blasts them.

"But I know everything about you, what you do and where you go. I know how you rage against me. I have received the report of that rage and that pride of yours, and now I will put a hook through your nose and a bit in your mouth, and take you back by the same road you came."

Then Isaiah said to King Hezekiah, "This is a sign of what will happen. This year and next you will have only wild grain to eat, but the following year you will be able to sow your corn and harvest it, and plant vines and eat grapes. Those in Judah who survive will flourish like plants that send roots deep into the ground and produce fruit. There will be people in Jerusalem and on Mount Zion who will survive, because the Lord is determined to make this happen.

"This is what the Lord has said about the Assyrian emperor: 'He will not enter this city or shoot a single arrow against it. No soldiers with shields will come near the city, and no siege-mounds will be built round it. He will go back by the same road he came, without entering this city. I, the Lord, have spoken. I will defend this city and protect it, for the sake of my own honour and because of the promise I made to my servant David.' "

That night an angel of the Lord went to the Assyrian camp and killed 185,000 soldiers. At dawn the next day, there they lay, all dead!

The Peaceful Kingdom

> *Isaiah looks forward to perfect peace under the perfect king.*

The royal line of David is like a tree that has been cut down; but just as new branches sprout from a stump, so a new king will arise from among David's descendants.

> The spirit of the Lord will give him wisdom,
> > and the knowledge and skill to rule his people.
>
> He will know the Lord's will and honour him,
> > and find pleasure in obeying him.
>
> He will not judge by appearance or hearsay;
> > he will judge the poor fairly
> > and defend the rights of the helpless.
>
> At his command the people will be punished,
> > and evil persons will die.
>
> He will rule his people with justice and integrity.
>
> Wolves and sheep will live together in peace,
> > and leopards will lie down with young goats.
>
> Calves and lion cubs will feed together,
> > and little children will take care of them.
>
> Cows and bears will eat together,
> > and their calves and cubs will lie down in peace.
>
> Lions will eat straw as cattle do.
>
> Even a baby will not be harmed
> > if it plays near a poisonous snake.
>
> On Zion, God's sacred hill,
> > there will be nothing harmful or evil.
>
> The land will be as full of knowledge of the Lord
> > as the seas are full of water.

The Nations Learn Peace

> *The prophet looks forward to the time when many nations will live in peace according to God's law.*

> In days to come
> > the mountain where the Temple stands
> > will be the highest one of all,
> > towering above all the hills.
>
> Many nations will come streaming to it,
> > and their people will say,
>
> "Let us go up the hill of the Lord,
> > to the Temple of Israel's God.
>
> For he will teach us what he wants us to do;
> > we will walk in the paths he has chosen.

> For the Lord's teaching comes from Jerusalem;
> from Zion he speaks to his people."

He will settle disputes among the nations,
> among the great powers near and far.
They will hammer their swords into ploughs
> and their spears into pruning-knives.
Nations will never again go to war,
> never prepare for battle again.
Everyone will live in peace
> among his own vineyards and fig-trees,
> and no one will make him afraid.
The Lord Almighty has promised this.

Peace at the End of War

In the 35th chapter of Isaiah's book we find a song which promises peace to a people weary with war.
> The desert will rejoice,
> and flowers will bloom in the wilderness.
> The desert will sing and shout for joy;
> it will be as beautiful as the Lebanon Mountains
> and as fertile as the fields of Carmel and Sharon.
> Everyone will see the Lord's splendour,
> see his greatness and power.
> Give strength to hands that are tired
> and to knees that tremble with weakness.
> Tell everyone who is discouraged,
> "Be strong and don't be afraid!
> God is coming to your rescue,
> coming to punish your enemies."

The blind will be able to see,
> and the deaf will hear.
The lame will leap and dance,
> and those who cannot speak will shout for joy.
Streams of water will flow through the desert;
> the burning sand will become a lake,
> and dry land will be filled with springs.
Where jackals used to live,
> marsh grass and reeds will grow.

There will be a highway there,
> called "The Road of Holiness."
No sinner will ever travel that road;
> no fools will mislead those who follow it.

> No lions will be there;
>> no fierce animals will pass that way.
> Those whom the Lord has rescued
>> will travel home by that road.
> They will reach Jerusalem with gladness,
>> singing and shouting for joy.
> They will be happy for ever,
>> for ever free from sorrow and grief.

The Law of God

The Book of the Law Is Found

> *Although the Assyrian army has retreated, many years pass before life in Judah and Jerusalem can be organised properly under the Law of God. Then this Law is discovered in the Temple.*

Josiah was eight years old when he became king of Judah, and he ruled in Jerusalem for thirty-one years. Josiah did what was pleasing to the Lord; he followed the example of his ancestor King David, strictly obeying all the laws of God.

In the eighteenth year of his reign, King Josiah sent the court secretary Shaphan, the son of Azaliah and grandson of Meshullam, to the Temple with the order: "Go to the High Priest Hilkiah and get a report on the amount of money that the priests on duty at the entrance to the Temple have collected from the people. Tell him to give the money to the men who are in charge of the repairs in the Temple. They are to pay the carpenters, the builders, and the masons, and buy the timber and the stones used in the repairs. The men in charge of the work are thoroughly honest, so there is no need to require them to account for the funds."

Shaphan delivered the king's order to Hilkiah, and Hilkiah told him that he had found the book of the Law in the Temple. Hilkiah gave him the book, and Shaphan read it. Then he went back to the king and reported: "Your servants have taken the money that was in the Temple and have handed it over to the men in charge of the repairs." And then he said, "I have here a book that Hilkiah gave me." And he read it aloud to the king.

When the king heard the book being read, he tore his clothes in dismay, and gave the following order to Hilkiah the priest, to Ahikam son of Shaphan, to Achbor son of Micaiah, to Shaphan, the court secretary, and to Asaiah, the king's attendant: "Go and consult the Lord for me and for all the people of Judah about the teachings of this book. The Lord is angry with us because our ancestors have not done what this book says must be done."

Josiah Does Away with Pagan Worship

King Josiah summoned all the leaders of Judah and Jerusalem, and together they went to the Temple, accompanied by the priests and the prophets and all the rest of the people, rich and poor alike. Before them all, the king read aloud the whole book of the covenant which had been found in the Temple. He stood by the royal column and made a covenant with the Lord to obey him, to keep his laws and commands with all his heart and soul, and to put into practice the demands attached to the covenant, as written in the book. And all the people promised to keep the covenant.

The Great Commandment

> *This is part of the Law of God which was read to King Josiah. It is printed in the Bible in the Book of Deuteronomy, and it includes the words which Jesus used to sum up our duty to God.*

"These are all the laws that the Lord your God commanded me to teach you. Obey them in the land that you are about to enter and occupy. As long as you live, you and your descendants are to honour the Lord your God and obey all his laws that I am giving you, so that you may live in that land a long time. Listen to them, people of Israel, and obey them! Then all will go well with you, and you will become a mighty nation and live in that rich and fertile land, just as the Lord, the God of our ancestors, has promised.

"Israel, remember this! The Lord — and the Lord alone — is our God. Love the Lord your God with all your heart, with all your soul, and with all your strength. Never forget these commands that I am giving you today. Teach them to your children. Repeat them when you are at home and when you are away, when you are resting and when you are working. Tie them on your arms and wear them on your foreheads as a reminder. Write them on the door-posts of your houses and on your gates."

Fall of the City

God Calls Jeremiah to be a Prophet

About six hundred years before the birth of Christ, a young man is commanded to speak up for the Lord.

The Lord said to me, "I chose you before I gave you life, and before you were born I selected you to be a prophet to the nations."

I answered, "Sovereign Lord, I don't know how to speak; I am too young."

But the Lord said to me, "Do not say that you are too young, but go to the people I send you to, and tell them everything I command you to say. Do not be afraid of them, for I will be with you to protect you. I, the Lord, have spoken!"

Then the Lord stretched out his hand, touched my lips, and said to me, "Listen, I am giving you the words you must speak. Today I give you authority over nations and kingdoms to uproot and to pull down, to destroy and to overthrow, to build and to plant."

Jeremiah Warns the People

This is an example of the brave prophet's preaching. He attacked the sins of the people of Judah and Jerusalem.

The Lord sent me to the gate of the Temple where the people of Judah went in to worship. He told me to stand there and announce what the Lord Almighty, the God of Israel, had to say to them: "Change the way you are living and the things you are doing, and I will let you go on living here. Stop believing those deceitful words, 'We are safe! This is the Lord's Temple, this is the Lord's Temple, this is the Lord's Temple!'

"Change the way you are living and stop doing the things you are doing. Be fair in your treatment of one another. Stop taking advantage of aliens, orphans, and widows. Stop killing innocent people in this land. Stop worshipping other gods, for that will destroy you. If you change, I will let you go on living here in the land which I gave your ancestors as a permanent possession.

"Look, you put your trust in deceitful words. You steal, murder, commit adultery, tell lies under oath, offer sacrifices to Baal, and worship gods that you had not known before. You do these things I hate, and then you come and stand in my presence, in my own Temple, and say, 'We are safe!' Do you think that my Temple is a hiding place for robbers?"

God's New Agreement

Most of what Jeremiah has to say is extremely unpopular, because he

Opposite: Jerusalem is captured (text on page 122)

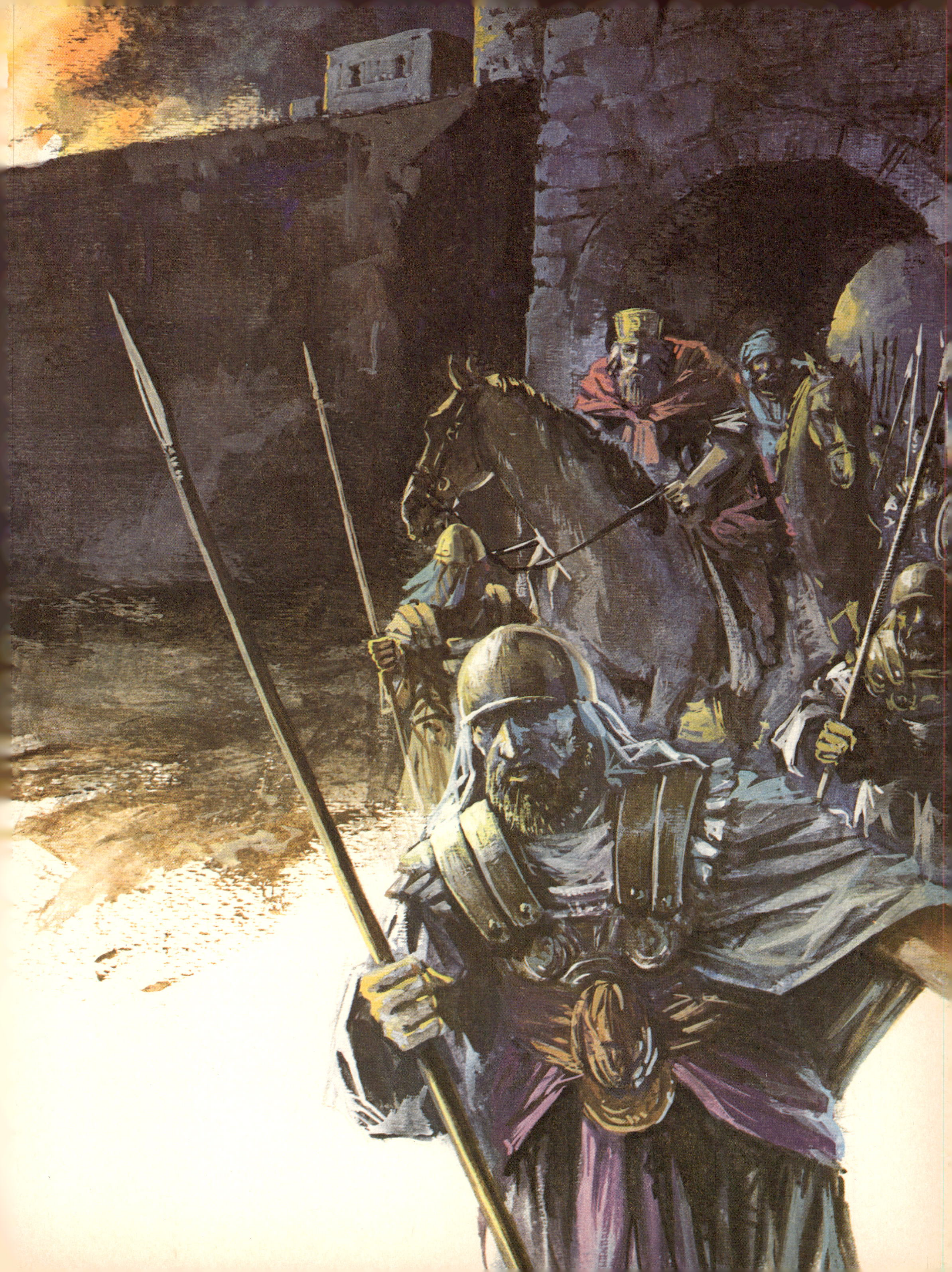

warns Jerusalem that it is now doomed. But beyond the disaster, he sees that God will make a new "covenant" or agreement with the people.

The Lord says, "The time is coming when I will make a new covenant with the people of Israel and with the people of Judah. It will not be like the old covenant that I made with their ancestors when I took them by the hand and led them out of Egypt. Although I was like a husband to them, they did not keep that covenant. The new covenant that I will make with the people of Israel will be this: I will put my law within them and write it on their hearts. I will be their God, and they will be my people. None of them will have to teach his fellow-countryman to know the Lord, because all will know me, from the least to the greatest. I will forgive their sins and I will no longer remember their wrongs. I, the Lord, have spoken."

Jerusalem Is Captured

Zedekiah and the other kings of Judah do not pay attention to the prophets' warnings. In the end Jerusalem is captured by the army of Nebuchadnezzar the emperor of Babylon. The disaster seems complete.

Zedekiah rebelled against King Nebuchadnezzar of Babylonia, so Nebuchadnezzar came with all his army and attacked Jerusalem on the tenth day of the tenth month of the ninth year of Zedekiah's reign. They set up camp outside the city, built siege walls round it, and kept it under siege until Zedekiah's eleventh year. On the ninth day of the fourth month of that same year, when the famine was so bad that the people had nothing left to eat, the city walls were broken through. Although the Babylonians were surrounding the city, all the soldiers escaped during the night. They left by way of the royal garden, went through the gateway connecting the two walls, and fled in the direction of the Jordan Valley. But the Babylonian army pursued King Zedekiah, captured him in the plains near Jericho, and all his soldiers deserted him. Zedekiah was taken to King Nebuchadnezzar, who was in the city of Riblah, and there Nebuchadnezzar passed sentence on him. While Zedekiah was looking on, his sons were put to death; then Nebuchadnezzar had Zedekiah's eyes put out, placed him in chains, and took him to Babylon.

A Song of the Exiles

Psalm 137 is one of the songs sung by the Jews forced to leave their homeland.

By the rivers of Babylon we sat down;
    there we wept when we remembered Zion.
On the willows near by
    we hung up our harps.
Those who captured us told us to sing;
    they told us to entertain them:

"Sing us a song about Zion."

How can we sing a song to the Lord
   in a foreign land?
May I never be able to play the harp again
   if I forget you, Jerusalem!
May I never be able to sing again
   if I do not remember you,
     if I do not think of you as my greatest joy!

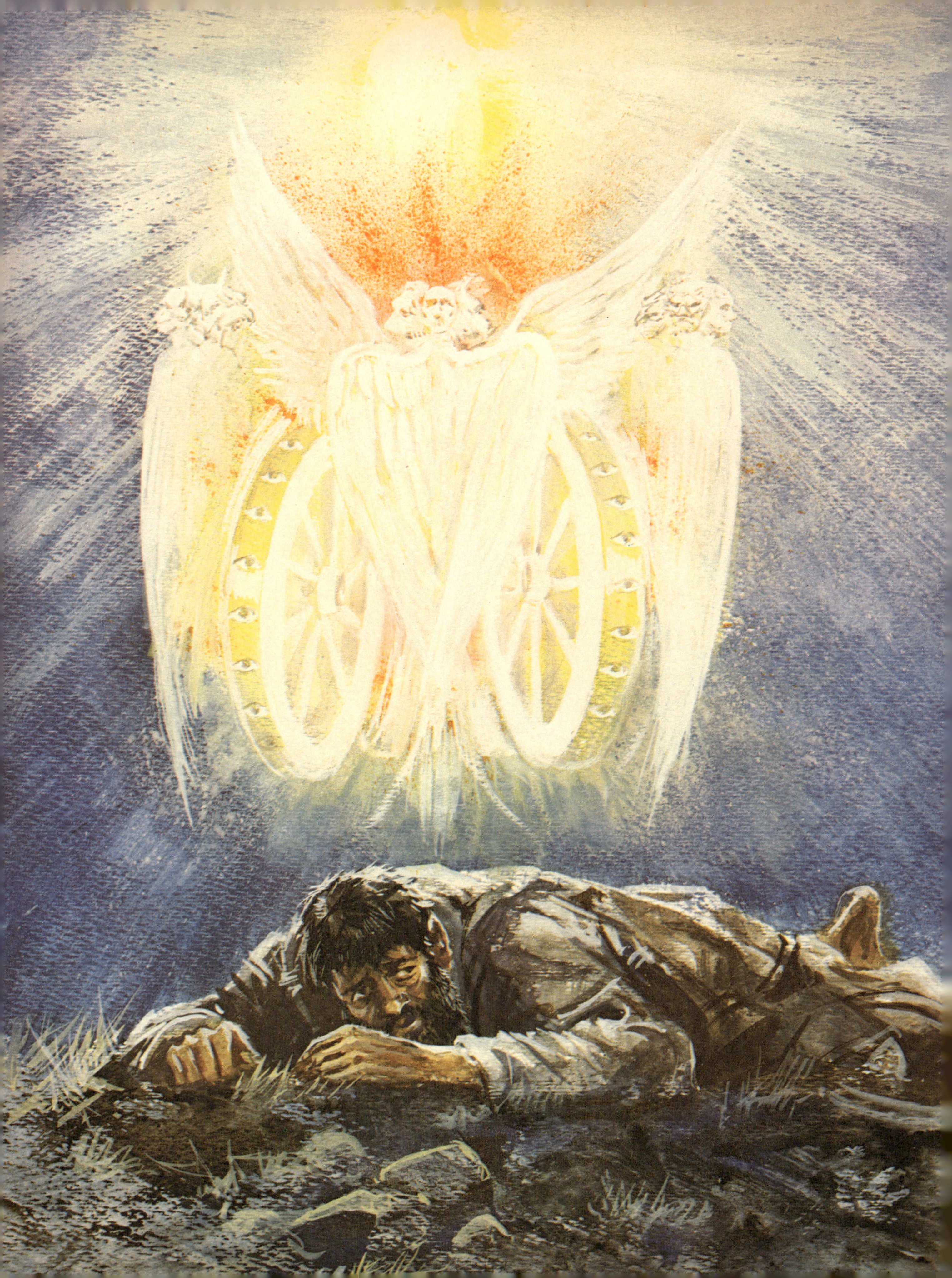

5
The Great Promise

All the leading Jews were forced to leave the land of Canaan, their beautiful and holy land. They went into exile in the empires of Assyria and Babylon. Some of them settled by the River Euphrates, where Abraham had lived many centuries before. But even in this defeat some of the prophets and leaders showed great courage because of their great faith. They told the people that God was near them in their exile and would take action to rescue them.

A Prophet in Exile

Ezekiel Sees the Glory of God

> *Far away from Jerusalem, among the Jews who were exiles in Babylonia, Ezekiel feels the power of the Lord.*

On the fifth day of the fourth month of the thirtieth year, I, Ezekiel the priest, son of Buzi, was living with the Jewish exiles by the River Chebar in Babylonia. The sky opened, and I saw a vision of God. There in Babylonia beside the River Chebar, I heard the Lord speak to me and I felt his power.

I looked up and saw a storm coming from the north. Lightning was flashing from a huge cloud, and the sky round it was glowing. Where the lightning was flashing, something shone like bronze. At the centre of the storm, I saw what looked like four living creatures in human form, but each of them had four faces and four wings. Their legs were straight, and they had hoofs like those of a bull. They shone like polished bronze. In addition to their four faces and four wings, they each had four human hands, one under each wing. Two wings of each creature were spread out so that they formed a square with their wing tips touching. When they moved they moved as a group without turning their bodies.

Above the heads of the animals there was something that looked like a dome made of dazzling crystal. There under the dome stood the animals, each stretching out two wings towards the ones next to it and covering its body with the other two wings. I heard the noise their wings made in flight; it sounded like the roar of the sea, like the noise of a huge army, like the voice of Almighty God. When they stopped flying, they folded their wings, but there was still a sound coming from above the dome over their heads.

Above the dome there was something that looked like a throne made of sapphire, and sitting on the throne was a figure that looked like a man. The figure seemed to be shining like bronze in the middle of a fire. It shone all over with a bright light that had in it all the colours of the rainbow. This was the dazzling light that shows the presence of the Lord.

God Calls Ezekiel to be a Prophet

When I saw this, I fell face downwards on the ground. Then I heard a voice saying, "Mortal man, stand up. I want to talk to you." While the voice was speaking, God's spirit entered me and raised me to my feet, and I heard the voice continue, "Mortal man, I am sending you to the people of Israel. They have rebelled and turned against me and are still rebels, just as their ancestors were. They are stubborn and do not respect me, so I am sending you to tell them what I, the Sovereign Lord, am saying to them. Whether those rebels listen to you or not, they will know that a prophet has been among them."

The Good Shepherd

Ezekiel sees that God is like a shepherd looking after the sheep — a comparison which Jesus himself used.

"I, the Sovereign Lord, tell you that I myself will look for my sheep and take care of them in the same way as a shepherd takes care of his sheep that were scattered and are brought together again. I will bring them back from all the places where they were scattered on that dark, disastrous day. I will take them out of foreign countries, gather them together, and bring them back to their own land. I will lead them back to the mountains and the streams of Israel and will feed them in pleasant pastures. I will let them graze in safety in the mountain meadows and the valleys and in all the green pastures of the land of Israel. I myself will be the shepherd of my sheep, and I will find them a place to rest. I, the Sovereign Lord, have spoken."

The Valley of Dry Bones

Ezekiel sees that God gives new life to the dead. This is a time of defeat, but God promises victory.

I felt the powerful presence of the Lord, and his spirit took me and set me down in a valley where the ground was covered with bones. He led me all round the valley, and I could see that there were very many bones and that they were very dry. He said to me, "Mortal man, can these bones come back to life?"

I replied, "Sovereign Lord, only you can answer that!"

He said, "Prophesy to the bones. Tell these dry bones to listen to the word of the Lord. Tell them that I, the Sovereign Lord, am saying to them: I am going to put breath into you and bring you back to life. I will give you sinews and muscles, and cover you with skin. I will put breath into you and bring you back to life. Then you will know that I am the Lord."

So I prophesied as I had been told. While I was speaking, I heard a rattling noise, and the bones began to join together. While I watched, the bones were covered with sinews and muscles, and then with skin. But there was no breath in the bodies.

God said to me, "Mortal man, prophesy to the wind. Tell the wind that the Sovereign Lord commands it to come from every direction, to breathe into these dead bodies, and to bring them back to life."

So I prophesied as I had been told. Breath entered the bodies, and they came to life and stood up. There were enough of them to form an army.

God said to me, "Mortal man, the people of Israel are like these bones. They say that they are dried up, without any hope and with no future. So prophesy to my people Israel and tell them that I, the Sovereign Lord, am going to open their graves. I am going to take them out and bring them back to the land of Israel. When I open the graves where my people are buried and bring them out, they will know that I am the Lord. I will put my breath in them, bring them back to life, and let them live in their own land. Then they will know that I am the Lord. I have promised that I would do this — and I will. I, the Lord, have spoken."

God Is with His People

Words of Hope

> *Another prophet cries out that the exiles will return to Jerusalem because that is the promise of the Lord.*
>
> "Comfort my people," says our God. "Comfort them!
> Encourage the people of Jerusalem.
> Tell them they have suffered long enough
>   and their sins are now forgiven.
> I have punished them in full for all their sins."
>
> A voice cries out,
> "Prepare in the wilderness a road for the Lord!
>   Clear the way in the desert for our God!
> Fill every valley;
>   level every mountain.
> The hills will become a plain,
>   and the rough country will be made smooth.
> Then the glory of the Lord will be revealed,
>   and all mankind will see it.
> The Lord himself has promised this."
>
> A voice cries out, "Proclaim a message!"
> "What message shall I proclaim?" I ask.
> "Proclaim that all mankind are like grass;
>   they last no longer than wild flowers.
>
> Grass withers and flowers fade,
>   when the Lord sends the wind blowing over them.
>   People are no more enduring than grass.

Yes, grass withers and flowers fade,
   but the word of our God endures for ever."

God's Suffering Servant

In another of his songs in exile, this prophet pictures his people as being like a criminal condemned to die. But this "criminal" is God's servant.

He was treated harshly, but endured it humbly;
   he never said a word.
Like a lamb about to be slaughtered,
like a sheep about to be sheared,
   he never said a word.
He was arrested and sentenced and led off to die,
   and no one cared about his fate.
He was put to death for the sins of our people.
He was placed in a grave with evil men,
he was buried with the rich,
even though he had never committed a crime
   or ever told a lie.
The Lord says,
"It was my will that he should suffer;
   his death was a sacrifice to bring forgiveness.
And so he will see his descendants;
   he will live a long life,
   and through him my purpose will succeed.
After a life of suffering, he will again have joy;
   he will know that he did not suffer in vain.
My devoted servant, with whom I am pleased,
   will bear the punishment of many
   and for his sake I will forgive them.
And so I will give him a place of honour,
   a place among great and powerful men.
He willingly gave his life
   and shared the fate of evil men.

Daniel Sees the Triumph of God

Victory Is Coming

In the Book of Daniel we read about a dream. It is a dream about a man who receives from God power over the people of all nations. When Jesus had done his work, the first Christians said: this is the man — God's suffering servant, now triumphant!

During this vision in the night, I saw what looked like a human being. He was approaching me, surrounded by clouds, and he went to the one

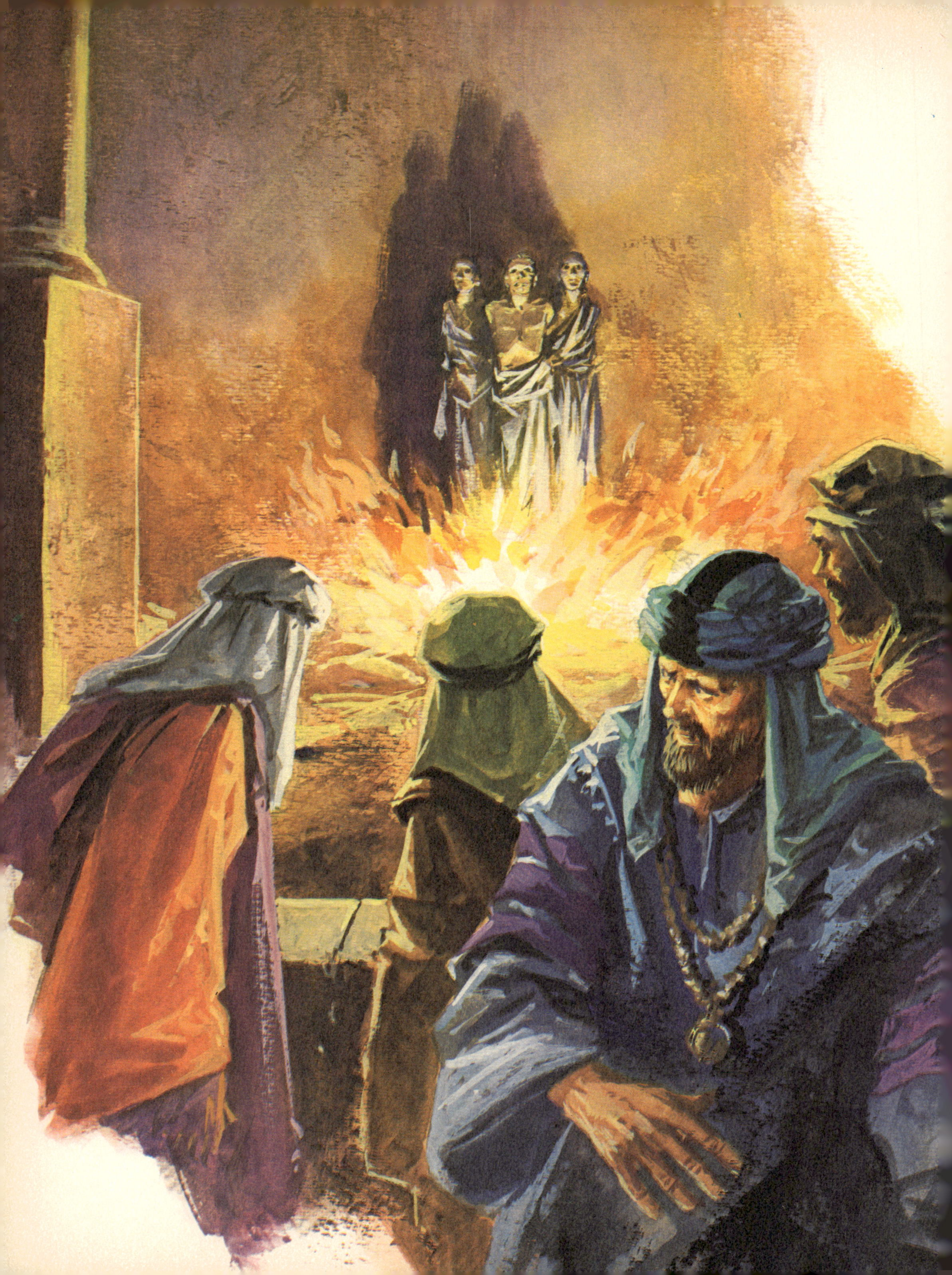

who had been living for ever and was presented to him. He was given authority, honour, and royal power, so that the people of all nations, races, and languages would serve him. His authority would last for ever, and his kingdom would never end.

While I was looking, thrones were put in place. One who had been living for ever sat down on one of the thrones. His clothes were white as snow, and his hair was like pure wool. His throne, mounted on fiery wheels, was blazing with fire, and a stream of fire was pouring out from it. There were many thousands of people there to serve him, and millions of people stood before him. The court began its session, and the books were opened.

In the Furnace

> *In the Book of Daniel there are some famous stories, told in order to show how God remains loyal to those who are loyal to him. There is a story about three loyal Jews who are thrown into a blazing furnace because they have refused to worship a gold statue set up by King Nebuchadnezzar. In the fire, God saves them.*

Then Nebuchadnezzar lost his temper, and his face turned red with anger at Shadrach, Meshach, and Abednego. So he ordered his men to heat the furnace seven times hotter than usual. And he commanded the strongest men in his army to tie the three men up and throw them into the blazing furnace. So they tied them up, fully dressed — shirts, robes, caps, and all — and threw them into the blazing furnace. Now because the king had given strict orders for the furnace to be made extremely hot, the flames burnt up the guards who took the men to the furnace. Then Shadrach, Meshach, and Abednego, still tied up, fell into the heart of the blazing fire.

Suddenly Nebuchadnezzar leapt to his feet in amazement. He asked his officials, "Didn't we tie up three men and throw them into the blazing furnace?"

They answered, "Yes, we did, Your Majesty."

"Then why do I see four men walking about in the fire?" he asked. "They are not tied up, and they show no sign of being hurt — and the fourth one looks like a god."

The Writing on the Wall

> *This is the story of a great banquet given by King Nebuchadnezzar's son, King Belshazzar. In the middle of the feast, some mysterious writing is seen on the wall of the palace. Only Daniel can understand it. It is a warning that Belshazzar's kingdom will soon be no more.*

One night King Belshazzar invited a thousand noblemen to a great banquet, and they drank wine together. While they were drinking, Belshazzar gave orders to bring in the gold and silver cups and bowls which his father Nebuchadnezzar had carried off from the Temple in Jerusalem. The king sent for them so that he, his noblemen, his wives, and his concubines could drink out of them. At once the gold cups and bowls were brought in, and they all drank wine out of them and praised gods made of gold, silver, bronze, iron, wood, and stone.

Suddenly a human hand appeared and began writing on the plaster wall of the palace, where the light from the lamps was shining most brightly. And the king saw the hand as it was writing. He turned pale and was so frightened that his knees began to shake. He shouted for someone to bring in the magicians, wizards, and astrologers. When they came in, the king said to them, "Anyone who can read this writing and tell me what it means will be dressed in robes of royal purple, wear a gold chain of honour round his neck, and be the third in power in the kingdom." The royal advisers came forward, but none of them could read the writing or tell the king what it meant. In his distress King Belshazzar grew even paler, and his noblemen had no idea what to do.

The queen mother heard the noise made by the king and his noblemen and entered the banqueting-hall. She said, "May Your Majesty live for ever! Please do not be so disturbed and look so pale. There is a man in your kingdom who has the spirit of the holy gods in him. When your father was king, this man showed good sense, knowledge, and wisdom like the wisdom of the gods. And King Nebuchadnezzar, your father, made him chief of the fortune-tellers, magicians, wizards, and astrologers. He has unusual ability and is wise and skilful in interpreting dreams, solving riddles, and explaining mysteries; so send for this man Daniel, and he will tell you what all this means."

Daniel Explains the Writing

Daniel was brought at once into the king's presence, and the king said to him, "Are you Daniel, that Jewish exile whom my father the king brought here from Judah? I have heard that the spirit of the holy gods is in you and that you are skilful and have knowledge and wisdom. The advisers and magicians were brought in to read this writing and tell me what it means, but they could not discover the meaning. Now I have heard that you can find hidden meanings and explain mysteries. If you can read this writing and tell me what it means, you will be dressed in robes of royal purple, wear a gold chain of honour round your neck, and be the third in power in the kingdom."

Daniel replied, "Keep your gifts for yourself or give them to someone

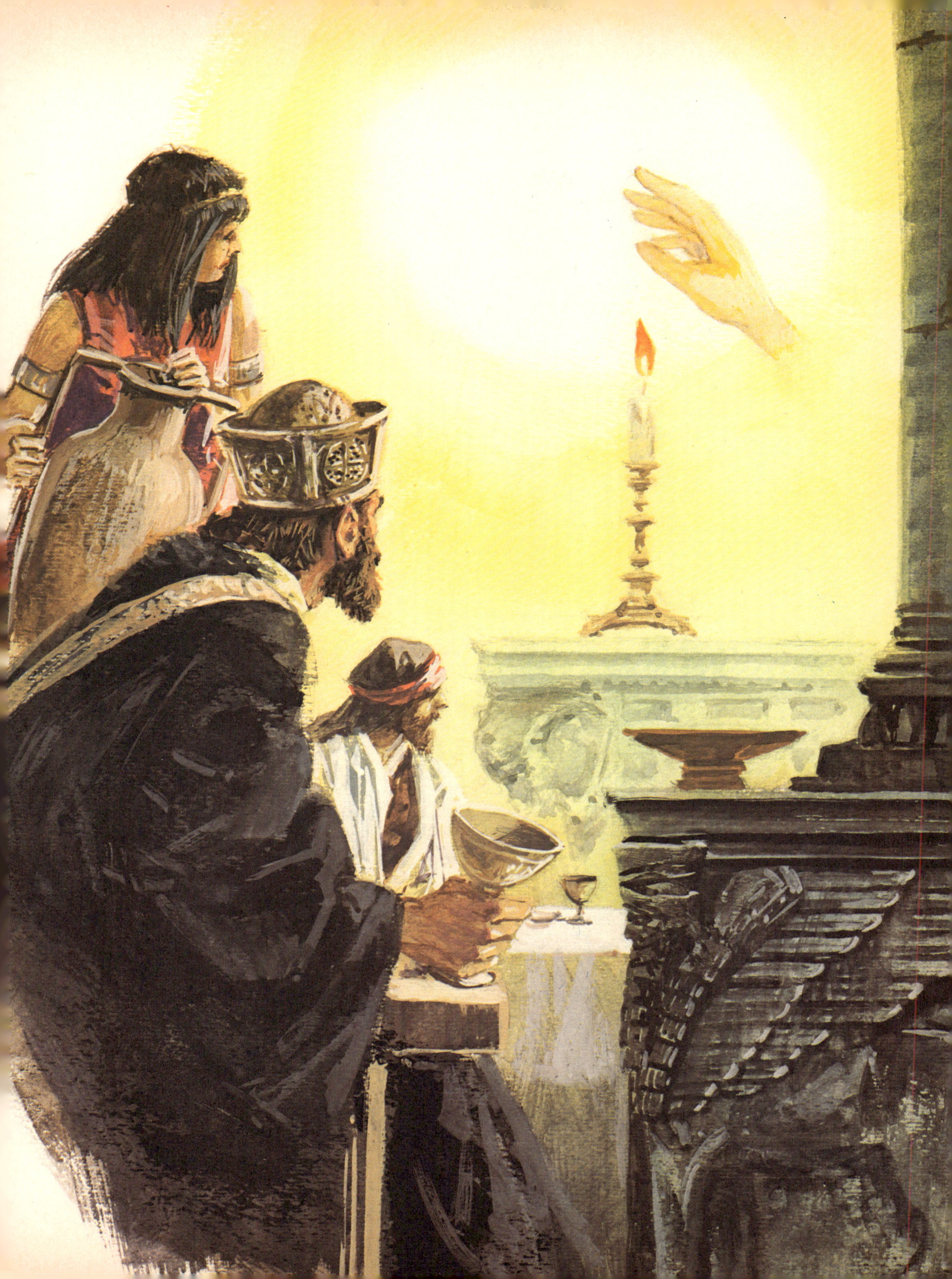

else. I will read for Your Majesty what has been written and tell you what it means.

"The Supreme God made your father Nebuchadnezzar a great king and gave him dignity and majesty. He was so great that people of all nations, races, and languages were afraid of him and trembled. If he wanted to kill someone, he did; if he wanted to keep someone alive, he did. He honoured or disgraced anyone he wanted to. But because he became proud, stubborn, and cruel, he was removed from his royal throne and lost his place of honour. He was driven away from human society, and his mind became like that of an animal. He lived with wild donkeys, ate grass like an ox, and slept in the open air with nothing to protect him from the dew. Finally he admitted that the Supreme God controls all human kingdoms and can give them to anyone he chooses.

"But you, his son, have not humbled yourself, even though you knew all this. You acted against the Lord of heaven and brought in the cups and bowls taken from his Temple. You, your noblemen, your wives, and your concubines drank wine out of them and praised gods made of gold, silver, bronze, iron, wood, and stone – gods that cannot see or hear and that do not know anything. But you did not honour the God who determines whether you live or die and who controls everything you do. That is why God has sent the hand to write these words.

"This is what was written: 'Number, weight, divisions.' And this is what it means: *number*, God has numbered the days of your kingdom and brought it to an end; *weight*, you have been weighed on the scales and found to be too light; *divisions*, your kingdom is divided up and given to the Medes and Persians."

Immediately Belshazzar ordered his servants to dress Daniel in a robe of royal purple and to hang a gold chain of honour round his neck. And he made him the third in power in the kingdom. That same night Belshazzar, the king of Babylonia, was killed; and Darius the Mede, who was then sixty-two years old, seized the royal power.

Daniel in the Den of Lions

Under the new king, Darius, Daniel becomes powerful. Then, because he continued to pray as a faithful Jew, he is put in a cage full of lions. But he escapes unhurt.

Darius decided to appoint a hundred and twenty governors to hold office throughout his empire. In addition, he chose Daniel and two others to supervise the governors and to look after the king's interests. Daniel soon showed that he could do better work than the other supervisors or governors. Because he was so outstanding, the king considered putting him in charge of the whole empire. Then the other supervisors and the governors tried to find something wrong with the way Daniel administered the empire, but they couldn't, because Daniel was reliable and did not do anything wrong or dishonest. They said to one another, "We are not going to find anything of which to accuse Daniel unless it is something in connection with his religion."

So they went to see the king and said, "King Darius, may Your Majesty live for ever! All of us who administer your empire — the supervisors, the governors, the lieutenant-governors, and the other officials — have agreed that Your Majesty should issue an order and enforce it strictly. Give orders that for thirty days no one be permitted to request anything from any god or from any man except from Your Majesty. Anyone who violates this order is to be thrown into a pit filled with lions. So let Your Majesty issue this order and sign it, and it will be in force, a law of the Medes and Persians, which cannot be changed." And so King Darius signed the order. When Daniel learnt that the order had been signed, he went home. In an upstairs room of his house there were windows that faced towards Jerusalem. There, just as he had always done, he knelt down at the open windows and prayed to God three times a day.

When Daniel's enemies observed him praying to God, all of them went together to the king to accuse Daniel. They said, "Your Majesty, you signed an order that for the next thirty days anyone who requested anything from any god or from any man except you, would be thrown into a pit filled with lions."

The king replied, "Yes, a strict order, a law of the Medes and Persians, which cannot be changed."

Then they said to the king, "Daniel, one of the exiles from Judah, does not respect Your Majesty or obey the order you issued. He prays regularly three times a day."

When the king heard this, he was upset and did his best to find some way to rescue Daniel. He kept trying until sunset. Then the men came back to the king and said to him, "Your Majesty knows that according to the laws of the Medes and Persians no order which the king issues can be changed."

So the king gave orders for Daniel to be arrested and he was thrown into the pit filled with lions. He said to Daniel, "May your God, whom you serve so loyally, rescue you." A stone was put over the mouth of the pit, and the king placed his own royal seal and the seal of his noblemen on the stone, so that no one could rescue Daniel. Then the king returned to the palace and spent a sleepless night, without food or any form of entertainment.

At dawn the king got up and hurried to the pit. When he got there, he called out anxiously, "Daniel, servant of the living God! Was the God you serve so loyally able to save you from the lions?"

Daniel answered, "May Your Majesty live for ever! God sent his angel

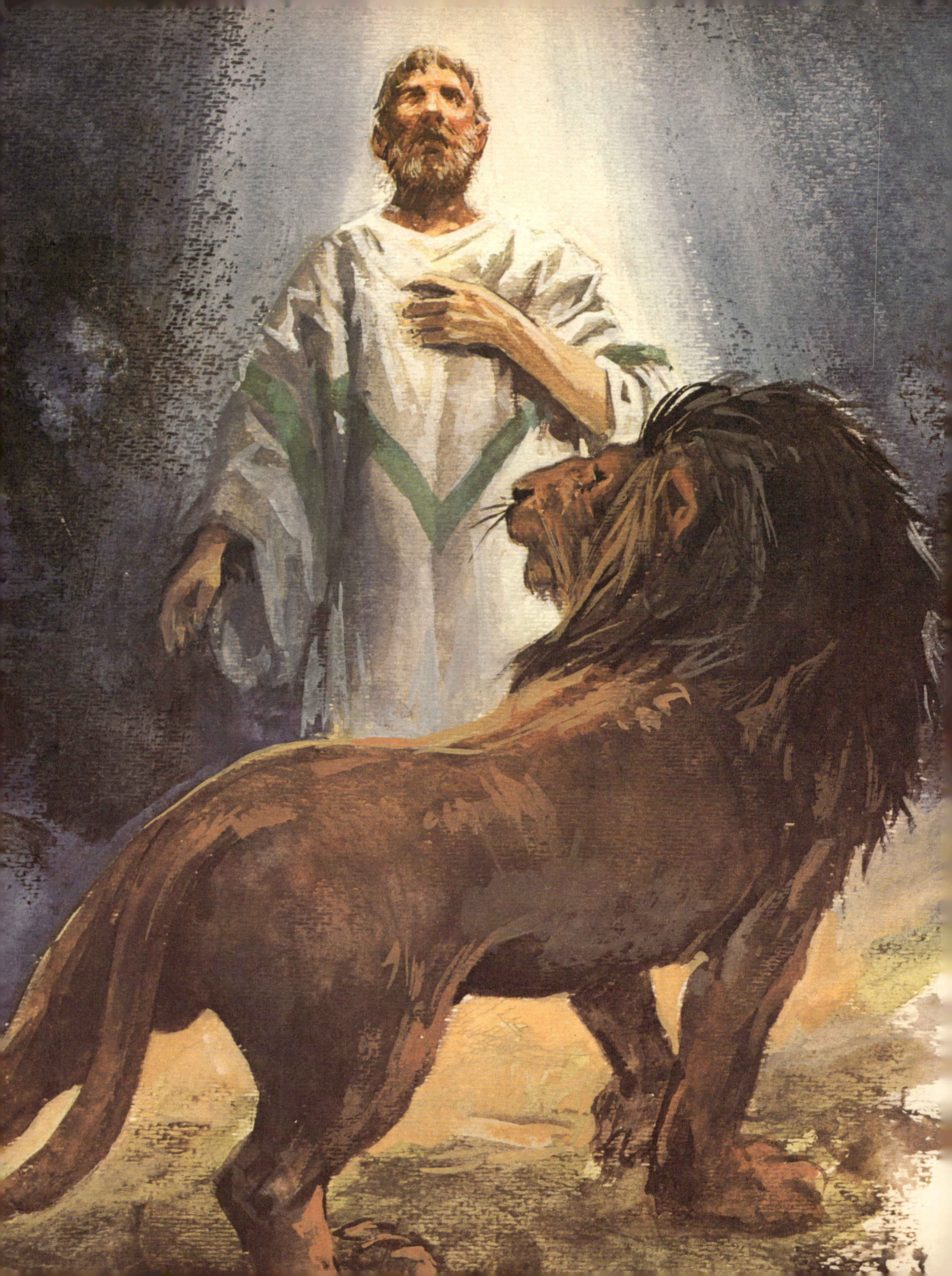

to shut the mouths of the lions so that they would not hurt me. He did this because he knew that I was innocent and because I have not wronged you, Your Majesty."

The king was overjoyed and gave orders for Daniel to be pulled up out of the pit. So they pulled him up and saw that he had not been hurt at all, for he trusted God.

Jonah is Sent to the Great City

Like the Book of Daniel, the Book of Jonah is full of stories with a meaning. Jonah, who represents the whole Jewish people, tries to escape from God, as the Jews have tried. Then he is swallowed by a whale, as the Jews have been swallowed by disaster and exile. But Jonah is told to proclaim God's message to the great city of Nineveh, the capital of the hated Assyrian empire. And Jonah finds that it is a message about God's love.

Jonah Disobeys the Lord

One day, the Lord spoke to Jonah son of Amittai. He said, "Go to Nineveh, that great city, and speak out against it; I am aware how wicked its people are." Jonah, however, set out in the opposite direction in order to get away from the Lord. He went to Joppa, he found a ship about to go to Spain. He paid his fare and went aboard with the crew to sail to Spain, where he would be away from the Lord. But the Lord sent a strong wind on the sea, and the storm was so violent that the ship was in danger of breaking up. The sailors were terrified and cried out for help, each one to his own god. Then, in order to lessen the danger, they threw the cargo overboard. Meanwhile, Jonah had gone below and was lying in the ship's hold, sound asleep.

The captain found him there and said to him, "What are you doing asleep? Get up and pray to your god for help. Maybe he will feel sorry for us and spare our lives."

The sailors said to one another, "Let's draw lots and find out who is to blame for getting us into this danger." They did so, and Jonah's name was drawn. So they said to him: "Now then, tell us! Are you to blame for this? What are you doing here? What country do you come from? What is your nationality?"

"I am a Hebrew," Jonah answered. "I worship the Lord, the God of heaven, who made land and sea." Jonah went on to tell them that he was running away from the Lord.

The sailors were terrified, and said to him, "That was an awful thing to do!" The storm was getting worse all the time, so the sailors asked him, "What should we do to you to stop the storm?"

Jonah answered, "Throw me into the sea, and it will calm down. I know it is my fault that you are caught in this violent storm."

Instead, the sailors tried to get the ship to shore, rowing with all their might. But the storm was getting worse and worse, and they got nowhere. So they cried out to the Lord, "O Lord, we pray, don't punish us with death for taking this man's life! You, O Lord, are responsible for all this; it is your doing." Then they picked Jonah up and threw him into the sea, and it calmed down at once. This made the sailors so afraid of the Lord that they offered a sacrifice and promised to serve him.

At the Lord's command a large fish swallowed Jonah, and he was inside the fish for three days and nights.

Then the Lord ordered the fish to spew Jonah up on the beach, and it did.

Jonah Obeys the Lord

Once again the Lord spoke to Jonah. He said, "Go to Nineveh, that great city, and proclaim to the people the message I have given you." So Jonah obeyed the Lord and went to Nineveh, a city so large that it took three days to walk through it. Jonah started through the city, and after walking a whole day, he proclaimed, "In forty days Nineveh will be destroyed!"

The people of Nineveh believed God's message. So they decided that everyone should fast, and all the people, from the greatest to the least, put on sackcloth to show that they had repented.

When the king of Nineveh heard about it, he got up from his throne, took off his robe, put on sackcloth, and sat down in ashes. He sent out a proclamation to the people of Nineveh: "This is an order from the king and his officials: No one is to eat anything; all persons, cattle, and sheep are forbidden to eat or drink. All persons and animals must wear sackcloth. Everyone must pray earnestly to God and must give up his wicked behaviour and his evil actions. Perhaps God will change his mind; perhaps he will stop being angry, and we will not die!"

God saw what they did; he saw that they had given up their wicked behaviour. So he changed his mind and did not punish them as he had said he would.

Jonah's Anger and God's Mercy

Jonah was very unhappy about this and became angry. So he prayed, "Lord, didn't I say before I left home that this is just what you would do? That's why I did my best to run away to Spain! I knew that you are a loving and merciful God, always patient, always kind, and always ready to change your mind and not punish. Now, Lord, let me die. I am better off dead than alive."

The Lord answered, "What right have you to be angry?"

Jonah went out east of the city and sat down. He made a shelter for himself and sat in its shade, waiting to see what would happen to Nineveh. Then the Lord God made a plant grow up over Jonah to give him some shade, so that he would be more comfortable. Jonah was extremely pleased with the plant. But at dawn the next day, at God's command, a worm attacked the plant, and it died. After the sun had risen, God sent a hot east wind, and Jonah was about to faint from the heat of the sun beating down on his head. So he wished he were dead.

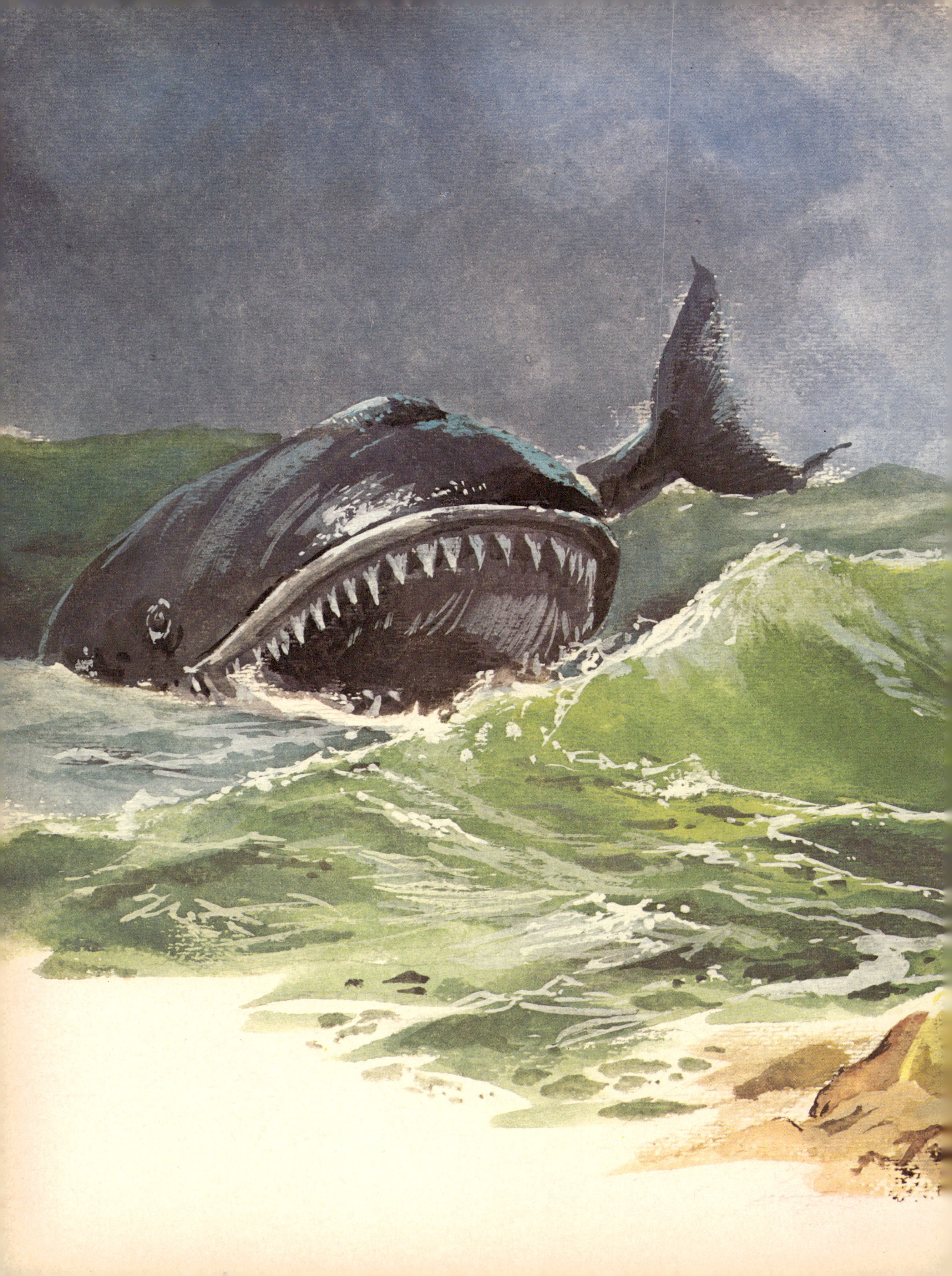

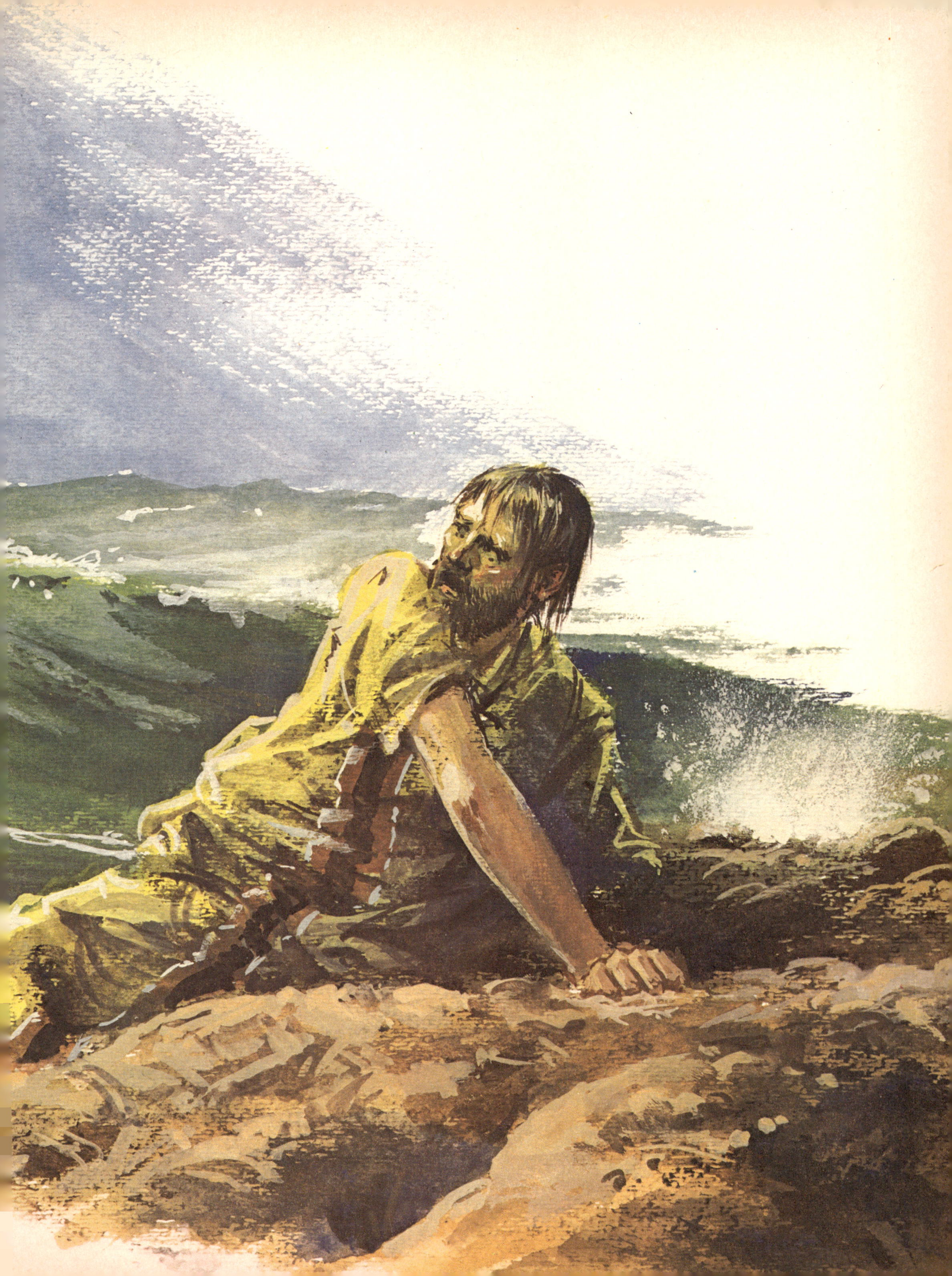

"I am better off dead than alive," he said.

But God said to him, "What right have you to be angry about the plant?"

Jonah replied, "I have every right to be angry — angry enough to die!"

The Lord said to him, "This plant grew up in one night and disappeared the next; you didn't do anything for it, and you didn't make it grow — yet you feel sorry for it! How much more, then, should I have pity on Nineveh, that great city. After all, it has more than 120,000 innocent children in it, as well as many animals!"

Three Songs about God

This is the faith which the Jews still held in their time of defeat. It is seen in Psalm 22, used by the dying Jesus.

My God, my God, why have you abandoned me?
I have cried desperately for help,
   but still it does not come.
During the day I call to you, my God,
   but you do not answer;
I call at night,
   but get no rest.
But you are enthroned as the Holy One,
   the one whom Israel praises.
Our ancestors put their trust in you;
   they trusted you, and you saved them.
They called to you and escaped from danger;
   they trusted you and were not disappointed.

God our Shepherd

The most famous of all the hymns in the Bible is Psalm 23, because it is a song about God's love.

The Lord is my shepherd;
   I have everything I need.
He lets me rest in fields of green grass
   and leads me to quiet pools of fresh water.
He gives me new strength.
He guides me in the right paths,
   as he has promised.
Even if I go through the deepest darkness,
   I will not be afraid, Lord,
     for you are with me.
Your shepherd's rod and staff protect me.

You prepare a banquet for me,
>   where all my enemies can see me;
> you welcome me as an honoured guest
>   and fill my cup to the brim.
> I know that your goodness and love will be with me all my life;
>   and your house will be my home as long as I live.

God our Refuge

Psalm 31 was a prayer used by devout Jews every night, and Jesus used it just before he died.
> I come to you, Lord, for protection;
>   never let me be defeated.
> You are a righteous God;
>   save me, I pray!
> Hear me! Save me now!
> Be my refuge to protect me;
>   my defence to save me.
>
> You are my refuge and defence;
>   guide me and lead me as you have promised.
> Keep me safe from the trap that has been set for me;
>   shelter me from danger.
> I place myself in your care.
> You will save me, Lord;
>   you are a faithful God.

Your King is Coming

In the Book of Zachariah we read the promise which people remembered when Jesus entered Jerusalem with his message of peace.
> Rejoice, rejoice, people of Zion!
>   Shout for joy, you people of Jerusalem!
>   Look, your king is coming to you!
> He comes triumphant and victorious,
>   but humble and riding on a donkey –
>   on a colt, the foal of a donkey.

The Lord says,
> "I will remove the war-chariots from Israel
>   and take the horses from Jerusalem;
>   the bows used in battle will be destroyed.
> Your king will make peace among the nations;
>   he will rule from sea to sea,
>   from the River Euphrates to the ends of the earth."

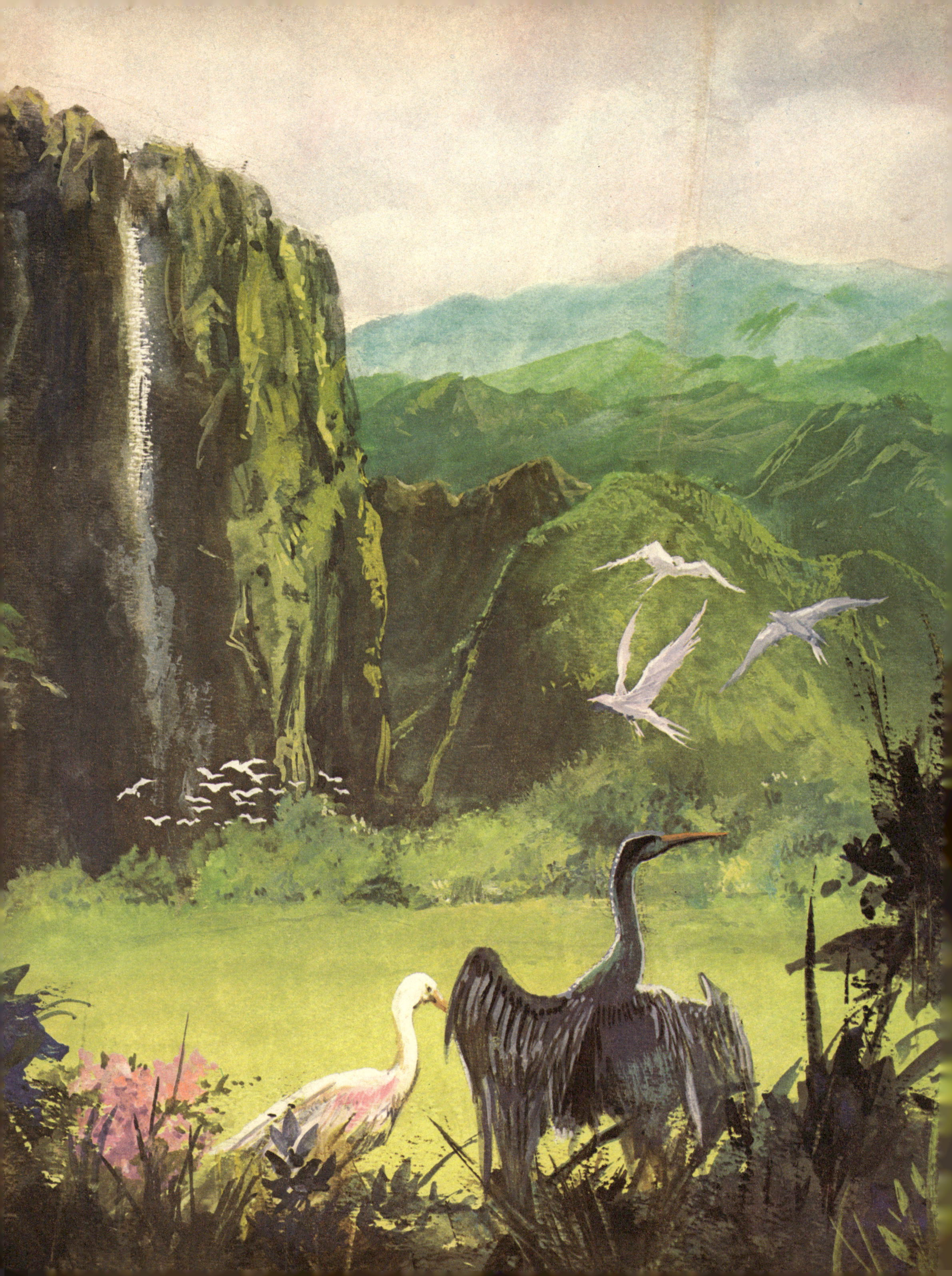

6
This is God's World

Here are the stories and songs which the people of Ancient Israel used in order to say: this is God's world. If we want to have an accurate account of how matter and life evolved in this amazingly vast and old universe, we must turn to science. But here is a wisdom even greater than science.

God's Good Creation

In the Beginning

This magnificent picture shows God at work everywhere.
In the beginning, when God created the universe, the earth was formless and desolate. The raging ocean that covered everything was engulfed in total darkness, and the power of God was moving over the water. Then God commanded, "Let there be light" – and light appeared. God was pleased with what he saw. Then he separated the light from the darkness, and he named the light "Day" and the darkness "Night". Evening passed and morning came – that was the first day.

Then God commanded, "Let there be a dome to divide the water and to keep it in two separate places" – and it was done. So God made a dome, and it separated the water under it from the water above it. He named the dome "Sky". Evening passed and morning came – that was the second day.

Then God commanded, "Let the water below the sky come together in one place, so that the land will appear" – and it was done. He named the land "Earth", and the water which had come together he named "Sea". And God was pleased with what he saw. Then he commanded, "Let the earth produce all kinds of plants, those that bear grain and those that bear fruit" – and it was done. So the earth produced all kinds of plants, and God was pleased with what he saw. Evening passed and morning came – that was the third day.

Then God commanded, "Let lights appear in the sky to separate day from night and to show the time when days, years, and religious festivals begin; they will shine in the sky to give light to the earth" – and it was done. So God made the two larger lights, the sun to rule over the day and the moon to rule over the night; he also made the stars. He placed the lights in the sky to shine on the earth, to rule over the day and the night, and to separate light from darkness. And God was pleased with what he saw. Evening passed and morning came — that was the fourth day.

Then God commanded, "Let the water be filled with many kinds of living beings, and let the air be filled with birds." So God created the great sea-monsters, all kinds of creatures that live in the water, and all kinds of birds. And God was pleased with what he saw. He blessed them all and told the creatures that live in the water to reproduce, and to fill the sea, and he told the birds to increase in number. Evening passed and morning came — that was the fifth day.

Then God commanded, "Let the earth produce all kinds of animal life: domestic and wild, large and small" — and it was done. So God made them all, and he was pleased with what he saw.

Then God said, "And now we will make human beings; they will be like us and resemble us. They will have power over the fish, the birds, and all animals, domestic and wild, large and small." So God created human beings, making them to be like himself. He created them male and female, blessed them, and said, "Have many children, so that your descendants will live all over the earth and bring it under their control. I am putting you in charge of the fish, the birds, and all the wild animals. I have provided all kinds of grain and all kinds of fruit for you to eat; but for all the wild animals and for all the birds I have provided grass and leafy plants for food" — and it was done. God looked at everything he had made, and he was very pleased. Evening passed and morning came — that was the sixth day.

And so the whole universe was completed. By the seventh day God finished what he had been doing and stopped working. He blessed the seventh day and set it apart as a special day, because by that day he had completed his creation and stopped working. And that is how the universe was created.

In Praise of the Creator

Psalm 104 is a song of joy about the world as God has made it.
Praise the Lord, my soul!
    O Lord, my God, how great you are!
You are clothed with majesty and glory;
    you cover yourself with light.
You spread out the heavens like a tent
    and built your home on the waters above.
You use the clouds as your chariot
    and ride on the wings of the wind.
You use the winds as your messengers
    and flashes of lightning as your servants.

You have set the earth firmly on its foundations,
    and it will never be moved.
You placed the ocean over it like a robe,
    and the water covered the mountains.
When you rebuked the waters, they fled;
    they rushed away when they heard your shout of command.
They flowed over the mountains and into the valleys,
    to the place you had made for them.
You set a boundary they can never pass,
    to keep them from covering the earth again.

You make springs flow in the valleys,
    and rivers run between the hills.
They provide water for the wild animals;
    there the wild donkeys quench their thirst.
In the trees near by,
    the birds make their nests and sing.
From the sky you send rain on the hills,
    and the earth is filled with your blessings.
You make grass grow for the cattle
    and plants for man to use,
so that he can grow his crops
    and produce wine to make him happy,
    olive-oil to make him cheerful,
    and bread to give him strength.

The cedars of Lebanon get plenty of rain —
    the Lord's own trees, which he planted.
There the birds build their nests;
    the storks nest in the fir-trees.
The wild goats live in the high mountains,
    and the badgers hide in the cliffs.

You created the moon to mark the months;
    the sun knows the time to set.
You made the night, and in the darkness
    all the wild animals come out.
The young lions roar while they hunt,
    looking for the food that God provides.
When the sun rises, they go back
    and lie down in their dens.
Then people go out to do their work
    and keep working until evening.
Lord, you have made so many things!
    How wisely you made them all!

The earth is filled with your creatures.
There is the ocean, large and wide,
    where countless creatures live,
    large and small alike.
The ships sail on it, and in it plays Leviathan,
    that sea-monster which you made.

All of them depend on you
    to give them food when they need it.
You give it to them, and they eat it;
    you provide food, and they are satisfied.
When you turn away, they are afraid;
    when you take away their breath, they die
    and go back to the dust from which they came.
But when you give them breath, they are created;
    you give new life to the earth.

May the glory of the Lord last for ever!
    May the Lord be happy with what he has made!
He looks at the earth, and it trembles;
    he touches the mountains, and they pour out smoke.

I will sing to the Lord all my life;
    as long as I live I will sing praises to my God.

God Created Them All

Underneath the Earth

Beneath the fields there are still more marvellous things: silver, gold, iron, copper and many jewels, all buried deep in the soil and the rocks. Sometimes miners dig them out. The Book of Job describes the miners' work, but adds: how much greater is the cleverness of the God who made all this!

There are mines where silver is dug;
There are places where gold is refined.
Men dig iron out of the ground
And melt copper out of the stones.
Men explore the deepest darkness.
They search the depths of the earth
And dig for rocks in the darkness.
Far from where anyone lives
Or human feet ever travel,
Men dig the shafts of mines.
There they work in loneliness,
Clinging to ropes in the pits.

Food grows out of the earth,
But underneath the same earth
All is torn up and crushed.
The stones of the earth contain sapphires.
And its dust contains gold.
No hawk sees the roads to the mines,
And no vulture ever flies over them.
No lion or other fierce beast
Ever travels those lonely roads.

Men dig the hardest rocks,
Dig mountains away at their base.
As they tunnel through the rocks,
They discover precious stones.
They dig to the sources of rivers
And bring to light what is hidden.

Horses

In the Book of Job, horses are described among the wonders of God's world.
   Was it you, Job, who made horses so strong
      and gave them their flowing manes?
   Did you make them leap like locusts
      and frighten men with their snorting?
   They eagerly paw the ground in the valley;
      they rush into battle with all their strength.
   They do not know the meaning of fear,
      and no sword can turn them back.
   The weapons which their riders carry
      rattle and flash in the sun.
   Trembling with excitement, the horses race ahead;
   when the trumpet blows, they can't stand still.
   At each blast of the trumpet they snort;
      they can smell a battle before they get near,
      and they hear the officers shouting commands.

Crocodiles

The crocodile is 'king of all wild beasts'. But God made him, too; and here is his picture in the Book of Job.
   Can you catch Leviathan with a fish-hook
      or tie his tongue down with a rope?
   Can you put a rope through his snout
      or put a hook through his jaws?
   Will he beg you to let him go?
      Will he plead with you for mercy?

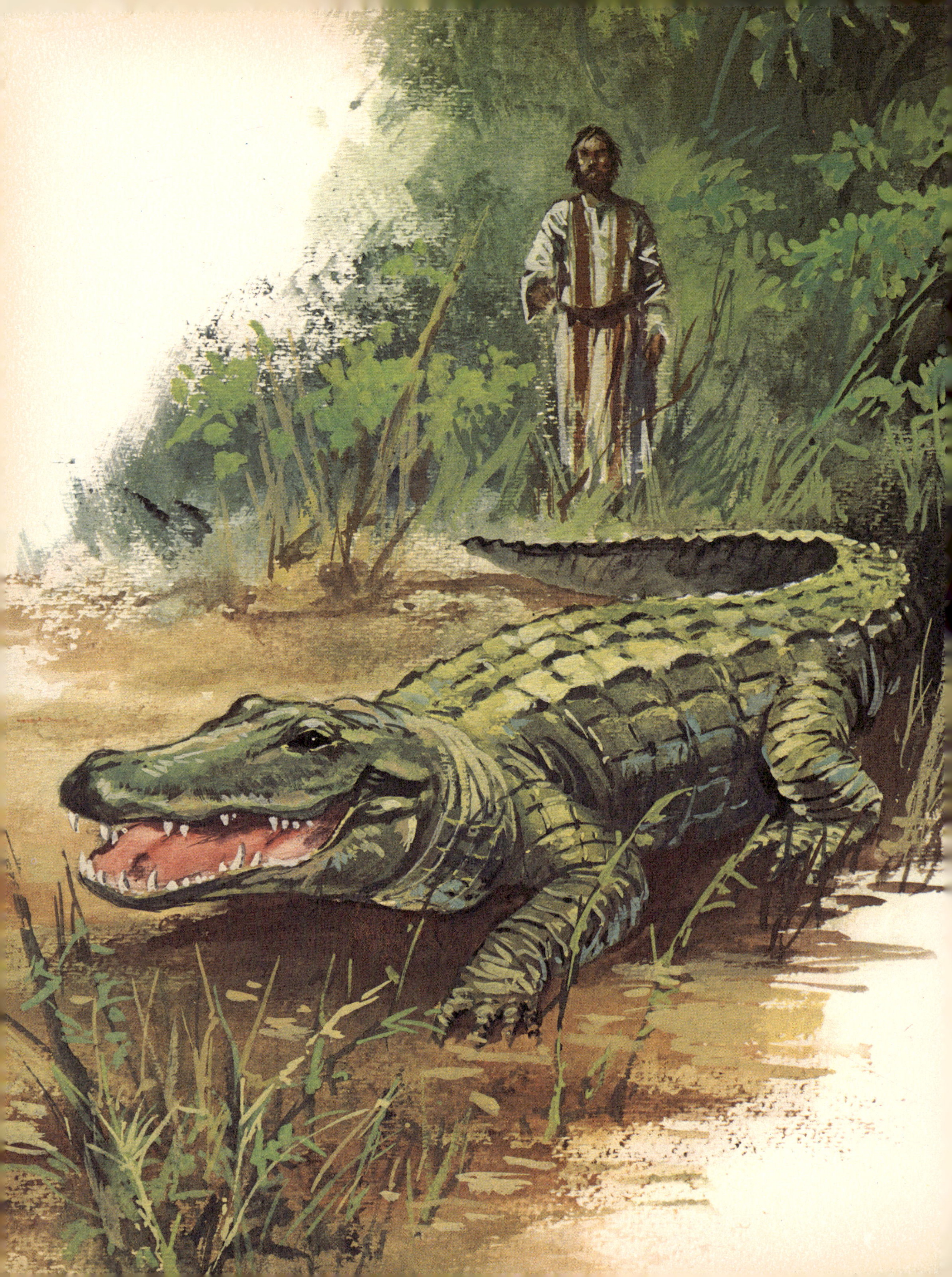

Will he make an agreement with you
  and promise to serve you for ever?
Will you tie him up like a pet bird,
  like something to amuse your servant-girls?
Will fishermen bargain over him?
  Will merchants cut him up to sell?
Can you fill his hide with fishing-spears
  or pierce his head with a harpoon?
Touch him once and you'll never try it again;
  you'll never forget the fight.

Anyone who sees Leviathan
  loses courage and falls to the ground
When he is aroused, he is fierce;
  no one would dare to stand before him.
Who can attack him and still be safe?
  No one in all the world can do it.

Let me tell you about Leviathan's legs
  and describe how great and strong he is.
No one can tear off his outer coat
  or pierce the armour he wears.
Who can make him open his jaws,
  ringed with those terrifying teeth?
His back is made of rows of shields,
  fastened together and hard as stone.
Each one is joined so tight to the next,
  not even a breath can come between.
They all are fastened so firmly together
  that nothing can ever pull them apart.
Light flashes when he sneezes,
  and his eyes glow like the rising sun.
Flames blaze from his mouth,
  and streams of sparks fly out.
Smoke comes pouring out of his nose,
  like smoke from weeds burning under a pot.
His breath starts first burning;
  flames leap out of his mouth.
His neck is so powerful
  that all who meet him are terrified.
There is not a weak spot in his skin;
  it is as hard and unyielding as iron.
His stony heart is without fear,
  as unyielding and hard as a millstone.
When he rises up, even the strongest are frightened;

they are helpless with fear.
There is no sword that can wound him;
  no spear or arrow or lance that can harm him.
For him iron is as flimsy as straw,
  and bronze as soft as rotten wood.
There is no arrow that can make him run;
  rocks thrown at him are like bits of straw.
To him a club is a piece of straw,
  and he laughs when men throw spears.
The scales on his belly are like jagged pieces of pottery;
  they tear up the muddy ground like a threshing-sledge.
He churns up the sea like boiling water
  and makes it bubble like a pot of oil.
He leaves a shining path behind him
  and turns the sea to white foam.
There is nothing on earth to compare with him;
  he is a creature that has no fear.
He looks down on even the proudest animals;
  he is king of all wild beasts.

Mankind Goes Wrong

And so we come to the tragic story of mankind. But first the Bible said a man and a woman could be happy together in peace, happy to do God's will in God's world. Adam means "Mankind" and Eve means "Life".

Adam and Eve

When the Lord God made the universe, there were no plants on the earth and no seeds had sprouted, because he had not sent any rain, and there was no one to cultivate the land; but water would come up from beneath the surface and water the ground.

Then the Lord God took some soil from the ground and formed a man out of it; he breathed life-giving breath into his nostrils and the man began to live.

Then the Lord God planted a garden in Eden, in the East, and there he put the man he had formed. He made all kinds of beautiful trees grow there and produce good fruit. In the middle of the garden stood the tree that gives life and the tree that gives knowledge of what is good and what is bad.

Then the Lord God placed the man in the Garden of Eden to cultivate it and guard it. He said to him, "You may eat the fruit of any tree in the garden, except the tree that gives knowledge of what is good and what is bad. You must not eat the fruit of that tree; if you do, you will die the same day."

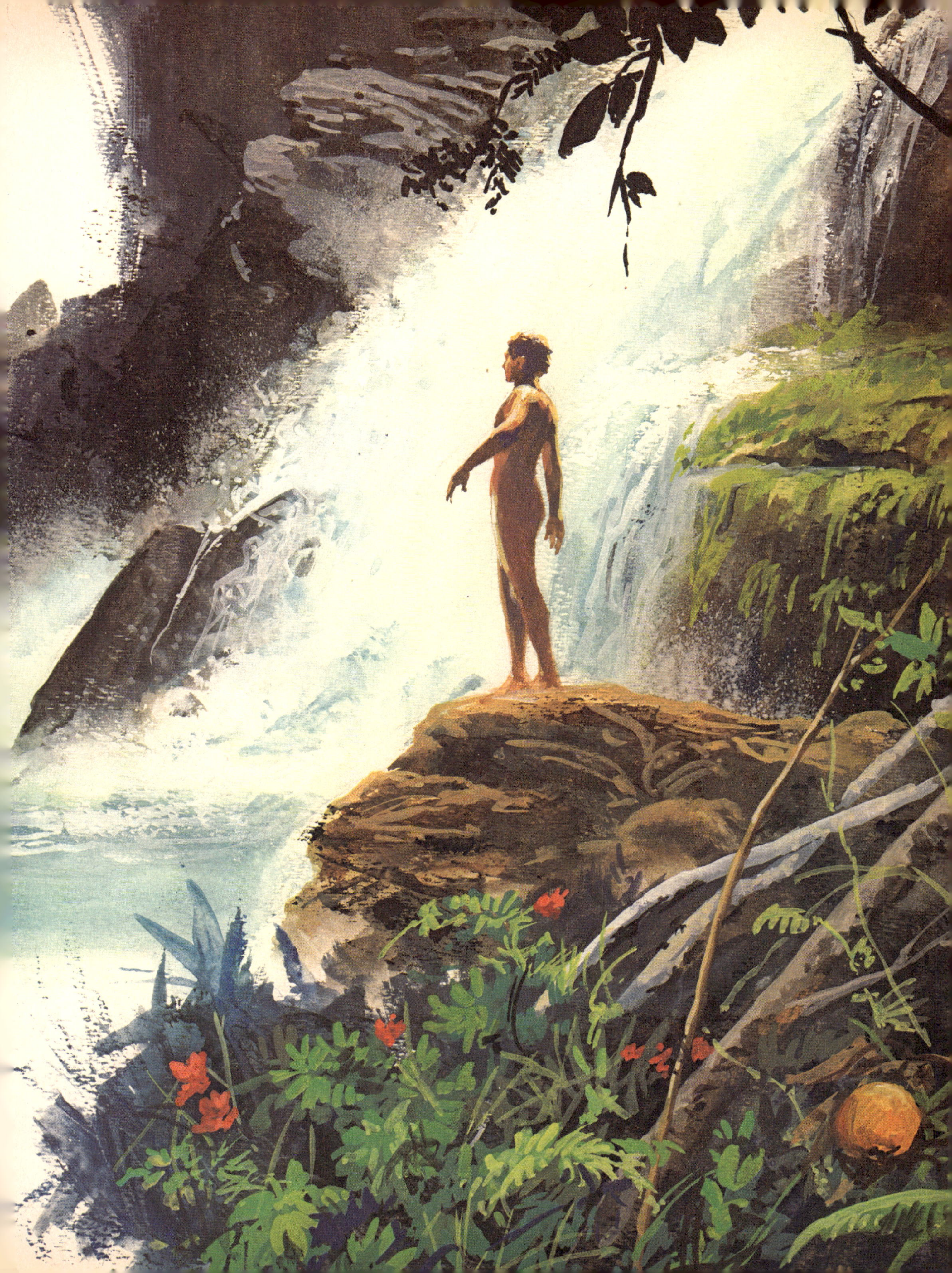

Then the Lord God said, "It is not good for the man to live alone. I will make a suitable companion to help him." So he took some soil from the ground and formed all the animals and all the birds. Then he brought them to the man to see what he would name them; and that is how they all got their names. So the man named all the birds and all the animals; but not one of them was a suitable companion to help him.

Then the Lord God made the man fall into a deep sleep, and while he was sleeping, he took out one of the man's ribs and closed up the flesh. He formed a woman out of the rib and brought her to him. Then the man said,

"At last, here is one of my own kind —
Bone taken from my bone, and flesh from my flesh.
'Woman' is her name because she was taken out of man."

That is why a man leaves his father and mother and is united with his wife, and they become one.

The man and the woman were both naked, but they were not embarrassed.

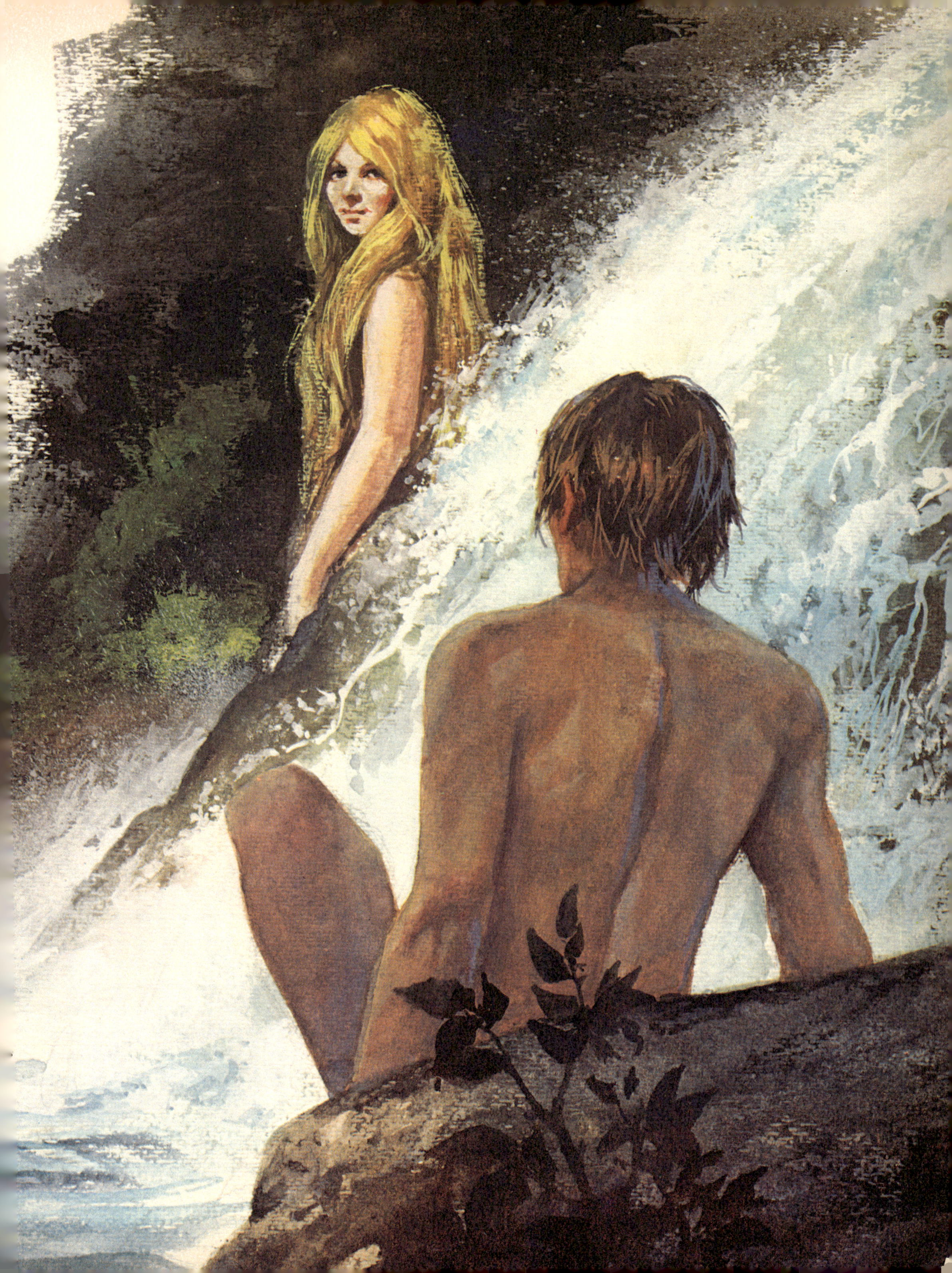

The Disobedience of Mankind

The story of when Adam and Eve first decided not to do what they were told.
Now the snake was the most cunning animal that the Lord God had made. The snake asked the woman, "Did God really tell you not to eat fruit from any tree in the garden?"

"We may eat the fruit of any tree in the garden," the woman answered, "except the tree in the middle of it. God told us not to eat the fruit of that tree or even touch it; if we do, we will die."

The snake replied, "That's not true; you will not die. God said that, because he knows that when you eat it you will be like God and know what is good and what is bad."

The woman saw how beautiful the tree was and how good its fruit would be to eat, and she thought how wonderful it would be to become wise. So she took some of the fruit and ate it. Then she gave some to her husband, and he also ate it. As soon as they had eaten it, they were given understanding and realized that they were naked; so they sewed fig leaves together and covered themselves.

That evening they heard the Lord God walking in the garden, and they hid from him among the trees. But the Lord God called out to the man, "Where are you?"

He answered, "I heard you in the garden; I was afraid and hid from you, because I was naked."

"Who told you that you were naked?" God asked. "Did you eat the fruit that I told you not to eat?"

The man answered, "The woman you put here with me gave me the fruit, and I ate it."

The Lord God asked the woman, "Why did you do this?"

She replied, "The snake tricked me into eating it."

Then the Lord God said, "Now the man has become like one of us and has knowledge of what is good and what is bad. He must not be allowed to eat fruit from the tree of life, and live for ever." So the Lord God sent him out of the Garden of Eden and made him cultivate the soil from which he had been formed. Then at the east side of the garden he put living creatures and a flaming sword which turned in all directions. This was to keep anyone from coming near the tree of life.

The First Hatred

Adam and Eve have two sons, Cain and Abel. Cain, the farmer, becomes jealous of Abel, the shepherd. And so Cain murders his own brother.
Abel became a shepherd, but Cain was a farmer. After some time, Cain brought some of his harvest and gave it as an offering to the Lord. Then Abel brought the first lamb born to one of his sheep, killed it, and gave the best parts of it as an offering. The Lord was pleased with Abel and his

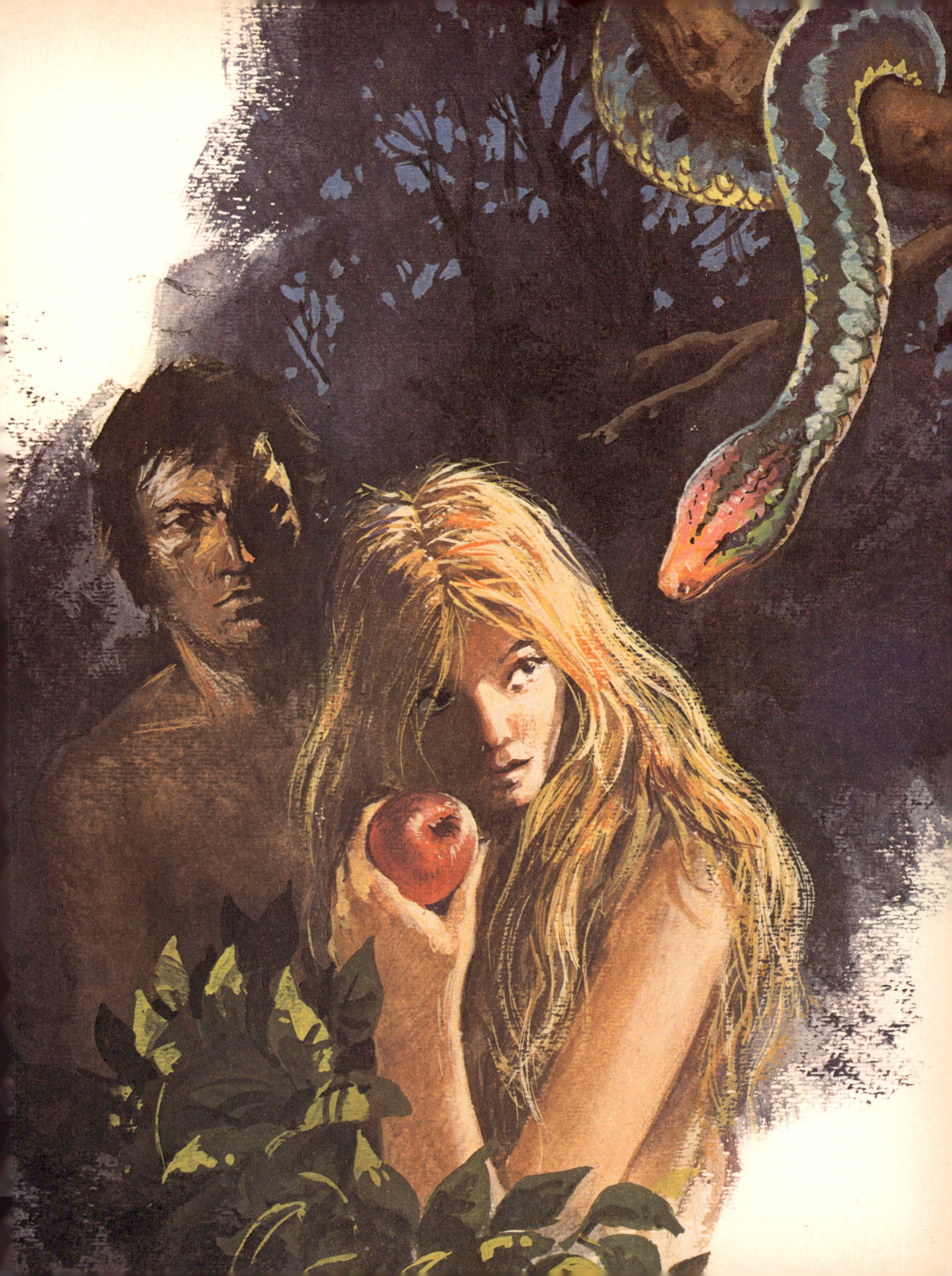

offering, but he rejected Cain and his offering. Cain became furious, and he scowled in anger. Then the Lord said to Cain, "Why are you angry? Why that scowl on your face? If you had done the right thing, you would be smiling; but because you have done evil, sin is crouching at your door. It wants to rule you, but you must overcome it."

The First Murder

Cain said to his brother Abel, "Let's go out in the fields." When they were out in the fields, Cain turned on his brother and killed him.

The Lord asked Cain, "Where is your brother Abel?"

He answered, "I don't know. Am I supposed to take care of my brother?"

Then the Lord said, "Why have you done this terrible thing? Your brother's blood is crying out to me from the ground, like a voice calling for revenge. You are placed under a curse and can no longer farm the soil. It has soaked up your brother's blood as if it had opened its mouth to receive it when you killed him. If you try to grow crops, the soil will not produce anything; you will be a homeless wanderer on the earth."

And Cain said to the Lord, "This punishment is too hard for me to bear. You are driving me off the land and away from your presence. I will be a homeless wanderer on the earth, and anyone who finds me will kill me."

But the Lord answered, "No. If anyone kills you, seven lives will be taken in revenge." So the Lord put a mark on Cain to warn anyone who met him not to kill him. And Cain went away from the Lord's presence and lived in a land called "Wandering," which is east of Eden.

The Great Tower of Pride

> In the ancient city of Babylon stood a high tower. When people saw it, they thought of a story. Perhaps it had been built to reach the sky? And perhaps the pride of its builders had been punished? Here is the story.

At first, the people of the whole world had only one language and used the same words. As they wandered about in the East, they came to a plain in Babylonia and settled there. They said to one another, "Come on! Let's make bricks and bake them hard." So they had bricks to build with and tar to hold them together. They said, "Now let's build a city with a tower that reaches the sky, so that we can make a name for ourselves and not be scattered all over the earth."

Then the Lord came down to see the city and the tower which those men had built, and he said, "Now then, these are all one people and they speak one language; this is just the beginning of what they are going to do. Soon they will be able to do anything they want! Let us

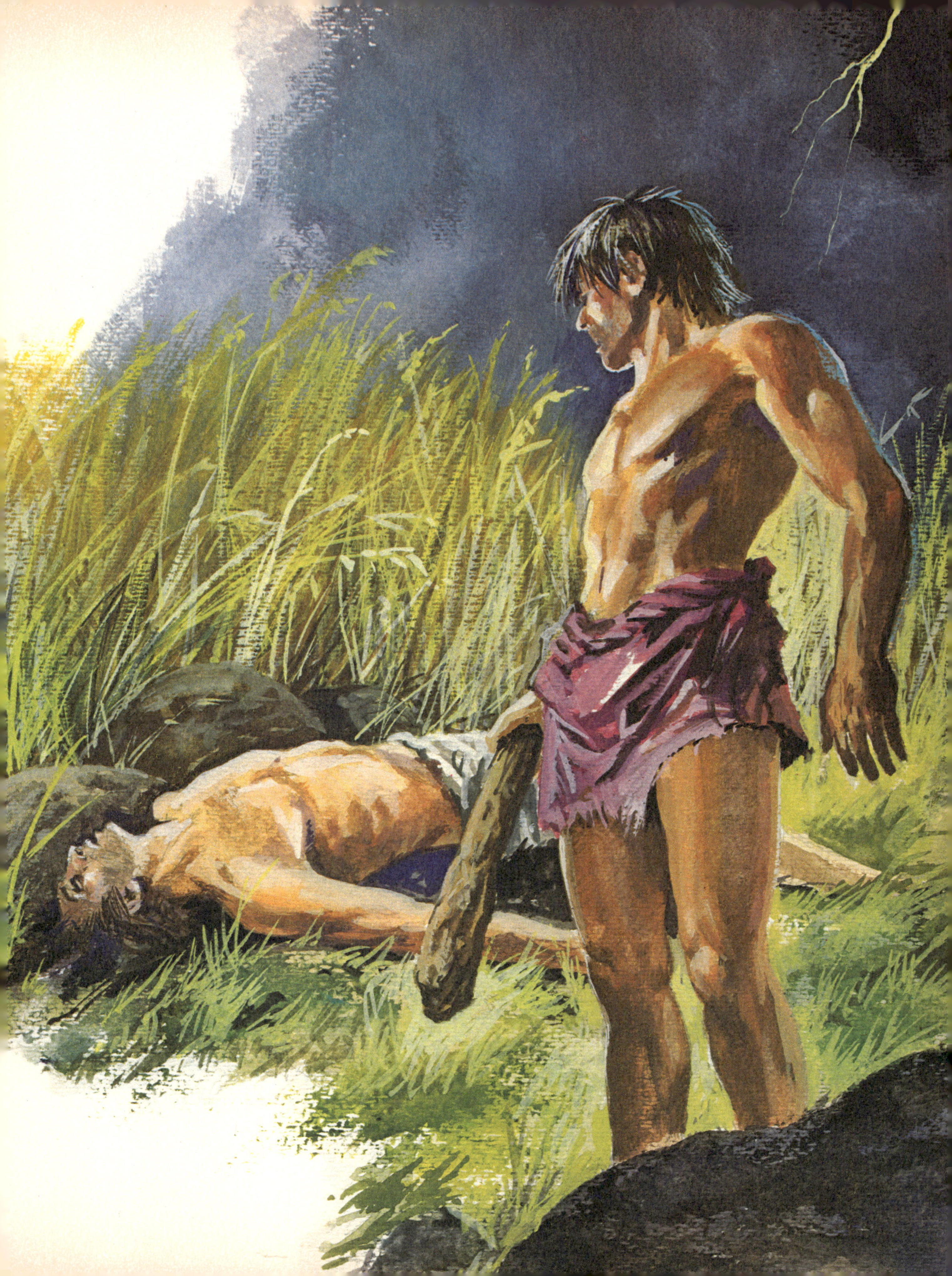

go down and mix up their language so that they will not understand one another." So the Lord scattered them all over the earth, and they stopped building the city. The city was called Babylon, because there the Lord mixed up the language of all the people, and from there he scattered them all over the earth.

Noah and the Flood

The great River Euphrates used to flood disastrously from time to time and there may be memory of that here. But the story of the Flood is really a story about "how wicked everyone on earth was" — and how merciful God remained.

God Calls Noah

When the Lord saw how wicked everyone on earth was and how evil their thoughts were all the time, he was sorry that he had ever made them and put them on the earth. He was so filled with regret that he said, "I will wipe out these people I have created, and also the animals and the birds, because I am sorry that I made any of them." But the Lord was pleased with Noah.

This is the story of Noah. He had three sons, Shem, Ham, and Japheth. Noah had no faults and was the only good man of his time. He lived in fellowship with God, but everyone else was evil in God's sight, and violence had spread everywhere. God looked at the world and saw that it was evil, for the people were all living evil lives.

God said to Noah, "I have decided to put an end to all mankind. I will destroy them completely, because the world is full of their violent deeds. Build a boat for yourself out of good timber; make rooms in it and cover it with tar inside and out. Build it with three decks and put a door in the side. I am going to send a flood on the earth to destroy every living being. Everything on the earth will die, but I will make a covenant with you. Go into the boat with your wife, your sons, and their wives. Take into the boat with you a male and a female of every kind of animal and of every kind of bird, in order to keep them alive. Take along all kinds of food for you and for them." Noah did everything that God commanded.

When Noah was six hundred years old, on the seventeenth day of the second month all the outlets of the vast body of water beneath the earth burst open, all the floodgates of the sky were opened, and rain fell on the earth for forty days and nights. On that same day Noah and his wife went into the boat with their three sons, Shem, Ham, and Japheth, and their wives. With them went every kind of animal, domestic and wild, large and small, and every kind of bird. A male and a female of each kind of living being went into the boat with Noah, as God had commanded. Then the Lord shut the door behind Noah.

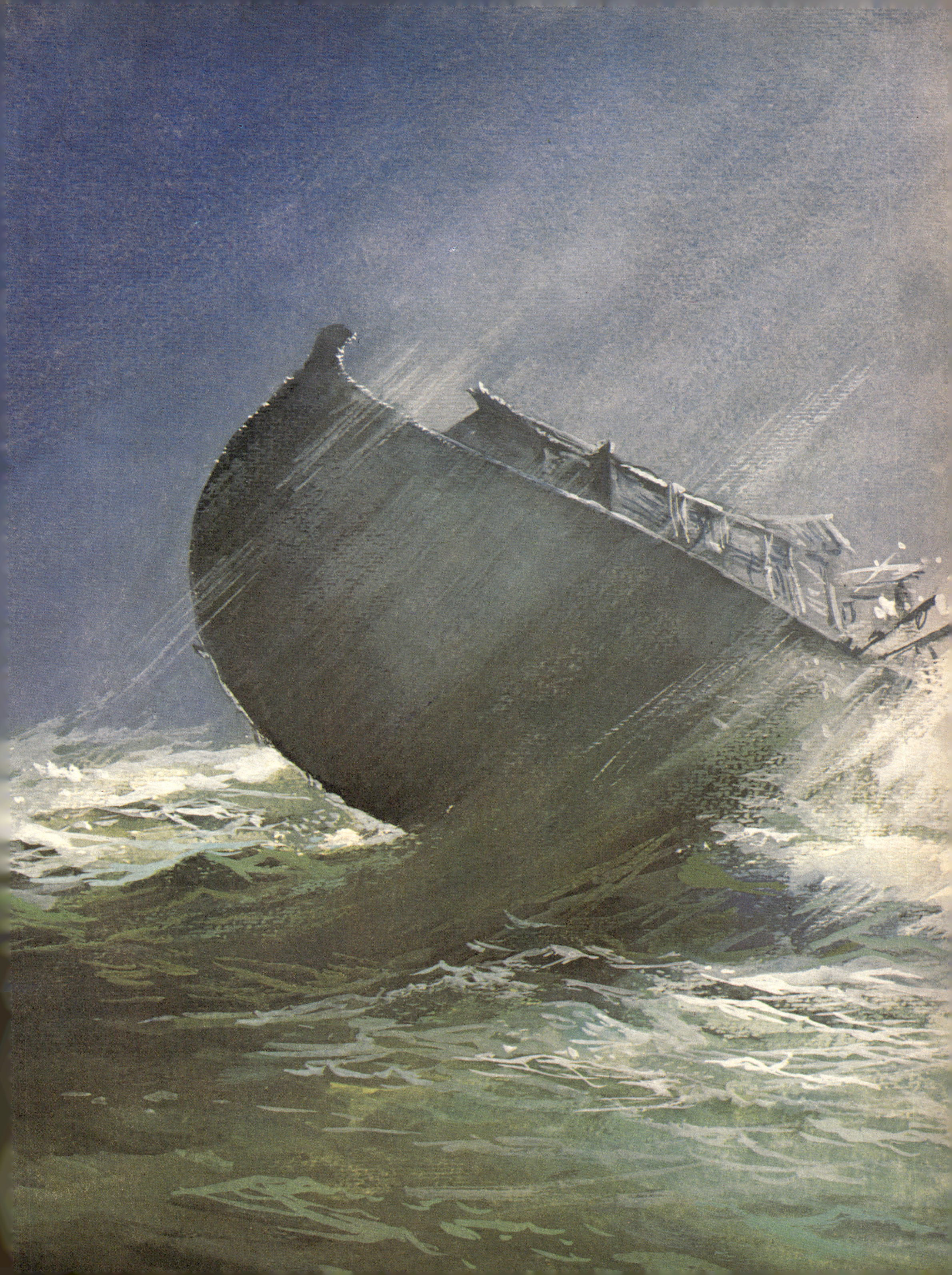

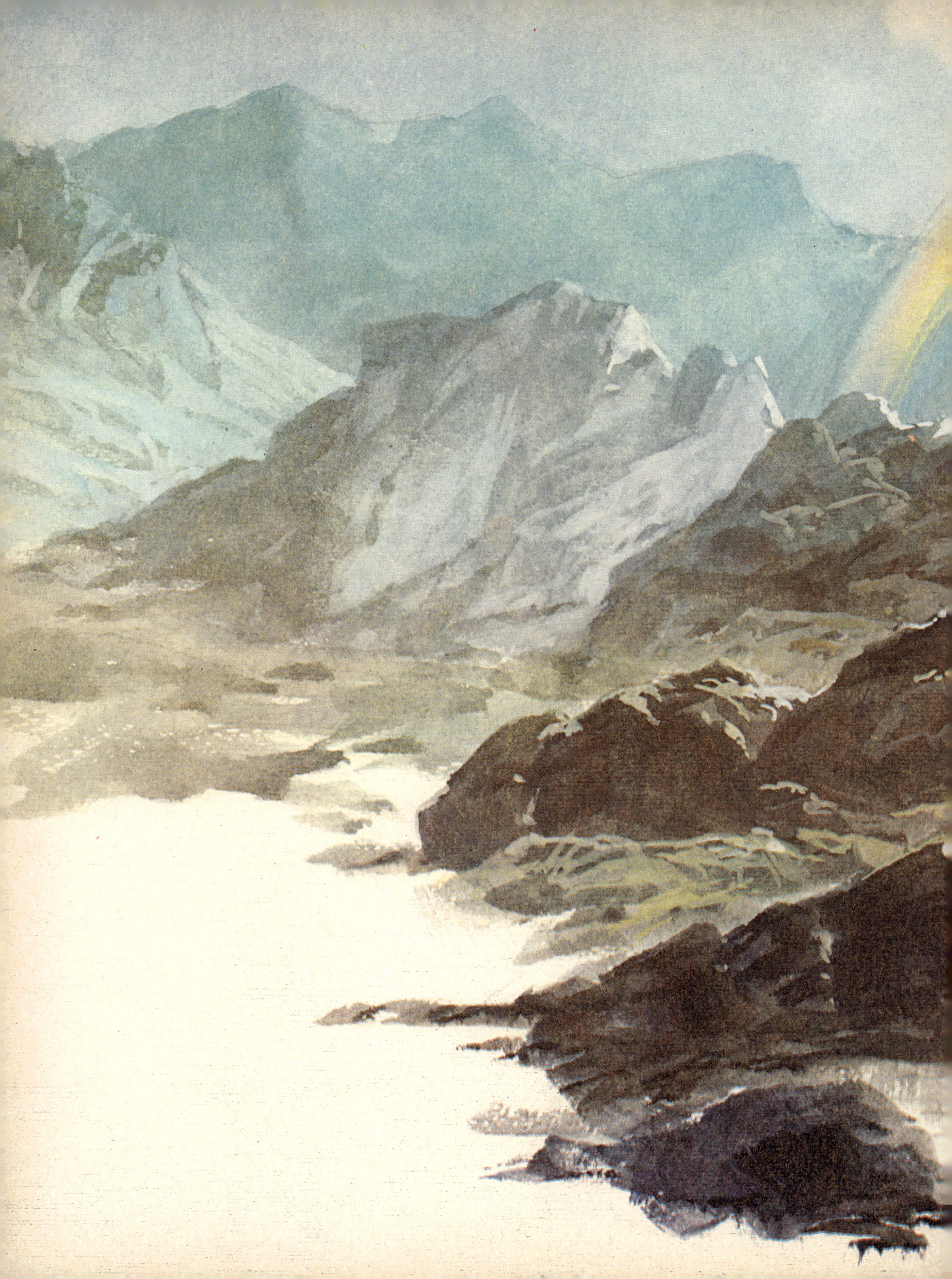

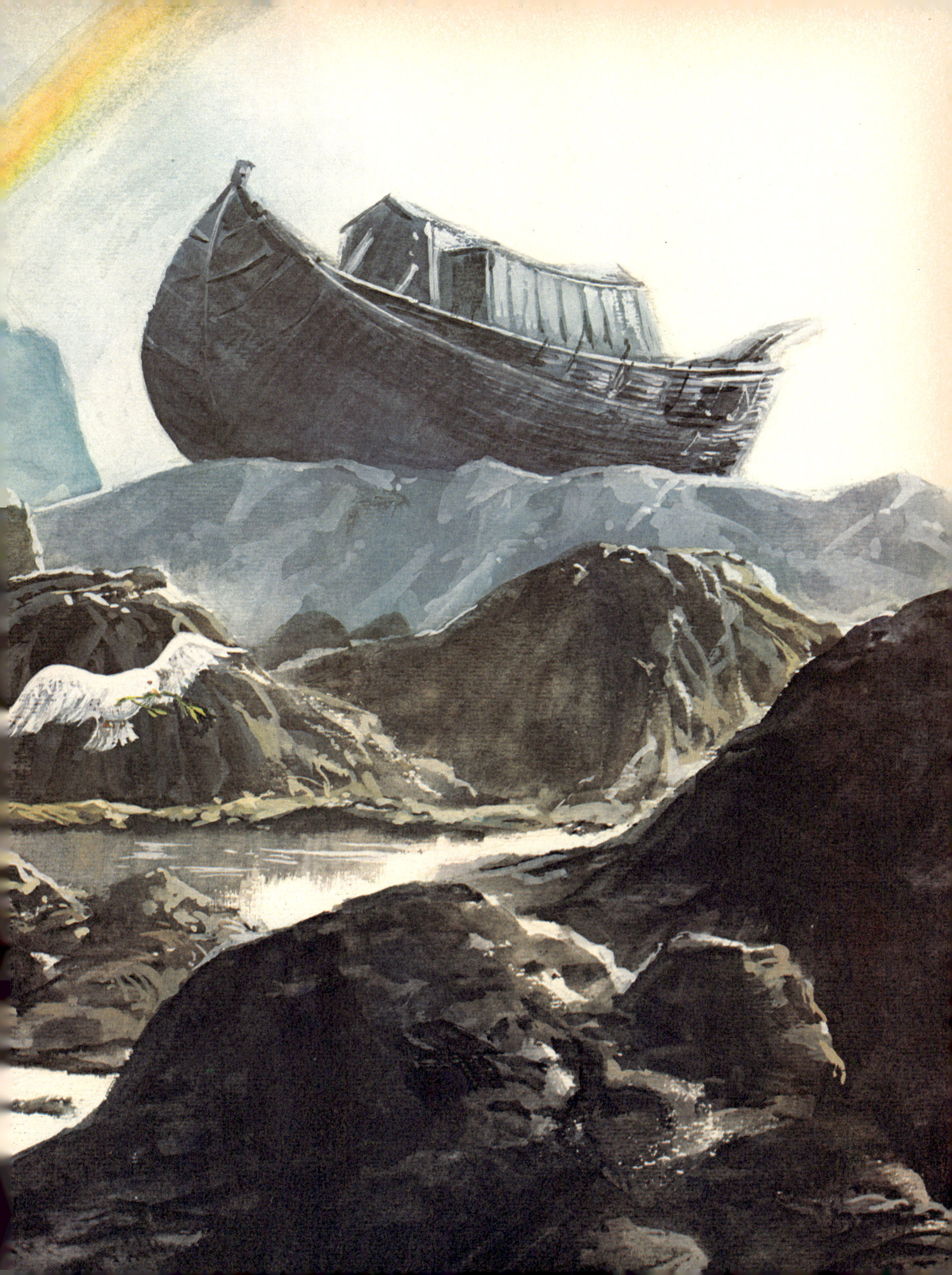

The flood continued for forty days, and the water became deep enough for the boat to float. The water became deeper, and the boat drifted on the surface. It became so deep that it covered the highest mountains; it went on rising until it was seven metres above the tops of the mountains. Every living being on the earth died — every bird, every animal, and every person. Everything on the earth that breathed died. The Lord destroyed all living beings on the earth — human beings, animals, and birds. The only ones left were Noah and those who were with him in the boat. The water did not start going down for a hundred and fifty days.

The Flood Ends with God's Promise

A new life starts after the disaster.
God had not forgotten Noah and all the animals with him in the boat; he caused a wind to blow, and the water started going down. The outlets of the water beneath the earth and the floodgates of the sky were closed. The rain stopped, and the water gradually went down for a hundred and fifty days. On the seventeenth day of the seventh month the boat came to rest on a mountain in the Ararat range. The water kept going down, and on the first day of the tenth month the tops of the mountains appeared.

After forty days Noah opened a window and sent out a raven. It did not come back, but kept flying around until the water was completely gone. Meanwhile, Noah sent out a dove to see if the water had gone down, but since the water still covered all the land, the dove did not find a place to alight. It flew back to the boat, and Noah reached out and took it in. He waited another seven days and sent out the dove again. It returned to him in the evening with a fresh olive leaf in its beak. So Noah knew that the water had gone down. Then he waited another seven days and sent out the dove once more; this time it did not come back.

On the first day of the first month, the water was gone. Noah removed the covering of the boat, looked round, and saw that the ground was getting dry. By the twenty-seventh day of the second month the earth was completely dry.

God said to Noah, "Go out of the boat with your wife, your sons, and their wives. Take all the birds and animals out with you, so that they may reproduce and spread over all the earth." So Noah went out of the boat with his wife, his sons, and their wives. All the animals and birds went out of the boat in groups of their own kind.

Noah built an altar to the Lord; he took one of each kind of ritually clean animal and bird, and burnt them whole as a sacrifice on the altar. The odour of the sacrifice pleased the Lord, and he said to himself, "Never again will I put the earth under a curse because of what man does; I know that from the time he is young his thoughts are evil. Never again will I destroy all living beings, as I have done this time. As long as the world exists, there will be a time for planting and a time for harvest. There will always be cold and heat, summer and winter, day and night."

God's Promise to Everyone

The rainbow in the sky after a storm is a sign that God is merciful not to the Jews only, and not to Mankind only, but to "all living beings".

God said to Noah and his sons, "I am now making my covenant with you and with your descendants, and with all living beings — all birds and all animals — everything that came out of the boat with you. With these words I make my covenant with you: I promise that never again will all living beings be destroyed by a flood; never again will a flood destroy the earth. As a sign of this everlasting covenant which I am making with you and with all living beings, I am putting my bow in the clouds. It will be the sign of my covenant with the world. Whenever I cover the sky with clouds and the rainbow appears, I will remember my promise to you and to all the animals that a flood will never again destroy all living beings. When the rainbow appears in the clouds, I will see it and remember the everlasting covenant between me and all living beings on earth. That is the sign of the promise which I am making to all living beings."

The Great Promise Comes True

St Luke tells how Jesus read the Bible which we have been reading.

Then Jesus went to Nazareth, where he had been brought up, and on the Sabbath he went as usual to the synagogue. He stood up to read the Scriptures and was handed the book of the prophet Isaiah. He unrolled the scroll and found the place where it is written,

"The Spirit of the Lord is upon me,
because he has chosen me to bring good news to the poor.
He has sent me to proclaim liberty to the captives
and recovery of sight to the blind;
to set free the oppressed
and announce that the time has come
when the Lord will save his people."

Jesus rolled up the scroll, gave it back to the attendant, and sat down. All the people in the synagogue had their eyes fixed on him, as he said to them, "This passage of scripture has come true today, as you heard it being read."

The New Testament

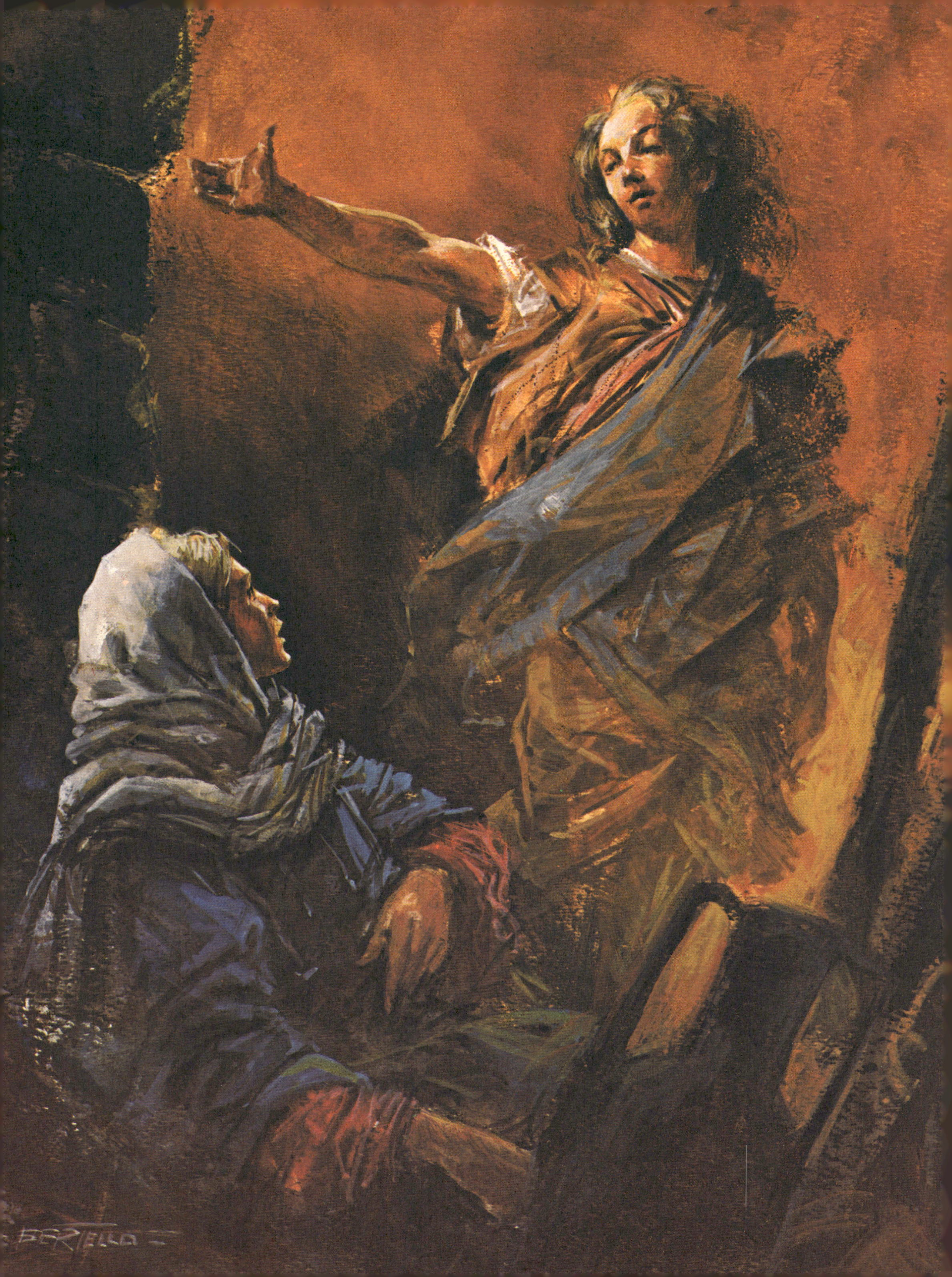

1
When Jesus was Young

Jesus was a poor boy. When he was young, people did not see how great he would be. But many years later Luke and Matthew told the stories which we remember every Christmas, and which give the message that Mary's son was really Christ the Lord, the "Messiah" born to be King of the Jews.

Only one story is told by Luke about Jesus as a boy: the story of his visit to the temple in Jerusalem. It shows that already Jesus knew God as his Father. To him, the temple was his Father's house.

There is another story told in these parts of the Bible, about a boy called John, the son of Zechariah and Elizabeth. This was John the Baptist, and about him it was said:

> *"You will go ahead of the Lord*
> *to prepare his way for him."*

The First Christmas

The Birth of Jesus Announced

God sent the angel Gabriel to a town in Galilee named Nazareth. He had a message for a girl promised in marriage to a man named Joseph, who was a descendant of King David. The girl's name was Mary. The angel came to her and said, "Peace be with you! The Lord is with you, and has greatly blessed you!"

Mary was deeply troubled by the angel's message, and she wondered what his words meant. The angel said to her, "Don't be afraid, Mary, because God has been gracious to you. You will become pregnant and give birth to a son, and you will name him Jesus. He will be great and will be called the Son of the Most High God. The Lord God will make him a king, as his ancestor David was, and he will be the king of the descendants of Jacob forever; his kingdom will never end!"

Mary said to the angel, "I am a virgin. How, then, can this be?"

The angel answered, "The Holy Spirit will come on you, and God's power will rest upon you. For this reason the holy child will be called the Son of God. Remember your relative Elizabeth. It is said that she cannot have children; but she herself is now six months pregnant, even though she is very old. For there is not a thing that God cannot do."

"I am the Lord's servant," said Mary; "may it happen to me as you have said." And the angel left her.

Mary Visits Elizabeth

Soon afterwards Mary got ready and hurried off to the hill country, to a town in Judea. She went into Zechariah's house and greeted Elizabeth. When Elizabeth heard Mary's greeting, the baby moved within her. Elizabeth was filled with the Holy Spirit, and spoke in a loud voice, "You are the most blessed of all women, and blessed is the child you will bear! Why should this great thing happen to me, that my Lord's mother comes to visit me? For as soon as I heard your greeting, the baby within me jumped with gladness. How happy are you to believe that the Lord's message to you will come true!"

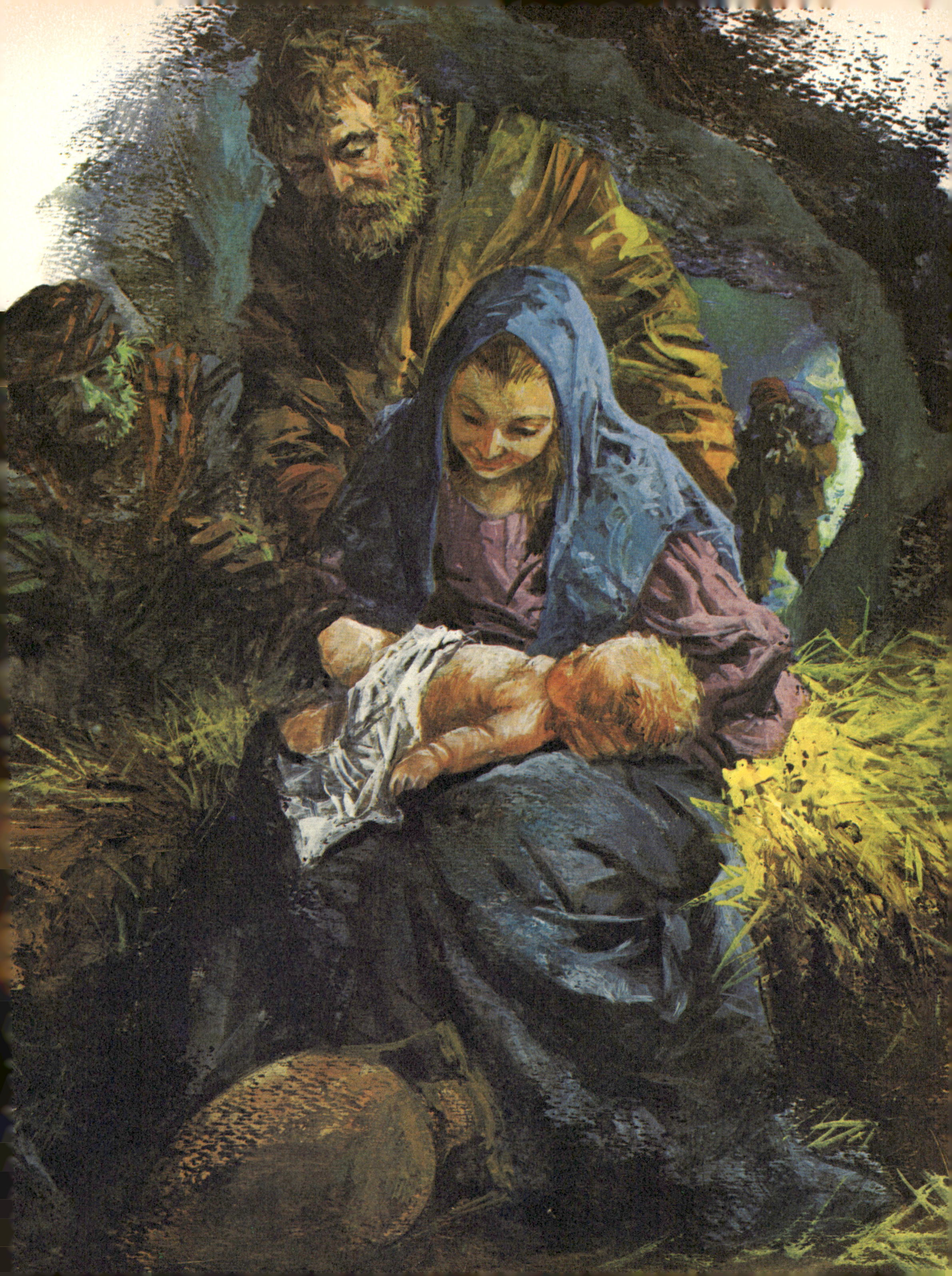

Mary's Song of Praise

Mary said,
"My heart praises the Lord;
my soul is glad because of God my Saviour,
because he has remembered me, his lowly servant!
From now on all people will call me happy because of the great
things the Mighty God has done for me.
His name is holy;
he shows mercy to those who fear him, from one generation
to another.
He stretched out his mighty arm
and scattered the proud with all their plans.
He brought down mighty kings from their thrones,
and lifted up the lowly.
He filled the hungry with good things, and sent the rich away
with empty hands.
He kept the promise he made to our ancestors,
and came to the help of his servant Israel;
He remembered to show mercy to Abraham,
and to all his descendants forever!"

Mary stayed about three months with Elizabeth, and then went back home.

The Birth of Jesus

At that time Emperor Augustus sent out an order for all the citizens of the Empire to register themselves for the census. When this first census took place, Quirinius was the governor of Syria. Everyone, then, went to register himself, each to his own town.

Joseph went from the town of Nazareth, in Galilee, to Judea, to the town named Bethlehem, where King David was born. Joseph went there because he was a descendant of David. He went to register himself with Mary, who was promised in marriage to him. She was pregnant, and while they were in Bethlehem, the time came for her to have her baby. She gave birth to her first son, wrapped him in cloths and laid him in a manger — there was no room for them to stay in the inn.

The Shepherds and the Angels

There were some shepherds in that part of the country who were spending the night in the fields, taking care of their flocks. An angel of the Lord appeared to them, and the glory of the Lord shone over them. They were terribly afraid, but the angel said to them, "Don't be afraid! I am here with good news for you, which will bring great joy to all the people. This very day in David's town your Saviour was born —

Christ the Lord! What will prove it to you is this: you will find a baby wrapped in cloths and lying in a manger."

Suddenly a great army of heaven's angels appeared with the angel, singing praises to God,

"Glory to God in the highest heaven,
and peace on earth to those with whom he is pleased!"

When the angels went away from them back into heaven, the shepherds said to one another, "Let us go to Bethlehem and see this thing that has happened, that the Lord has told us."

So they hurried off and found Mary and Joseph, and saw the baby lying in the manger. When the shepherds saw him they told them what the angel had said about this child. All who heard it were filled with wonder at what the shepherds told them. Mary remembered all these things and thought deeply about them. The shepherds went back, singing praises to God for all they had heard and seen; it had been just as the angel had told them.

Jesus is Named

A week later, when the time came for the baby to be circumcised, he was named Jesus, the name which the angel had given him before he had been conceived.

Jesus is Presented in the Temple

The time came for Joseph and Mary to do what the Law of Moses commanded and perform the ceremony of purification. So they took the child to Jerusalem to present him to the Lord, as written in the law of the Lord, "Every firstborn male shall be dedicated to the Lord." They also went to offer a sacrifice of a pair of doves or two young pigeons, as required by the law of the Lord.

Now there was a man living in Jerusalem whose name was Simeon. He was a good and God-fearing man, and was waiting for Israel to be saved. The Holy Spirit was with him, and he had been assured by the Holy Spirit that he would not die before he had seen the Lord's promised Messiah. Led by the Spirit, Simeon went into the temple. When the parents brought the child Jesus into the temple to do for him what the Law required, Simeon took the child in his arms, and gave thanks to God:

"Now, Lord, you have kept your promise,
and you may let your servant go in peace.
With my own eyes I have seen your salvation,
which you have prepared in the presence of all peoples:
A light to reveal your way to the Gentiles, and bring glory to your
people Israel."

The child's father and mother were amazed at the things Simeon said about him. Simeon blessed them and said to Mary, his mother, "This child is chosen by God for the destruction and the salvation of many in Israel. He will be a sign from God which many people will speak against, and so reveal their secret thoughts. And sorrow, like a sharp sword, will break your own heart."

There was a prophetess named Anna, daughter of Phanuel, of the tribe of Asher. She was an old woman who had been married for seven years, and then had been a widow for eighty-four years. She never left the temple; day and night she worshipped God, fasting and praying. That very same hour she arrived and gave thanks to God, and spoke about the child to all who were waiting for God to redeem Jerusalem.

The Wise Men in Matthew's Gospel

Visitors from the East

Jesus was born in the town of Bethlehem, in the land of Judea, during the time when Herod was king. Soon afterwards some men who studied the stars came from the east to Jerusalem and asked, "Where is the baby born to be king of the Jews? We saw his star when it came up in the east, and we have come to worship him."

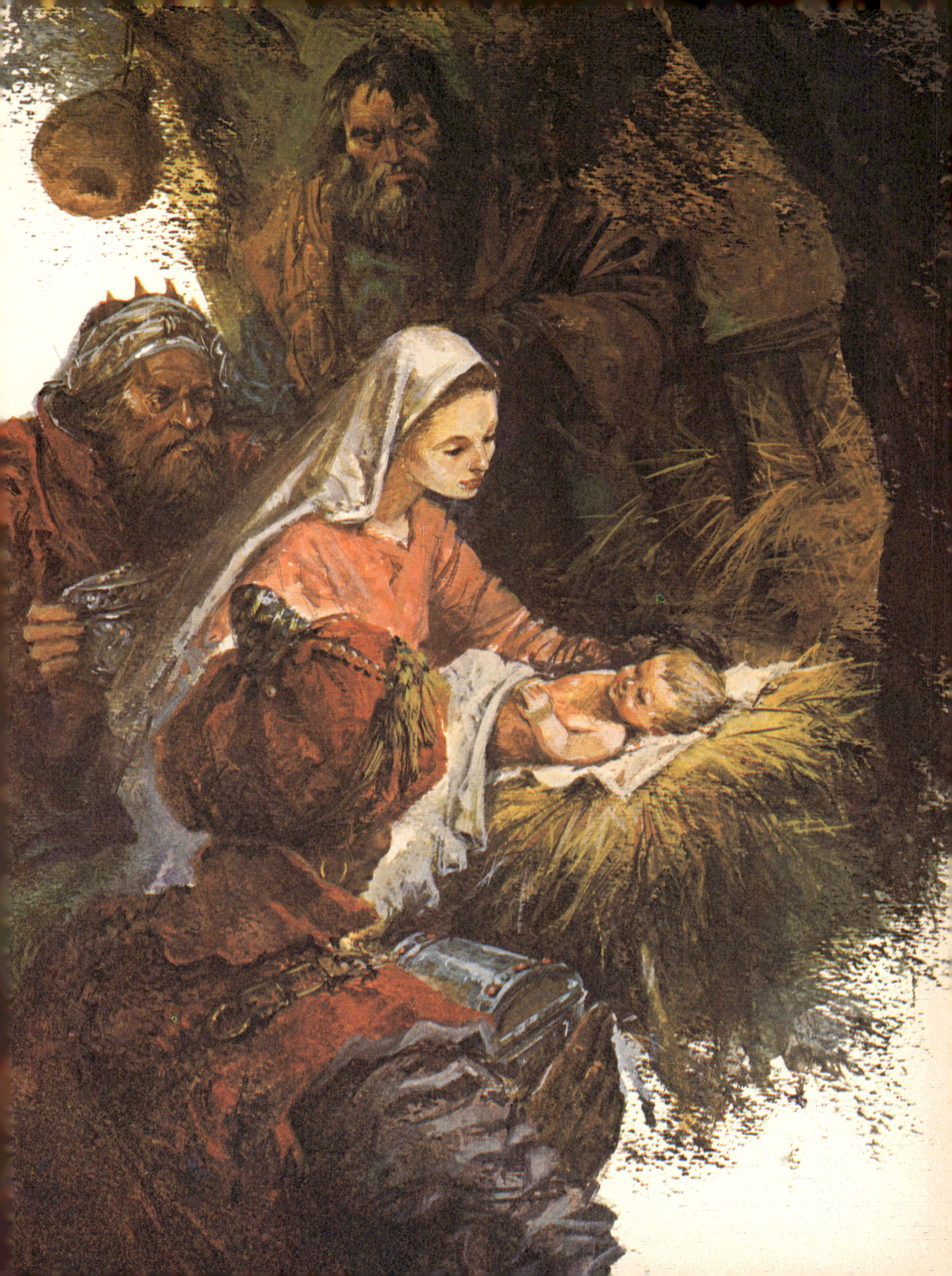

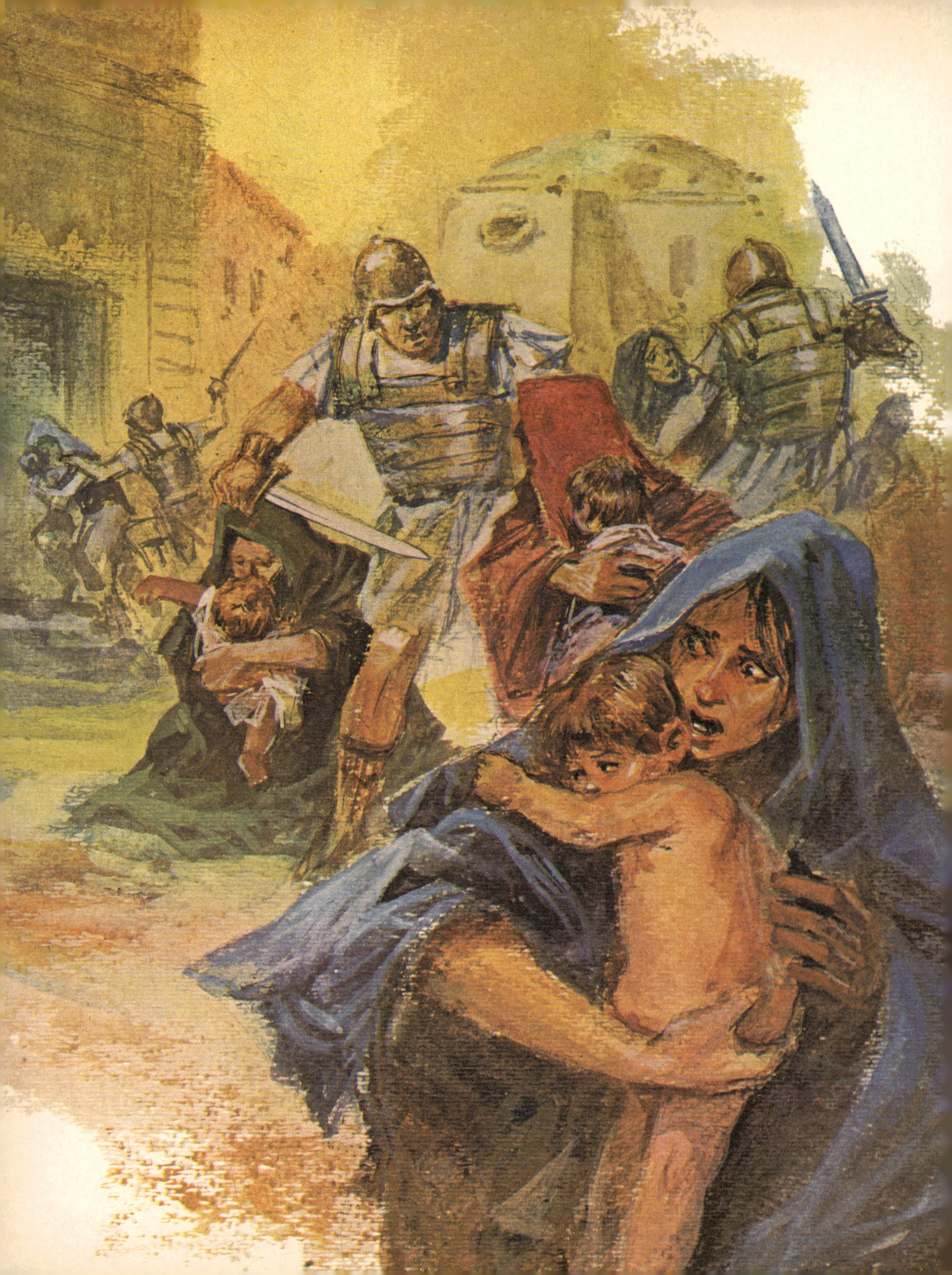

When King Herod heard about this he was very upset, and so was everyone else in Jerusalem. He called together all the chief priests and the teachers of the Law and asked them, "Where will the Messiah be born?"

"In the town of Bethlehem, in Judea," they answered. "This is what the prophet wrote,

'Bethlehem, in the land of Judah,
you are by no means the least among the rulers of Judah;
for from you will come a leader who will guide my people Israel.'"

So Herod called the visitors from the east to a secret meeting and found out from them the exact time the star had appeared. Then he sent them to Bethlehem with these instructions: "Go and make a careful search for the child, and when you find him let me know, so that I may go and worship him too."

With this they left, and on their way they saw the star – the same they had seen in the east – and it went ahead of them until it came and stopped over the place where the child was. How happy they were, what joy was theirs, when they saw the star! They went into the house and saw the child with his mother Mary. They knelt down and worshipped him; then they opened their bags and offered him presents: gold, frankincense, and myrrh.

God warned them in a dream not to go back to Herod; so they went back to their country by another road.

The Escape to Egypt

After they had left, an angel of the Lord appeared in a dream to Joseph and said, "Get up, take the child and his mother and run away to Egypt, and stay there until I tell you to leave. Herod will be looking for the child to kill him."

Joseph got up, took the child and his mother, and left during the night for Egypt, where he stayed until Herod died.

The Killing of the Children

When Herod realized that the visitors from the east had tricked him, he was furious. He gave orders to kill all the boys in Bethlehem and its neighbourhood who were two years old and younger – in accordance with what he had learned from the visitors about the time when the star had appeared.

The Return from Egypt

After Herod had died, an angel of the Lord appeared in a dream to Joseph, in Egypt, and said, "Get up, take the child and his mother, and go back to the land of Israel, because those who tried to kill the child are dead." So Joseph got up, took the child and his mother, and went back to Israel.

When he heard that Archelaus had succeeded his father Herod as king of Judea, Joseph was afraid to settle there. He was given more instructions in a dream, and so he went to the province of Galilee and made his home in a town named Nazareth.

The Boy Jesus in the Temple

Every year the parents of Jesus went to Jerusalem for the Feast of Passover. When Jesus was twelve years old, they went to the feast as usual.

When the days of the feast were over, they started back home, but the boy Jesus stayed in Jerusalem. His parents did not know this; they thought that he was with the group, so they travelled a whole day, and then started looking for him among their relatives and friends. They did not find him, so they went back to Jerusalem looking for him. On the third day they found him in the temple, sitting with the Jewish teachers, listening to them and asking questions. All who heard him were amazed at his intelligent answers. His parents were amazed when they saw him, and his mother said to him, "Son, why have you done this to us? Your father and I have been terribly worried trying to find you."

He answered them, "Why did you have to look for me? Didn't you know that I had to be in my Father's house?"

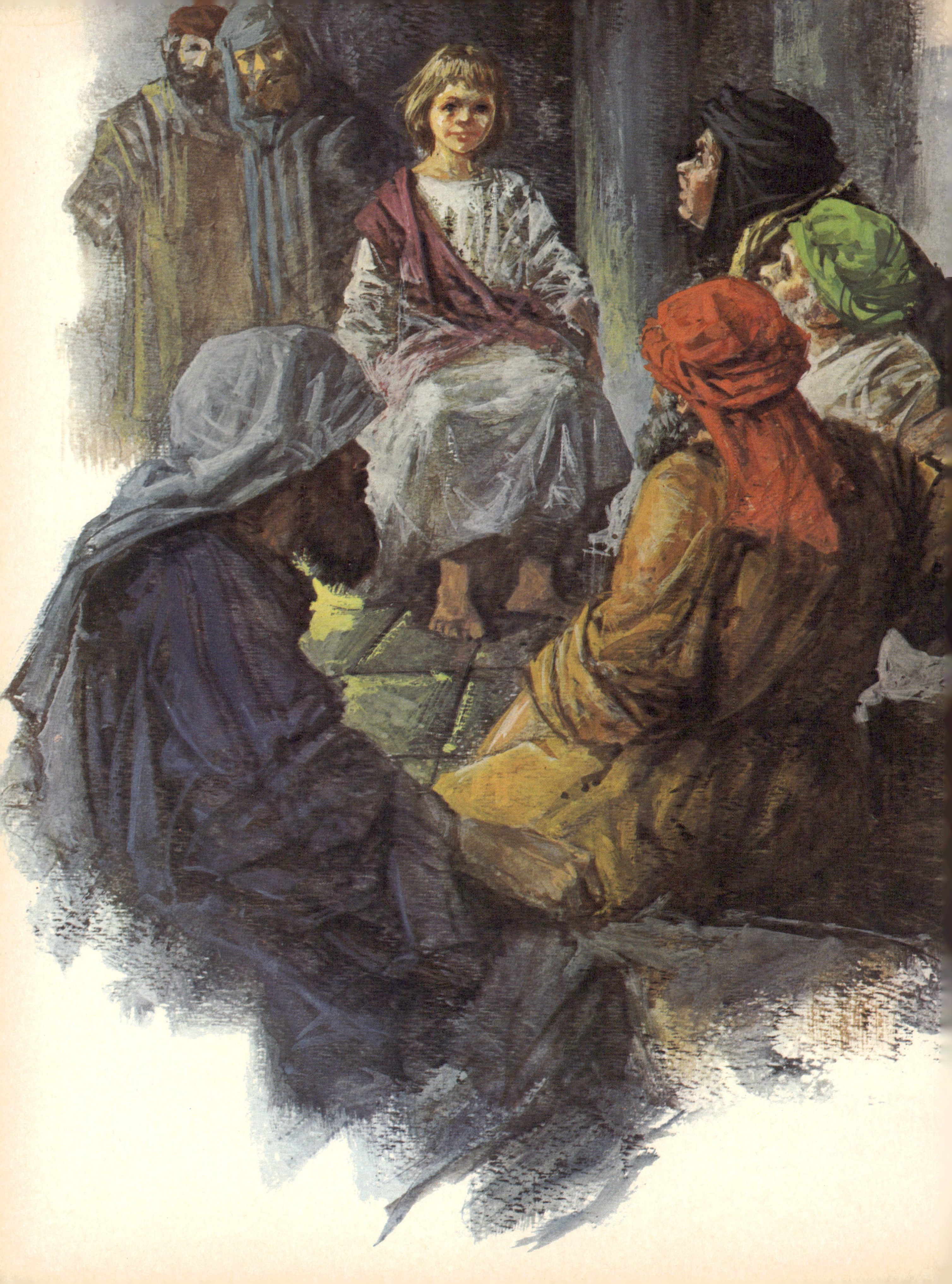

So Jesus went back with them to Nazareth, where he was obedient to them. His mother treasured all these things in her heart. And Jesus grew, both in body and in wisdom, gaining favour with God and men.

John the Baptist, God's Messenger

The Birth of John the Baptist

The time came for Elizabeth to have her baby, and she gave birth to a son. Her neighbours and relatives heard how wonderfully good the Lord had been to her, and they all rejoiced with her.

When the baby was a week old they came to circumcise him; they were going to name him Zechariah, his father's name. But his mother said, "No! His name will be John."

Zechariah's Prophecy

John's father Zechariah was filled with the Holy Spirit, and he spoke God's message,
"Let us praise the Lord, the God of Israel!
   He came to the help of his people and set them free.
He provided a mighty Saviour for us,
   who is a descendant of his servant David.
Long ago by means of his holy prophets he said this:
   He promised to save us from our enemies,
   and from the power of all those who hate us.
He said he would show mercy to our ancestors,
   and remember his sacred covenant.
He made a solemn promise to our ancestor Abraham,
   and vowed that he would rescue us from our enemies,
   and allow us to serve him without fear;
   to be holy and righteous before him, all the days of our life.

"You, my child, will be called a prophet of the Most High God.
You will go ahead of the Lord to prepare his road for him;
   to tell his people that they will be saved, by having their sins forgiven.
Our God is merciful and tender.
He will cause the bright dawn of salvation to rise on us,
   and shine from heaven on all those who live in the dark shadow of death,
   to guide our steps into the path of peace."

The child grew and developed in body and spirit. He lived in the desert until the day when he would appear publicly to the people of Israel.

The Preaching of John the Baptist

It was the fifteenth year of the rule of Emperor Tiberius; Pontius Pilate was governor of Judea, Herod was ruler of Galilee, and his brother Philip ruler of the territory of Iturea and Trachonitis; Lysanias was ruler of Abilene, and Annas and Caiaphas were high priests. It was at this time that the word of God came to John, the son of Zechariah, in the desert. So John went throughout the whole territory of the Jordan River. "Turn away from your sins and be baptized," he preached, "and God will forgive your sins," As the prophet Isaiah had written in his book,

"Someone is shouting in the desert:
  'Get the Lord's road ready for him;
  make a straight path for him to travel!
All low places must be filled up,
  all hills and mountains levelled off.
The winding roads must be made straight,
  and the rough paths made smooth.
All mankind will see God's salvation!' "

Crowds of people came out to John to be baptized by him. "You snakes!" he said to them. "Who told you that you could escape from God's wrath that is about to come? Do the things that will show that you have turned from your sins. And don't start saying among yourselves, 'Abraham is our ancestor.' I tell you that God can take these rocks and make descendants for Abraham! The axe is ready to cut down the trees at the roots; every tree that does not bear good fruit will be cut down and thrown in the fire."

The people asked him. "What are we to do, then?"

He answered, "Whoever has two shirts must give one to the man who has none, and whoever has food must share it."

Some tax collectors came to be baptized, and they asked him, "Teacher, what are we to do?"

"Don't collect more than is legal," he told them.

Some soldiers also asked him, "What about us? What are we to do?"

He said to them, "Don't take money from anyone by force or accuse anyone falsely. Be content with your pay."

People's hopes began to rise, and they began to wonder about John, thinking that perhaps he might be the Messiah. So John said to all of them, "I baptize you with water, but one who is much greater than I is coming. I am not good enough even to untie his sandals. He will baptize you with the Holy Spirit and fire. He has his winnowing shovel with him, to thresh out all the grain and gather the wheat into his barn; but he will burn the chaff in a fire that never goes out."

In many different ways John urged the people as he preached the Good News to them.

2
How Jesus Lived

When he had been baptized by John in the river Jordan, Jesus had to think out what it was God wanted him to do. He was tempted to take wrong ways, but he decided to depend humbly on God. So he began his work for God, healing many people.

In those days everyone thought that diseases were caused by demons, or evil spirits, who lived inside the sick person. So when people saw Jesus healing minds and bodies by the power of his love and faith, they said: "This man is able to give orders to the evil spirits!" But Jesus not only cured diseases. He also set people free from their sins — from everything that separated them from true life and true joy. People said, "We have never seen anything like this!" And some of them, specially the twelve apostles, gave up everything in order to follow him when he called them. Jesus said, "Whoever does what God wants him to do is my brother, my sister, my mother."

Jesus spread the good news of God's reign giving people peace and health. He gave them courage by being with them. Strange stories are told about his powers; it is said that he stopped a storm, fed thousands and walked on water. We do not know exactly what happened in these miracles, but we do know that the whole life of Jesus showed a strange power. Jesus himself claimed that it was the power of God in action. The strange things which Jesus did were not intended to draw attention to him. They were intended to show that God's Kingdom was a kingdom of peace and health.

Jesus is Baptized and Tempted

The Baptism of Jesus

At that time Jesus went from Galilee to the Jordan, and came to John to be baptized by him. But John tried to make him change his mind. "I ought to be baptized by you," John said, "yet you come to me!"

But Jesus answered him, "Let it be so for now. For in this way we shall do all that God requires."

So John agreed. As soon as he was baptized, Jesus came up out of the water. The heaven was opened to him, and he saw the Spirit of God coming down like a dove and lighting on him. And then a voice said from heaven, "This is my own dear Son, with whom I am well pleased."

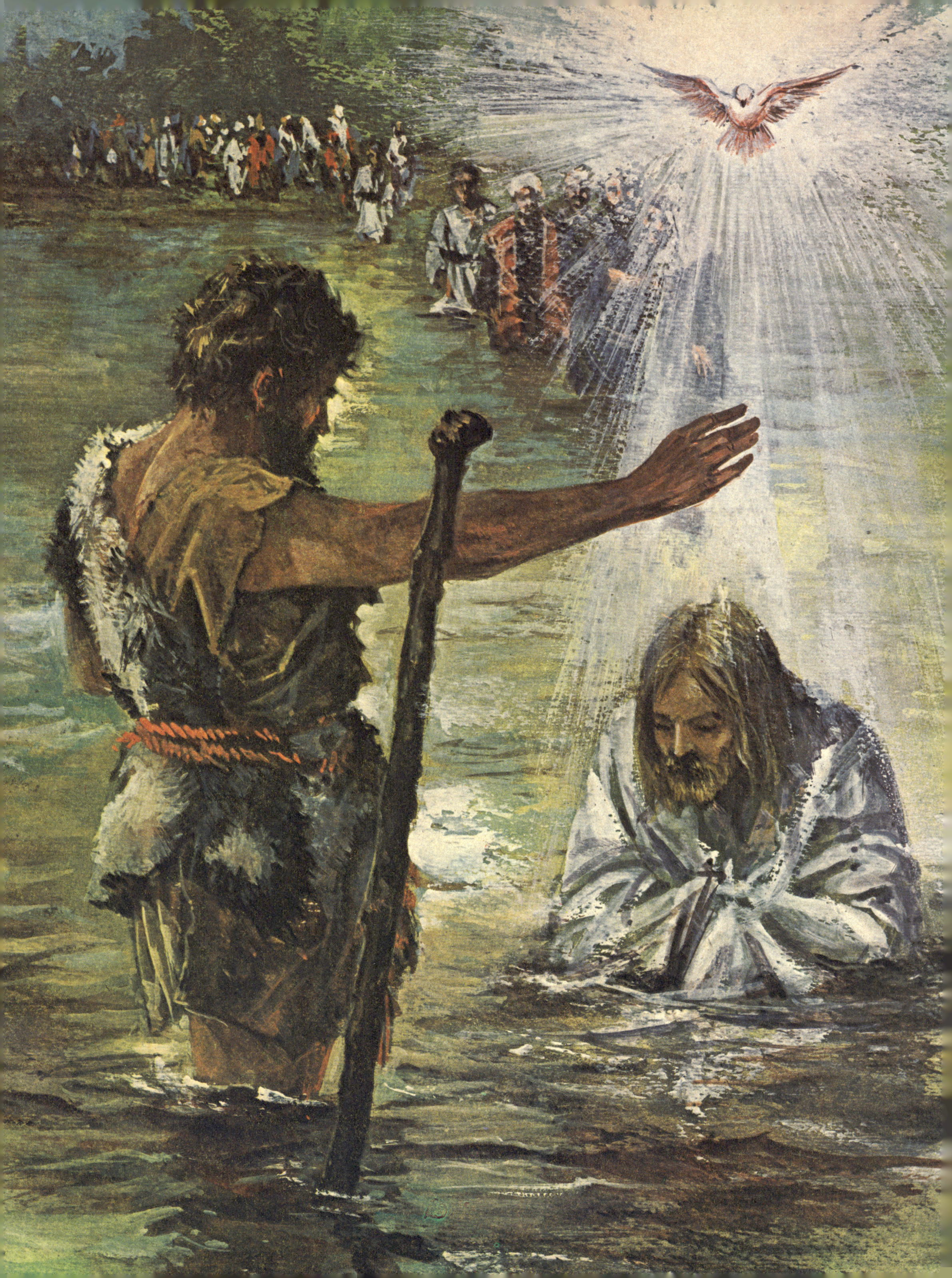

The Temptation of Jesus

Then the Spirit led Jesus into the desert to be tempted by the Devil. After spending forty days and nights without food, Jesus was hungry. The Devil came to him and said, "If you are God's Son, order these stones to turn into bread."

Jesus answered, "The scripture says, 'Man cannot live on bread alone, but on every word that God speaks.'"

Then the Devil took Jesus to the Holy City, set him on the highest point of the temple, and said to him, "If you are God's Son, throw yourself down to the ground; because the scripture says,

'God will give orders to his angels about you:
they will hold you up with their hands,
so that not even your feet will be hurt on the stones.'"

Jesus answered, "But the scripture also says, 'You must not put the Lord your God to the test.'"

Then the Devil took Jesus to a very high mountain and showed him all the kingdoms of the world, in all their greatness. "All this I will give you," the Devil said, "if you kneel down and worship me."

Then Jesus answered, "Go away, Satan! The scripture says, 'Worship the Lord your God and serve only him!'"

Then the Devil left him; and angels came and helped Jesus.

Jesus Begins his Work

Jesus Calls Four Fishermen

After John had been put in prison, Jesus went to Galilee and preached the Good News from God. "The right time has come," he said, "and the Kingdom of God is near! Turn away from your sins and believe the Good News!"

As Jesus walked by Lake Galilee, he saw two fishermen, Simon and his brother Andrew, catching fish in the lake with a net. Jesus said to them, "Come with me and I will teach you to catch men." At once they left their nets and went with him.

He went a little farther on and saw two other brothers, James and John, the sons of Zebedee. They were in their boat getting their nets ready. As soon as Jesus saw them he called them; they left their father Zebedee in the boat with the hired men and went with Jesus.

A Man with an Evil Spirit

They came to the town of Capernaum, and on the next Sabbath day Jesus went into the synagogue and began to teach. The people who heard him were amazed at the way he taught. He wasn't like the teachers of the Law; instead, he taught with authority.

Opposite: The baptism of Jesus (text on page 183)

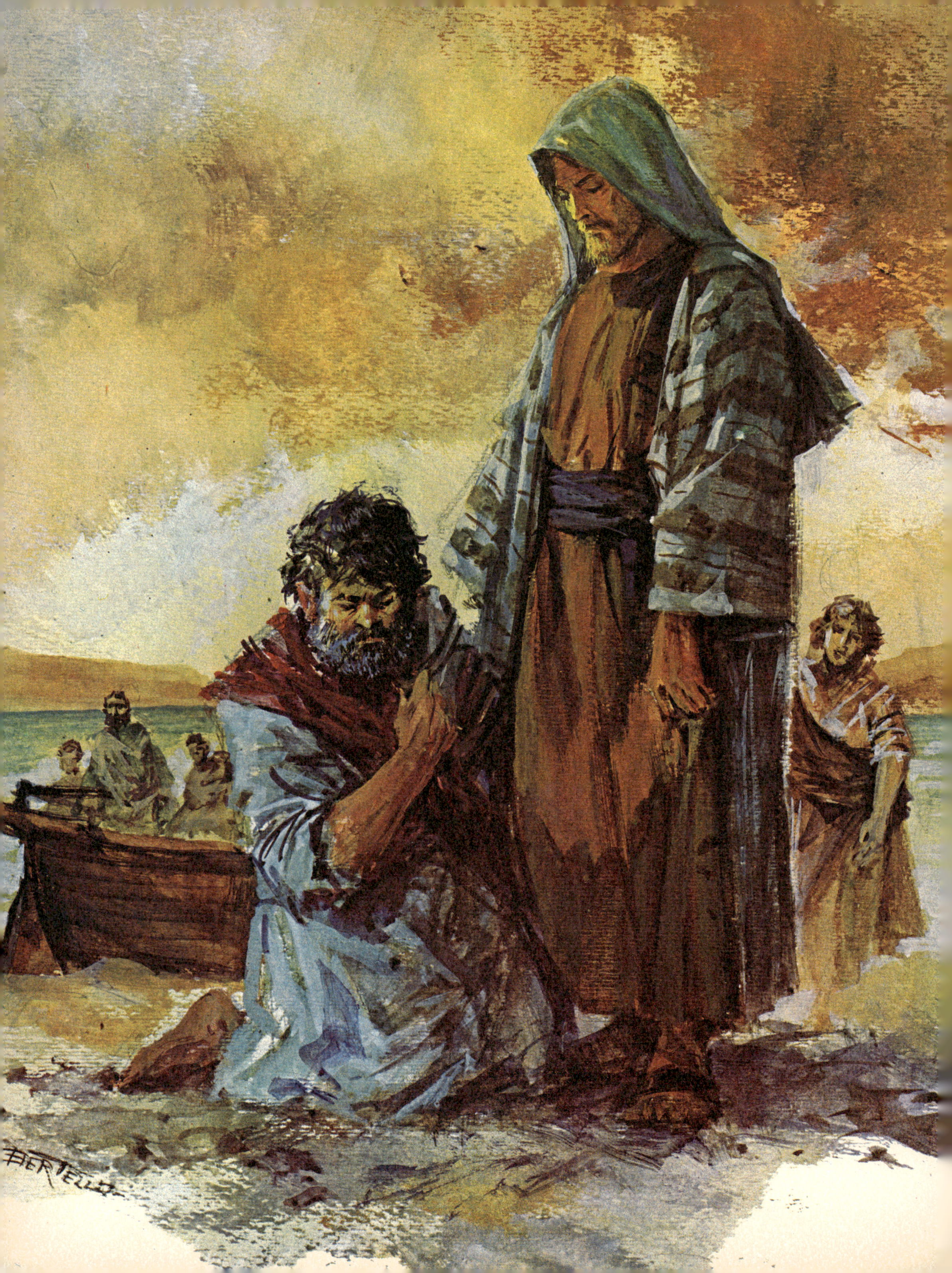
BERTELLI

Just then a man with an evil spirit in him came into the synagogue and screamed, "What do you want with us, Jesus of Nazareth? Are you here to destroy us? I know who you are: you are God's holy messenger!"

Jesus commanded the spirit, "Be quiet, and come out of the man!"

The evil spirit shook the man hard, gave a loud scream and came out of him. The people were all so amazed that they started saying to each other, "What is this? Some kind of new teaching? This man has authority to give orders to the evil spirits, and they obey him!"

And so the news about Jesus spread quickly everywhere in the region of Galilee.

Jesus Heals Many People

They left the synagogue and went straight to the home of Simon and Andrew; and James and John went with them. Simon's mother-in-law was sick in bed with a fever, and as soon as Jesus got there he was told about her. He went to her, took her by the hand and helped her up. The fever left her and she began to wait on them.

When evening came, after the sun had set, people brought to Jesus all the sick and those who had demons. All the people of the town gathered in front of the house. Jesus healed many who were sick with all kinds of diseases and drove out many demons. He would not let the demons say anything, because they knew who he was.

Jesus Preaches in Galilee

Very early the next morning, long before daylight, Jesus got up and left the house. He went out of town to a lonely place, where he prayed. But Simon and his companions went out searching for him; when they found him they said, "Everyone is looking for you."

But Jesus answered, "We must go on to the other villages round here. I have to preach in them also, because that is why I came."

So he travelled all over Galilee, preaching in the synagogues and driving out demons.

Jesus Makes a Leper Clean

A leper came to Jesus, knelt down, and begged him for help. "If you want to," he said, "you can make me clean."

Jesus was filled with pity, and reached out and touched him. "I do want to," he answered. "Be clean!" At once the leprosy left the man and he was clean. Then Jesus spoke harshly with him and sent him away at once. "Listen," he said, "don't tell this to anyone. But go straight to the priest and let him examine you; then offer the sacrifice that Moses ordered, to prove to everyone that you are now clean."

But the man went away and began to spread the news everywhere.

Opposite: Jesus calls the fishermen (text on page 185)

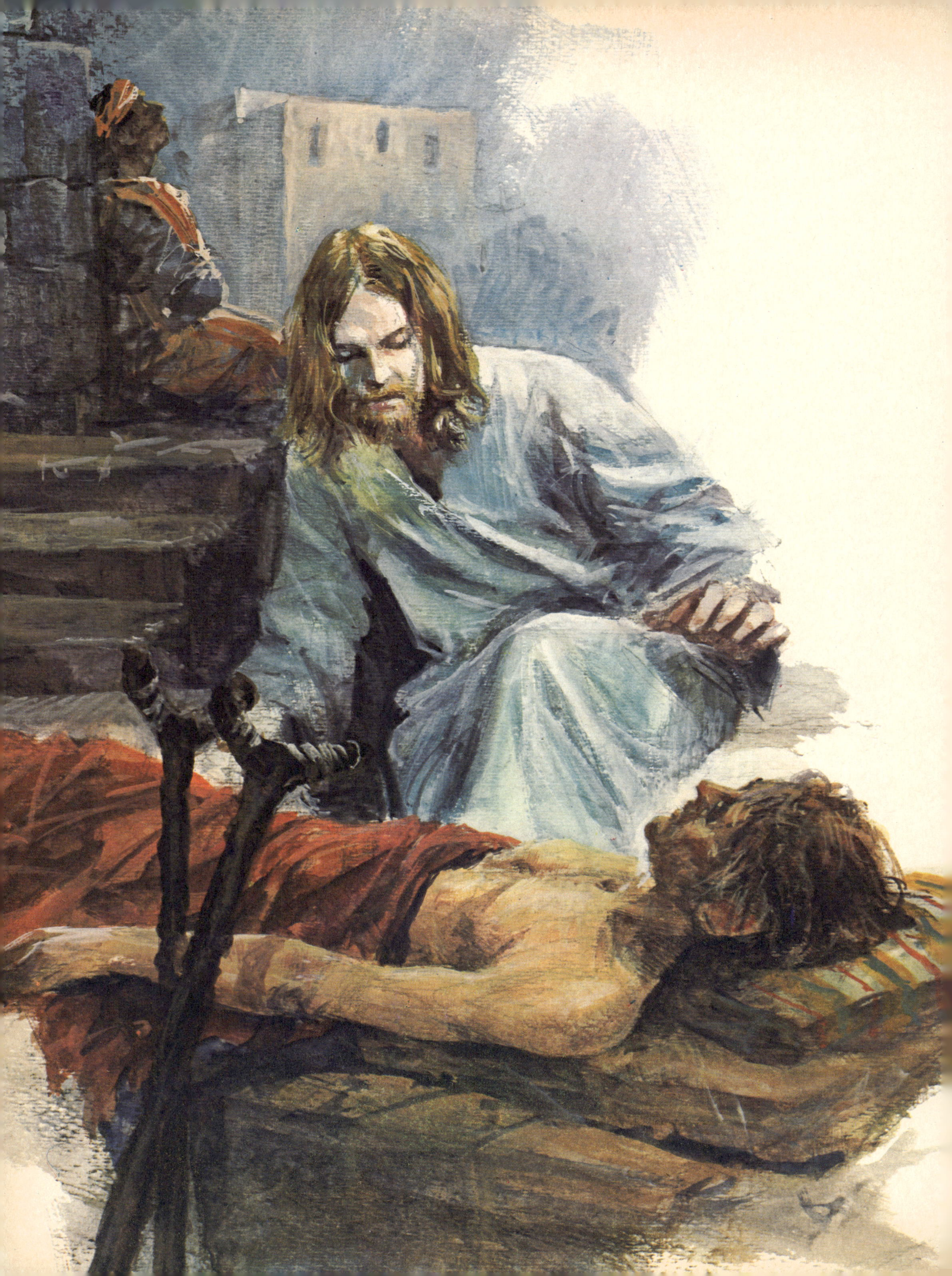

Indeed, he talked so much that Jesus could not go into a town publicly. Instead, he stayed out in lonely places, and people came to him from everywhere.

Jesus Heals a Paralysed Man

A few days later Jesus came back to Capernaum, and the news spread that he was at home. So many people came together that there wasn't any room left, not even out in front of the door. Jesus was preaching the message to them, when a paralysed man, carried by four men, was brought to him. Because of the crowd, however, they could not get the man to Jesus. So they made a hole in the roof right above the place where Jesus was. When they had made an opening, they let the man down, lying on his mat. Jesus saw how much faith they had, and said to the paralysed man, "My son, your sins are forgiven."

Some teachers of the Law who were sitting there thought to themselves, "How does he dare talk against God like this? No man can forgive sins; only God can!"

At once Jesus knew their secret thoughts, so he said to them, "Why do you think such things? Is it easier to say to this paralysed man, 'Your sins are forgiven,' or to say. 'Get up, pick up your mat, and walk'? I will prove to you, then, that the Son of Man has authority on earth to forgive sins." So he said to the paralysed man, "I tell you, get up, pick up your mat, and go home!"

While they all watched, the man got up, picked up his mat and hurried away. They were all completely amazed and praised God, saying, "We have never seen anything like this!"

Jesus Calls Matthew

Jesus left that place, and as he walked along he saw a tax collector, named Matthew, sitting in his office. He said to him, "Follow me."

Matthew got up and followed him.

While Jesus was having dinner at his house, many tax collectors and outcasts came and joined him and his disciples at the table. Some Pharisees saw this and said to his disciples, "Why does your teacher eat with tax collectors and outcasts?"

Jesus heard them and answered, "People who are well do not need a doctor, but only those who are sick. Go and find out what this scripture means, 'I do not want animal sacrifices, but kindness.' I have not come to call the respectable people, but the outcasts."

The Question about Fasting

On one occasion the followers of John the Baptist and the Pharisees were fasting. Some people came to Jesus and asked him, "Why is it that the disciples of John the Baptist and the disciples of the Pharisees fast, but yours do not?"

Jesus answered, "Do you expect the guests at a wedding party to go without food? Of course not! As long as the bridegroom is with them they will not do that. But the time will come when the bridegroom will be taken away from them; when that day comes then they will go without food.

"No one uses a piece of new cloth to patch up an old coat. If he does, the new patch will tear off some of the old cloth, making an even bigger hole. Nor does anyone pour new wine into used wineskins. If he does, the wine will burst the skins, and both the wine and the skins will be ruined. No! Fresh skins for new wine!"

Jesus Has Pity for the People

So Jesus went round visiting all the towns and villages. He taught in their synagogues, preached the Good News of the Kingdom, and healed people from every kind of disease and sickness. As he saw the crowds, his heart was filled with pity for them, because they were worried and helpless, like sheep without a shepherd. So he said to his disciples, "There is a large harvest, but few workers to gather it in. Pray to the owner of the harvest that he will send out workers to gather in his harvest."

The New Family Chosen by Jesus

A Crowd by the Lake

Jesus and his disciples went away to Lake Galilee, and a large crowd followed him. They came from Galilee, from Judea, from Jerusalem, from the territory of Idumea, from the territory on the other side of the Jordan, and from the neighbourhood of the cities of Tyre and Sidon. This large crowd came to Jesus because they heard of the things he was doing. The crowd was so large that Jesus told his disciples to get a boat ready for him, so the people would not crush him. He had healed many people, and all the sick kept pushing their way to him in order to touch him. And whenever the people who had evil spirits in them saw him they would fall down before him and scream, "You are the Son of God!"

Jesus gave a stern command to the evil spirits not to tell who he was.

Jesus Chooses the Twelve Apostles

Then Jesus went up a hill and called to himself the men he wanted. They came to him and he chose twelve, whom he named apostles. "I have chosen you to be with me," he told them; "I will also send you out to preach, and you will have authority to drive out demons."

These are the twelve he chose: Simon (Jesus gave him the name Peter); James and his brother John, the sons of Zebedee (Jesus gave them the name Boanerges, which means "Men of Thunder"); Andrew, Philip, Bartholomew, Matthew, Thomas, James, the son of Alphaeus, Thaddaeus, Simon the Patriot, and Judas Iscariot, who betrayed Jesus.

Jesus' Mother and Brothers

Then Jesus went home. Again such a large crowd gathered that Jesus and his disciples had no time to eat. When his family heard about this they set out to get him, because people were saying, "He's gone mad!" Then Jesus' mother and brothers arrived. They stood outside the house and sent in a message, asking for him. A crowd was sitting round Jesus, and they told him, "Look, your mother and brothers are outside, and they want you."

Jesus answered, "Who is my mother? Who are my brothers?" He looked over the people sitting round him and said, "Look! Here are my mother and my brothers! Whoever does what God wants him to do is my brother, my sister, my mother."

Jesus Rejected at Nazareth

Then Jesus went to Nazareth, where he had been brought up, and on the Sabbath day he went as usual to the synagogue. He stood up to read the Scriptures, and was handed the book of the prophet Isaiah. He unrolled the scroll and found the place where it is written,

"The Spirit of the Lord is upon me,
  because he has chosen me to preach the Good News to the poor.
He has sent me to proclaim liberty to the captives,
  and recovery of sight to the blind;
to set free the oppressed,
  and announce the year when the Lord will save his people."

Jesus rolled up the scroll, gave it back to the attendant, and sat down. All the people in the synagogue had their eyes fixed on him. He began speaking to them, "This passage of scripture has come true today, as you heard it being read."

They were all well impressed with him, and marvelled at the beautiful words that he spoke. They said, "Isn't he the son of Joseph?"

He said to them, "I am sure that you will quote this proverb to me,

'Doctor, heal yourself.' You will also say to me, 'Do here in your own home town the same things we were told happened in Capernaum.' I tell you this," Jesus added. "A prophet is never welcomed in his own home town. Listen to me: it is true that there were many widows in Israel during the time of Elijah, when there was no rain for three and a half years and there was a great famine throughout the whole land. Yet Elijah was not sent to a single one of them, but only to a widow of Zarephath, in the territory of Sidon. And there were many lepers in Israel during the time of the prophet Elisha; yet not one of them was made clean, but only Naaman the Syrian."

All the people in the synagogue were filled with anger when they heard this. They rose up, dragged Jesus out of town and took him to the top of the hill on which their town was built, to throw him over the cliff. But he walked through the middle of the crowd and went his way.

The Good News is Spread by Word and Deed

Jesus Heals a Roman Officer's Servant

Jesus went to Capernaum. A Roman officer there had a servant who was very dear to him; the man was sick and about to die. When the officer heard about Jesus, he sent to him some Jewish elders to ask him to come and heal his servant. They came to Jesus and begged him earnestly, "This man really deserves your help. He loves our people and he himself built a synagogue for us."

So Jesus went with them. He was not far from the house when the officer sent friends to tell him, "Sir, don't trouble yourself. I do not deserve to have you come into my house, neither do I consider myself worthy to come to you in person. Just give the order and my servant will get well. I, too, am a man placed under the authority of superior officers, and I have soldiers under me. I order this one, 'Go!' and he goes; I order that one, 'Come!' and he comes; and I order my slave, 'Do this!' and he does it."

Jesus was surprised when he heard this; he turned round and said to the crowd following him, "I have never found such faith as this, I tell you, not even in Israel!"

The messengers went back to the officer's house and found his servant well.

Jesus Raises a Widow's Son

Soon afterwards Jesus went to a town named Nain; his disciples and a large crowd went with him. Just as he arrived at the gate of the town, a funeral procession was coming out. The dead man was the only son of a

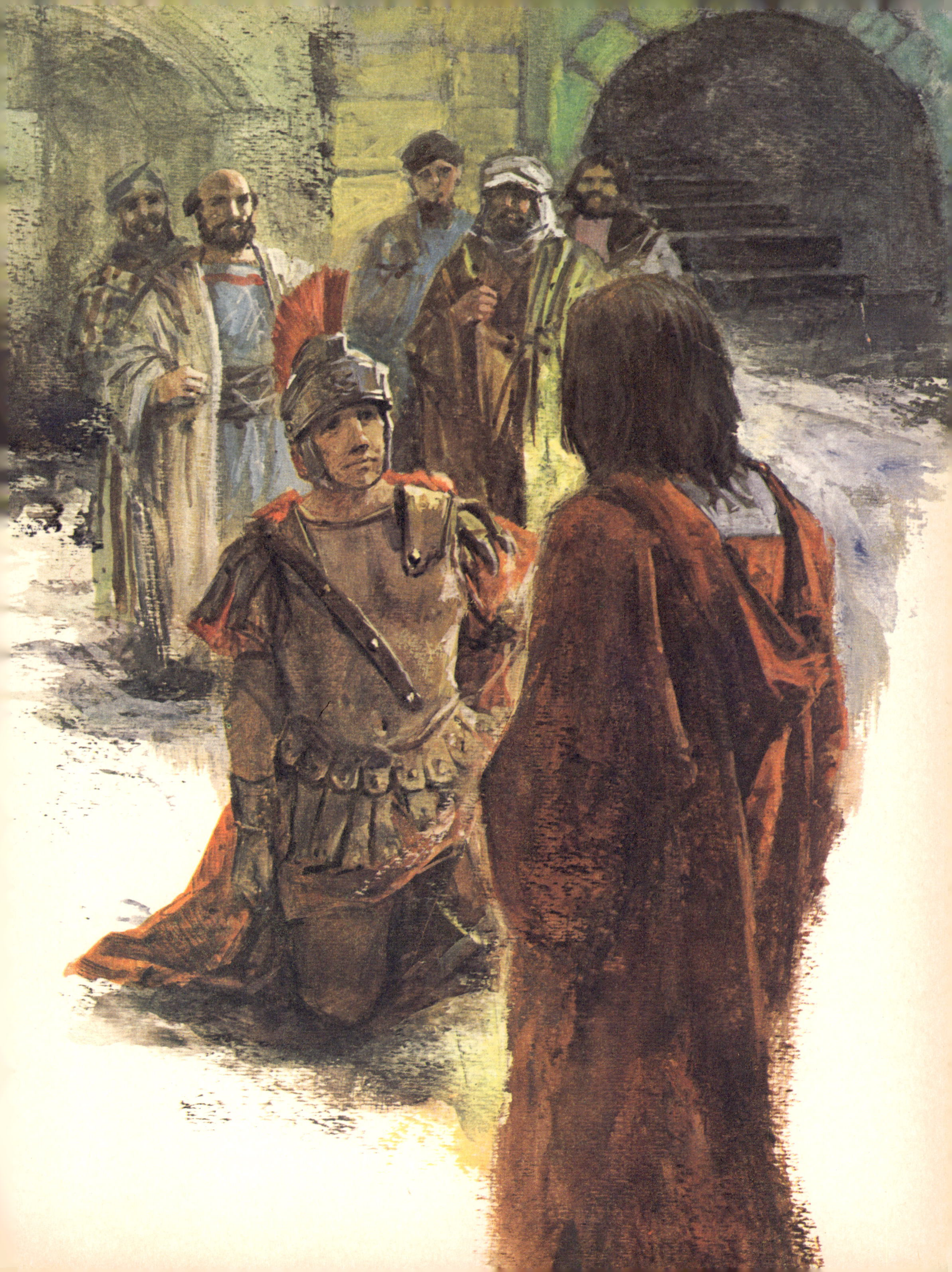

woman who was a widow, and a large crowd from the city was with her. When the Lord saw her his heart was filled with pity for her and he said to her, "Don't cry." Then he walked over and touched the coffin, and the men carrying it stopped. Jesus said, "Young man! Get up, I tell you!" The dead man sat up and began to talk, and Jesus gave him back to his mother.

Everyone was filled with fear, and they praised God, "A great prophet has appeared among us!" and, "God has come to save his people!"

The Messengers from John the Baptist

John's disciples told him about all these things. He called two of them to him and sent them to the Lord to ask him, "Are you the one John said was going to come, or should we expect someone else?"

When they came to Jesus they said, "John the Baptist sent up to ask, 'Are you the one he said was going to come, or should we expect someone else?'"

At that very time Jesus healed many people from their sicknesses, diseases, and evil spirits, and gave sight to many blind people. He answered John's messengers, "Go back and tell John what you have seen and heard: the blind can see, the lame can walk, the lepers are made clean, the deaf can hear, the dead are raised to life, and the Good News is preached to the poor. How happy is he who has no doubts about me!"

After John's messengers had left, Jesus began to speak about John to the crowds, "When you went out to John in the desert, what did you expect to see? A blade of grass bending in the wind? What did you go out to see? A man dressed up in fancy clothes? Really, those who dress like that and live in luxury are found in palaces! Tell me, what did you go out to see? A prophet? Yes, I tell you — you saw much more than a prophet. For John is the one of whom the Scripture says, 'Here is my messenger, says God; I will send him ahead of you to open the way for you.' I tell you," Jesus added, "John is greater than any man ever born; but he who is least in the Kingdom of God is greater than he."

"Now, to what can I compare the people of this day? What are they like? They are like children sitting in the market place. One group shouts to the other, 'We played wedding music for you, but you would not dance! We sang funeral songs, but you would not cry!' John the Baptist came, and he fasted and drank no wine, and you said, 'He has a demon in him!' The Son of Man came, and he ate and drank, and you said, 'Look at this man! He is a glutton and wine-drinker, a friend of tax collectors and outcasts!' God's wisdom, however, is shown to be true by all who accept it."

Jesus at the Home of Simon the Pharisee

A Pharisee invited Jesus to have dinner with him. Jesus went to his house and sat down to eat. There was a woman in that town who lived a sinful life. She heard that Jesus was eating in the Pharisee's house, so she brought an alabaster jar full of perfume and stood behind Jesus, by his feet, crying and wetting his feet with her tears. Then she dried his feet with her hair, kissed them, and poured the perfume on them. When the Pharisee who had invited Jesus saw this, he said to himself, "If this man really were a prophet, he would know who this woman is who is touching him; he would know what kind of sinful life she leads!"

Jesus spoke up and said to him, "Simon, I have something to tell you."

"Yes, Teacher," he said, "tell me."

"There were two men who owed money to a moneylender," Jesus began; "one owed him fifty pounds and the other one five pounds. Neither one could pay him back, so he cancelled the debts of both. Which one, then, will love him more?"

"I suppose," answered Simon, "that it would be the one who was forgiven more."

"Your answer is correct," said Jesus. Then he turned to the woman and said to Simon, "Do you see this woman? I came into your home, and you gave me no water for my feet, but she has washed my feet with her tears and dried them with her hair. You did not welcome me with a kiss, but she has not stopped kissing my feet since I came. You provided no oil for my head, but she has covered my feet with perfume. I tell you, then, the great love she has shown proves that her many sins have been forgiven. Whoever has been forgiven little, however, shows only a little love."

Then Jesus said to the woman, "Your sins are forgiven."

The others sitting at the table began to say to themselves, "Who is this, who even forgives sins?"

But Jesus said to the woman, "Your faith has saved you; go in peace."

Women who Accompanied Jesus

Some time later Jesus travelled through towns and villages, preaching the Good News about the Kingdom of God. The twelve disciples went with him, and so did some women who had been healed of evil spirits and diseases: Mary (who was called Magdalene), from whom seven demons had been driven out; Joanna, the wife of Chuza who was an officer in Herod's court; Susanna, and many other women who used their own resources to help Jesus and his disciples.

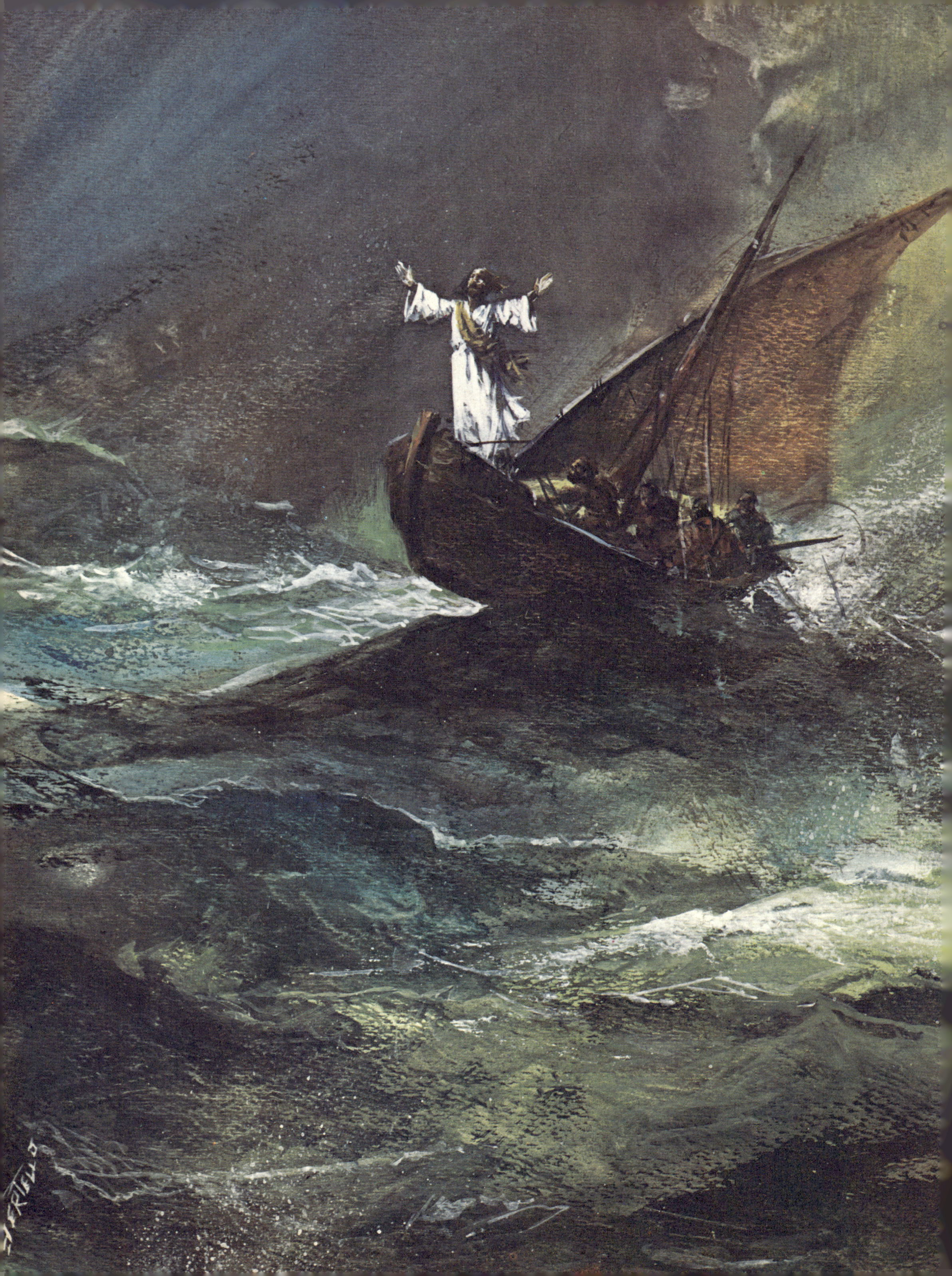

Jesus Heals a Boy with an Evil Spirit

Some teachers of the Law were arguing with the disciples. As soon as the people saw Jesus, they were greatly surprised and ran to him and greeted him. Jesus asked his disciples, "What are you arguing with them about?"

A man in the crowd answered, "Teacher, I brought my son to you, because he has an evil spirit in him and cannot talk. Whenever the spirit attacks him, it throws him to the ground, and he foams at the mouth, grits his teeth, and becomes stiff all over. I asked your disciples to drive the spirit out, but they could not."

Jesus said to them, "How unbelieving you people are! How long must I stay with you? How long do I have to put up with you? Bring the boy to me!" They brought him to Jesus.

As soon as the spirit saw Jesus, it threw the boy into a fit, so that he fell on the ground and rolled around, foaming at the mouth. "How long has he been like this?" Jesus asked the father.

"Ever since he was a child," he replied. "Many times it has tried to kill him by throwing him in the fire and in the water. Have pity on us and help us, if you possibly can!"

"Yes," said Jesus, "if *you* can! Everything is possible for the person who has faith."

The father at once cried out, "I do have faith, but not enough. Help me have more!"

Jesus noticed that the crowd was closing in on them, so he gave a command to the evil spirit. "Deaf and dumb spirit," he said, "I order you to come out of the boy and never go into him again!"

The spirit screamed, threw the boy into a bad fit, and came out. The boy looked like a corpse, so that everyone said, "He is dead!" But Jesus took the boy by the hand and helped him rise, and he stood up.

After Jesus had gone indoors, his disciples asked him privately, "Why couldn't we drive the spirit out?"

"Only prayer can drive this kind out," answered Jesus; "nothing else can."

Jesus Calms a Storm

One evening Jesus said to his disciples, "Let us go across to the other side of the lake." So they left the crowd; the disciples got into the boat that Jesus was already in, and took him with them. Other boats were there too. A very strong wind blew up and the waves began to spill over into the boat, so that it was about to fill with water. Jesus was in the back of the boat, sleeping with his head on a pillow. The disciples woke him up and said, "Teacher, don't you care that we are about to die?"

Jesus got up and commanded the wind, "Be quiet!" and said to the waves, "Be still!" The wind died down, and there was a great calm. Then Jesus said to his disciples, "Why are you frightened? Are you still without faith?"

But they were terribly afraid, and began to say to each other, "Who is this man? Even the wind and the waves obey him!"

Jesus Heals a Man with Evil Spirits

They arrived on the other side of Lake Galilee, at the territory of the Gerasenes. As soon as Jesus got out of the boat he was met by a man who came out of the burial caves. This man had an evil spirit in him and lived among the graves. Nobody could keep him tied with chains any more; many times his feet and hands had been tied, but every time he broke the chains, and smashed the irons on his feet. He was too strong for anyone to stop him. Day and night he wandered among the graves and through the hills, screaming and cutting himself with stones.

He was some distance away when he saw Jesus; so he ran, fell on his knees before him, and screamed in a loud voice, "Jesus, Son of the Most High God! What do you want with me? For God's sake, I beg you, don't punish me!" (He said this because Jesus was saying to him, "Evil spirit, come out of this man!")

So Jesus asked him, "What is your name?"

The man answered, "My name is 'Mob' — there are so many of us!" And he kept begging Jesus not to send the evil spirits out of that territory.

A large herd of pigs was near by, feeding on the hillside. The spirits begged Jesus, "Send us to the pigs, and let us go into them." So he let them. The evil spirits went out of the man and went into the pigs. The whole herd — about two thousand pigs in all — rushed down the side of the cliff into the lake and were drowned.

The men who had been taking care of the pigs ran away and spread the news in the town and among the farms. The people went out to see what had happened. They came to Jesus and saw the man who used to have the mob of demons in him. He was sitting there, clothed and in his right mind; and they were all afraid. Those who had seen it told the people what had happened to the man with the demons, and about the pigs. So they began to ask Jesus to leave their territory.

As Jesus was getting into the boat, the man who had had the demons begged him, "Let me go with you!"

But Jesus would not let him. Instead he told him, "Go back home to your family and tell them how much the Lord has done for you, and how kind he has been to you."

So the man left and went all through the Ten Towns telling what Jesus had done for him; and all who heard it were filled with wonder.

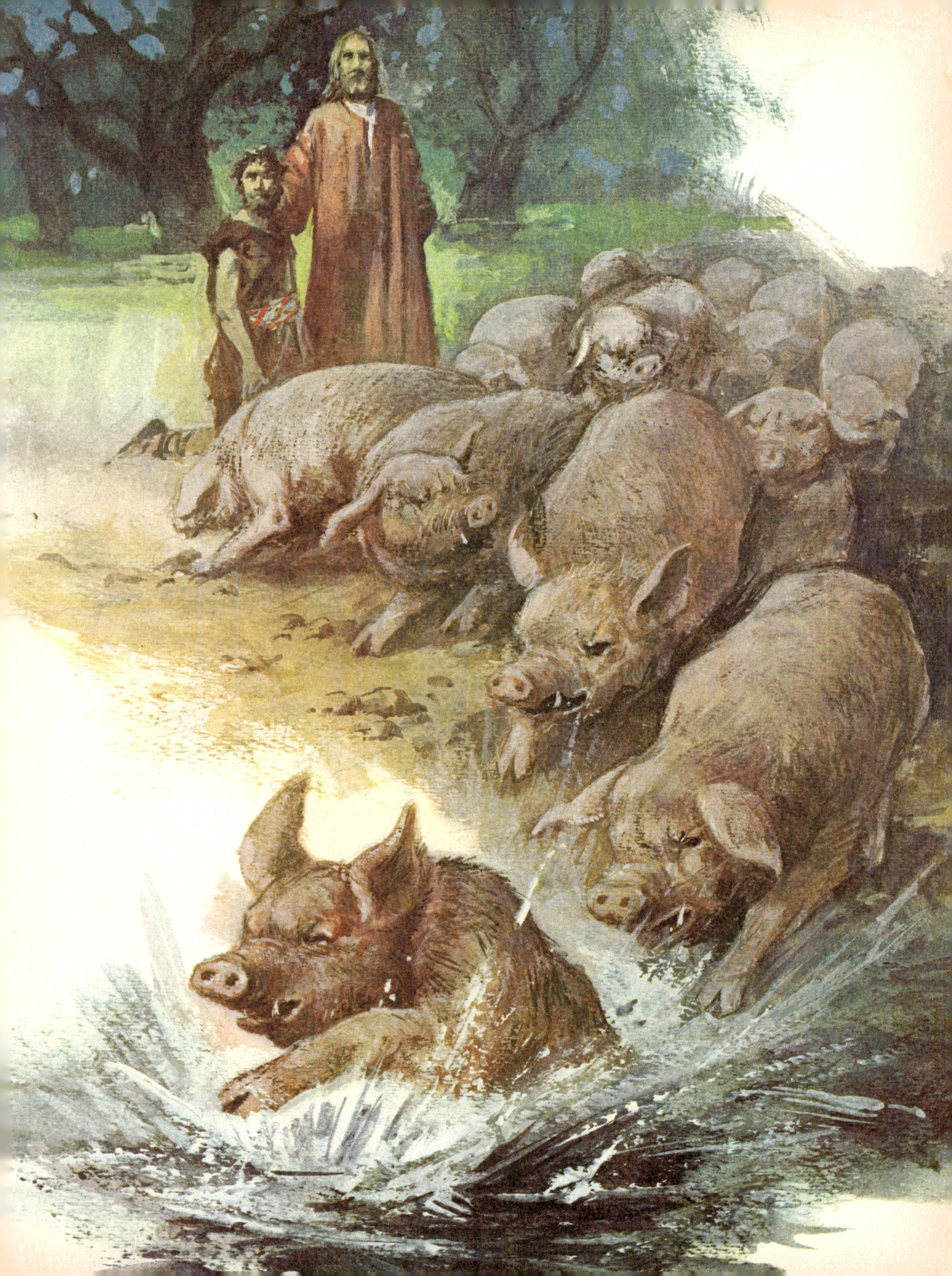

Jairus' Daughter and the Woman who Touched Jesus' Cloak

Jesus went back across to the other side of the lake. There at the lakeside a large crowd gathered round him. Jairus, an official of the local synagogue, came up, and when he saw Jesus he threw himself down at his feet and begged him with all his might, "My little daughter is very sick. Please come and place your hands on her, so that she will get well and live!"

Then Jesus started off with him. So many people were going along with him that they were crowding him from every side.

There was a woman who had suffered terribly from severe bleeding for twelve years, even though she had been treated by many doctors. She had spent all her money, but instead of getting better she got worse all the time. She had heard about Jesus, so she came in the crowd behind him. "If I touch just his clothes," she said to herself, "I shall get well."

She touched his cloak and her bleeding stopped at once; and she had the feeling inside herself that she was cured of her trouble. At once Jesus knew that power had gone out of him. So he turned round in the crowd and said, "Who touched my clothes?"

His disciples answered, "You see how the people are crowding you; why do you ask who touched you?"

But Jesus kept looking round to see who had done it. The woman realized what had happened to her; so she came, trembling with fear, fell at his feet, and told him the whole truth. Jesus said to her, "My daughter, your faith has made you well. Go in peace, and be healed from your trouble."

While Jesus was saying this, some messengers came from Jairus' house and told him, "Your daughter has died. Why should you bother the Teacher any longer?"

Jesus paid no attention to what they said, but told him, "Don't be afraid, only believe." Then he did not let anyone else go on with him except Peter and James and his brother John. They arrived at the official's house, where Jesus saw the confusion and heard all the loud crying and wailing. He went in and said to them, "Why all this confusion? Why are you crying? The child is not dead — she is only sleeping!"

They started making fun of him, so he put them all out, took the child's father and mother, and his three disciples, and went into the room where the child was lying. He took her by the hands and said to her, *"Talitha, koum,"* which means, "Little girl! Get up, I tell you!"

She got up at once and started walking around. (She was twelve years old.) When this happened they were completely amazed! But Jesus gave them strict orders not to tell anyone, and said, "Give her something to eat."

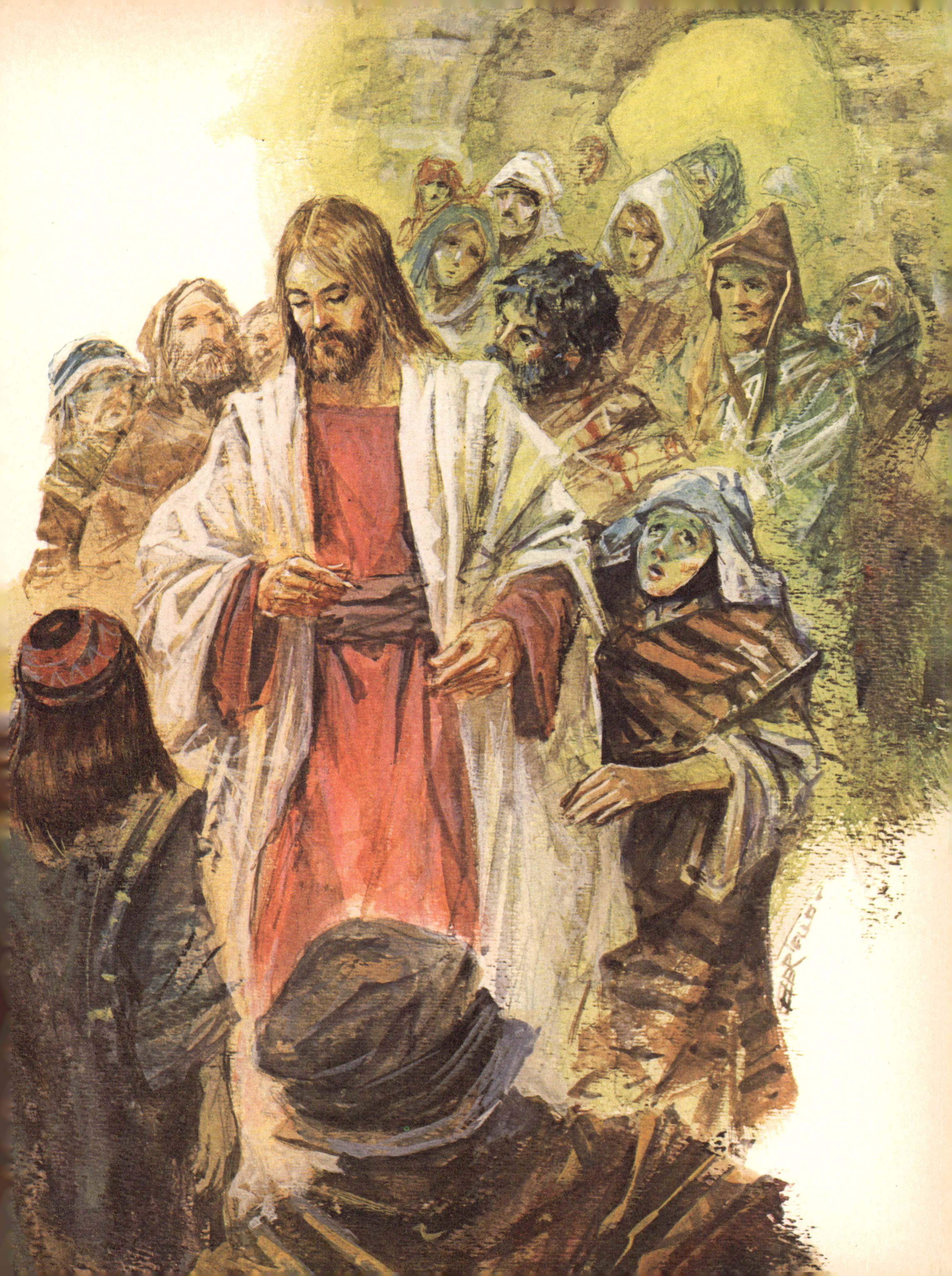

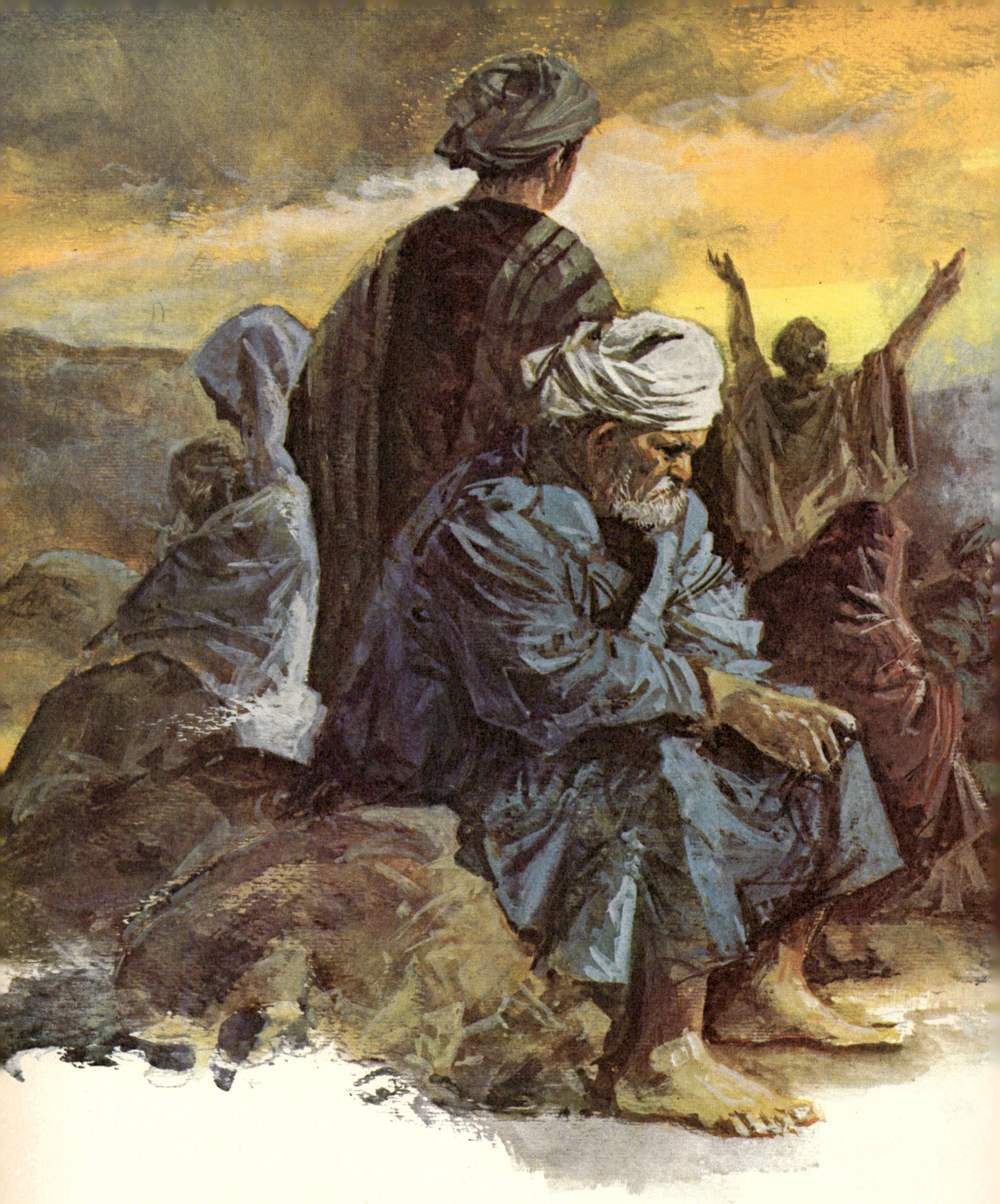

Jesus Sends the Apostles to Heal and Preach

Then Jesus went to the villages round there, teaching the people. He called the twelve disciples together and sent them out two by two. He gave them authority over the evil spirits and ordered them, "Don't take anything with you on the journey except a walking stick; no bread, no beggar's bag, no money in your pockets. Wear sandals, but don't wear an extra shirt." He also told them, "Wherever you are welcomed, stay in the same house until you leave that town. If you come to a place where people do not welcome you or will not listen to you, leave it and shake the dust off your feet. This will be a warning to them!"

Jesus Feeds the Five Thousand

The apostles returned and met with Jesus, and told him all they had done and taught. There were so many people coming and going that Jesus and his disciples didn't even have time to eat. So he said to them, "Let us go off by ourselves to some place where we will be alone and you can rest a while." So they started out in the boat by themselves to a lonely place.

Many people, however, saw them leave and knew at once who they were; so they went from all the towns and ran ahead by land and got to the place ahead of Jesus and his disciples. When Jesus got out of the boat, he saw this large crowd, and his heart was filled with pity for them, because they were like sheep without a shepherd. So he began to teach them many things. When it was getting late, his disciples came to him and said, "It is already very late, and this is a lonely place. Send the people away, and let them go to the nearby farms and villages and buy themselves something to eat."

"You yourselves give them something to eat," Jesus answered.

They asked, "Do you want us to go and buy twenty pounds' worth of bread and feed them?"

So Jesus asked them, "How much bread do you have? Go and see."

When they found out they told him, "Five loaves, and two fish also."

Jesus then told his disciples to make all the people divide into groups and sit down on the green grass. So the people sat down in rows, in groups of a hundred and groups of fifty. Then Jesus took the five loaves and the two fish, looked up to heaven, and gave thanks to God. He broke the loaves and gave them to his disciples to distribute to the people. He also divided the two fish among them all. Everyone ate and had enough. Then the disciples took up twelve baskets full of what was left of the bread and of the fish. The number of men who ate the bread was five thousand.

Jesus Walks on the Water

At once Jesus made his disciples get into the boat and go ahead of him to Bethsaida, on the other side of the lake, while he sent the crowd away. After saying good-bye to the disciples, he went away to a hill to pray. When evening came the boat was in the middle of the lake, while Jesus was alone on land. He saw that his disciples were having trouble rowing the boat, because the wind was blowing against them; so sometime between three and six o'clock in the morning he came to them walking on the water. He was going to pass them by. But they saw him walking on the water. "It's a ghost!" they thought, and screamed. For when they all saw him they were terrified.

Jesus spoke to them at once, "Courage!" he said. "It is I. Don't be afraid!" Then he got into the boat with them, and the wind died down. The disciples were completely amazed, because they had not understood what the loaves of bread meant; their minds could not grasp it.

Jesus Heals the Sick in Gennesaret

They crossed the lake and came to land at Gennesaret, where they tied up the boat. As they left the boat, people recognized Jesus at once. So they ran throughout the whole region and brought the sick lying on their mats to him, wherever they heard he was. And everywhere Jesus went, to villages, towns, or farms, people would take their sick to the market places and beg him to let the sick at least touch the edge of his cloak; and all who touched it were made well.

A Woman's Faith

Then Jesus left and went away to the territory near the city of Tyre. He went into a house, and did not want anyone to know he was there; but he could not stay hidden. A certain woman, whose daughter had an evil spirit in her, heard about Jesus and came to him at once and fell at his feet. The woman was a foreigner, born in Phoenicia of Syria. She begged Jesus to drive the demon out of her daughter. But Jesus answered, "Let us feed the children first; it isn't right to take the children's food and throw it to the dogs."

"Sir," she answered, "even the dogs under the table eat the children's leftovers!"

So Jesus said to her, "For such an answer you may go home; the demon has gone out of your daughter!"

She went back home and found her child lying on the bed; the demon had indeed gone out of her.

Jesus Heals a Deaf and Dumb Man

Jesus then left the neighbourhood of Tyre and went on through Sidon to Lake Galilee, going by way of the territory of the Ten Towns. Some people brought him a man who was deaf and could hardly speak, and begged Jesus to place his hand on him. So Jesus took him off alone, away from the crowd, put his fingers in the man's ears, spat, and touched the man's tongue. Then Jesus looked up to heaven, gave a deep groan, and said to the man, "*Ephphatha*," which means, "Open up!"

At once the man's ears were opened, his tongue was set loose, and he began to talk without any trouble. Then Jesus ordered them all not to speak of it to anyone; but the more he ordered them, the more they told it. And all who heard were completely amazed. "How well he does everything!" they exclaimed.

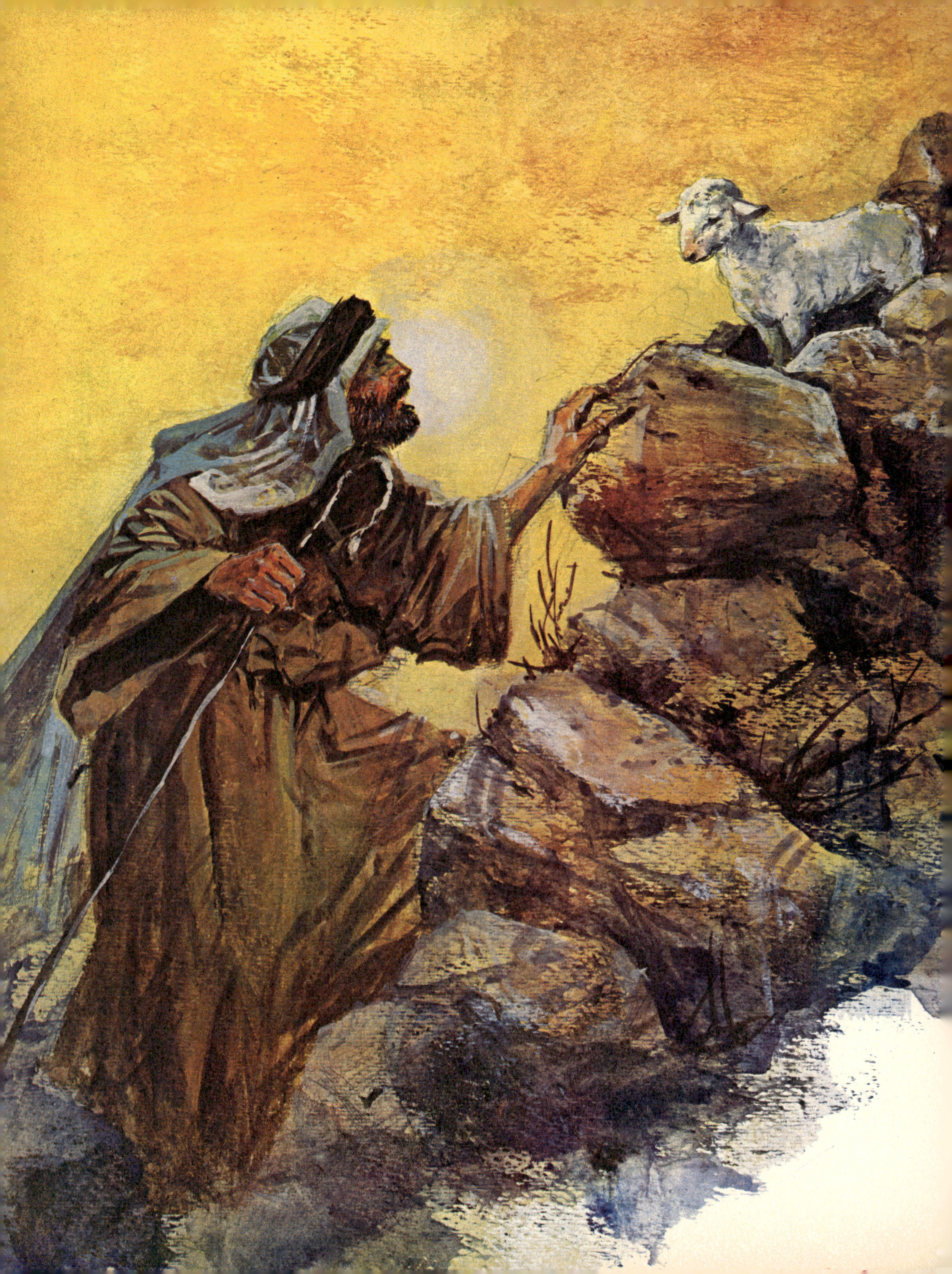

3
Stories Told by Jesus

Everyone enjoys a story. That is why Jesus taught people by telling them stories or parables. They were such good stories that they have never been forgotten. But as we read any one of them, we ought to ask: what lesson does it teach?

Some of these stories were parables told in order to show God's love and patience. Others were told in order to show our danger and our duty.

Stories about God's Love: The Lost Sheep

One time many tax collectors and outcasts came to listen to Jesus. The Pharisees and the teachers of the Law started grumbling, "This man welcomes outcasts and even eats with them!" So Jesus told them this parable

"Suppose one of you has a hundred sheep and loses one of them — what does he do? He leaves the other ninety-nine sheep in the pasture and goes looking for the one that got lost until he finds it. When he finds it, he is so happy that he puts it on his shoulders, and carries it back home. Then he calls his friends and neighbours together, and says to them, 'I am so happy I found my lost sheep. Let us celebrate!' In the same way, I tell you, there will be more joy in heaven over one sinner who repents than over ninety-nine respectable people who do not need to repent."

The Parable of the Lost Coin

"Or suppose a woman who has ten silver coins loses one of them — what does she do? She lights a lamp, sweeps her house, and looks carefully everywhere until she finds it. When she finds it, she calls her friends and neighbours together, and says to them, 'I am so happy I found the coin I lost. Let us celebrate!' In the same way, I tell you, the angels of God rejoice over one sinner who repents."

The Parable of the Lost Son

Jesus went on to say, "There was a man who had two sons. The younger one said to him, 'Father, give me now my share of the property.' So the man divided the property between his two sons. After a few days the younger son sold his part of the property and left home with the money. He went to a country far away, where he wasted his money in reckless living. He spent everything he had. Then a severe famine spread over that country, and he was left without a thing. So he went to work for one of the citizens of that country, who sent him out to his farm to take care of the pigs. He wished he could fill himself with the bean pods the pigs ate, but no one gave him anything to eat. At last he came to his senses and said, 'All my father's hired workers have more than they can eat, and here I am, about to starve! I will get up and go to my father and say, "Father, I have sinned against God and against you. I am no longer fit to be called your son; treat me as one of your hired workers."' So he got up and started back to his father.

"He was still a long way from home when his father saw him; his heart was filled with pity and he ran, threw his arms around his son, and kissed him. 'Father,' the son said, 'I have sinned against God and against you. I am no longer fit to be called your son.' But the father called his servants: 'Hurry!' he said. 'Bring the best robe and put it on him. Put a ring on his finger and shoes on his feet. Then go get the prize calf and kill it, and let us celebrate with a feast! Because this son of mine was dead, but now he is alive; he was lost, but now he has been found.' And so the feasting began.

"The older son, in the meantime, was out in the field. On his way back, when he came close to the house, he heard the music and dancing. He called one of the servants and asked him, 'What's going on?' 'Your brother came back home,' the servant answered, 'and your father killed the prize calf, because he got him back safe and sound.' The older brother was so angry that he would not go into the house; so his father came out and begged him to come in. 'Look,' he answered back to his father, 'all these years I have worked like a slave for you, and I never disobeyed your orders. What have you given me? Not even a goat for me to have a feast with my friends! But this son of yours wasted all your property on prostitutes, and when he comes back home you kill the prize calf for him!' 'My son,' the father answered, 'you are always here with me and everything I have is yours. But we had to have a feast and be happy, because your brother was dead, but now he is alive; he was lost, but now he has been found.'"

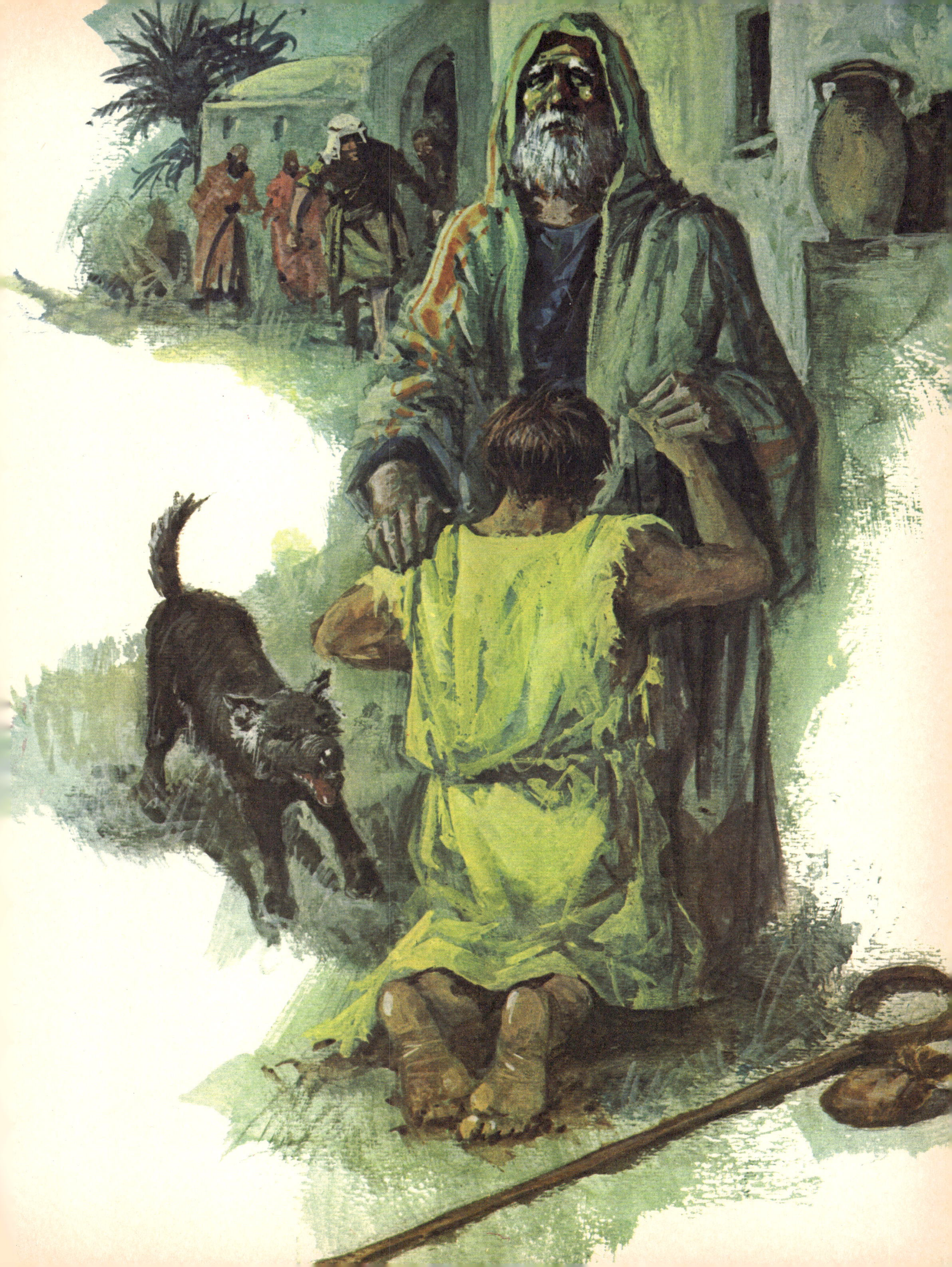

The Parable of the Workers in the Vineyard

"The Kingdom of heaven is like the owner of a vineyard who went out early in the morning to hire some men to work in his vineyard. He agreed to pay them the regular wage, a silver coin a day, and sent them to work in his vineyard. He went out again to the market place at nine o'clock and saw some men standing there doing nothing, so he told them, 'You also go to work in the vineyard, and I will pay you a fair wage.' So they went. Then at twelve o'clock and again at three o'clock he did the same thing. It was nearly five o'clock when he went to the market place and saw some other men still standing there. Why are you wasting the whole day here doing nothing?' he asked them. 'It is because no one hired us,' they answered. 'Well, then, you also go to work in the vineyard,' he told them.

"When evening came, the owner told his foreman, 'Call the workers and pay them their wages, starting with those who were hired last, and ending with those who were hired first.' The men who had begun to work at five o'clock were paid a silver coin each. So when the men who were the first to be hired came to be paid, they thought they would get more; but they too were given a silver coin each. They took their money and started grumbling against the employer. These men who were hired last worked only one hour,' they said, 'while we put up with a whole day's work in the hot sun — yet you paid them the same as you paid us!' 'Listen, friend,' the owner answered one of them. 'I have not cheated you. After all, you agreed to do a day's work for a silver coin. Now, take your pay and go home. I want to give this man who was hired last as much as I have given you. Don't I have the right to do as I wish with my own money? Or are you jealous because I am generous?' "

The Parable of the Hidden Treasure

"The Kingdom of heaven is like a treasure hidden in a field. A man happens to find it, so he covers it up again. He is so happy that he goes and sells everything he has, and then goes back and buys the field."

The Parable of the Pearl

"Also, the Kingdom of heaven is like a buyer looking for fine pearls. When he finds one that is unusually fine, he goes and sells everything he has, and buys the pearl."

The Parable of the Net

"Also, the Kingdom of heaven is like a net thrown out in the lake, which catches all kinds of fish. When it is full, the fishermen pull it to shore and sit down to divide the fish: the good ones go into their buckets, the worthless ones are thrown away. It will be like this at the end of the age: the angels will go out and gather up the evil people from among the good, and throw them into the fiery furnace. There they will cry and gnash their teeth."

The Parable of the Storage Room

"Do you understand these things?" Jesus asked them.
"Yes," they answered.
So he replied, "This means, then, that every teacher of the Law who becomes a disciple in the Kingdom of heaven is like a homeowner who takes new and old things out of his storage room."

Stories about God's Patience: The Growing Seed

Jesus went on to say, "The Kingdom of God is like a man who scatters seed in his field. He sleeps at night, is up and about during the day, and all the while the seeds are sprouting and growing. Yet he does not know how it happens. The soil itself makes the plants grow and bear fruit: first the tender stalk appears, then the head, and finally the head full of grain. When the grain is ripe the man starts working with his sickle because harvest time has come."

The Parable of the Sower

Jesus began to teach by Lake Galilee. The crowd that gathered round him was so large that he got into a boat and sat in it. The boat was out in the water, while the crowd stood on the shore, at the water's edge. He used parables to teach them many things, and in his teaching said to them,
"Listen! There was a man who went out to sow. As he scattered the seed in the field, some of it fell along the path, and the birds came and ate it up. Some of it fell on rocky ground, where there was little soil. The seeds soon sprouted, because the soil wasn't deep. Then when the sun came up it burned the young plants, and because the roots had not grown deep enough the plants soon dried up. Some of the seed fell among thorns, which grew up and choked the plants, and they didn't bear grain. But some seeds fell in good soil, and the plants sprouted, grew, and bore grain: some had thirty grains, others sixty, and others one hundred."
And Jesus concluded, "Listen, then, if you have ears to hear with!"

The Parable of the Weeds

Jesus told them another parable, "The Kingdom of heaven is like a man who sowed good seed in his field. One night, when everyone was asleep, an enemy came and sowed weeds among the wheat, and went away. When the plants grew and the heads of grain began to form, then the weeds showed up. The man's servants came to him and said, 'Sir, it was good seed you sowed in your field; where did the weeds come from?' 'It was some enemy who did this,' he answered. 'Do you want us to go and pull up the weeds?' they asked him. 'No,' he answered, 'because as you gather the weeds you might pull up some of the wheat along with them. Let the wheat and the weeds both grow together until harvest, and then I will tell the harvest workers: Pull up the weeds first and tie them in bundles to throw in the fire; then gather in the wheat and put it in my barn.'"

The Parable of the Mustard Seed

Jesus asked, "What is the Kingdom of God like? What shall I compare it with? It is like a mustard seed, which a man took and planted in his field; the plant grew and became a tree, and the birds made their nests in its branches."

The Parable of the Yeast

Again Jesus asked, "What shall I compare the Kingdom of God with? It is like the yeast which a woman takes and mixes in a bushel of flour, until the whole batch of dough rises."

The Lesson of the Fig Tree

Then Jesus told them this parable, "Remember the fig tree and all the other trees. When you see their leaves beginning to appear you know that summer is near. In the same way, when you see these things happening, you will know that the Kingdom of God is about to come.

"Remember this! All these things will take place before the people now living have all died. Heaven and earth will pass away; my words will never pass away."

The Parable of the Unfruitful Fig Tree

Then Jesus told them this parable, "A man had a fig tree growing in his vineyard. He went looking for figs on it but found none. So he said to his gardener, 'Look, for three years I have been coming here looking for figs on this fig tree and I haven't found any. Cut it down! Why should it go on using up the soil?' But the gardener answered, 'Leave it alone, sir, just this one year; I will dig a trench round it and fill it up with fertilizer. Then if the tree bears figs next year, so much the better; if not, then you will have it cut down.' "

The Parable of the Great Feast

One of the men sitting at the table heard this and said to Jesus, "How happy are those who will sit at the table in the Kingdom of God!"

Jesus said to him, "There was a man who was giving a great feast, to which he invited many people. At the time for the feast he sent his servant to tell his guests, 'Come, everything is ready!' But they all began, one after another, to make excuses. The first one told the servant, 'I bought a field, and have to go and look at it; please accept my apologies.' Another one said, 'I bought five pairs of oxen and am on my way to try them out; please accept my apologies.' Another one said, 'I have just got married, and for this reason I cannot come.' The servant went back and told all this to his master. The master of the house was furious and said to his servant, 'Hurry out to the streets and alleys of the town, and bring back the poor, the crippled, the blind, and the lame.' Soon the servant said, 'Your order has been carried out, sir, but there is room for more.' So the master said to the servant, 'Go out to the country roads and lanes, and make people come in, so that my house will be full. I tell you all that none of those men who were invited will taste my dinner!' "

Stories about our Danger: the Ten Girls

(Jesus is speaking of what it will be like on the day of his second coming.) "On that day the Kingdom of heaven will be like ten girls who took their oil lamps and went out to meet the bridegroom. Five of them were foolish, and the other five were wise. The foolish ones took their lamps but did not take any extra oil with them, while the wise ones took containers full of oil with their lamps. The bridegroom was late in coming, so the girls began to nod and fall asleep.

"It was already midnight when the cry rang out, 'Here is the bridegroom! Come and meet him!' The ten girls woke up and trimmed their lamps. Then the foolish ones said to the wise ones, 'Let us have some of your oil, because our lamps are going out.' 'No, indeed,' the wise ones answered back, 'there is not enough for you and us. Go to the store and buy some for yourselves.' So the foolish girls went off to buy some oil, and while they were gone the bridegroom arrived. The five girls who were ready went in with him to the wedding feast, and the door was closed.

"Later the other girls arrived. 'Sir, sir! Let us in!' they cried. 'But I really don't know you,' the bridegroom answered."

And Jesus concluded, "Watch out, then, because you do not know the day or hour."

The Parable of the Three Servants

"It will be like a man who was about to leave home on a journey; he called his servants and put them in charge of his property. He gave to each one according to his ability: to one he gave five thousand pounds, to the other two thousand pounds, and to the other one thousand pounds. Then he left on his journey. The servant who had received five thousand pounds went at once and invested his money and earned another five thousand pounds. In the same way the servant who received two thousand pounds earned another two thousand pounds. But the servant who received one thousand pounds went off, dug a hole in the ground, and hid his master's money.

"After a long time the master of those servants came back and settled accounts with them. The servant who had received five thousand pounds came in and handed over the other five thousand pounds. 'You gave me five thousand pounds, sir,' he said. 'Look! Here are another five thousand pounds that I have earned.' 'Well done, good and faithful servant!' said his master. 'You have been faithful in managing small amounts, so I will put you in charge of large amounts. Come on in and share my happiness!' Then the servant who had been given two thousand pounds came in and said, 'You gave me two thousand pounds, sir. Look! Here are another two thousand pounds that I have earned.' 'Well done, good and faithful servant!' said his master. 'You have been faithful in managing small amounts, so I will put you in charge of large amounts. Come on in and share my happiness!' Then the servant who had received one thousand pounds came in and said, 'Sir, I know you are a hard man; you reap harvests where you did not plant, and gather crops where you did not scatter seed. I was afraid, so I went off and hid your money in the ground. Look! Here is what belongs to you.' 'You bad and lazy servant!' his master said. 'You knew, did you, that I reap harvests where I did not plant, and gather crops where I did not scatter seed? Well, then, you should have deposited my money in the bank, and I would have received it all back with interest when I returned. Now, take the money away from him and give it to the one who has ten thousand pounds. For to everyone who has, even more will be given, and he will have more than enough; but the one who has nothing, even the little he has will be taken away from him. As for this useless servant — throw him outside in the darkness; there he will cry and gnash his teeth.'"

Watchful Servants

"Be ready for whatever comes, with your clothes fastened tight at the waist and your lamps lit, like servants who are waiting for their master to come back from a wedding feast. When he comes and knocks, they will open the door for him at once. How happy are those servants whose master finds them awake and ready when he returns! I tell you, he will fasten his belt, have them sit down, and wait on them. How happy are they if he finds them ready, even if he should come as late as midnight or even later! And remember this! If the man of the house knew the time when the thief would come, he would not let the thief break into his house. And you, too, be ready, because the Son of Man will come at an hour when you are not expecting him."

The Faithful or the Unfaithful Servant

Peter said, "Lord, are you telling this parable to us, or do you mean it for everyone?"

The Lord answered, "Who, then, is the faithful and wise servant? He is the one whom his master will put in charge, to run the household and give the other servants their share of the food at the proper time. How happy is that servant if his master finds him doing this when he comes home! Indeed, I tell you, the master will put that servant in charge of all his property. But if that servant says to himself, 'My master is taking a long time to come back,' and begins to beat the other servants, both the men and the women, and eats and drinks and gets drunk, then the master will come back some day when the servant does not expect him and at a time he does not know. The master will cut him to pieces, and make him share the fate of the disobedient.

"The servant who knows what his master wants him to do, but does not get himself ready and do what his master wants, will be punished with a heavy whipping; but the servant who does not know what his master wants, and does something for which he deserves a whipping, will be punished with a light whipping. The man to whom much is given, of him much is required; the man to whom more is given, of him much more is required."

The Parable of the Rich Fool

A man in the crowd said to him, "Teacher, tell my brother to divide with me the property our father left us."

Jesus answered him, "Man, who gave me the right to judge, or to divide the property between you two?" And he went on to say to them all, "Watch out, and guard yourselves from all kinds of greed; because a man's true life is not made up of the things he owns, no matter how rich he may be."

Then Jesus told them this parable, "A rich man had land which bore good crops. He began to think to himself, 'I don't have a place to keep all my crops. What can I do? This is what I will do,' he told himself; 'I will tear my barns down and build bigger ones, where I will store the grain and all my other goods. Then I will say to myself, Lucky man! You have all the good things you need for many years. Take life easy, eat, drink, and enjoy yourself!' But God said to him, 'You fool! This very night you will have to give up your life; then who will get all these things you have kept for yourself?' "

And Jesus concluded, "This is how it is with those who pile up riches for themselves but are not rich in God's sight."

The Rich Man and Lazarus

"There was once a rich man who dressed in the most expensive clothes and lived in great luxury every day. There was also a poor man, named Lazarus, full of sores, who used to be brought to the rich man's door, hoping to fill himself with the bits of food that fell from the rich man's table. Even the dogs would come and lick his sores. The poor man died and was carried by the angels to Abraham's side, at the feast in heaven; the rich man died and was buried. He was in great pain in Hades; and he looked up and saw Abraham, far away, with Lazarus at his side. So he called out, 'Father Abraham! Take pity on me, and send Lazarus to dip his finger in some water and cool off my tongue, because I am in great pain in this fire!' But Abraham said, 'Remember, my son, that in your lifetime you were given all the good things, while Lazarus got all the bad things; but now he is enjoying himself here, while you are in pain. Besides all that, there is a deep pit lying between us, so that those who want to cross over from here to you cannot do it, nor can anyone cross over to us from where you are.' The rich man said, 'Well, father, I beg you, send Lazarus to my father's house, where I have five brothers; let him go and warn them so that they, at least, will not come to this place of pain.' Abraham said, 'Your brothers have Moses and the prophets to warn them; let your brothers listen to what they say.' The rich man answered, 'That is not enough, father Abraham! But if someone were to rise from death and go to them, then they would turn from their sins.' But Abraham said, 'If they will not listen to Moses and the prophets, they will not be convinced even if someone were to rise from death.' "

The Parable of the Tenants in the Vineyard

Then Jesus told the people this parable, "A man planted a vineyard, rented it out to tenants, and then left home for a long time. When the time came for harvesting the grapes, he sent a slave to the tenants to receive from them his share of the harvest. But the tenants beat the

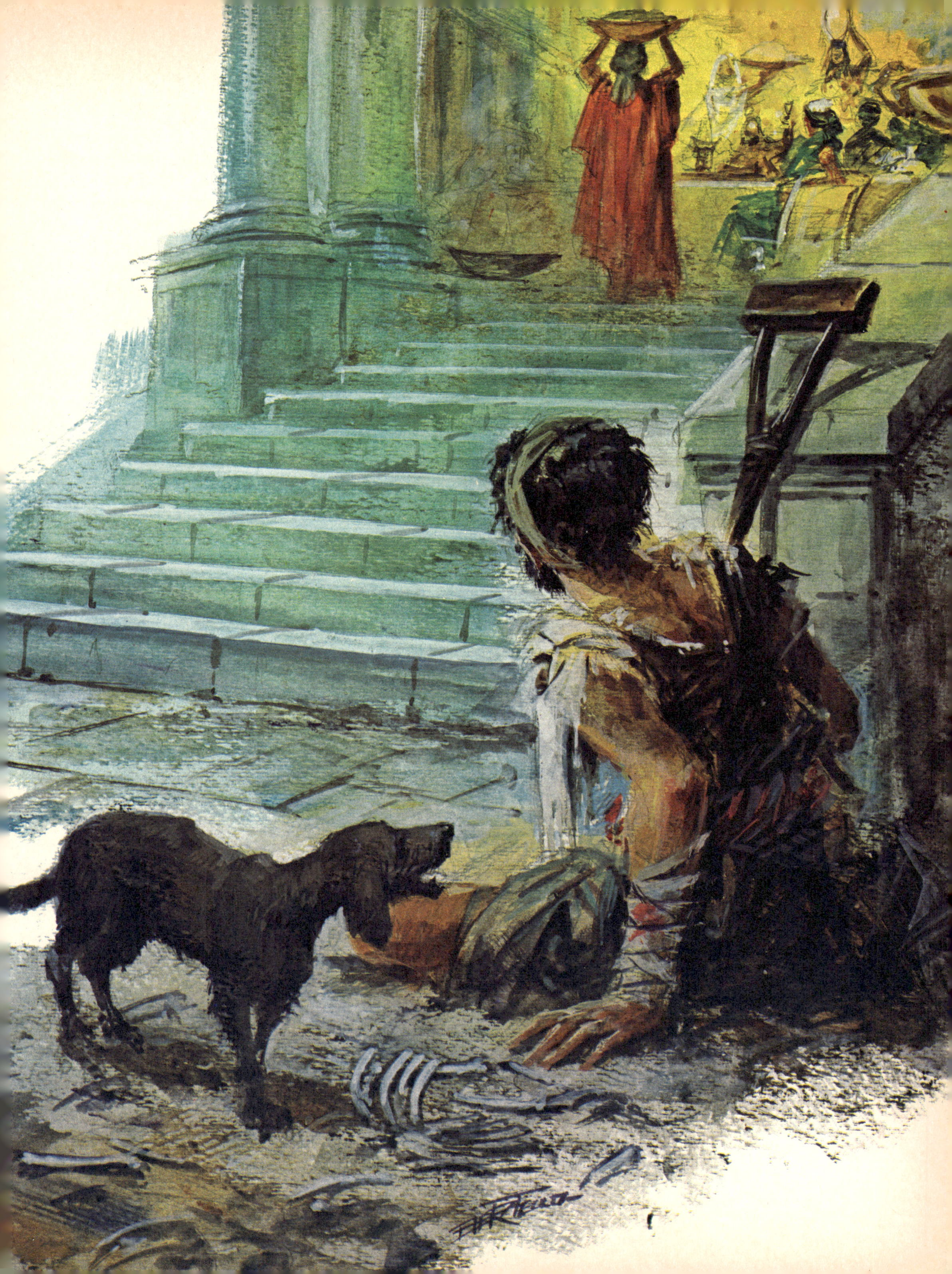

slave and sent him back without a thing. So he sent another slave; but the tenants beat him also, treated him shamefully, and sent him back without a thing. Then he sent a third slave; the tenants hurt him, too, and threw him out. Then the owner of the vineyard said, 'What shall I do? I will send my own dear son; surely they will respect him!' But when the tenants saw him they said to one another, 'This is the owner's son. Let us kill him, and his property will be ours!' So they threw him out of the vineyard and killed him.

"What, then, will the owner of the vineyard do to the tenants?" Jesus asked. "He will come and kill those men, and turn over the vineyard to other tenants."

The Parable of the Unforgiving Servant

Then Peter came to Jesus and asked, "Lord, how many times can my brother sin against me and I have to forgive him? Seven times?"

"No, not seven times," answered Jesus, "but seventy times seven. Because the Kingdom of heaven is like a king who decided to check on his servants' accounts. He had just begun to do so when one of them was brought in who owed him millions of pounds. The servant did not have enough to pay his debt, so his master ordered him to be sold as a slave, with his wife and his children and all that he had, in order to pay the debt. The servant fell on his knees before his master. 'Be patient with me,' he begged, 'and I will pay you everything!' The master felt sorry for him, so he forgave him the debt and let him go.

"The man went out and met one of his fellow servants who owed him a few pounds. He grabbed him and started choking him. 'Pay back what you owe me!' he said. His fellow servant fell down and begged him, 'Be patient with me and I will pay you back!' But he would not; instead, he had him thrown into jail until he should pay the debt. When the other servants saw what had happened, they were very upset, and went to their master and told him everything. So the master called the servant in. 'You worthless slave!' he said. 'I forgave you the whole amount you owed me, just because you asked me to. You should have had mercy on your fellow servant, just as I had mercy on you.' The master was very angry, and he sent the servant to jail to be punished until he should pay back the whole amount."

And Jesus concluded, "That is how my Father in heaven will treat you if you do not forgive your brother, every one of you, from your heart."

The Parable of the Two Sons

"Now, what do you think? There was a man who had two sons. He went to the older one and said, 'Son, go work in the vineyard today.' 'I don't want to,' he answered, but later he changed his mind and went to the vineyard. Then the father went to the other son and said the same thing. 'Yes, sir,' he answered, but he did not go. Which one of the two did what his father wanted?"

"The older one," they answered.

"And I tell you this," Jesus said to them. "The tax collectors and the prostitutes are going into the Kingdom of God ahead of you. For John the Baptist came to you showing you the right path to take, and you would not believe him; but the tax collectors and the prostitutes believed him. Even when you saw this you did not change your minds later on and believe him."

The Return of the Evil Spirit

"When an evil spirit goes out of a man, it travels over dry country looking for a place to rest. If it can't find one, it says to itself, 'I will go back to my house which I left.' So it goes back and finds the house clean and all fixed up. Then it goes out and brings seven other spirits even worse than itself, and they come and live there. So that man is in worse shape, when it is all over, than he was at the beginning."

Stories about our Duty

The Parable of the Widow and the Judge

Then Jesus told them this parable, to teach them that they should always pray and never become discouraged. "There was a judge in a certain town who neither feared God nor respected men. And there was a widow in that same town who kept coming to him and pleading for her rights: 'Help me against my opponent!' For a long time the judge was not willing, but at last he said to himself, 'Even though I don't fear God or respect men, yet because of all the trouble this widow is giving me I will see to it that she gets her rights; or else she will keep on coming and finally wear me out!'"

And the Lord continued, "Listen to what that corrupt judge said. Now, will God not judge in favour of his own people who cry to him for help day and night? Will he be slow to help them? I tell you, he will judge in their favour, and do it quickly. But will the Son of Man find faith on earth when he comes?"

The Parable of the Friend at Midnight

And Jesus said to his disciples, "Suppose one of you should go to a friend's house at midnight and tell him, 'Friend, let me borrow three loaves of bread. A friend of mine who is on a journey has just come to my house and I haven't got any food for him! And suppose your friend should answer from inside, 'Don't bother me! The door is already locked, and my children and I are in bed. I can't get up to give you anything.' Well, what then? I tell you, even if he will not get up and give you the bread because he is your friend, yet he will get up and give you everything you need because you are not ashamed to keep on asking."

The Parable of the Pharisee and the Tax Collector

Jesus also told this parable to people who were sure of their own goodness and despised everybody else. "Two men went up to the temple to pray; one was a Pharisee, the other a tax collector. The Pharisee stood apart by himself and prayed, 'I thank you, God, that I am not greedy, dishonest, or immoral, like everybody else; I thank you that I am not like that tax collector. I fast two days every week, and I give you one tenth of all my income.' But the tax collector stood at a distance and would not even raise his face to heaven, but beat on his breast and said, 'God, have pity on me, a sinner!'" "I tell you," said Jesus, "this man, and not the other, was in the right with God when he went home. Because everyone who makes himself great will be humbled, and everyone who humbles himself will be made great."

The Parable of the Good Samaritan

A certain teacher of the Law came up and tried to trap Jesus. "Teacher," he asked, "what must I do to receive eternal life?"

Jesus answered him, "What do the Scriptures say? How do you interpret them?"

The man answered, " 'You must love the Lord your God with all your heart, with all your soul, with all your strength, and with all your mind;' and, 'You must love your fellow-man as yourself.' "

"Your answer is correct," replied Jesus; "do this and you will live."

But the teacher of the Law wanted to put himself in the right, so he asked Jesus, "Who is my fellow-man?"

Jesus answered, "There was a man who was going down from Jerusalem to Jericho, when robbers attacked him, stripped him and beat him up, leaving him half dead. It so happened that a priest was going down that road; when he saw the man he walked on by, on the other side. In the same way a Levite also came there, went over and looked at the man, and then walked on by, on the other side. But a certain Samaritan who was travelling that way came upon him, and when he saw the man his heart was filled with pity. He went over to him, poured oil and wine on his wounds and bandaged them; then he put the man on his own animal and took him to an inn, where he took care of him. The

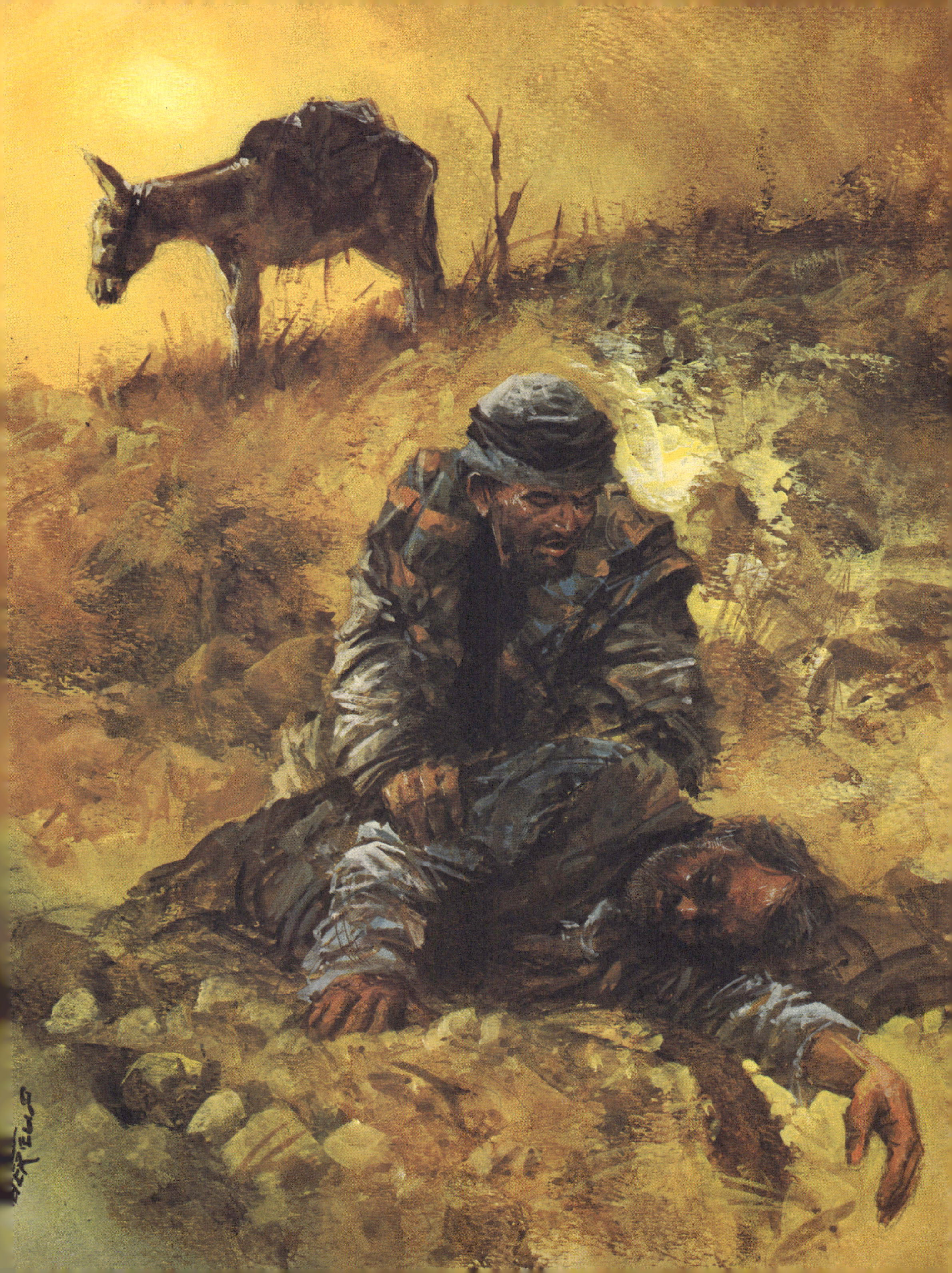

next day he took out two silver coins and gave them to the innkeeper. 'Take care of him,' he told the innkeeper, 'and when I come back this way I will pay you back whatever you spend on him.'"

And Jesus concluded, "In your opinion, which one of these three acted like a fellow-man towards the man attacked by the robbers?"

The teacher of the Law answered, "The one who was kind to him."

Jesus replied, "You go, then, and do the same."

The Final Judgment

"When the Son of Man comes as King, and all the angels with him, he will sit on his royal throne, and all the earth's people will be gathered before him. Then he will divide them into two groups, just as a shepherd separates the sheep from the goats: he will put the sheep at his right and the goats at his left. Then the King will say to the people on his right, 'You that are blessed by my Father: come! Come and receive the kingdom which has been prepared for you ever since the creation of the world. I was hungry and you fed me, thirsty and you gave me drink; I was a stranger and you received me in your homes, naked and you clothed me; I was sick and you took care of me, in prison, and you visited me.' The righteous will then answer him, 'When, Lord, did we ever see you hungry and feed you, or thirsty and give you drink? When did we ever see you a stranger and welcome you in our homes, or naked and clothe you? When did we ever see you sick or in prison, and visit you?' The King will answer back, 'I tell you, indeed, whenever you did this for one of the least important of these brothers of mine, you did it for me!'

"Then he will say to those on his left, 'Away from me, you that are are under God's curse! Away to the eternal fire which has been prepared for the Devil and his angels! I was hungry but you would not feed me, thirsty but you would not give me drink; I was a stranger but you would not welcome me in your homes, naked but you would not clothe me; I was sick and in prison but you would not take care of me.' Then they will answer him, 'When, Lord, did we ever see you hungry, or thirsty, or a stranger, or naked, or sick, or in prison, and we would not help you?' The King will answer them back, 'I tell you, indeed, whenever you refused to help one of these least important ones, you refused to help me.' These, then, will be sent off to eternal punishment; the righteous will go to eternal life."

4
Jesus Teaches

Matthew has collected much of the teaching of Jesus into the Sermon on the Mount. This shows how Jesus' followers ought to live, knowing that God is their Father and King.

But Jesus said many other things while he was teaching. He warned people against many of the teachers of the religious Law and the Pharisees. These Pharisees were proud because they obeyed all the religious Law, and they despised ordinary people. Jesus called them hypocrites, a word which means actors in a play. They were just acting. But it is important to remember that Jesus was not criticizing Jewish teachers only, and that many Christians have been hypocrites.

The Sermon on the Mount

Jesus saw the crowds and went up a hill, where he sat down. His disciples gathered round him, and he began to teach them:

True Happiness

"Happy are those who know they are spiritually poor;
   the Kingdom of heaven belongs to them!
"Happy are those who mourn;
   God will comfort them!
"Happy are the meek;
   they will receive what God has promised!
"Happy are those whose greatest desire is to do what God
      requires;
   God will satisfy them fully!
"Happy are those who are merciful to others;
   God will be merciful to them!
"Happy are the pure in heart;
   they will see God!
"Happy are those who work for peace among men;
   God will call them his sons!
"Happy are those who are persecuted because they do what
      God requires;
   the Kingdom of heaven belongs to them!
"Happy are you when men insult you, and persecute you, and tell all

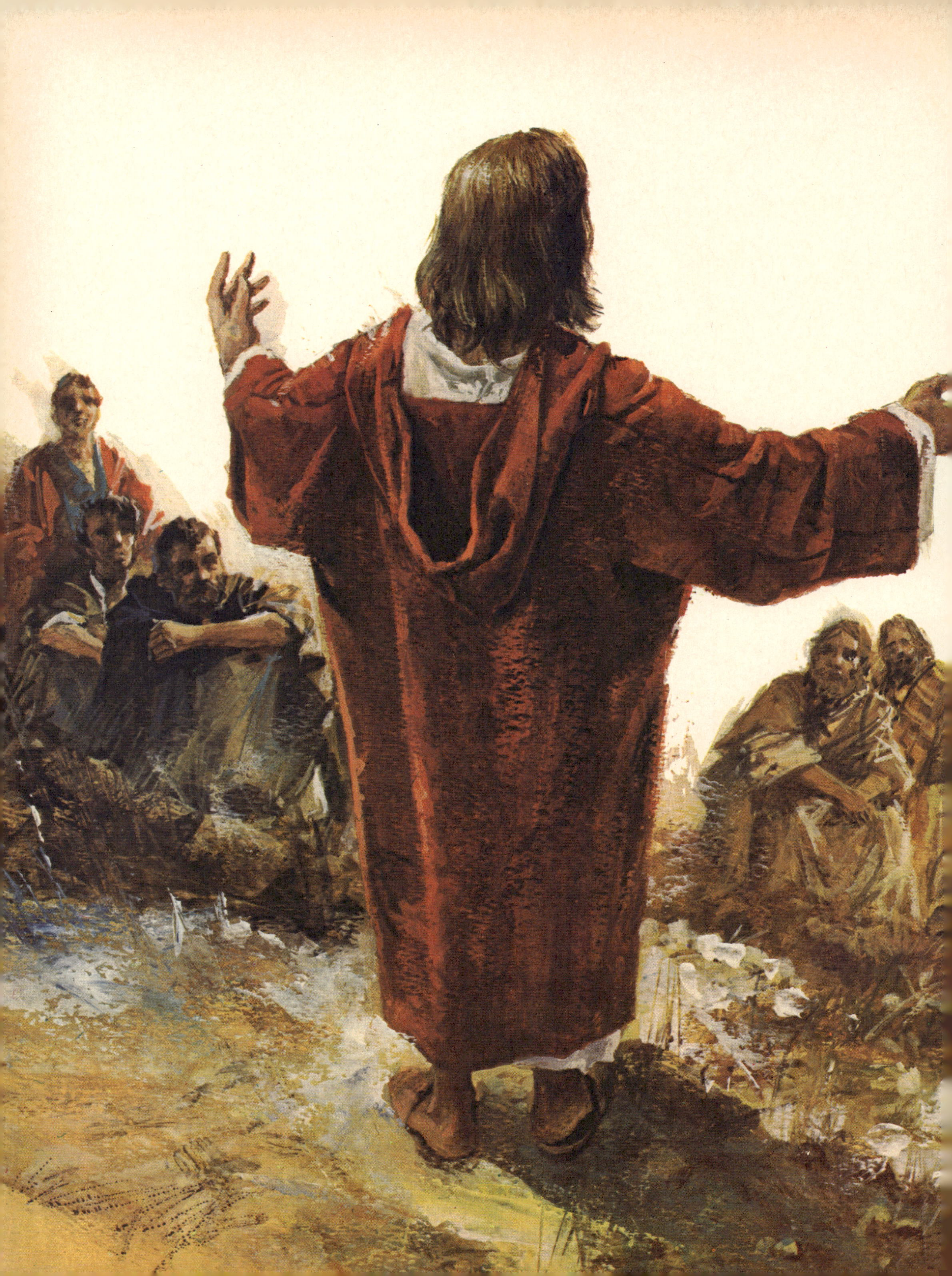

kinds of evil lies against you because you are my followers. Be glad and happy, because a great reward is kept for you in heaven. This is how men persecuted the prophets who lived before you."

Salt and Light

"You are like salt for all mankind. But if salt loses its taste, there is no way to make it salty again. It has become worthless, so it is thrown away and people walk on it.

"You are like light for the whole world. A city built on a hill cannot be hid. No one lights a lamp to put it under a bowl; instead he puts it on the lampstand, where it gives light for everyone in the house. In the same way your light must shine before people, so that they will see the good things you do and give praise to your Father in heaven."

Teaching about the Law

"Do not think that I have come to do away with the Law of Moses and the teachings of the prophets. I have not come to do away with them, but to make their teachings come true. Remember this! As long as heaven and earth last, the least point or the smallest detail of the Law will not be done away with — not until the end of all things. So then, whoever disobeys even the smallest of the commandments, and teaches others to do the same, will be least in the Kingdom of heaven. On the other hand, whoever obeys the Law, and teaches others to do the same, will be great in the Kingdom of heaven. I tell you, then, that you will be able to enter the Kingdom of heaven only if you are more faithful than the teachers of the Law and the Pharisees in doing what God requires."

Teaching about Anger

"You have heard that men were told in the past, 'Do not murder; anyone who commits murder will be brought before the judge.' But now I tell you: whoever is angry with his brother will be brought before the judge; whoever calls his brother 'You good-for-nothing!' will be brought before the Council; and whoever calls his brother a worthless fool will be in danger of going to the fire of hell. So if you are about to offer your gift to God at the altar and there you remember that your brother has something against you, leave your gift there in front of the altar and go at once to make peace with your brother; then come back and offer your gift to God.

"If a man brings a lawsuit against you and takes you to court, be friendly with him while there is time, before you get to court; once you are there he will turn you over to the judge, who will hand you over to the police, and you will be put in jail. There you will stay, I tell you, until you pay the last penny of your fine."

Teaching about Adultery

"You have heard that it was said, 'Do not commit adultery.' But now I tell you: anyone who looks at a woman and wants to possess her is guilty of committing adultery with her in his heart. So if your right eye causes you to sin, take it out and throw it away! It is much better for you to lose a part of your body than to have your whole body thrown into hell. If your right hand causes you to sin, cut if off and throw it away! It is much better for you to lose one of your limbs than to have your whole body go off to hell."

Teaching about Divorce

"It was also said, 'Anyone who divorces his wife must give her a written notice of divorce.' But now I tell you: if a man divorces his wife, and she has not been unfaithful, then he is guilty of making her commit adultery if she marries again; and the man who marries her also commits adultery."

Teaching about Vows

"You have also heard that men were told in the past, 'Do not break your promise, but do what you have sworn to the Lord to do.' But now I tell you: do not use any vow when you make a promise; do not swear by heaven, because it is God's throne; nor by earth, because its is the resting place for his feet; nor by Jerusalem, because it is the city of the great King. Do not even swear by your head, because you cannot make a single hair white or black. Just say 'Yes' or 'No' — anything else you have to say comes from the Evil One."

Teaching about Revenge

"You have heard that it was said, 'An eye for an eye, and a tooth for a tooth.' But now I tell you: do not take revenge on someone who does you wrong. If anyone slaps you on the right cheek, let him slap your left cheek too. And if someone takes you to court to sue you for your shirt, let him have your coat as well. And if one of the occupation troops forces you to carry his pack one mile, carry it another mile. When someone asks you for something, give it to him; when someone wants to borrow something, lend it to him."

Love for Enemies

"You have heard that it was said, 'Love your friends, hate your enemies.' 'But now I tell you: love your enemies, and pray for those who persecute you, so that you will become the sons of your Father in heaven. For he makes his sun to shine on bad and good people alike, and gives rain to those who do good and those who do evil. Why should God reward you if you love only the people who love you? Even the tax collectors do that! And if you speak only to your friends, have you done anything out of the ordinary? Even the pagans do that! You must be perfect — just as your Father in heaven is perfect."

Teaching about Charity

"Be careful not to perform your religious duties in public so that people will see what you do. If you do these things publicly you will not have any reward from your Father in heaven.

"So when you give something to a needy person, do not make a big show of it, as the hypocrites do in the synagogues and on the streets. They do it so that people will praise them. Remember this! They have already been paid in full. But when you help a needy person, do it in such a way that even your closest friend will not know about it, but it will be a private matter. And your Father, who sees what you do in private, will reward you."

Teaching about Prayer

"When you pray, do not be like the hypocrites! They love to stand up and pray in the synagogues and on the street corners so that everyone will see them. Remember this! They have already been paid in full. But when you pray, go to your room and close the door, and pray to your Father, who is unseen. And your Father, who sees what you do in private, will reward you.

"In your prayers do not use a lot of meaningless words, as the pagans do, who think that God will hear them because of their long prayers. Do not be like them; your Father already knows what you need before you ask him. This, then, is how you should pray:
'Our Father in heaven:
May your holy name be honoured;
may your kingdom come;
may your will be done on earth as it is in heaven.
Give us today the food we need.
Forgive us the wrongs that we have done, as we forgive the wrongs that others have done us.
Do not bring us to hard testing,
but keep us safe from the Evil One.' "

Teaching about Forgiveness

"If you forgive others the wrongs they have done you, your Father in heaven will also forgive you. But if you do not forgive the wrongs of others, then your Father in heaven will not forgive the wrongs you have done."

Teaching about Fasting

"And when you fast, do not put on a sad face as the hypocrites do. They go around with a hungry look so that everyone will see that they are fasting. Remember this! They have already been paid in full. When you go without food, wash your face and comb your hair, so that others cannot know that you are fasting — only your Father, who is unseen, will know. And your Father, who sees what you do in private, will reward you."

Riches in Heaven

"Do not save riches for yourselves here on earth, where moths and rust destroy, and robbers break in and steal. Instead, save riches for yourselves in heaven, where moths and rust cannot destroy, and robbers cannot break in and steal. For your heart will always be where your riches are."

The Light of the Body

"The eyes are like a lamp for the body. If your eyes are clear, your whole body will be full of light; but if your eyes are bad, your body will be in darkness. So if the light in you is darkness, how terribly dark it will be!"

God and Possessions

"No one can be a slave to two masters; he will hate one and love the other; he will be loyal to one and despise the other. You cannot serve both God and money.

"This is why I tell you: do not be worried about the food and drink you need to stay alive, or about clothes for your body. After all, isn't life worth more than food? And isn't the body worth more than clothes? Look at the birds flying around: they do not plant seeds, gather a harvest, and put it in barns; your Father in heaven takes care of them! Aren't you worth much more than birds? Which one of you can live a few more years by worrying about it?

"And why worry about clothes? Look how the wild flowers grow: they do not work or make clothes for themselves. But I tell you that not even Solomon, as rich as he was, had clothes as beautiful as one of these flowers. It is God who clothes the wild grass — grass that is here today, gone tomorrow, burned up in the oven. Won't he be all the more sure to clothe you? How little faith you have! So do not start worrying: 'Where will my food come from? or my drink? or my clothes?' (These are the things the heathen are always concerned about.) Your Father in heaven knows that you need all these things. Instead, be concerned above everything else within his Kingdom and with what he requires, and he will provide you with all these other things. So do not worry about tomorrow; it will have enough worries of its own. There is no need to add to the troubles each day brings."

Judging Others

"Do not judge others, so that God will not judge you — because God will judge you in the same way you judge others, and he will apply to you the same rules you apply to others. Why, then, do you look at the speck in your brother's eye, and pay no attention to the log in your own eye? How dare you say to your brother, 'Please, let me take that speck out of your eye,' when you have a log in your own eye? You hypocrite! Take the log out of your own eye first, and then you will be able to see and take the speck out of your brother's eye.

"Do not give what is holy to dogs — they will only turn and attack you; do not throw your pearls in front of pigs — they will only trample them underfoot."

Ask, Seek, Knock

"Ask, and you will receive; seek, and you will find; knock, and the door will be opened to you. For everyone who asks will receive, and he who seeks will find, and the door will be opened to him who knocks. Would any of you who are fathers give your son a stone, when he asks you for bread? Or would you give him a snake, when he asks you for fish? As bad as you are, you know how to give good things to your children. How much more, then, your Father in heaven will give good things to those who ask him!

"Do for others what you want them to do for you: this is the meaning of the Law of Moses and the teaching of the prophets."

The Narrow Gate

"Go in through the narrow gate, because the gate is wide and the road is easy that leads to hell, and there are many who travel it. The gate is narrow and the way is hard that leads to life, and few people find it."

A Tree and its Fruit

"Watch out for false prophets; they come to you looking like sheep on the outside, but they are really like wild wolves on the inside. You will know them by the way they act. Thorn bushes do not bear grapes, and briers do not bear figs. A healthy tree bears good fruit, while a poor tree bears bad fruit. A healthy tree cannot bear bad fruit, and a poor tree cannot bear good fruit. Any tree that does not bear good fruit is cut down and thrown in the fire. So, then, you will know the false prophets by the way they act."

I Never Knew You

"Not everyone who calls me 'Lord, Lord,' will enter into the Kingdom of heaven, but only those who do what my Father in heaven wants them to do. When that Day comes, many will say to me, 'Lord, Lord! In your name we spoke God's message, by your name we drove out many demons and performed many miracles!' Then I will say to them, 'I never knew you. Away from me, you evildoers!'"

The Two House Builders

"So then, everyone who hears these words of mine and obeys them will be like a wise man who built his house on the rock. The rain poured down, the rivers flooded over, and the winds blew hard against that house. But it did not fall, because it had been built on the rock.

"But everyone who hears these words of mine and does not obey them will be like a foolish man who built his house on the sand. The rain poured down, the rivers flooded over, the winds blew hard against that house, and it fell. What a terrible fall that was!"

The Authority of Jesus

Jesus finished saying these things, and the crowd was amazed at the way he taught. He wasn't like their teachers of the Law; instead, he taught with authority.

Some Other Teaching Given by Jesus

Whom to Fear

"Do not be afraid of men. Whatever is covered up will be uncovered, and every secret will be made known. What I am telling you in the dark you must repeat in broad daylight, and what you have heard in private you must tell from the housetops. Do not be afraid of those who kill the body but cannot kill the soul; rather be afraid of God, who can destroy both body and soul in hell. You can buy two sparrows for a penny; yet not a single one of them falls to the ground without your Father's consent. As for you, even the hairs of your head have all been counted. So do not be afraid; you are worth much more than many sparrows!"

Who Belongs

"Whoever declares publicly that he belongs to me, I will do the same for him before my Father in heaven. But whoever denies publicly that he belongs to me, then I will deny him before my Father in heaven."

Not Peace, but a Sword

"Do not think that I have come to bring peace to the world; no, I did not come to bring peace, but a sword. I came to set sons against their fathers, daughters against their mothers, daughters-in-law against their mothers-in-law; a man's worst enemies will be the members of his own family.

"Whoever loves his father or mother more than me is not worthy of me; whoever loves his son or daughter more than me is not worthy of me. Whoever does not take up his cross and follow in my steps is not worthy of me. Whoever tries to gain his own life will lose it; whoever loses his life for my sake will gain it."
"Whoever welcomes you, welcomes me; and whoever welcomes me, welcomes the one who sent me. Whoever welcomes God's messenger because he is God's messenger will share in his reward; and whoever

welcomes a truly good man, because he is that, will share in his reward. And remember this! Whoever gives even a drink of cold water to one of the least of these my followers, because he is my follower, will certainly receive his reward."

Come to Me and Rest

"Come to me, all of you who are tired from carrying your heavy loads, and I will give you rest. Take my yoke and put it on you, and learn from me, because I am gentle and humble in spirit; and you will find rest. The yoke I will give you is easy, and the load I will put on you is light."

The Question about Paying Taxes

The Pharisees went off and made a plan to trap Jesus with questions. Then they sent some of their disciples and some members of Herod's party to Jesus. "Teacher," they said, "we know that you tell the truth. You teach the truth about God's will for man, without worrying about what people think, because you pay no attention to a man's status. Tell us, then, what do you think? Is it against our Law to pay taxes to the Roman Emperor, or not?"

Jesus was aware of their evil plan, however, and so he said, "You hypocrites! Why are you trying to trap me? Show me the coin to pay the tax!"

They brought him the coin, and he asked them, "Whose face and name are these?"

"The Emperor's," they answered.

So Jesus said to them, "Well, then, pay to the Emperor what belongs to him, and pay to God what belongs to God."

When they heard this, they were filled with wonder; and they left him and went away.

The Question about Rising from Death

That same day some Sadducees came to Jesus. (They are the ones who say that people will not rise from death.) "Teacher," they said, "Moses taught: 'If a man who has no children dies, his brother must marry the widow so they can have children for the dead man.' Now, there were seven brothers who used to live here. The oldest got married, and died without having children, so he left his widow to his brother. The same thing happened to the second brother, to the third, and finally to all seven. Last of all, the woman died. Now, on the day when the dead rise to life, whose wife will she be? All of them had married her."

Jesus answered them, "How wrong you are! It is because you don't know the Scriptures or God's power. For when the dead rise to life they will be like the angels in heaven, and men and women will not marry. Now, as for the dead rising to life: haven't you ever read what God has told you? He said, I am the God of Abraham, the God of Isaac, and the God of Jacob.' This means that he is the God of the living, not of the dead."

When the crowds heard this they were amazed at his teaching.

The Great Commandment

When the Pharisees heard that Jesus had silenced the Sadducees, they came together, and one of them, a teacher of the Law, tried to trap him with a question. "Teacher," he asked, "which is the greatest commandment in the Law?"

Jesus answered, "'You must love the Lord your God with all your heart, with all your soul, and with all your mind.' This is the greatest and the most important commandment. The second most important commandment is like it: 'You must love your fellow-man as yourself.' The whole Law of Moses and the teachings of the prophets depend on these two commandments."

Jesus Warns against Hypocrisy

Jesus Warns against the Teachers of the Law and the Pharisees

Then Jesus spoke to the crowds and to his disciples. "The teachers of the Law and the Pharisees," he said, "are the authorized interpreters of Moses' Law. So you must obey and follow everything they tell you to do; do not, however, imitate their actions, because they do not practise what they preach. They fix up heavy loads and tie them on men's backs, yet they aren't willing even to lift a finger to help them carry those loads. They do everything just so people will see them. See how big are the containers with scripture verses on their foreheads and arms, and notice how long are the hems of their cloaks! They love the best places at feasts and the reserved seats in the synagogues; they love to be greeted with respect in the market places and have people call them 'Teacher'. You must not be called 'Teacher', because you are all brothers of one another and have only one Teacher. And you must not call anyone here on earth 'Father', because you have only the one Father in heaven. Nor should you be called 'Leader', because your one and only leader is the Messiah. The greatest one among you must be your servant. Whoever makes himself great will be humbled, and whoever humbles himself will be made great."

Jesus Condemns their Hypocrisy

"How terrible for you, teachers of the Law and Pharisees! Hypocrites!

You lock the door to the Kingdom of heaven in men's faces, but you yourselves will not go in, and neither will you let people in who are trying to go in!

["How terrible for you, teachers of the Law and Pharisees! Hypocrites! You take advantage of widows and rob them of their homes, and then make a show of saying long prayers! Because of this your punishment will be all the worse!]

"How terrible for you, teachers of the Law and Pharisees! Hypocrites! You sail the seas and cross whole countries to win one convert; and when you succeed, you make him twice as deserving of going to hell as you yourselves are!

"How terrible for you, blind guides! You teach, 'If a man swears by the temple he isn't bound by his vow; but if he swears by the gold in the temple, he is bound.' Blind fools! Which is more important, the gold or the temple which makes the gold holy? You also teach, 'If a man swears by the altar he isn't bound by his vow; but if he swears by the gift on the altar, he is bound.' How blind you are! Which is more important, the gift or the altar which makes the gift holy? So then, when a man swears by the altar he is swearing by it and by all the gifts on it; and when a man swears by the temple he is swearing by it and by God, the one who lives there; and when a man swears by heaven he is swearing by God's throne and by him who sits on it.

"How terrible for you, teachers of the Law and Pharisees! Hypocrites! You give to God one tenth even of the seasoning herbs, such as mint, dill, and cummin, but you neglect to obey the really important teachings of the Law, such as justice and mercy and honesty. These you should practise, without neglecting the others. Blind guides! You strain a fly out of your drink, but swallow a camel!

"How terrible for you, teachers of the Law and Pharisees! Hypocrites! You clean the outside of your cup and plate, while the inside is full of things you have got by violence and selfishness. Blind Pharisee! Clean what is inside the cup first, and then the outside will be clean too!

"How terrible for you, teachers of the Law and Pharisees! Hypocrites! You are like whitewashed tombs, which look fine on the outside, but are full of dead men's bones and rotten stuff on the inside. In the same way, on the outside you appear to everybody as good, but inside you are full of hypocrisy and sins."

The Things that Make a Person Unclean

Then Jesus called the crowd to him and said to them, "Listen, and understand! It is not what goes into a person's mouth that makes him unclean; rather, what comes out of it makes him unclean."

Then the disciples came to him and said, "Do you know that the Pharisees had their feelings hurt by what you said?"

"Every plant which my Father in heaven did not plant will be pulled up," answered Jesus. "Don't worry about them! They are blind leaders; and when one blind man leads another one, both fall into a ditch."

Peter spoke up, "Tell us what this parable means."

Jesus said to them, "You are still no more intelligent than the others. Don't you understand? Anything that goes into a person's mouth goes into his stomach and then on out of the body. But things that come out of the mouth come from the heart; such things make a man unclean. For from his heart come the evil ideas which lead him to kill, commit adultery, and do other immoral things; to rob, lie, and slander others. These are the things that make a man unclean. But to eat without washing your hands as they say you should – this does not make a man unclean."

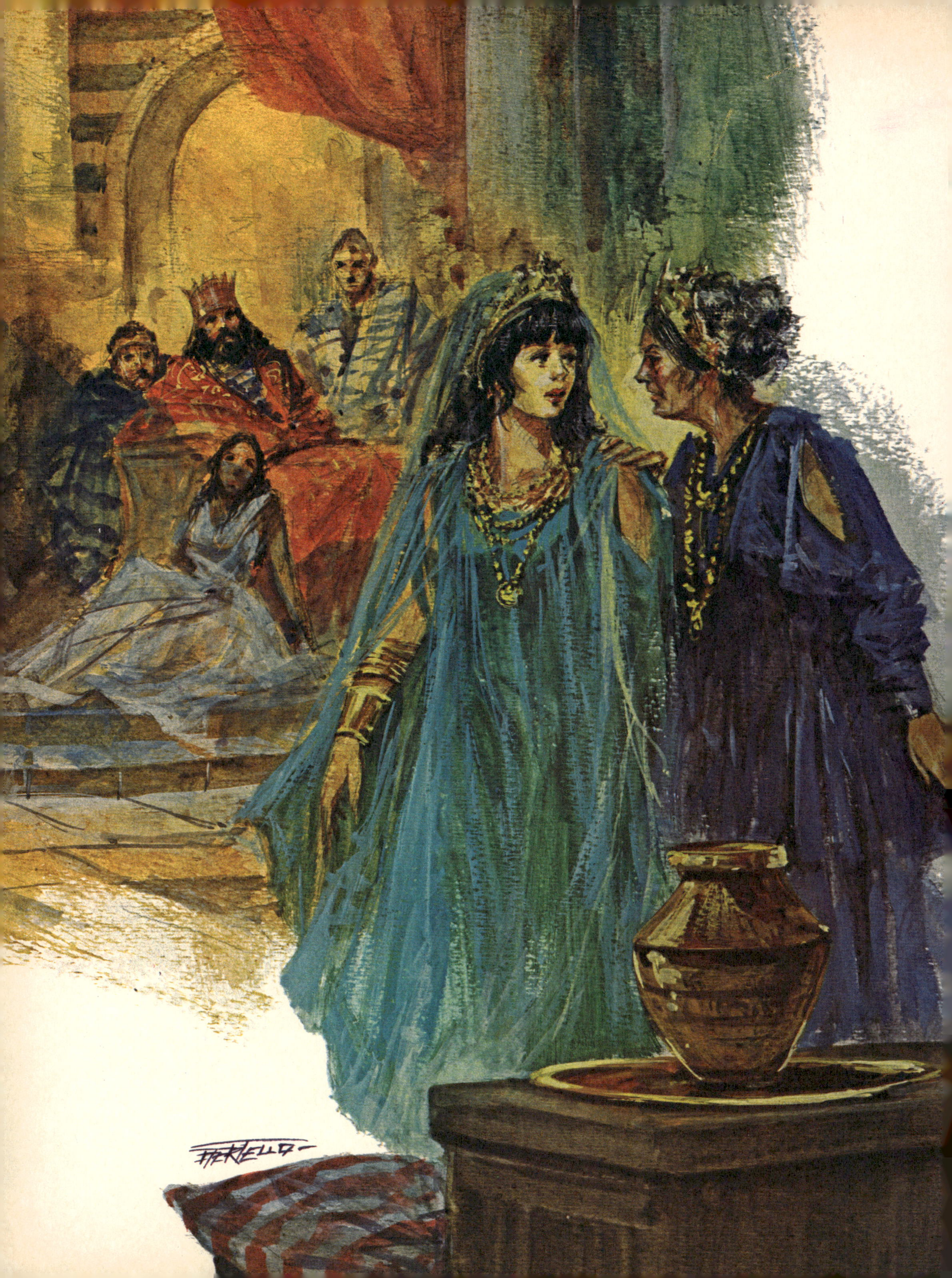

5
The Road to the Cross

What Jesus taught by living was even more important than what he taught by speaking. He taught us to be brave, although when his cousin John the Baptist was killed he saw clearly that he, too, would have to die because he was doing God's work. He taught us to be humble, because he himself humbly did what God asked him to do. As he said, he did not come to be served; he came to serve.

So he entered Jerusalem and taught in its temple.

John the Baptist is Killed

King Herod heard about Jesus' reputation, which had spread everywhere. Some people were saying, "John the Baptist has come back to life! That is why these powers are at work in him."

Others, however, said, "He is Elijah."

Others said, "He is a prophet, like one of the prophets of long ago."

When Herod heard it he said, "He is John the Baptist! I had his head cut off, but he has come back to life!" Herod himself had ordered John's arrest, and had him tied up and put in prison. Herod did this because of Herodias, whom he had married, even though she was the wife of his brother Philip. John the Baptist kept telling Herod, "It isn't right for you to marry your brother's wife!"

So Herodias held a grudge against John and wanted to kill him, but she could not because of Herod. Herod was afraid of John because he knew that John was a good and holy man, and so he kept him safe. He liked to listen to him, even though he became greatly disturbed every time he heard him.

Finally Herodias got her chance. It was on Herod's birthday, when he gave a feast for all the top government officials, the military chiefs, and the leading citizens of Galilee. The daughter of Herodias came in and danced, and pleased Herod and his guests. So the king said to the girl, "What would you like to have? I will give you anything you want." With many vows he said to her, "I promise that I will give you anything you ask for, even as much as half my kingdom!"

So the girl went out and asked her mother, "What shall I ask for?"

"The head of John the Baptist," she answered.

The girl hurried back at once to the king and demanded, "I want you to give me right now the head of John the Baptist on a plate!"

This made the king very sad; but he could not refuse her, because of the vows he had made in front of all his guests. So he sent off a guard at once with orders to bring John's head. The guard left, went to the prison and cut John's head off; then he brought it on a plate and gave it to the girl, who gave it to her mother. When John's disciples heard about this, they came and got his body and laid it in a grave.

Jesus Sees that he Must Die

Peter's Declaration about Jesus

Jesus went to the territory near the town of Caesarea Philippi, where he asked his disciples, "Who do men say the Son of Man is?"

"Some say John the Baptist," they answered. "Others say Elijah, while others say Jeremiah or some other prophet."

"What about you?" he asked them. "Who do you say I am?"

Simon Peter answered, "You are the Messiah, the Son of the living God."

"Good for you, Simon, son of John!" answered Jesus. "Because this truth did not come to you from any human being, but it was given to you directly by my Father in heaven. And so I tell you: you are a rock, Peter, and on this rock foundation I will build my church, which not even death will ever be able to overcome. I will give you the keys of the Kingdom of heaven; what you prohibit on earth will be prohibited in heaven; what you permit on earth will be permitted in heaven."

Then Jesus ordered his disciples not to tell anyone that he was the Messiah.

Jesus Speaks about his Suffering and Death

Then Jesus began to teach his disciples: "The Son of Man must suffer much, and be rejected by the elders, the chief priests, and the teachers of the Law. He will be put to death, and after three days he will rise to life." He made this very clear to them. So Peter took him aside and began to rebuke him. But Jesus turned round, looked at his disciples, and rebuked Peter. "Get away from me, Satan," he said. "Your thoughts are men's thoughts, not God's!"

Then Jesus called the crowd and his disciples to him. "If anyone wants to come with me," he told them, "he must forget himself, carry his cross, and follow me. For whoever wants to save his own life will lose it; but whoever loses his life for me and for the gospel will save it. Does a man gain anything if he wins the whole world but loses his life? Of course not! There is nothing a man can give to regain his life. If, then, a man is ashamed of me and of my teaching in this godless and wicked day, then the Son of Man will be ashamed of him when he comes in the glory of his Father with the holy angels."

And he went on to say, "Remember this! There are some here who will not die until they have seen the kingdom of God come with power."

The Transfiguration

Six days later Jesus took Peter, James, and John with him, and led them up a high mountain by themselves. As they looked on, a change came over him, and his clothes became shining white, whiter than anyone in the world could wash them. Then the three disciples saw Elijah and Moses, who were talking with Jesus. Peter spoke up and said to Jesus, "Teacher, it is a good thing that we are here. We will make three tents, one for you, one for Moses, and one for Elijah." He and the others were so frightened that he did not know what to say.

A cloud appeared and covered them with its shadow, and a voice came from the cloud, "This is my own dear Son — listen to him!" They took a quick look round but did not see anyone else; only Jesus was with them.

As they came down the mountain Jesus ordered them, "Don't tell anyone what you have seen, until the Son of Man has risen from death."

They obeyed his order, but among themselves they started discussing the matter, "What does this 'rising from death' mean?" And they asked Jesus, "Why do the teachers of the Law say that Elijah has to come first?"

His answer was, "Elijah does indeed come first to get everything ready. Yet why do the Scriptures say that the Son of Man will suffer much and be rejected? I tell you, however, that Elijah has already come, and that people did to him what they wanted to, just as the Scriptures say about him."

Jesus Teaches Humility

Who Is the Greatest?

They came to Capernaum, and after going indoors Jesus asked his disciples, "What were you arguing about on the road?"

But they would not answer him, because on the road they had been arguing among themselves about who was the greatest. Jesus sat down, called the twelve disciples and said to them, "Whoever wants to be first must place himself last of all and be the servant of all." He took a child and made him stand in front of them. Then he put his arms round him and said to them, "Whoever in my name welcomes one of these children, welcomes me; and whoever welcomes me, welcomes not only me but also the one who sent me."

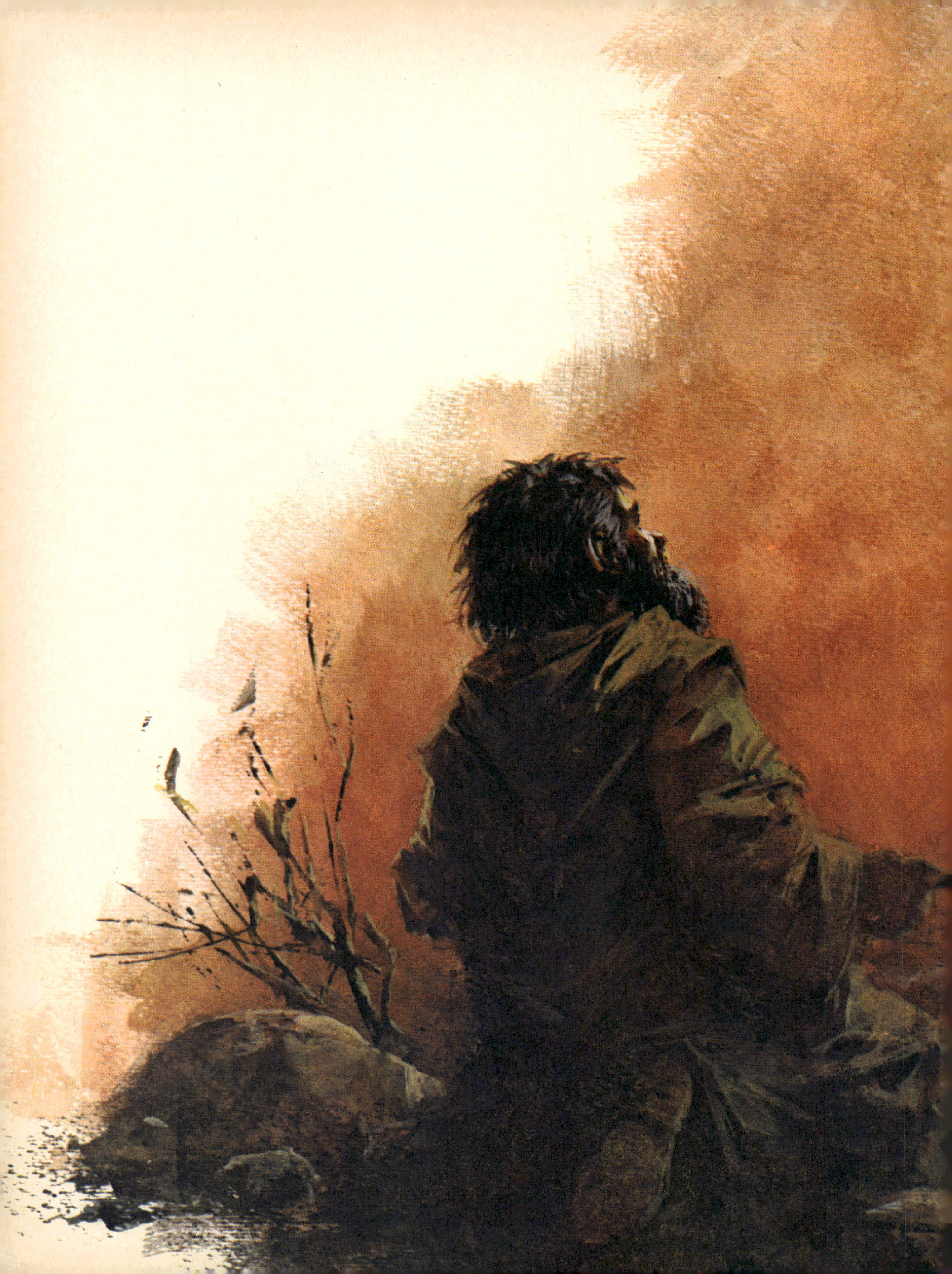

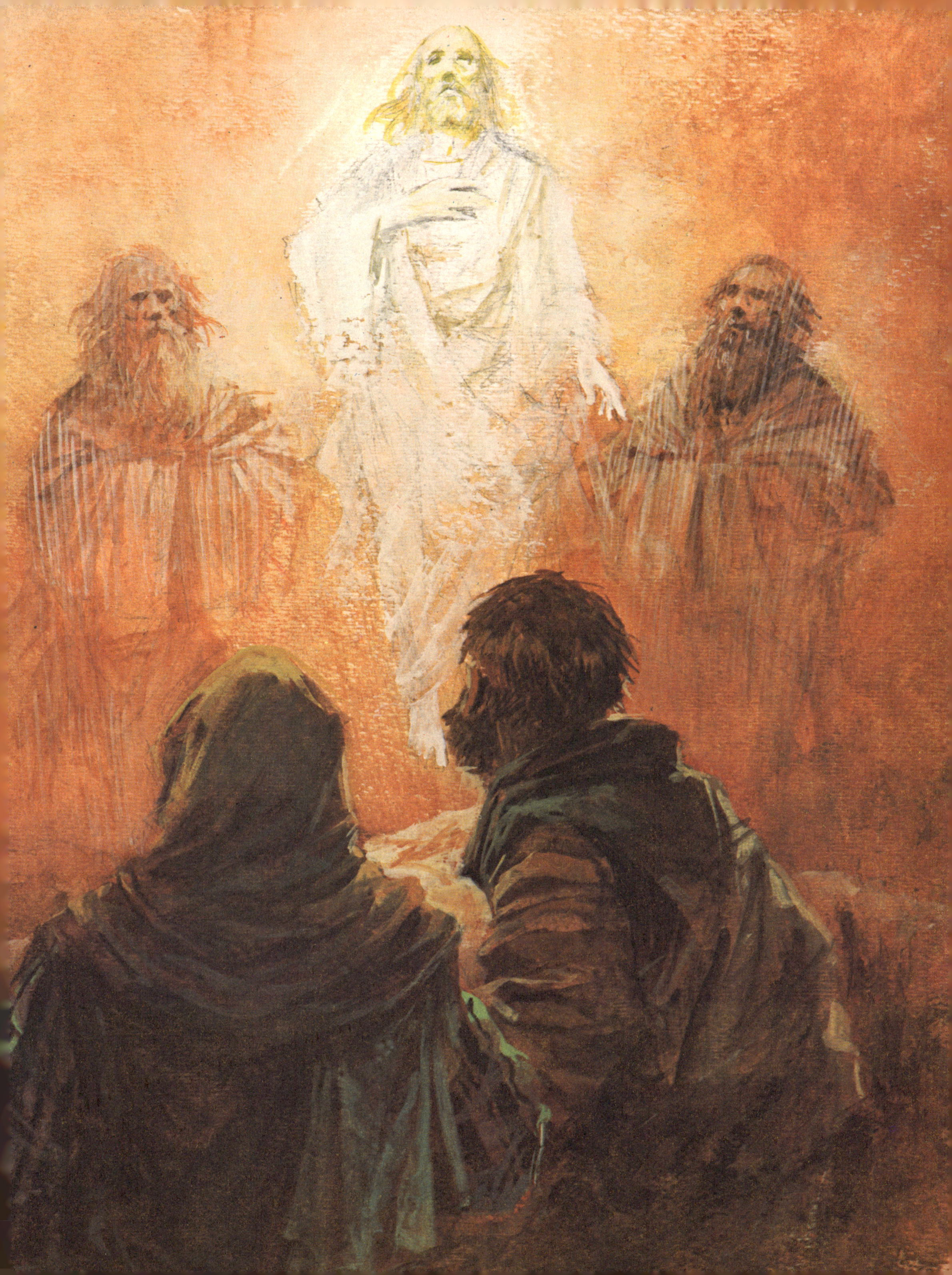

Who Is not against Us Is for Us

John said to him, "Teacher, we saw a man who was driving out demons in your name, and we told him to stop, because he doesn't belong to our group."

"Do not try to stop him," Jesus told them, "because no one who performs a miracle in my name will be able soon after to say bad things about me. For whoever is not against us is for us. Remember this! Anyone who gives you a drink of water because you belong to Christ will certainly receive his reward."

Jesus Blesses Little Children

Some people brought children to Jesus for him to touch them, but the disciples scolded those people. When Jesus noticed it, he was angry and said to his disciples, "Let the children come to me, and do not stop them, because the Kingdom of God belongs to such as these. Remember this! Whoever does not receive the Kingdom of God like a child will never enter it." Then he took the children in his arms, placed his hands on each of them, and blessed them.

The Rich Man

As Jesus was starting again on his way, a man ran up, knelt before him, and asked him, "Good Teacher, what must I do to receive eternal life?"

"Why do you call me good?" Jesus asked him. "No one is good except God alone. You know the commandments: 'Do not murder; do not commit adultery; do not steal; do not lie; do not cheat; honour your father and mother.'"

"Teacher," the man said, "ever since I was young I have obeyed all these commandments."

Jesus looked straight at him with love and said, "You need only one thing. Go and sell all you have and give the money to the poor, and you will have riches in heaven; then come and follow me." When the man heard this, gloom spread over his face and he went away sad, because he was very rich.

Jesus looked round at his disciples and said to them, "How hard it will be for rich people to enter the Kingdom of God!"

The disciples were shocked at these words, but Jesus went on to say, "My children, how hard it is to enter the Kingdom of God! It is much harder for a rich man to enter the Kingdom of God than for a camel to go through the eye of a needle."

A Samaritan Village Refuses to Receive Jesus

As the days drew near when Jesus would be taken up to heaven, he

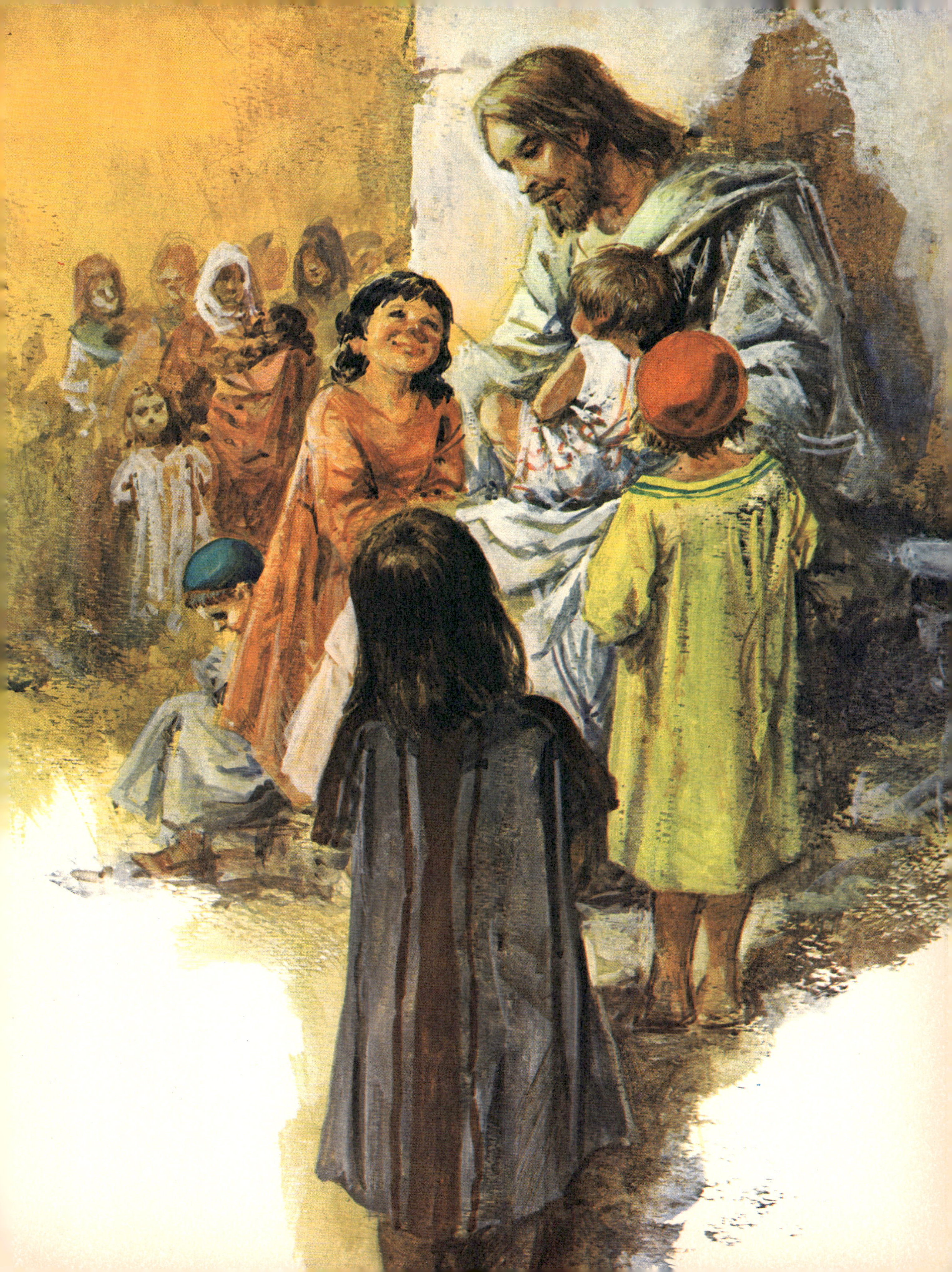

made up his mind and set out on his way to Jerusalem. He sent messengers ahead of him, who left and went into a Samaritan village to get everything ready for him. But the people there would not receive him, because it was plain that he was going to Jerusalem. When the disciples James and John saw this they said, "Lord, do you want us to call fire down from heaven and destroy them?"

Jesus turned and rebuked them; and they went on to another village.

The Would-be Followers of Jesus

As they went on their way, a certain man said to Jesus, "I will follow you wherever you go."

Jesus said to him, "Foxes have holes, and birds have nests, but the Son of Man has no place to lie down and rest." He said to another man, "Follow me."

But that man said, "Sir, first let me go back and bury my father."

Jesus answered, "Let the dead bury their own dead. You go and preach the Kingdom of God."

Another man said, "I will follow you, sir; but first let me go and say good-bye to my family."

Jesus said to him, "Anyone who starts to plough and then keeps looking back is of no use for the Kingdom of God."

Jesus Sends out the Seventy-two

After this the Lord chose another seventy-two men and sent them out, two by two, to go ahead of him to every town and place where he himself was about to go. He said to them, "There is a large harvest, but few workers to gather it in. Pray to the owner of the harvest that he will send out workers to gather in his harvest. Go! I am sending you like lambs among wolves. Don't take a purse, or a beggar's bag, or shoes; don't stop to greet anyone on the road. Whenever you go into a house, first say, 'Peace be with this house.' If a peace-loving man lives there, let your greeting of peace remain on him; if not, take back your greeting of peace. Stay in that same house, eating and drinking what they offer you, because a worker should be given his pay. Don't move round from one house to another. Whenever you go into a town and are made welcome, eat what is set before you, heal the sick in that town, and say to the people there, 'The Kingdom of God has come near you.' But whenever you go into a town and are not welcomed there, go out in the streets and say, 'Even the dust from your town that sticks to our feet we wipe off against you; but remember this, the Kingdom of God has come near you!' I tell you that on the Judgment Day God will show more mercy to Sodom than to that town!"

The Unbelieving Towns

"How terrible it will be for you, Chorazin! How terrible for you too, Bethsaida! If the miracles which were performed in you had been performed in Tyre and Sidon, long ago the people there would have sat down, put on sackcloth, and sprinkled ashes on themselves to show that they had turned from their sins! God will show more mercy on the Judgment Day to Tyre and Sidon than to you. And as for you, Capernaum! You wanted to lift yourself up to heaven? You will be thrown down to hell!"

Jesus said to his disciples, "Whoever listens to you, listens to me; whoever rejects you, rejects me; and whoever rejects me, rejects the one who sent me."

The Return of the Seventy-two

The seventy-two men came back in great joy. "Lord," they said, "even the demons obeyed us when we commanded them in your name!"

Jesus answered them, "I saw Satan fall like lightning from heaven. Listen! I have given you authority, so that you can walk on snakes and scorpions, and over all the power of the Enemy, and nothing will hurt you. But don't be glad because the evil spirits obey you; rather be glad because your names are written in heaven."

At that time Jesus was filled with joy by the Holy Spirit, and said, "Father, Lord of heaven and earth! I thank you because you have shown to the unlearned what you have hidden from the wise and learned. Yes, Father, this was done by your own choice and pleasure.

"My Father has given me all things. No one knows who the Son is except the Father, and no one knows who the Father is except the Son and those to whom the Son wants to reveal him."

Then Jesus turned to the disciples and said to them privately, "How fortunate you are, to see the things you see! Many prophets and kings, I tell you, wanted to see what you see, but they could not, and to hear what you hear, but they did not."

Jesus Heals a Sick Man

One Sabbath day Jesus went to eat a meal at the home of one of the leading Pharisees; and people were watching Jesus closely. A man whose legs and arms were swollen came to Jesus, and Jesus spoke up and asked the teachers of the Law and the Pharisees, "Does our Law allow healing on the Sabbath, or not?"

But they would not say a thing. Jesus took the man, healed him and sent him away. Then he said to them, "If any one of you had a son or an ox that happened to fall in a well on a Sabbath, would you not pull him out at once on the Sabbath itself?"

But they were not able to answer him about this.

Humility and Hospitality

Jesus noticed how some of the guests were choosing the best places, so he told this parable to all of them, "When someone invites you to a wedding feast, do not sit down in the best place. It could happen that someone more important than you had been invited, and your host, who invited both of you, would come and say to you, 'Let him have this place.' Then you would be ashamed and have to sit in the lowest place. Instead, when you are invited, go and sit in the lowest place, so that your host will come to you and say, 'Come on up, my friend, to a better place.' This will bring you honour in the presence of all the other guests. Because everyone who makes himself great will be humbled, and everyone who humbles himself will be made great."

Then Jesus said to his host, "When you give a lunch or a dinner, do not invite your friends, or your brothers, or your relatives, or your rich neighbours — because they will invite you back and in this way you will be paid for what you did. When you give a feast, invite the poor, the crippled, the lame, and the blind, and you will be blessed; because they are not able to pay you back. You will be paid by God when the good people rise from death."

Jesus Visits Martha and Mary

As Jesus and his disciples went on their way, he came to a certain village where a woman named Martha welcomed him in her home. She had a sister named Mary, who sat down at the feet of the Lord and listened to his teaching. Martha was upset over all the work she had to do; so she came and said, "Lord, don't you care that my sister has left me to do all the work by myself? Tell her to come and help me!"

The Lord answered her, "Martha, Martha! You are worried and troubled over so many things, but just one is needed. Mary has chosen the right thing, and it will not be taken away from her."

The Request of James and John

Then James and John, the sons of Zebedee, came to Jesus. "Teacher," they said, "there is something we want you to do for us."

"What do you want me to do for you?" Jesus asked them.

They answered, "When you sit on your throne in the glorious Kingdom, we want you to let us sit with you, one at your right and one at your left."

Jesus said to them, "You don't know what you are asking for. Can you drink the cup that I must drink? Can you be baptized in the way I must be baptized?"

"We can," they answered.

Jesus said to them, "You will indeed drink the cup I must drink and be baptized in the way I must be baptized. But I do not have the right to choose who will sit at my right and my left. It is God who will give these places to those for whom he has prepared them."

When the other ten disciples heard about this they became angry with James and John. So Jesus called them all together to him and said, "You know that the men who are considered rulers have power over the people, and their leaders rule over them. This, however, is not the way it is among you. If one of you wants to be great, he must be the servant of the rest; and if one of you wants to be first, he must be the slave of all. For even the Son of Man did not come to be served; he came to serve and to give his life to redeem many people."

Jesus' Love for Jerusalem

Some Pharisees came to Jesus and said to him. "You must get out of here and go somewhere else, because Herod wants to kill you."

Jesus answered them, "Go tell that fox: 'I am driving out demons and performing cures today and tomorrow, and on the third day I shall finish my work.' Yet I must be on my way today, tomorrow, and the

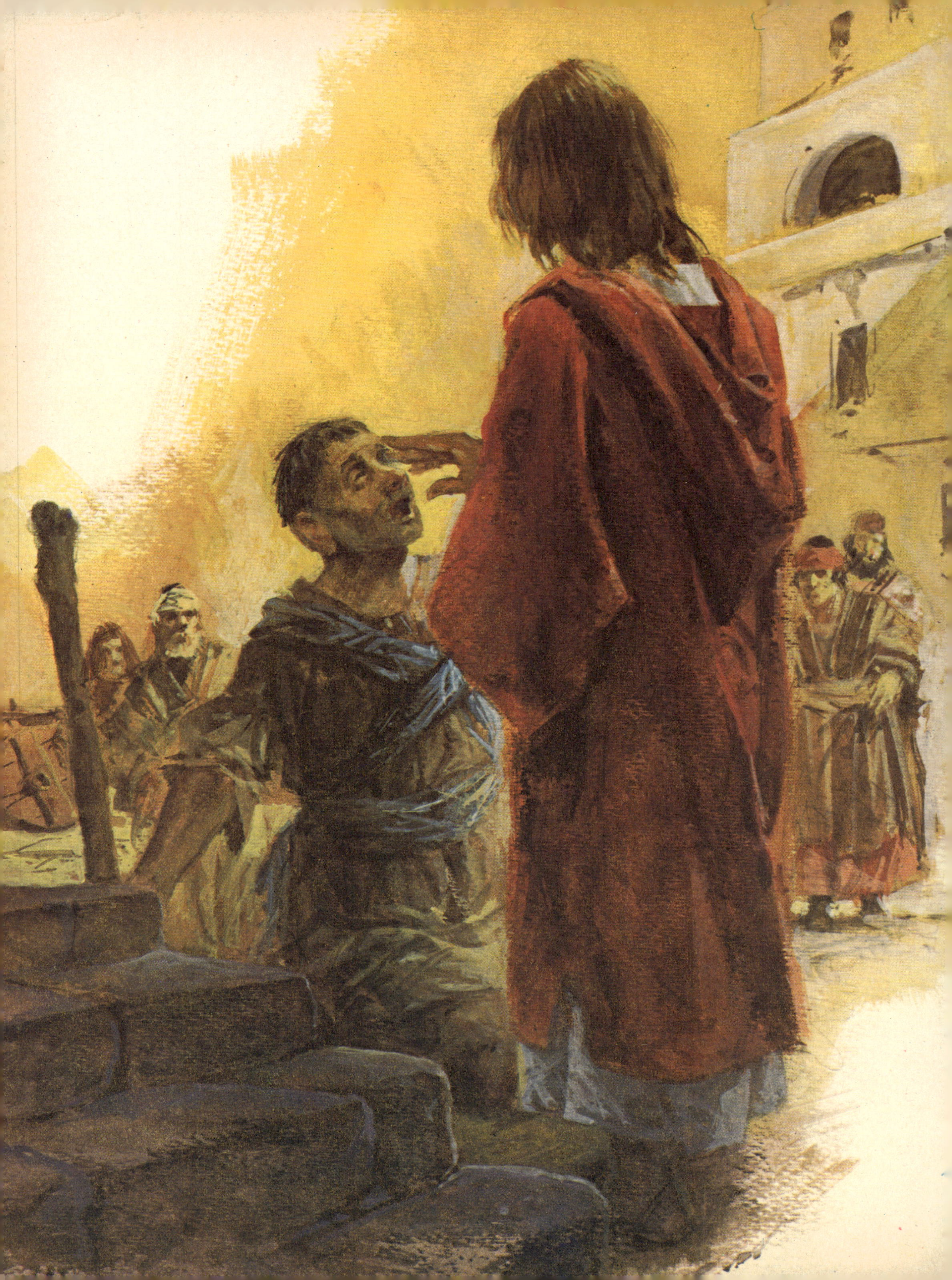

next day; it is not right for a prophet to be killed anywhere except in Jerusalem.

"Jerusalem, Jerusalem! You kill the prophets, you stone the messengers God has sent you! How many times I wanted to put my arms round all your people, just as a hen gathers her chicks under her wings, but you would not let me! Now your home will be completely forsaken. You will not see me, I tell you, until the time comes when you say, 'God bless him who comes in the name of the Lord.'"

Jesus Enters Jerusalem

Jesus Heals a Blind Beggar

Jesus was coming near Jericho, and a certain blind man was sitting by the road, begging. When he heard the crowd passing by he asked, "What is this?"

"Jesus of Nazareth is passing by," they told him.

He cried out, "Jesus! Son of David! Have mercy on me!"

The people in front scolded him and told him to be quiet. But he shouted even more loudly, "Son of David! Have mercy on me!"

When he came near, Jesus asked him, "What do you want me to do for you?"

"Sir," he answered, "I want to see again."

Then Jesus said to him, "See! Your faith has made you well."

At once he was able to see, and he followed Jesus, giving thanks to God. When the crowd saw it, they all praised God.

Jesus and Zacchaeus

Jesus went on into Jericho and was passing through. There was a chief tax collector there, named Zacchaeus, who was rich. He was trying to see who Jesus was, but he was a little man and could not see Jesus because of the crowd. So he ran ahead of the crowd and climbed a sycamore tree to see Jesus, who would be going that way. When Jesus came to that place he looked up and said to Zacchaeus, "Hurry down, Zacchaeus, because I must stay in your house today."

Zacchaeus hurried down and welcomed him with great joy. All the people who saw it started grumbling, "This man has gone as a guest to the home of a sinner!"

Zacchaeus stood up and said to the Lord, "Listen, sir! I will give half my belongings to the poor; and if I have cheated anyone, I will pay him back four times as much."

Jesus said to him, "Salvation has come to this house today; this man, also, is a descendant of Abraham. For the Son of Man came to seek and to save the lost."

The Triumphant Entry into Jerusalem

As they came near Jerusalem, at the towns of Bethphage and Bethany they came to the Mount of Olives. Jesus sent two of his disciples on ahead with these instructions. "Go to the village there ahead of you. As soon as you get there you will find a colt tied up that has never been ridden. Untie it and bring it here. And if someone asks you, 'Why are you doing that?' tell him, 'The Master needs it and will send it back here at once.'"

So they went and found a colt out in the street, tied to the door of a house. As they were untying it, some of the bystanders asked them, "What are you doing untying that colt?"

They answered just as Jesus had told them, so the men let them go. They brought the colt to Jesus, threw their cloaks over the animal, and Jesus got on. Many people spread their cloaks on the road, while others

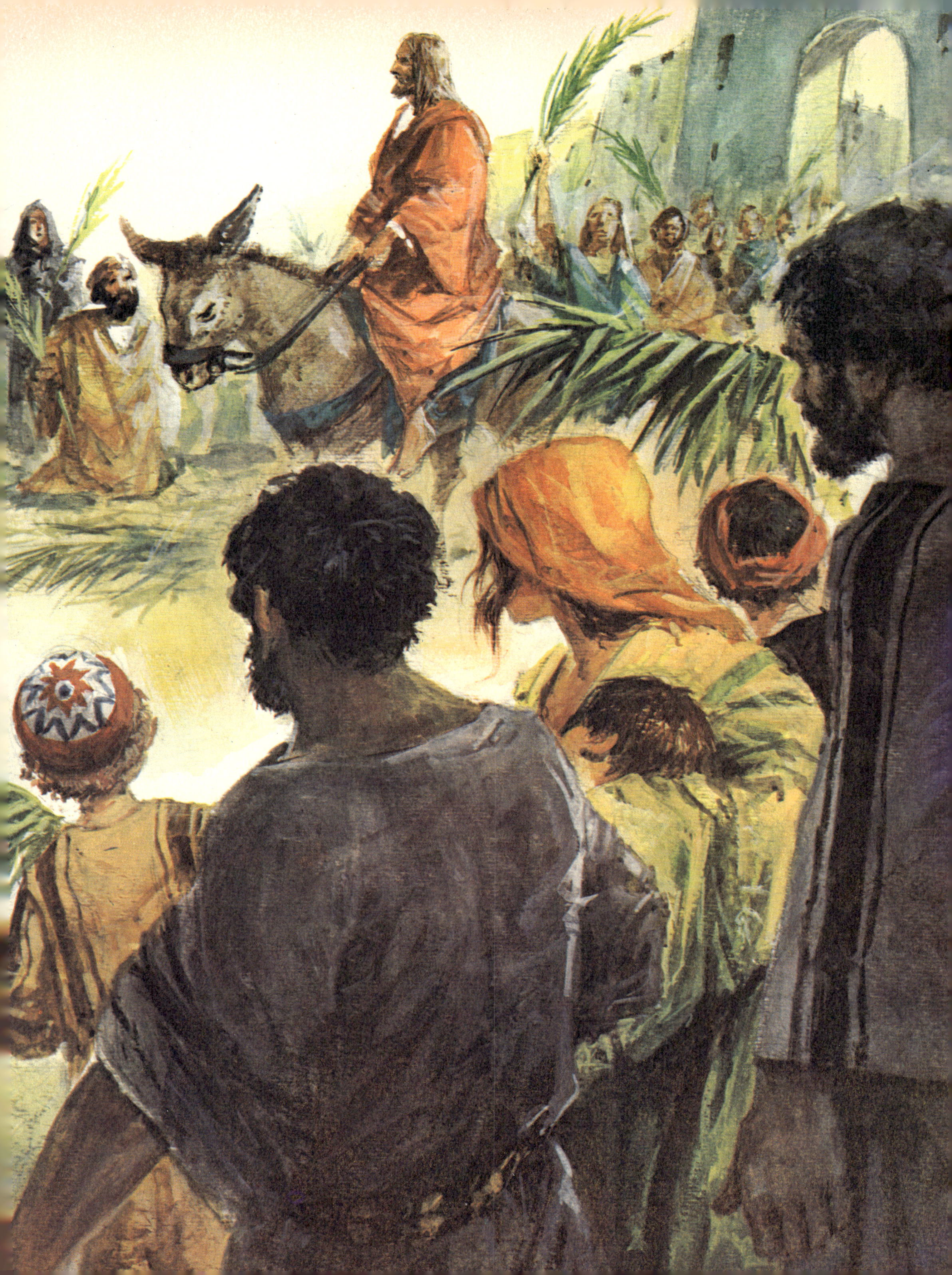

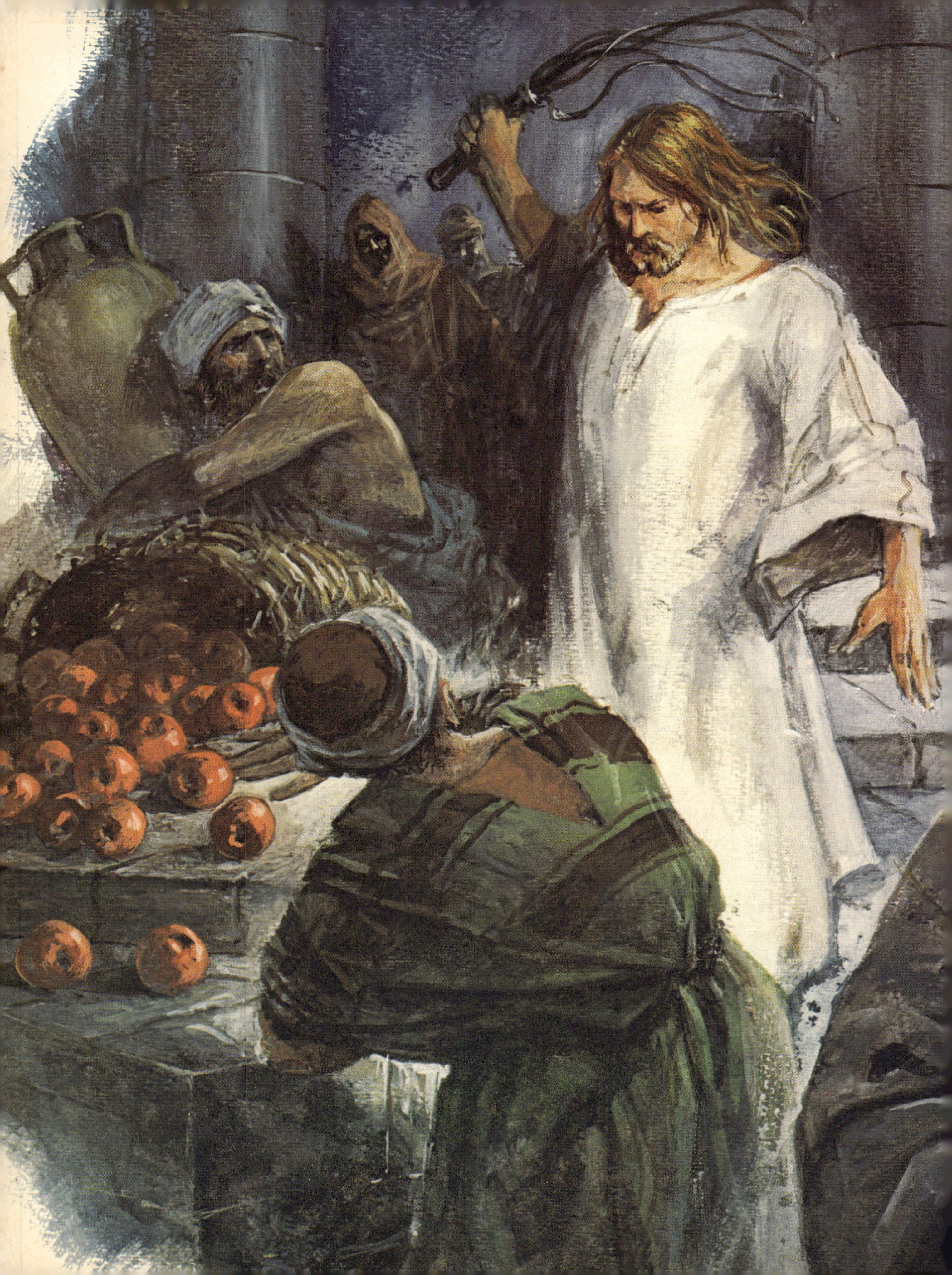

cut branches in the fields and spread them on the road. The people who were in front and those who followed behind began to shout, "Praise God! God bless him who comes in the name of the Lord! God bless the coming kingdom of our father David! Praise be to God!"

Jesus entered Jerusalem, went into the temple, and looked round at everything. But since it was already late in the day, he went out to Bethany with the twelve disciples.

Jesus Goes to the Temple

When they arrived in Jerusalem, Jesus went to the temple and began to drive out all those who bought and sold in the temple. He overturned the tables of the moneychangers and the stools of those who sold pigeons, and would not let anyone carry anything through the temple courts. He then taught the people, "It is written in the Scriptures that God said,

'My house will be called a house of prayer for all peoples.' But you have turned it into a hideout for thieves!" The chief priest and the teachers of the Law heard of this, so they began looking for some way to kill Jesus. They were afraid of him, because the whole crowd was amazed at his teaching. When evening came, Jesus and his disciples left the city.

The Question about Jesus' Authority

They came back to Jerusalem. As Jesus was walking in the temple, the chief priests, the teachers of the Law, and the elders came to him and asked him, "What right do you have to do these things? Who gave you the right to do them?"

Jesus answered them, "I will ask you just one question, and if you give me an answer I will tell you what right I have to do these things. Tell me, where did John's right to baptize come from: from God or from men?"

They started to argue among themselves, "What shall we say? If we answer, 'From God,' he will say, 'Why, then, did you not believe John?' But if we say, 'From men . . .' " (They were afraid of the people, because everyone was convinced that John had been a prophet.) So their answer to Jesus was, "We don't know."

Jesus said to them, "Neither will I tell you, then, by what right I do these things."

The Widow's Offering

As Jesus sat near the temple treasury he watched the people as they dropped in their money. Many rich men dropped in much money; then a poor widow came along and dropped in two little copper coins, worth about a penny. He called his disciples together and said to them, "I tell you that this poor widow put more in the offering box than all the others. For the others put in what they had to spare of their riches; but she, poor as she is, put in all she had — she gave all she had to live on."

Jesus Speaks of the Destruction of the Temple

As Jesus was leaving the temple, one of his disciples said, "Look, Teacher! What wonderful stones and buildings!"

Jesus answered, "You see these great buildings? Not a single stone here will be left in its place; every one of them will be thrown down."

Troubles and Persecutions

Jesus was sitting on the Mount of Olives, across from the temple, when

Peter, James, John, and Andrew came to him in private. "Tell us when this will be," they said, "and tell us what will happen to show that the time has come for all these things to take place."

Jesus said to them, "Watch out, and don't let anyone fool you. 'Many men will come in my name, saying, 'I am he!' and fool many people. And don't be troubled when you hear the noise of battles close by and news of battles far away. Such things must happen, but they do not mean that the end has come. Countries will fight each other, kingdoms will attack one another. There will be earthquakes everywhere, and there will be famines. These things are like the first pains of childbirth.

You yourselves must watch out. You will be arrested and taken to court. You will be beaten in the synagogues; you will stand before rulers and kings for my sake, to tell them the Good News. The gospel must first be preached to all peoples. And when they arrest you and take you to court, do not worry ahead of time about what you are going to say; when the time comes, say whatever is given to you then. For the words you speak will not be yours; they will come from the Holy Spirit. Men will hand over their own brothers to be put to death, and fathers will do the same to their children; children will turn against their parents and have them put to death. Everyone will hate you because of me. But whoever holds out to the end will be saved."

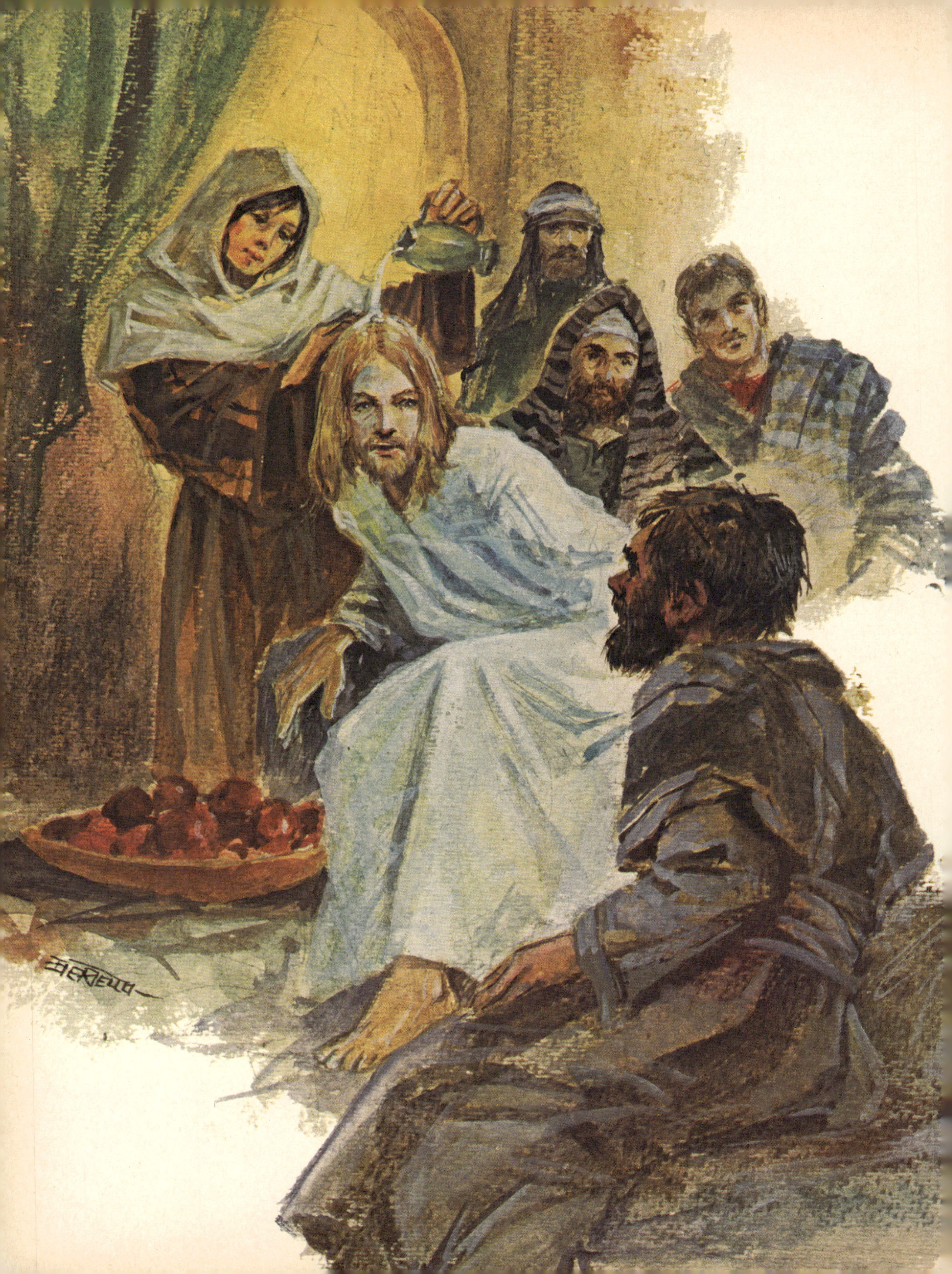

6
How Jesus Died

Jesus died as he lived. He was the humble servant of God, the loving brother of everyone. The story tells of how he was betrayed and left alone, how he was condemned to torture and death, and how he died full of courage and love. He gave his spirit back to God his Father, after this perfect sacrifice of his own life.

Many millions of people have been grateful for this, and their lives have been changed by this story. It is given here in the words of Mark, although at the end a few sentences are added from John and Luke.

The Plot against Jesus

It was now two days before the Feast of Passover and Unleavened Bread. The chief priests and the teachers of the Law were looking for a way to arrest Jesus secretly and put him to death. "We must not do it during the feast," they said, "or the people might riot."

Jesus Anointed at Bethany

Jesus was in the house of Simon the leper, in Bethany; while he was eating, a woman came in with an alabaster jar full of a very expensive perfume, made of pure nard. She broke the jar and poured the perfume on Jesus' head. Some of the people there became angry, and said to each other, "What was the use of wasting the perfume? It could have been sold for more than thirty pounds, and the money given to the poor!" And they criticized her harshly.

But Jesus said, "Leave her alone! Why are you bothering her? She has done a fine and beautiful thing for me. You will always have poor people with you, and any time you want to you can help them. But I shall not be with you always. She did what she could; she poured perfume on my body to prepare it ahead of time for burial. Now, remember this! Wherever the gospel is preached, all over the world, what she has done will be told in memory of her."

Judas Agrees to Betray Jesus

Then Judas Iscariot, one of the twelve disciples, went off to the chief priests in order to hand Jesus over to them. They were greatly pleased to hear what he had to say, and promised to give him money. So Judas started looking for a good chance to betray Jesus.

Jesus Eats the Passover Meal with his Disciples

On the first day of the Feast of Unleavened Bread, the day the lambs for the Passover meal were killed, Jesus' disciples asked him, "Where do you want us to go and get your Passover meal ready?"

Then Jesus sent two of them out with these instructions: "Go into the city, and a man carrying a jar of water will meet you. Follow him to the house he enters, and say to the owner of the house: 'The Teacher says, Where is my room where my disciples and I will eat the Passover meal?' Then he will show you a large upstairs room, fixed up and furnished, where you will get everything ready for us."

The disciples left, went to the city, and found everything just as Jesus had told them; and they prepared the Passover meal.

When it was evening, Jesus came with the twelve disciples. While they were at the table eating, Jesus said, "I tell you this: one of you will betray me — one who is eating with me."

The disciples were upset and began to ask him, one after the other, "Surely you don't mean me, do you?"

Jesus answered, "It will be one of you twelve, one who dips his bread in the dish with me. The Son of Man will die as the Scriptures say he will; but how terrible for that man who will betray the Son of Man! It would have been better for that man if he had never been born!"

The Lord's Supper

While they were eating, Jesus took the bread, gave a prayer of thanks, broke it, and gave it to his disciples. "Take it," he said, "this is my body."

Then he took the cup, gave thanks to God, and handed it to them; and they all drank from it. Jesus said, "This is my blood which is poured out for many, my blood which seals God's covenant. I tell you, I will never again drink this wine until the day I drink the new wine in the Kingdom of God."

Then they sang a hymn and went out to the Mount of Olives.

Jesus Predicts Peter's Denial

Jesus said to them, "All of you will run away and leave me, because the scripture says, 'God will kill the shepherd and the sheep will all be scattered.' But after I am raised to life I will go to Galilee ahead of you."

Peter answered, "I will never leave you, even though all the rest do!"

"Remember this!" Jesus said to Peter. "Before the cock crows two times tonight, you will say three times that you do not know me."

Peter answered even more strongly, "I will never say I do not know you, even if I have to die with you!"

And all the disciples said the same thing.

Jesus Prays in Gethsemane

They came to a place called Gethsemane, and Jesus said to his disciples, "Sit here while I pray."

Then he took Peter, James, and John with him. Distress and anguish came over him, and he said to them, "The sorrow in my heart is so great that it almost crushes me. Stay here and watch."

He went a little farther on, threw himself on the ground and prayed that, if possible, he might not have to go through the hour of suffering. "Father!" he prayed, "my Father! All things are possible for you. Take this cup away from me. But not what I want, but what you want."

Then he returned and found the three disciples asleep, and said to Peter, "Simon, are you asleep? Weren't you able to stay awake for one hour?" And he said to them, "Keep watch, and pray that you will not fall into temptation. The spirit is willing, but the flesh is weak."

He went away once more and prayed, saying the same words. Then he came back to the disciples and found them asleep; they could not keep their eyes open. And they did not know what to say to him.

When he came back the third time, he said to them, "Are you still sleeping and resting? Enough! The hour has come! Look, the Son of Man is now handed over to the power of sinful men. Get up, let us go. Look, here is the man who is betraying me!"

The Arrest of Jesus

Jesus was still speaking when Judas, one of the twelve disciples, arrived. With him was a crowd carrying swords and clubs, sent by the chief priests, the teachers of the Law, and the elders. The traitor had given the crowd a signal: "The man I kiss is the one you want. Arrest him and take him away under guard."

As soon as Judas arrived he went up to Jesus and said, "Teacher!" and kissed him. So they arrested Jesus and held him tight. But one of those standing by drew his sword and struck at the High Priest's slave, cutting off his ear. Then Jesus spoke up and said to them, "Did you have to come with swords and clubs to capture me, as though I were an outlaw? Day after day I was with you teaching in the temple, and you did not arrest me. But the Scriptures must come true."

Then all the disciples left him and ran away.

A certain young man, dressed only in a linen cloth, was following Jesus. They tried to arrest him, but he ran away naked, leaving the linen cloth behind.

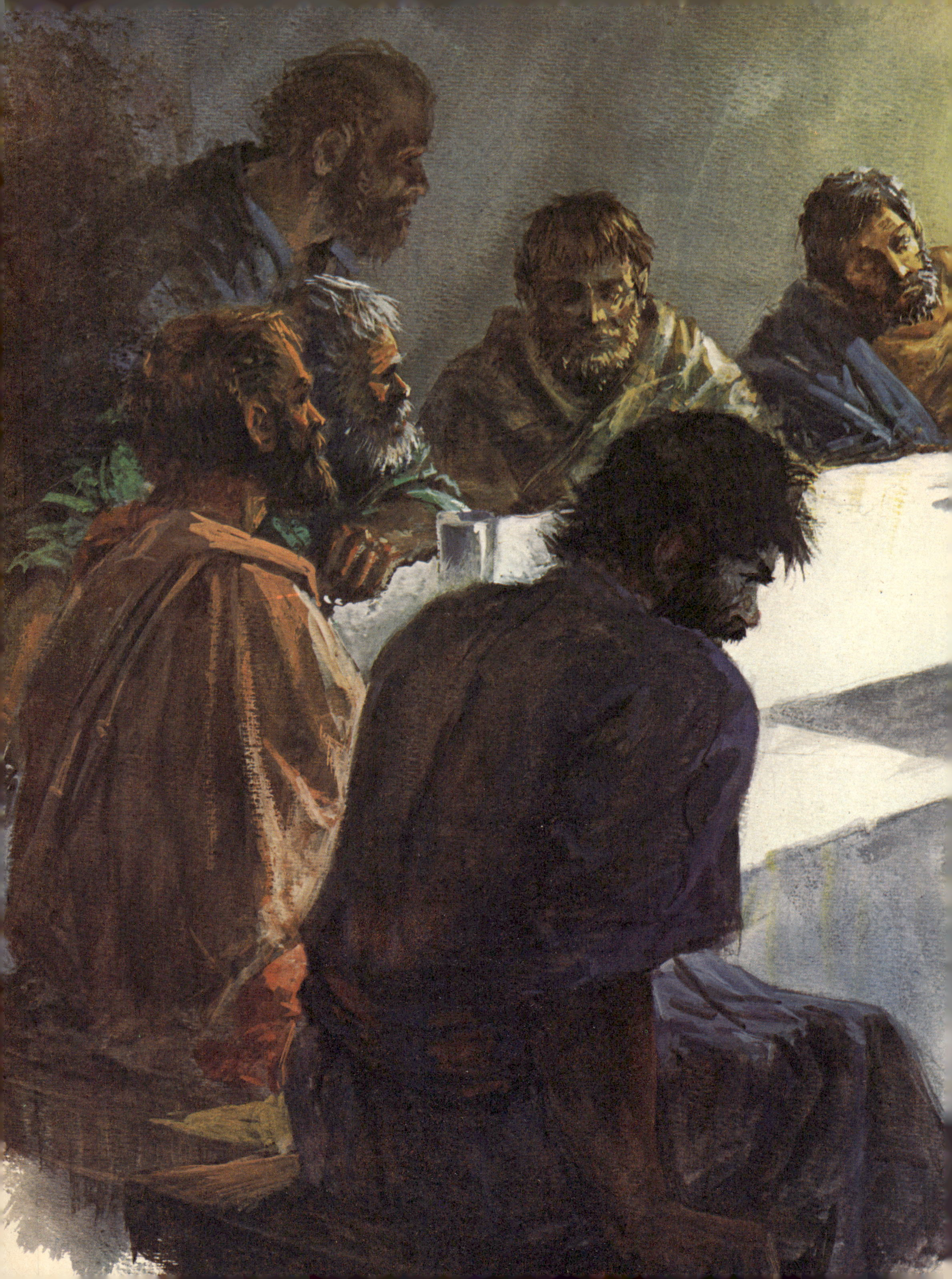

Jesus before the Council

Then they took Jesus to the High Priest's house, where all the chief priests, the elders, and the teachers of the Law were gathering. Peter followed from a distance and went into the courtyard of the High Priest's house. There he sat down with the guards, keeping himself warm by the fire. The chief priests and the whole Council tried to find some evidence against Jesus, in order to put him to death; but they could not find any. Many witnesses told lies against Jesus, but their stories did not agree.

Then some men stood up and told this lie against Jesus, "We heard him say, 'I will tear down this temple which men made, and after three days I will build one that is not made by men.'" Not even they, however, could make their stories agree.

The High Priest stood up in front of them all and questioned Jesus, "Have you no answer to the accusation they bring against you?"

But Jesus kept quiet and would not say a word. Again the High Priest questioned him, "Are you the Messiah, the Son of the Blessed God?"

"I am," answered Jesus, "and you will all see the Son of Man seated at the right side of the Almighty, and coming with the clouds of heaven!"

The High Priest tore his robes and said, "We don't need any more witnesses! You heard his wicked words. What is your decision?"

They all voted against him: he was guilty and should be put to death.

Some of them began to spit on Jesus, and they blindfolded him and hit him. "Guess who hit you!" they said. And the guards took him and slapped him.

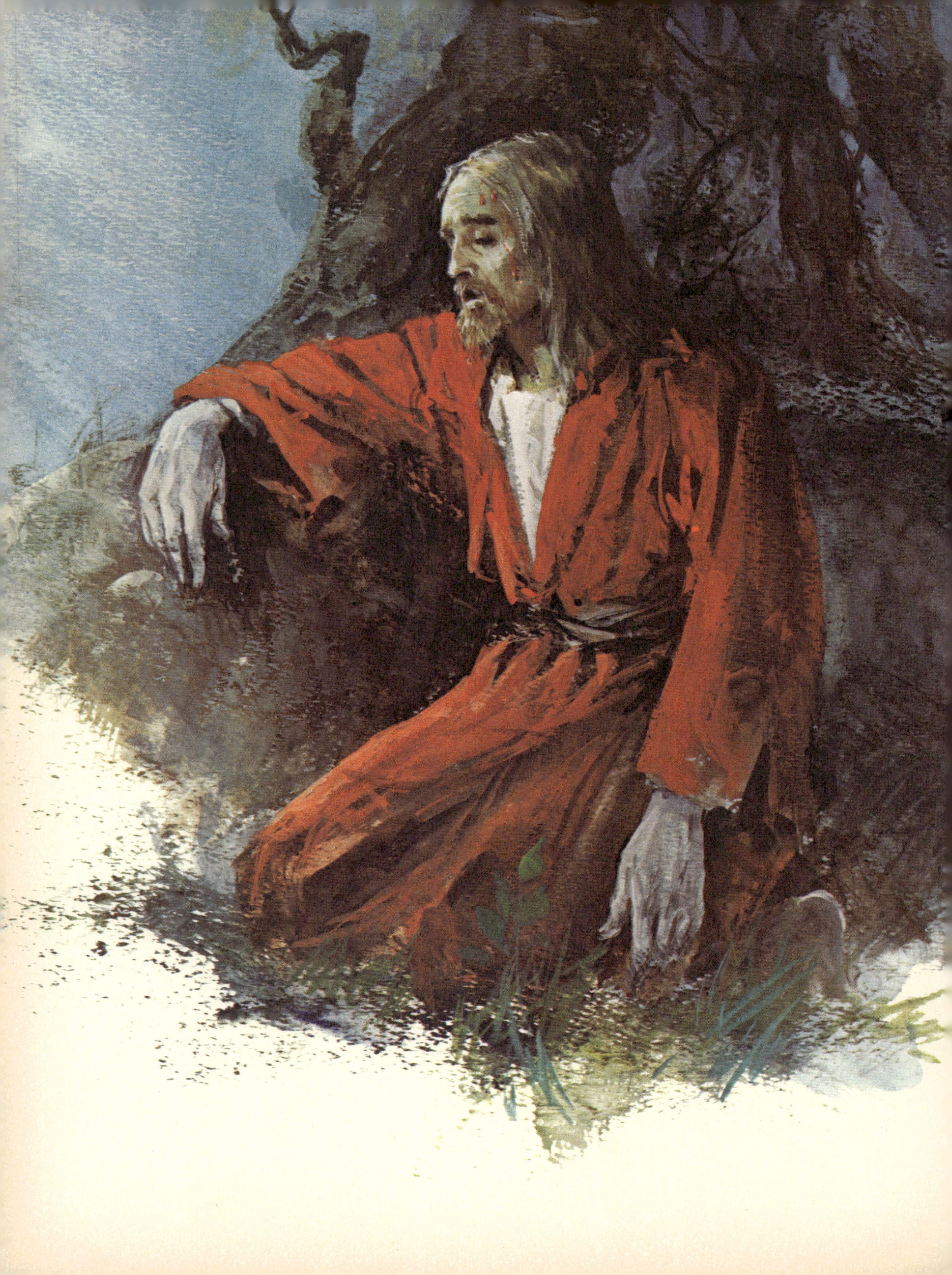

Peter Denies Jesus

Peter was still down in the courtyard when one of the High Priest's servant girls came by. When she saw Peter warming himself, she looked straight at him and said, "You, too, were with Jesus of Nazareth."

But he denied it. "I don't know . . . I don't understand what you are talking about," he answered, and went into the passageway; just then a cock crowed.

The servant girl saw him there and began to repeat to the bystanders, "He is one of them!" But Peter denied it again.

A little while later the bystanders accused Peter again, "You can't deny that you are one of them, because you, too, are from Galilee."

Then Peter made a vow: "May God punish me if I am not telling the truth! I do not know the man you are talking about!"

Just then a cock crowed a second time, and Peter remembered how Jesus had said to him, "Before the cock crows two times you will say three times that you do not know me." And he broke down and cried.

Jesus before Pilate

Early in the morning the chief priests met hurriedly with the elders, the teachers of the Law, and the whole Council, and made their plans. They put Jesus in chains, took him away and handed him over to Pilate. Pilate questioned him, "Are you the king of the Jews?"

Jesus answered, "So you say."

The chief priests accused Jesus of many things, so Pilate questioned him again, "Aren't you going to answer? See how many things they accuse you of!"

Again Jesus refused to say a word, and Pilate was filled with surprise.

Jesus Sentenced to Death

At every Passover Feast Pilate would set free any prisoner the people asked for. At that time a man named Barabbas was in prison with the rebels who had committed murder in the riot. When the crowd gathered and began to ask Pilate for the usual favour, he asked them, "Do you want me to set free for you the king of the Jews?" He knew very well that the chief priests had handed Jesus over to him because they were jealous.

But the chief priests stirred up the crowd to ask, instead, for Pilate to set Barabbas free for them. Pilate spoke again to the crowd, "What, then, do you want me to do with the one you call the king of the Jews?"

They shouted back, "Nail him to the cross!"

"But what crime has he committed?" Pilate asked.

They shouted all the louder, "Nail him to the cross!"

Pilate wanted to please the crowd, so he set Barabbas free for them. Then he had Jesus whipped and handed over to be nailed to the cross.

The Soldiers Make Fun of Jesus

The soldiers took Jesus inside the courtyard (that is, of the governor's palace) and called together the rest of the company. They put a purple robe on Jesus, made a crown out of thorny branches, and put it on his head. Then they began to salute him: "Long live the King of the Jews!" They beat him over the head with a stick, spat on him, fell on their knees and bowed down to him. When they had finished making fun of him, they took off the purple robe and put his own clothes back on him. Then they led him out to nail him to the cross.

Jesus Nailed to the Cross

On the way they met a man named Simon, who was coming into the city from the country, and they forced him to carry Jesus' cross. (This was Simon from Cyrene, the father of Alexander and Rufus.) They brought Jesus to a place called Golgotha, which means "The Place of the Skull". There they tried to give him wine mixed with a drug called myrrh, but Jesus would not drink it. So they nailed him to the cross and divided his clothes among themselves, throwing dice to see who would get which piece of clothing. It was nine o'clock in the morning when they nailed him to the cross. The notice of the accusation against him was written, "The King of the Jews". They also nailed two bandits to crosses with Jesus, one on his right and the other on his left. In this way the scripture came true which says, "He was included with criminals."

"Jesus said, "Forgive them, Father! They don't know what they are doing."

People passing by shook their heads and hurled insults at Jesus: "Aha! You were going to tear down the temple and build it up in three days! Now come down from the cross and save yourself!"

In the same way the chief priests and the teachers of the Law made fun of Jesus, saying to each other, "He saved others, but he cannot save himself! Let us see the Messiah, the king of Israel, come down from the cross now, and we will believe in him!"

One of the criminals hanging there hurled insults at him, "Aren't you the Messiah? Save yourself and us!"

The other one, however, rebuked him, saying, "Don't you fear God? We are all under the same sentence. Ours, however, is only right, because we are getting what we deserve for what we did; but he has done no wrong." And he said to Jesus, "Remember me, Jesus, when you come as King!"

Jesus said to him, "I tell you this: today you will be in Paradise with me."

Standing close to Jesus' cross were his mother, his mother's sister, Mary the wife of Clopas, and Mary Magdalene. Jesus saw his mother and the disciple he loved standing there; so he said to his mother, "Woman, here is your son."

Then he said to the disciple, "Here is your mother." From that time the disciple took her to live in his home.

The Death of Jesus

At noon the whole country was covered with darkness, which lasted for three hours. At three o'clock Jesus cried out with a loud shout, "*Eloi, Eloi, lema sabachthani?*" which means, "My God, my God, why did you abandon me?"

Some of the people who were there heard him and said, "Listen, he is calling for Elijah!" One of them ran up with a sponge, soaked it in cheap wine, and put it on the end of a stick. Then he held it up to Jesus' lips and said, "Wait! Let us see if Elijah is coming to bring him down from the cross!"

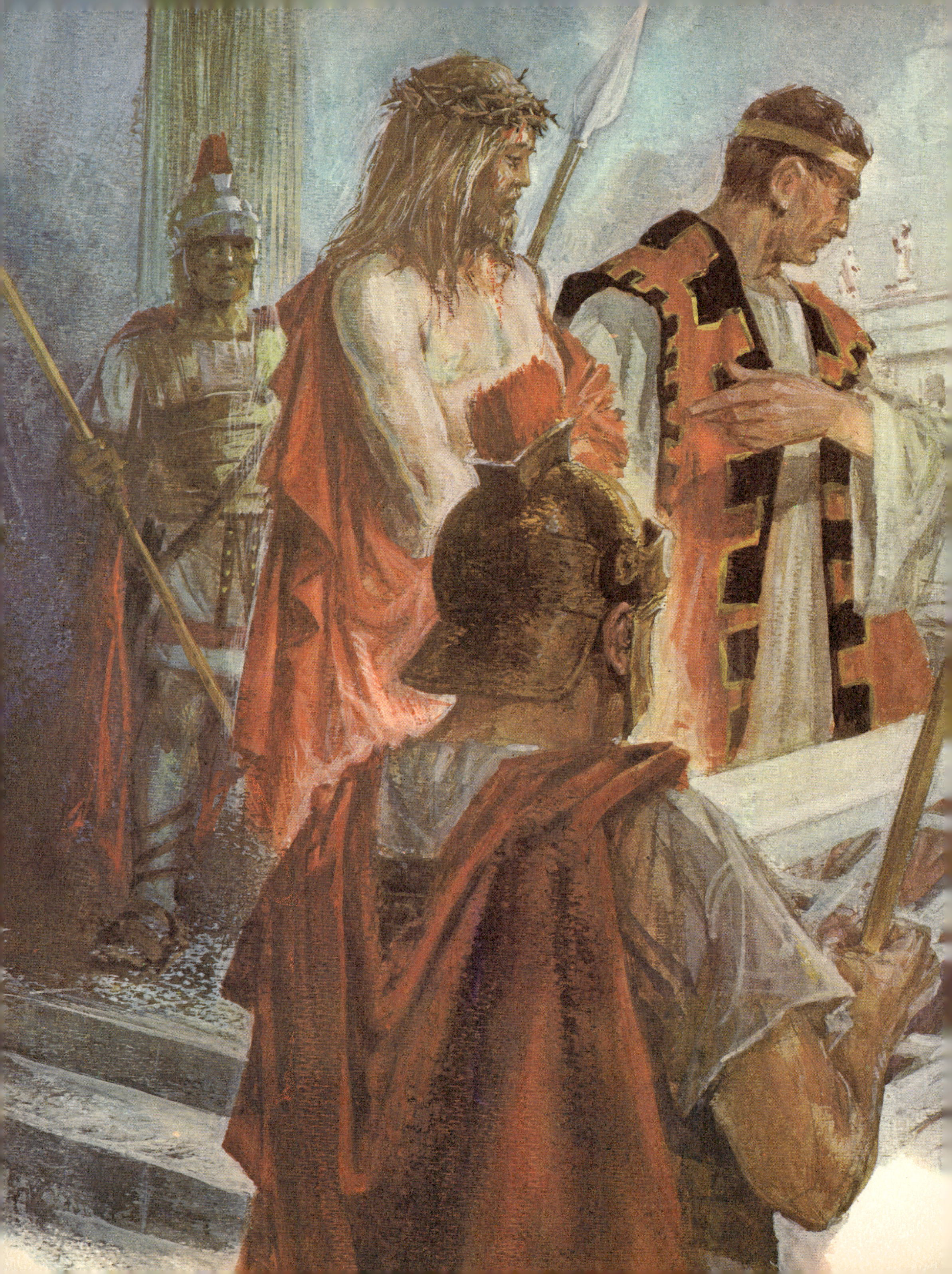

Jesus knew that by now everything had been completed; and in order to make the scripture come true he said, "I am thirsty."

A bowl was there, full of cheap wine; they soaked a sponge in the wine, put it on a branch of hyssop, and lifted it up to his lips. Jesus took the wine and said, "It is finished!"

Jesus cried out in a loud voice, "Father! In your hands I place my spirit!" He said this and died.

The army officer saw what had happened, and he praised God, saying, "Certainly he was a good man!"

When the people who had gathered there to watch the spectacle saw what happened, they all went back home, beating their breasts. All those who knew Jesus personally, including the women who had followed him from Galilee, stood off at a distance to see these things.

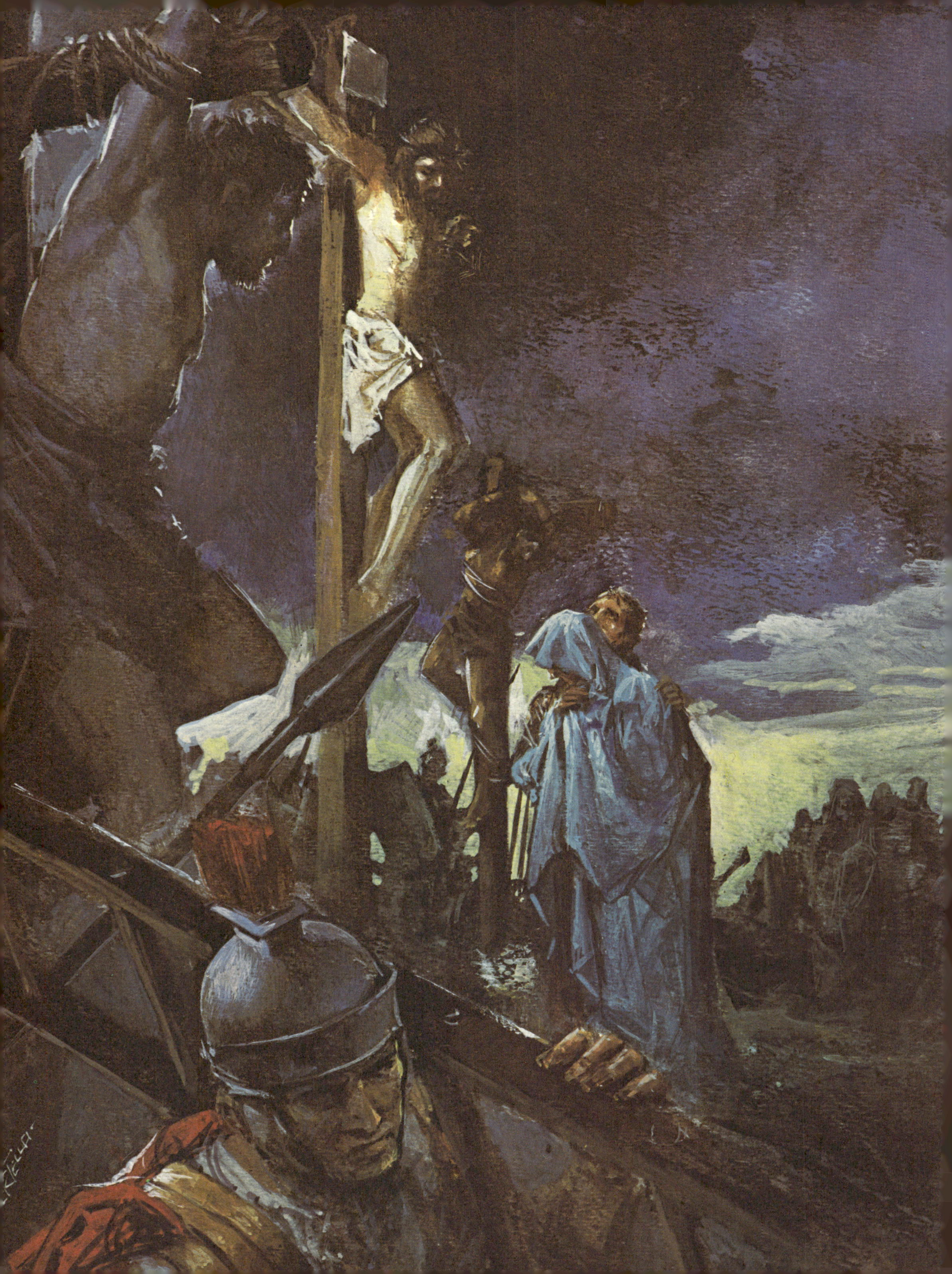

The Burial of Jesus

There was a man named Joseph, from the Jewish town of Arimathea. He was a good and honourable man, and waited for the coming of the Kingdom of God. Although a member of the Council, he had not agreed with their decision and action. He went into the presence of Pilate and asked for the body of Jesus. Then he took the body down, wrapped it in a linen sheet, and placed it in a grave which had been dug out of the rock —a grave which had never been used. It was Friday, and the Sabbath was about to begin.

The women who had followed Jesus from Galilee went with Joseph and saw the grave and how Jesus' body was placed in it. Then they went back home and prepared the spices and ointments for his body.

On the Sabbath they rested, as the Law commanded.

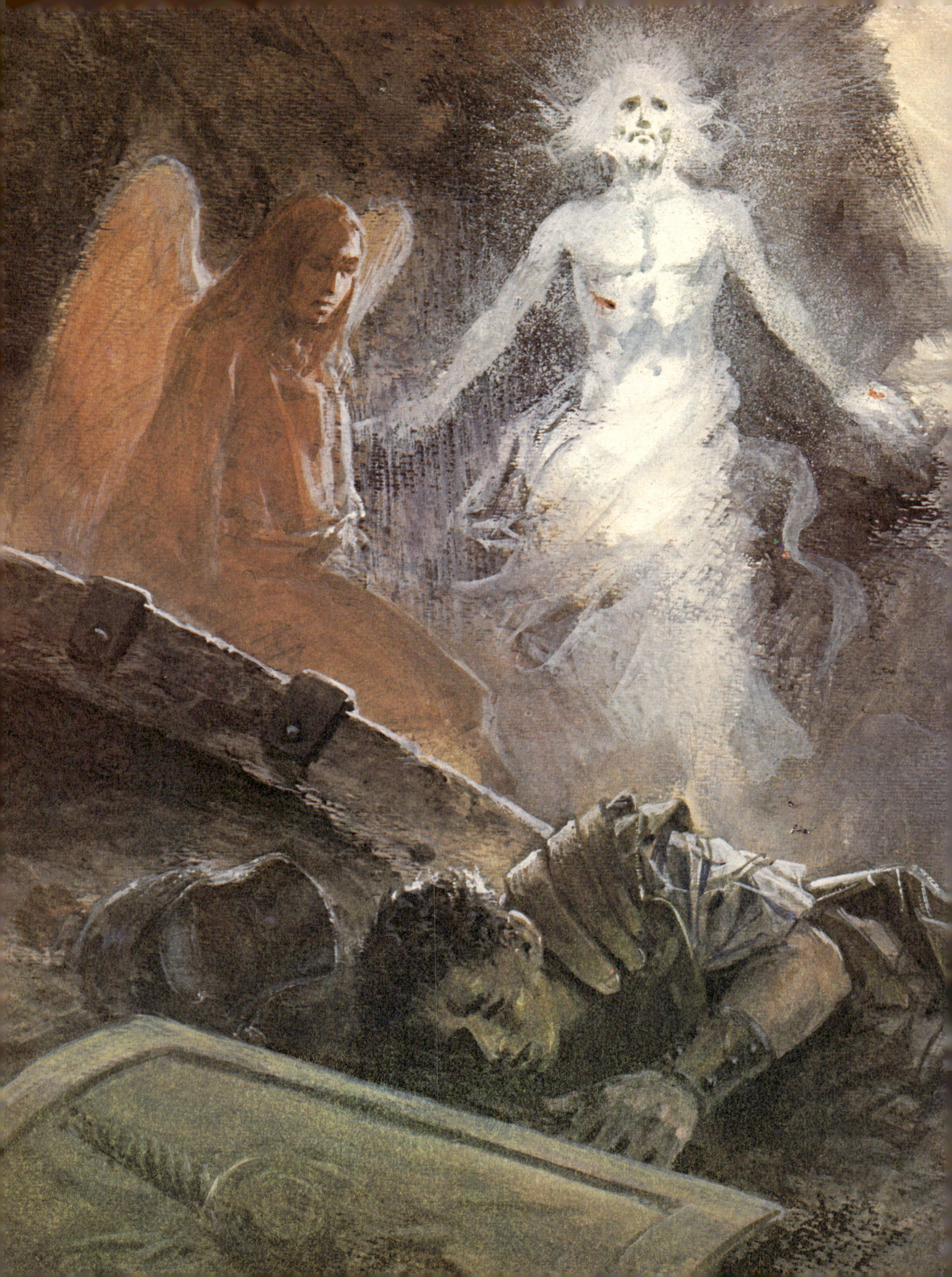

7
The Victory of Jesus

The death of Jesus was not the end. His followers became sure that he was alive, and that he was, after all, Lord and Saviour. No one can understand completely how these first Christians became so certain about the victory of Jesus, but we can read some of the stories they told about the resurrection. Here, extracts are given from three gospels—by John, Luke and Matthew—giving glimpses of the first Christians and their living Lord. And as we read, we can join in the prayer of the doubter, Thomas, to Jesus: "My Lord and my God!" This certainty that Jesus was Lord did not grow less when the first Easter had passed. The stories of Stephen and of Saul (who became Saint Paul) show how men still saw Jesus in his glory and his power. The Revelation written by John "the Divine" is the record of another vision of King Jesus.

The Empty Tomb

Early on Sunday morning, while it was still dark, Mary Magdalene went to the tomb and saw that the stone had been taken away from the entrance. She ran and went to Simon Peter and the other disciple, whom Jesus loved, and told them, "They have taken the Lord from the tomb and we don't know where they have put him!"

Then Peter and the other disciple left and went to the tomb. The two of them were running, but the other disciple ran faster than Peter and reached the tomb first. He bent over and saw the linen cloths, but he did not go in. Behind him came Simon Peter, and he went straight into the tomb. He saw the linen cloths lying there and the cloth which had been round Jesus' head. It was not lying with the linen cloths but was rolled up by itself. Then the other disciple, who had reached the tomb first, also went in; he saw and believed. (They still did not understand the Scripture which said that he must rise from death.) Then the disciples went back home.

Jesus Appears to Mary Magdalene

Mary stood crying outside the tomb. Still crying, she bent over and looked in the tomb, and saw two angels there, dressed in white, sitting where the body of Jesus had been, one at the head, the other at the feet. "Woman, why are you crying?" they asked her.

She answered, "They have taken my Lord away, and I do not know where they have put him!"

When she had said this, she turned round and saw Jesus standing there; but she did not know that it was Jesus. "Woman, why are you crying?" Jesus asked her. "Who is it that you are looking for?"

She thought he was the gardener, so she said to him, "If you took him away, sir, tell me where you have put him, and I will go and get him."

Jesus said to her, "Mary!"

She turned towards him and said in Hebrew, "Rabboni!" (This means "Teacher".)

"Do not hold on to me," Jesus told her, "because I have not yet gone back up to the Father. But go to my brothers and tell them for me, 'I go back up to him who is my Father and your Father, my God and your God.' "

So Mary Magdalene went and told the disciples that she had seen the Lord, and that he had told her this.

The Walk to Emmaus

On that same day two of them were going to a village named Emmaus, about seven miles from Jerusalem, and they were talking to each other

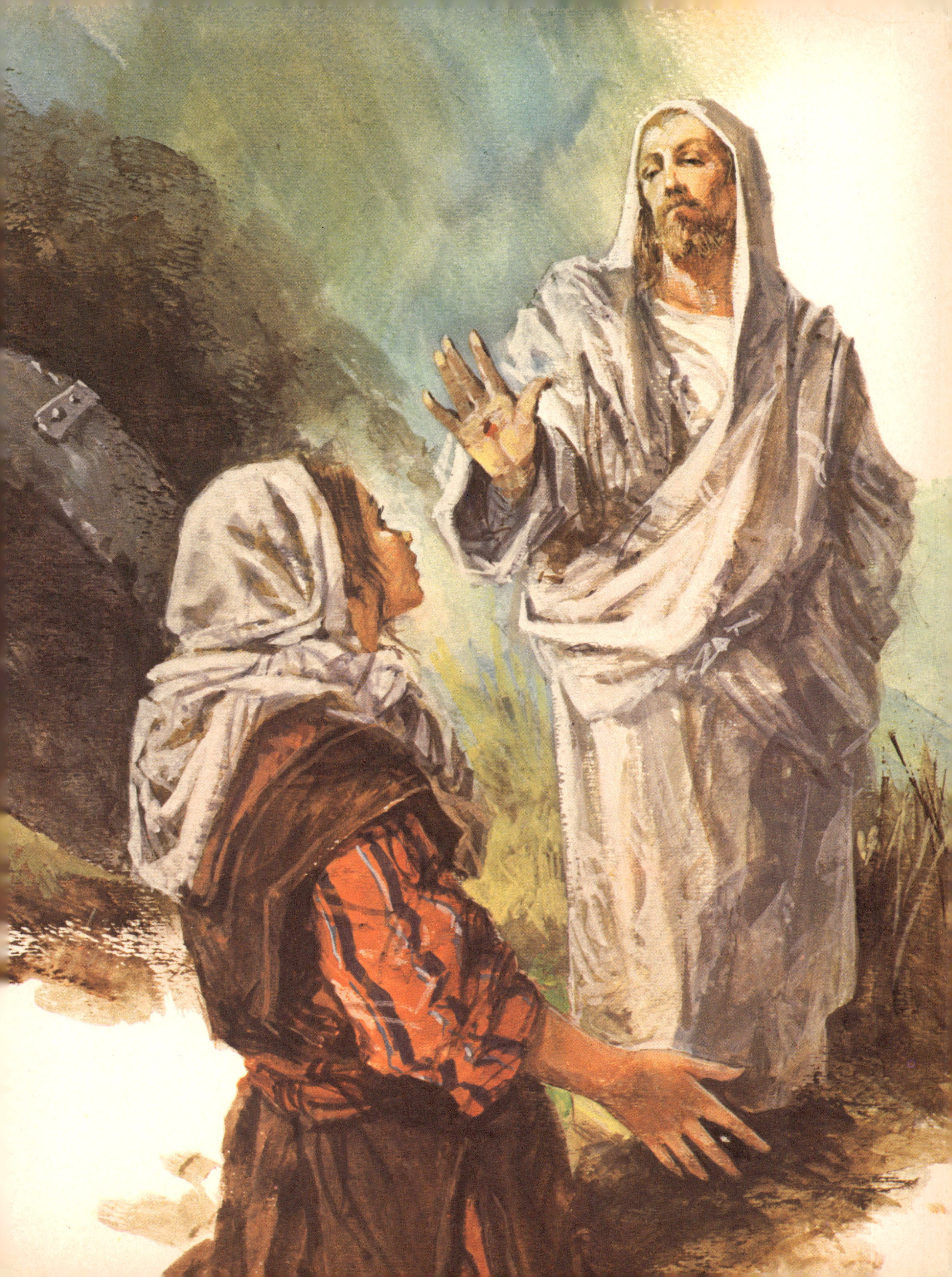

about all the things that had happened. As they talked and discussed, Jesus himself drew near and walked along with them; they saw him, but somehow did not recognize him. Jesus said to them, "What are you talking about, back and forth, as you walk along?"

They stood still, with sad faces. One of them, named Cleopas, asked him, "Are you the only man living in Jerusalem who does not know what has been happening there these last few days?"

"What things?" he asked.

"The things that happened to Jesus of Nazareth," they answered. "This man was a prophet, and was considered by God and by all the people to be mighty in words and deeds. Our chief priests and rulers handed him over to be sentenced to death, and he was nailed to the cross. And we had hoped that he would be the one who was going to redeem Israel! Besides all that, this is now the third day since it happened. Some of the women of our group surprised us; they went at dawn to the grave, but could not find his body. They came back saying they had seen a vision of angels who told them that he is alive. Some of our group went to the grave and found it exactly as the women had said; but they did not see him."

Then Jesus said to them, "How foolish you are, how slow you are to believe everything the prophets said! Was it not necessary for the Messiah to suffer these things and enter his glory?" And Jesus explained to them what was said about him in all the Scriptures, beginning with the books of Moses and the writings of all the prophets.

They came near the village to which they were going, and Jesus acted as if he were going farther; but they held him back, saying, "Stay with us; the day is almost over and it is getting dark." So he went in to stay with them. He sat at table with them, took the bread, and said the blessing; then he broke the bread and gave it to them. Their eyes were opened and they recognized him; but he disappeared from their sight. They said to each other, "Wasn't it like a fire burning in us when he talked to us on the road and explained the Scriptures to us?"

They got up at once and went back to Jerusalem, where they found the eleven disciples gathered together with the others and saying, "The Lord is risen indeed! He has appeared to Simon!"

The two then explained to them what had happened on the road, and how they had recognized the Lord when he broke the bread.

Jesus Appears to his Disciples

It was late that Sunday evening, and the disciples were gathered together behind locked doors, because they were afraid of the Jewish authorities. Then Jesus came and stood among them. "Peace be with you," he said. After saying this he showed them his hands and his side. The disciples were filled with joy at seeing the Lord. Then Jesus said to

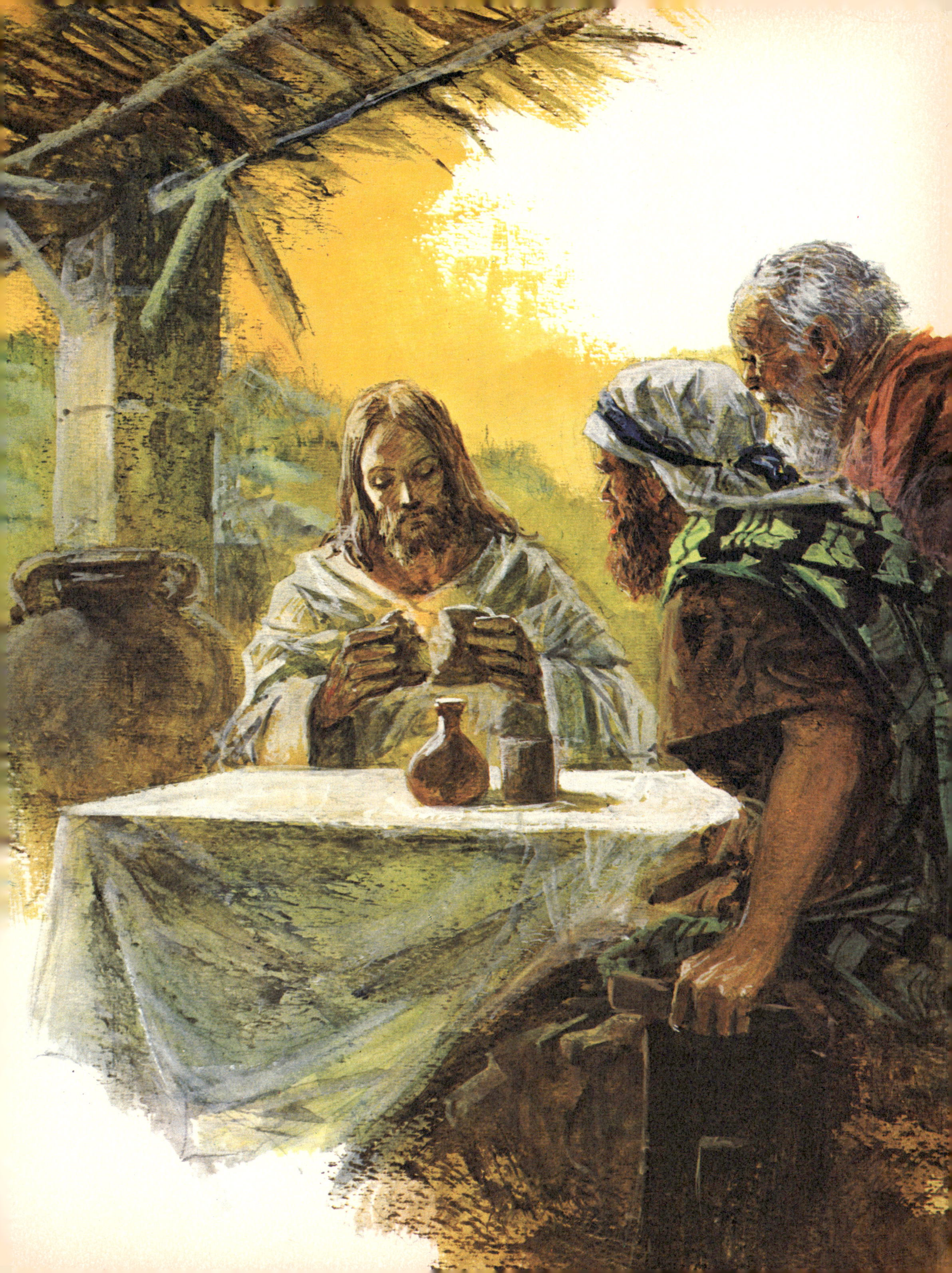

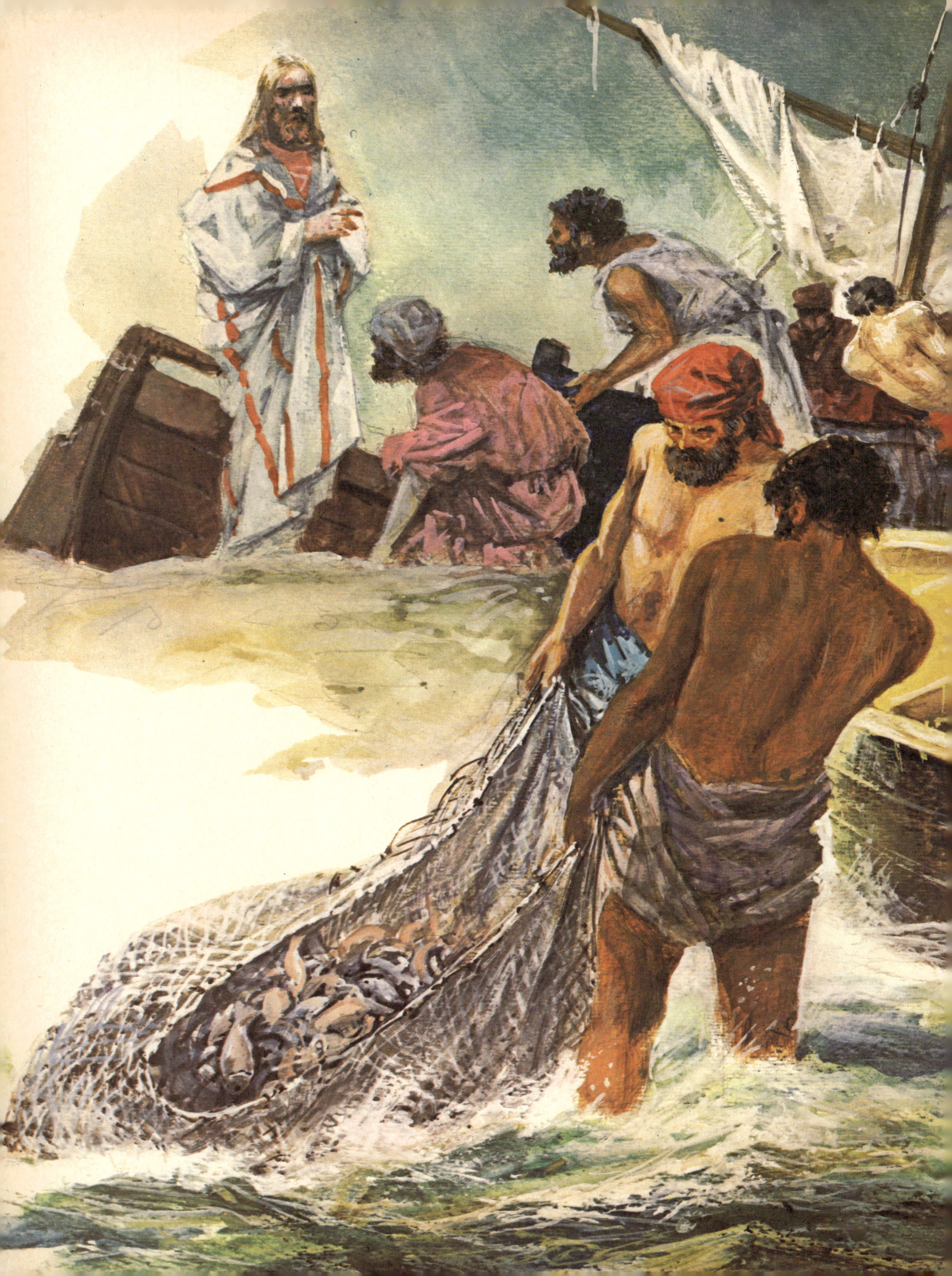

them again, "Peace be with you. As the Father sent me, so I send you," He said this, and then he breathed on them and said, "Receive the Holy Spirit. If you forgive men's sins, they are forgiven; if you do not forgive them, they are not forgiven."

Jesus and Thomas

One of the twelve disciples, Thomas (called the Twin), was not with them when Jesus came. So the other disciples told him, "We saw the Lord!"

Thomas said to them, "If I do not see the scars of the nails in his hands, and put my finger on those scars, and my hand in his side, I will not believe."

A week later the disciples were together indoors again, and Thomas was with them. The doors were locked, but Jesus came and stood among them and said, "Peace be with you." Then he said to Thomas, "Put your finger here, and look at my hands; then stretch out your hand and put it in my side. Stop your doubting, and believe!"

Thomas answered him, "My Lord and my God!"

Jesus said to him, "Do you believe because you see me? How happy are those who believe without seeing me!"

Jesus Appears to Seven Disciples

After this, Jesus showed himself once more to his disciples at Lake Tiberias. This is how he did it. Simon Peter, Thomas (called the Twin), Nathanael (the one from Cana in Galilee), the sons of Zebedee, and two other disciples of Jesus were all together. Simon Peter said to the others, "I am going fishing."

"We will come with you," they told him. So they went and got into the boat; but all that night they did not catch a thing. As the sun was rising, Jesus stood at the water's edge, but the disciples did not know that it was Jesus. Then he said to them, "Young men, haven't you caught anything?"

"Not a thing," they answered.

He said to them, "Throw your net out on the right side of the boat, and you will find some." So they threw the net out, and could not pull it back in, because they had caught so many fish.

The disciple whom Jesus loved said to Peter, "It is the Lord!" When Simon Peter heard that it was the Lord, he wrapped his outer garment round him (for he had taken his clothes off) and jumped into the water. The other disciples came to shore in the boat, pulling the net full of fish. They were not very far from land, about a hundred yards away. When they stepped ashore they saw a charcoal fire there with fish on it, and some bread. Then Jesus said to them, "Bring some of the fish you have just caught."

Simon Peter went aboard and dragged the net ashore, full of big fish, a hundred and fifty-three in all; even though there were so many, still the net did not tear. Jesus said to them, "Come and eat." None of the disciples dared ask him, "Who are you?" because they knew it was the Lord. So Jesus went over, took the bread and gave it to them; he did the same with the fish.

This, then, was the third time Jesus showed himself to the disciples after he was raised from death.

Jesus and Peter

After they had eaten, Jesus said to Simon Peter, "Simon, son of John, do you love me more than these?"

"Yes, Lord," he answered, "you know that I love you."

Jesus said to him, "Take care of my lambs." A second time Jesus said to him, "Simon, son of John, do you love me?"

"Yes, Lord," he answered, "you know that I love you."

Jesus said to him, "Take care of my sheep." A third time Jesus said, "Simon, son of John, do you love me?"

Peter became sad because Jesus asked him the third time, "Do you love me?" and said to him, "Lord, you know everything; you know that I love you!"

Jesus said to him, "Take care of my sheep. I tell you the truth: when you were young you used to fasten your belt and go anywhere you wanted to; but when you are old you will stretch out your hands and someone else will tie them and take you where you don't want to go." (In saying this Jesus was indicating the way in which Peter would die and bring glory to God.) Then Jesus said to him, "Follow me!"

Jesus and the Other Disciple

Peter turned round and saw behind him that other disciple, whom Jesus loved—the one who had leaned close to Jesus at the meal and asked, "Lord, who is going to betray you?" When Peter saw him, he said to Jesus, "Lord, what about this man?"

Jesus answered him, "If I want him to live until I come, what is that to you? Follow me!"

So a report spread among the followers of Jesus that this disciple would not die. But Jesus did not say that he would not die; he said, "If I want him to live until I come, what is that to you?"

He is the disciple who spoke of these things, the one who also wrote them down; and we know that what he said is true.

Jesus Appears to his Disciples

The eleven disciples went to the hill in Galilee where Jesus had told them to go. When they saw him they worshipped him, even though some of them doubted. Jesus drew near and said to them, "I have been given all authority in heaven and on earth. Go, then, to all peoples everywhere and make them my disciples: baptize them in the name of the Father, the Son, and the Holy Spirit, and teach them to obey everything I have commanded you. And remember! I will be with you always, to the end of the age."

Stephen and Saul See Jesus in his Glory

The Arrest of Stephen

Stephen, a man richly blessed by God and full of power, performed great miracles and wonders among the people. But some men opposed him; they were members of the synagogue of the Free Men (as it was called), which had Jews from Cyrenia and Alexandria. They and other Jews from Cilicia and Asia started arguing with Stephen. But the Spirit gave Stephen such wisdom that when he spoke they could not resist him. So they bribed some men to say, "We heard him speaking against Moses and against God!" In this way they stirred up the people, the elders, and the teachers of the Law. They came to Stephen, seized him, and took him before the Council. Then they brought in some men to tell lies about him. "This man," they said, "is always talking against our sacred temple and the Law of Moses. We heard him say that this Jesus of Nazareth will tear down the temple and change all the customs which have come down to us from Moses!" All those sitting in the Council fixed their eyes on Stephen and saw that his face looked like the face of an angel.

The Stoning of Stephen

As the members of the Council listened to Stephen they became furious and ground their teeth at him in anger. But Stephen, full of the Holy Spirit, looked up to heaven and saw God's glory, and Jesus standing at the right side of God. "Look!" he said. "I see heaven opened and the Son of Man standing at the right side of God!"

With a loud cry they covered their ears with their hands. Then they all rushed together at him at once, threw him out of the city and stoned him. The witnesses left their cloaks in charge of a young man named Saul. They kept on stoning Stephen as he called on the Lord, "Lord Jesus, receive my spirit!" He knelt down and cried out in a loud voice, "Lord! Do not remember this sin against them!" He said this and died.

And Saul approved of his murder.

Saul Persecutes the Church

That very day the church in Jerusalem began to suffer cruel persecution. All the believers, except the apostles, were scattered throughout the provinces of Judea and Samaria. Some devout men buried Stephen, mourning for him with loud cries.

But Saul tried to destroy the church; going from house to house, he dragged out the believers, both men and women, and threw them into jail.

The Conversion of Saul

Saul kept up his violent threats of murder against the disciples of the Lord. He went to the High Priest and asked for letters of introduction to the Jewish synagogues in Damascus, so that if he should find any followers of the Way of the Lord there, he would be able to arrest them, both men and women, and take them back to Jerusalem.

On his way to Damascus, as he came near the city, suddenly a light from the sky flashed round him. He fell to the ground and heard a voice saying to him, "Saul, Saul! Why do you persecute me?"

"Who are you, Lord?" he asked.

"I am Jesus, whom you persecute," the voice said. "But get up and go into the city, where you will be told what you must do."

The men who were travelling with Saul had stopped, not saying a word; they heard the voice but could not see anyone. Saul got up from the ground and opened his eyes, but could not see a thing. So they took him by the hand and led him into Damascus. For three days he was not able to see, and during that time he did not eat or drink anything.

There was a disciple in Damascus named Ananias. He had a vision, in which the Lord said to him, "Ananias!"

"Here I am, Lord," he answered.

The Lord said to him, "Get ready and go to Straight Street, and at the house of Judas ask for a man from Tarsus named Saul. He is praying, and in a vision he saw a man named Ananias come in and place his hands on him so that he might see again."

Ananias answered, "Lord, many people have told me about this man, about all the terrible things he has done to your people in Jerusalem. And he has come to Damascus with authority from the chief priests to arrest all who call on your name."

The Lord said to him, "Go, because I have chosen him to serve me, to make my name known to Gentiles and kings, and to the people of Israel. And I myself will show him all that he must suffer for my sake."

So Ananias went, entered the house and placed his hands on Saul. "Brother Saul," he said, "the Lord has sent me — Jesus himself, who appeared to you on the road as you were coming here. He sent me so

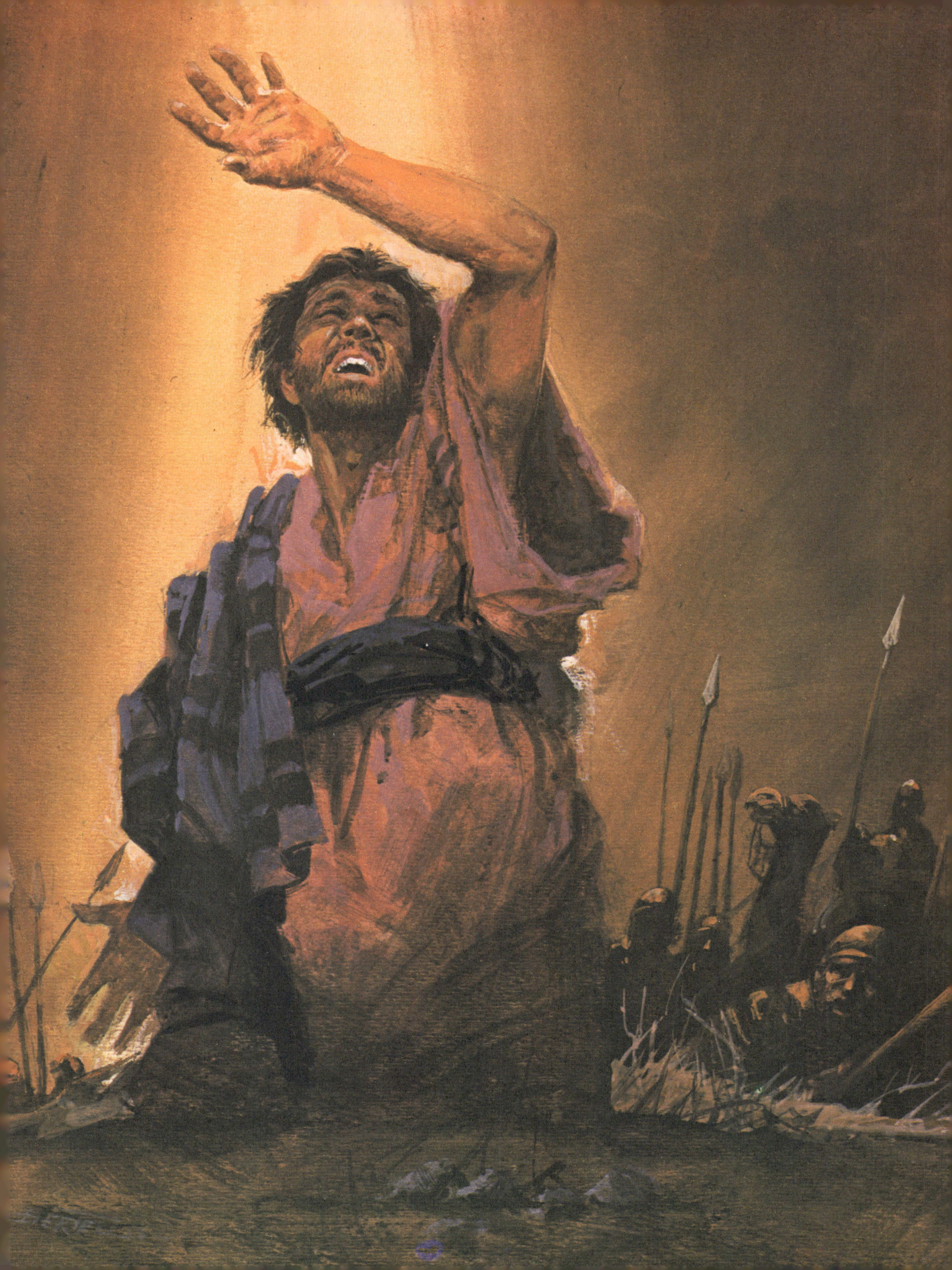

that you might see again and be filled with the Holy Spirit." At once something like fish scales fell from Saul's eyes and he was able to see again. He stood up and was baptized; and after he had eaten, his strength came back.

Saul Preaches in Damascus

Saul stayed for a few days with the disciples in Damascus. He went straight to the synagogues and began to preach about Jesus. "He is the Son of God," he said.

All who heard him were amazed, and asked, "Isn't this the man who in Jerusalem was killing those who call on this name? And didn't he come here for the very purpose of arresting them and taking them back to the chief priests?"

The Victory through our Lord Jesus Christ

Paul, previously Saul the enemy of the Church, writes to the Corinthians

The Resurrection of Christ

And now I want to remind you, brothers, of the Good News which I preached to you, which you received, and on which your faith stands firm. That is the gospel, the message that I preached to you. You are saved by the gospel if you hold firmly to it — unless it was for nothing that you believed.

I passed on to you what I received, which is of the greatest importance: that Christ died for our sins, as written in the Scriptures; that he was buried, and was raised to life on the third day, as written in the Scriptures; that he appeared to Peter, and then to all twelve apostles. Then he appeared to more than five hundred of his followers at once, most of whom are still alive, although some have died. Then he appeared to James, and then to all the apostles.

Last of all he appeared also to me — even though I am like one who was born in a most unusual way. For I am the least of all the apostles — I do not even deserve to be called an apostle, because I persecuted God's church. But by God's grace I am what I am, and the grace that he gave me was not without effect. On the contrary, I have worked harder than all the apostles, although it was not really my own doing, but God's grace working with me. So then, whether it came from me or from them, this is what we all preach, this is what you believe.

The Resurrection Body

Someone will ask, "How can the dead be raised to life? What kind of body will they have?" You fool! When you plant a seed in the ground it does not sprout to life unless it dies. And what you plant in the ground is a bare seed, perhaps a grain of wheat, or of some other kind, not the full-bodied plant that will grow up. God provides that seed with the body he wishes; he gives each seed its own proper body.

And the flesh of living beings is not all the same kind of flesh; men have one kind of flesh, animals another, birds another, and fish another.

And there are heavenly bodies and earthly bodies; there is a beauty that belongs to heavenly bodies, and another kind of beauty that belongs to earthly bodies. The sun has its own beauty, the moon another beauty, and the stars a different beauty; and even among stars there are different kinds of beauty.

This is how it will be when the dead are raised to life. When the body is buried it is mortal; when raised, it will be immortal. When buried, it is ugly and weak; when raised, it will be beautiful and strong. When buried, it is a physical body; when raised, it will be a spiritual body. There is, of course, a physical body, so there has to be a spiritual body. For the scripture says, "The first man, Adam, was created a living being"; but the last Adam is the life-giving Spirit. It is not the spiritual that comes first, but the physical, and then the spiritual. The first Adam was made of the dust of the earth; the second Adam came from heaven. Those who belong to the earth are like the one who was made of earth; those who are of heaven are like the one who came from heaven. Just as we wear the likeness of the man made of earth, so we will wear the likeness of the Man from heaven.

What I mean, brothers, is this: what is made of flesh and blood cannot share in God's Kingdom, and what is mortal cannot possess immortality.

Listen to this secret: we shall not all die, but in an instant we shall all be changed, as quickly as the blinking of an eye, when the last trumpet sounds. For when it sounds, the dead will be raised immortal beings, and we shall all be changed. For what is mortal must clothe itself with what is immortal; what will die must clothe itself with what cannot die. So when what is mortal has been clothed with what is immortal, and when what will die has been clothed with what cannot die, then the Scripture will come true: "Death is destroyed; victory is complete!"

"Where, Death, is your victory?

Where, Death is your power to hurt?"

Death gets its power to hurt from sin, and sin gets its power from the Law. But thanks be to God who gives us the victory through our Lord Jesus Christ!

So then, my dear brothers, stand firm and steady. Keep busy always in your work for the Lord, since you know that nothing you do in the Lord's service is ever without value.

The New Life is Stronger than Death

Paul writes to the Romans

Life in the Spirit

There is no condemnation now for those who live in union with Christ Jesus. For the law of the Spirit, which brings us life in union with Christ Jesus, has set me free from the law of sin and death. What the Law could not do, because human nature was weak, God did. He condemned sin in human nature by sending his own Son, who came with a nature like man's sinful nature to do away with sin. God did this so that the righteous demands of the Law might be fully satisfied in us who live according to the Spirit, not according to human nature. Those who live as their human nature tells them to, have their minds controlled by what human nature wants. Those who live as the Spirit tells them to, have their minds controlled by what the Spirit wants. To have your mind controlled by human nature results in death; to have your mind controlled by the Spirit results in life and peace. And so a man becomes an enemy of God when his mind is controlled by human nature; for he does not obey God's law, and in fact he cannot obey it. Those who obey their human nature cannot please God.

But you do not live as your human nature tells you to; you live as the Spirit tells you to – if, in fact, God's Spirit lives in you. Whoever does not have the Spirit of Christ does not belong to him. But if Christ lives in you, although your bodies are going to die because of sin, yet the Spirit is life for you because you have been put right with God. If the Spirit of God, who raised Jesus from death, lives in you, then he who raised Christ from death will also give life to your mortal bodies by the presence of his Spirit in you.

So then, my brothers, we have an obligation, but not to live as our human nature wants us to. For if you live according to your human nature, you are going to die; but if, by the Spirit, you kill your sinful actions, you will live. Those who are led by God's Spirit are God's sons. For the Spirit that God has given you does not make you a slave and cause you to be afraid; instead, the Spirit makes you God's sons, and by the Spirit's power we cry to God, "Father! my Father!" God's Spirit joins himself to our spirits to declare that we are God's children. Since we are his children, we will possess the blessings he keeps for his people, and we will also possess with Christ what God has kept for him; for if we share Christ's suffering, we will also share his glory.

The Future Glory

I consider that what we suffer at this present time cannot be compared at all with the glory that is going to be revealed to us. All of creation waits with eager longing for God to reveal his sons. For creation was condemned to become worthless, not of its own will, but because God willed it to be so. Yet there was this hope, that creation itself would one day be set free from its slavery to decay, and share the glorious freedom of the children of God. For we know that up to the present time all of creation groans with pain like the pain of childbirth. But not just creation alone; we who have the Spirit as the first of God's gifts, we also groan within ourselves as we wait for God to make us his sons and set our whole being free. For it was by hope that we were saved; but if we see what we hope for, then it is not really hope. For who hopes for something that he sees? But if we hope for what we do not see, we wait for it with patience.

In the same way the Spirit also comes to help us, weak that we are. For we do not know how we ought to pray; the Spirit himself pleads with God for us, in groans that words cannot express. And God, who sees into the hearts of men, knows what the thought of the Spirit is; because the Spirit pleads with God on behalf of his people and in accordance with his will.

We know that in all things God works for good with those who love him, those whom he has called according to his purpose. Those whom God had already chosen he had also set apart to become like his Son, so that the Son would be the first among many brothers. And so God called those that he had set apart; and those that he called he also put right with himself; and with those that he put right with himself he also shared his glory.

God's Love in Christ Jesus

Faced with all this, what can we say? If God is for us, who can be against us? He did not even keep back his own Son, but offered him for us all! He gave us his Son — will he not also freely give us all things? Who will accuse God's chosen people? God himself declares them not guilty! Can anyone, then, condemn them? Christ Jesus is the one who died, or rather, who was raised to life and is at the right side of God. He pleads with God for us! Who then, can separate us from the love of Christ? Can trouble do it, or hardship, or persecution, or hunger, or poverty, or danger, or death? As the scripture says,
>"For your sake we are in danger of death the whole day long;
>>we are treated like sheep that are going to be slaughtered."

No, in all these things we have complete victory through him who loved us! For I am certain that nothing can separate us from his love: neither death nor life; neither angels nor other heavenly rulers or powers; neither the present nor the future; neither the world above nor the world below — there is nothing in all creation that will ever be able to separate us from the love of God which is ours through Christ Jesus our Lord.

Jesus is Lord

John the Divine writes to Christians in Asia from the prison on the island of Patmos

From John to the seven churches in the province of Asia:
Grace and peace be yours from God, who is, who was, and who is to come, and from the seven spirits in front of his throne, and from Jesus Christ, the faithful witness, the firstborn Son who was raised from death, who is also the ruler of the kings of earth.

He loves us, and by his death he has freed us from our sins and made us a kingdom of priests to serve his God and Father. To Jesus Christ be the glory and power forever and ever! Amen.

Look, he is coming with the clouds! Everyone will see him, including those who pierced him. All peoples of earth will mourn over him. Certainly so! Amen.

"I am the Alpha and the Omega," says the Lord God Almighty, who is, who was, and who is to come.

A Vision of Christ

I am John, your brother, and in union with Jesus I share with you in suffering, and in his Kingdom, and in enduring. I was put on the island named Patmos because I had proclaimed God's word and the truth that Jesus revealed. On the Lord's day the Spirit took control of me, and I heard a loud voice, that sounded like a trumpet, speaking behind me. It said, "Write down what you see, and send the book to these seven churches: in Ephesus, Smyrna, Pergamum, Thyatira, Sardis, Philadelphia, and Laodicea."

I turned round to see who was talking to me. There I saw seven gold lampstands. Among them stood a being who looked like a man, wearing a robe that reached to his feet, and a gold band round his chest. His hair was white as wool, or as snow, and his eyes blazed like fire; his feet shone like brass melted in the furnace and then polished, and his voice sounded like a mighty waterfall. He held seven stars in his right hand, and a sharp two-edged sword came out of his mouth. His face was as bright as the midday sun. When I saw him I fell down at his feet like a dead man. He placed his right hand on me and said, "Don't be afraid! I am the first and the last. I am the living one! I was dead, but look, I am alive forever and ever. I have authority over death and the world of the dead. Write, then, the things you see, both the things that are now, and the things that will happen afterwards. Here is the secret meaning of the seven stars that you see in my right hand, and of the seven gold lampstands: the seven stars are the angels of the seven churches, and the seven lampstands are the seven churches."

The New Heaven and the New Earth

Then I saw a new heaven and a new earth. The first heaven and the first earth disappeared, and the sea vanished. And I saw the Holy City, the new Jerusalem, coming down out of heaven from God, prepared and ready, like a bride dressed to meet her husband. I heard a loud voice speaking from the throne, "Now God's home is with men! He will live with them, and they shall be his people. God himself will be with them, and he will be their God. He will wipe away all tears from their eyes. There will be no more death, no more grief, crying, or pain. The old things have disappeared."

Then the one who sits on the throne said, "And now I make all things new!" He also said to me, "Write this, because these words are true and can be trusted." And he said, "It is done! I am the Alpha and the Omega, the beginning and the end. To anyone who is thirsty I will give a free drink of water from the spring of the water of life. Whoever wins the victory will receive this from me: I will be his God, and he will be my son. But the cowards, the traitors, and the perverts, the murderers and the immoral, those who practise magic and those who worship idols, and all liars — the place for them is the lake burning with fire and sulphur, which is the second death."

The New Jerusalem

One of the seven angels who had the seven bowls full of the seven last plagues came to me and said, "Come, and I will show you the Bride, the wife of the Lamb." The Spirit took control of me, and the angel carried me to the top of a very high mountain. He showed me Jerusalem, the Holy City, coming down out of heaven from God, shining with the glory of God. The city shone like a precious stone, like a jasper, clear as crystal. It had a great, high wall, with twelve gates, and with twelve angels in charge of the gates. On the gates were written the names of the twelve tribes of the people of Israel. There were three gates on each side: three on the east, three on the south, three on the north, and three on the west. The city's wall was built on twelve stones, on which were written the names of the twelve apostles of the Lamb.

I did not see a temple in the city, because its temple is the Lord God, the Almighty, and the Lamb. The city has no need of the sun or the moon to shine on it, because the glory of God shines on it, and the Lamb is its lamp. The peoples of the world will walk by its light, and the kings of the earth will bring their wealth into it. The gates of the city will stand open all day; they will never be closed, because there will be no night there. The greatness and the wealth of the nations will be brought into the city. But nothing that is impure will enter the city, nor anyone who

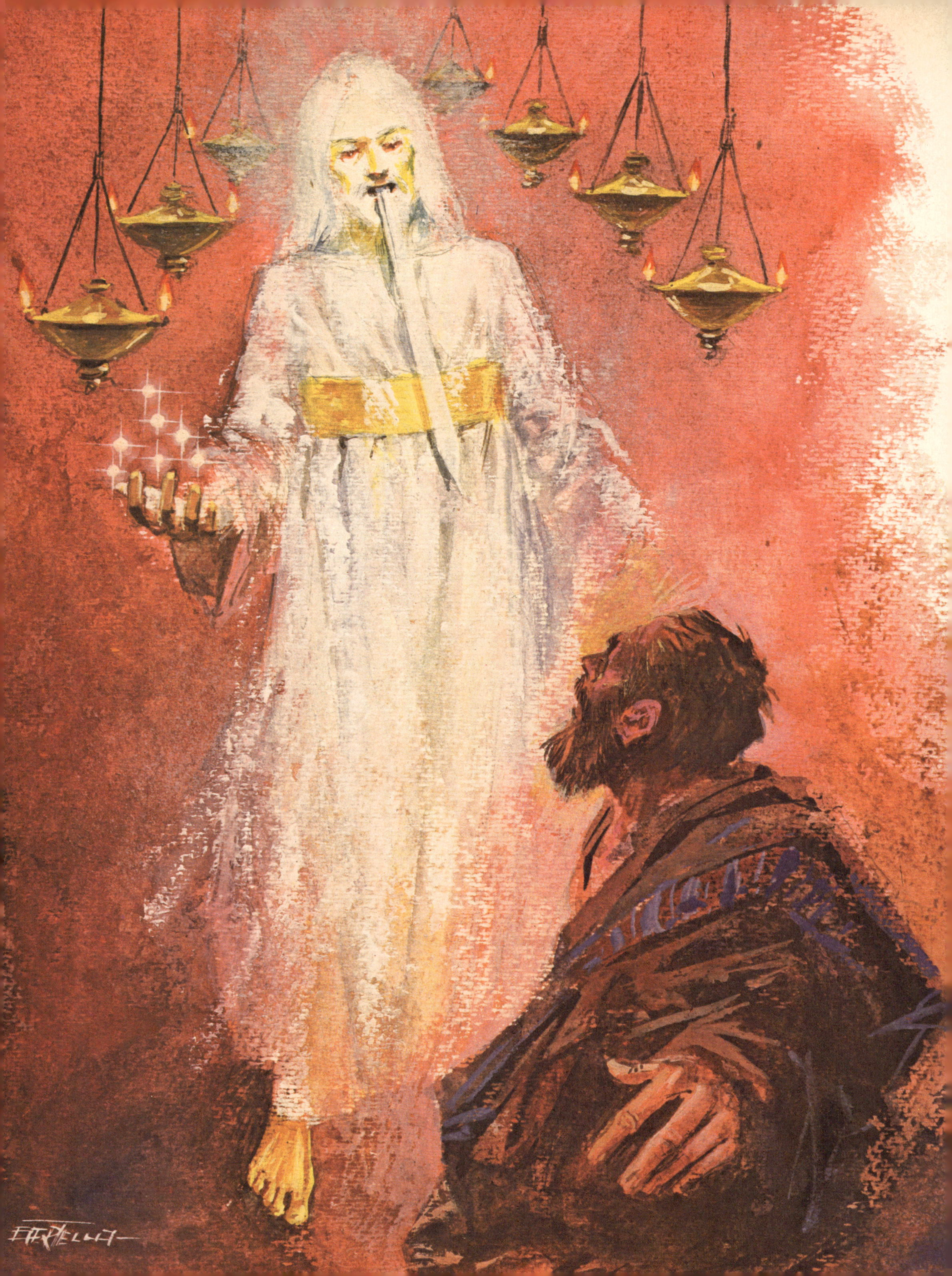

does shameful things or tells lies. Only those whose names are written in the Lamb's book of the living will enter the city.

The angel also showed me the river of the water of life, sparkling like crystal, which comes from the throne of God and of the Lamb, and flows down the middle of the city's street. On each side of the river was the tree of life, which bears fruit twelve times a year, once every month; and its leaves are for the healing of the nations.

The throne of God and of the Lamb will be in the city, and his servants will worship him. They will see his face, and his name will be written on their foreheads. There shall be no more night, and they will not need lamps or sunlight, because the Lord God will be their light, and they will rule as kings forever and ever.

Two Early Christian Hymns

quoted by Paul to the Philippians

He always had the very nature of God,
    but he did not think that by force he should try to become
        equal with God.
Instead, of his own free will he gave it all up,
    and took the nature of a servant.
He became like man,
    and appeared in human likeness.
He was humble and walked the path of obedience to death —
    his death on the cross.
For this reason God raised him to the highest place above,
    and gave him the name that is greater than any other name.
And so, in honour of the name of Jesus,
    all beings in heaven, on earth, and in the world below
    will fall on their knees,
and all will openly proclaim that Jesus Christ is the Lord,
    to the glory of God the Father.

and to Timothy

If we have died with him,
    we shall also live with him.
If we continue to endure,
    we shall also rule with him.
If we deny him,
    he also will deny us.
If we are not faithful,
    he remains faithful,
        because he cannot be false to himself.

8
We Saw his Glory

The fourth gospel was written by John. It includes some facts about Jesus which are not given to us in the other three gospels, but its main purpose is to explain the meaning of Jesus' life. John was a very wise and holy man who saw deeply into this meaning.

We learn from this gospel that the life of Jesus is God's Word: "the Word became a human being and lived among us." The life of Jesus brings new joy, a new birth, a new knowledge of God. The life of Jesus is like bread to feed us, and it is like light to make us see; for Jesus is like a shepherd guiding us, and like a servant washing us.

When in John's gospel Jesus speaks to his friends at his last supper, and when he prays for them before his death, we are allowed to see the glory which John saw. It is the glory of perfect love.

The Light Shines

The Word of Life

Before the world was created, the Word already existed; he was with God, and he was the same as God. From the very beginning, the Word was with God. Through him God made all things; not one thing in all creation was made without him. The Word was the source of life, and this life brought light to men. The light shines in the darkness, and the darkness has never put it out.

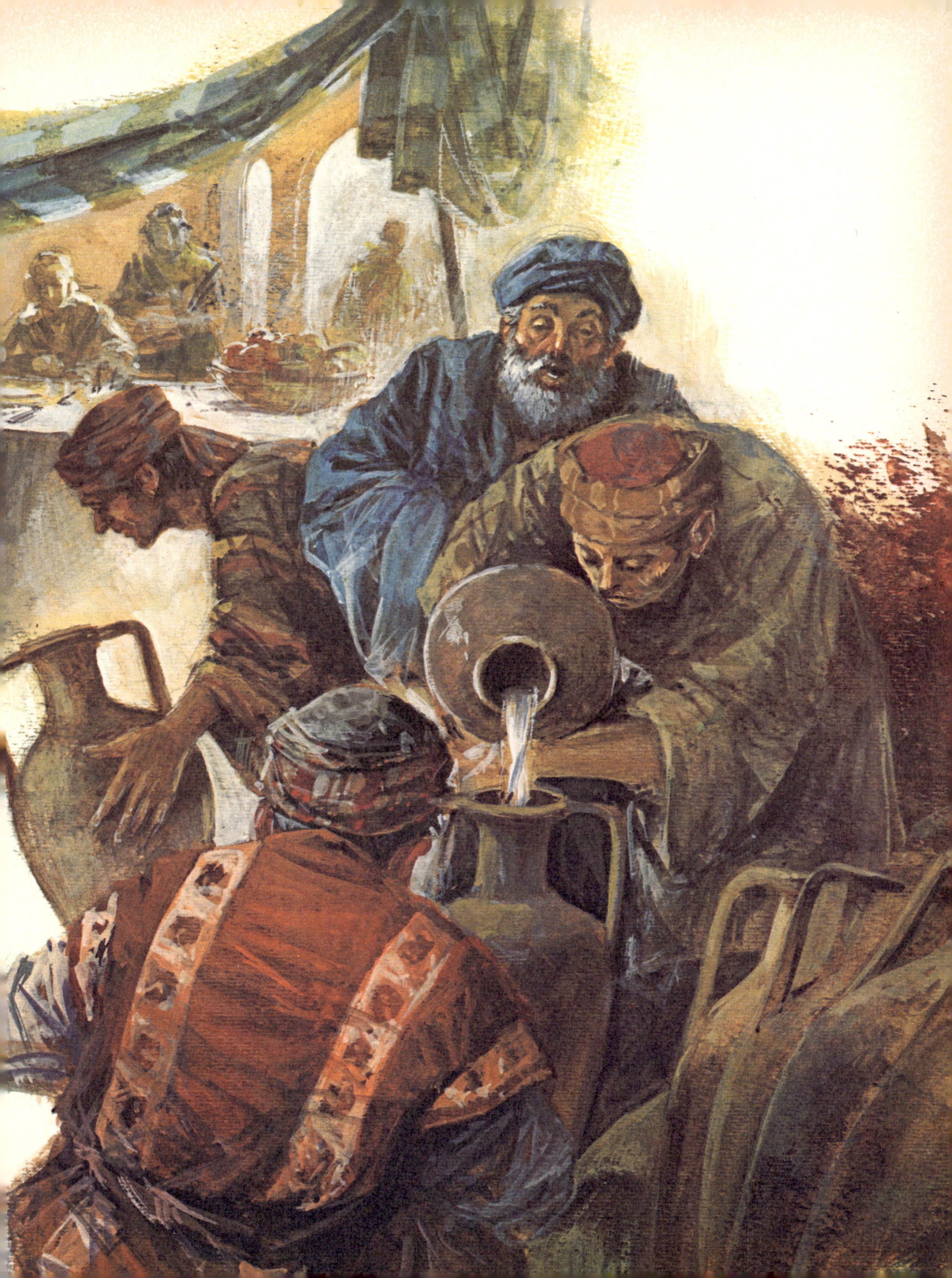

God sent his messenger, a man named John, who came to tell people about the light. He came to tell them, so that all should hear the message and believe. He himself was not the light; he came to tell about the light. This was the real light, the light that comes into the world and shines on all men.

The Word, then, was in the world. God made the world through him, yet the world did not know him. He came to his own country, but his own people did not receive him. Some, however, did receive him and believed in him; so he gave them the right to become God's children. They did not become God's children by natural means, by being born as the children of a human father; God himself was their Father.

The Word became a human being and lived among us. We saw his glory, full of grace and truth. This was the glory which he received as the Father's only Son.

John told about him. He cried out, "This is the one I was talking about when I said, 'He comes after me, but he is greater than I am, because he existed before I was born.'"

Out of the fulness of his grace he has blessed us all, giving us one blessing after another. God gave the Law through Moses; but grace and truth came through Jesus Christ. No one has ever seen God. The only One, who is the same as God and is at the Father's side, he has made him known.

The Wedding at Cana

There was a wedding in the town of Cana, in Galilee. Jesus' mother was there, and Jesus and his disciples had also been invited to the wedding. When all the wine had been drunk, Jesus' mother said to him, "They are out of wine."

"You must not tell me what to do, woman," Jesus replied. "My time has not yet come."

Jesus' mother then told the servants, "Do whatever he tells you."

The Jews have religious rules about washing, and for this purpose six stone water jars were there, each one large enough to hold between twenty and thirty gallons. Jesus said to the servants, "Fill these jars with water." They filled them to the brim, and then he told them. "Now draw some water out and take it to the man in charge of the feast." They took it to him, and he tasted the water, which had turned into wine. He did not know where this wine had come from (but the servants who had drawn out the water knew); so he called the bridegroom and said to him, "Everyone else serves the best wine first, and after the guests have drunk a lot he serves the ordinary wine. But you have kept the best wine until now!"

Jesus performed this first of his mighty works in Cana of Galilee; there he revealed his glory, and his disciples believed in him.

You Must All Be Born Again

Jesus and Nicodemus

There was a man named Nicodemus, a leader of the Jews, who belonged to the party of the Pharisees. One night he went to Jesus and said to him, "We know, Rabbi, that you are a teacher sent by God. No one could do the mighty works you are doing unless God were with him."

Jesus answered, "I tell you the truth: no one can see the Kingdom of God unless he is born again."

"How can a grown man be born again?" Nicodemus asked. "He certainly cannot enter his mother's womb and be born a second time!"

"I tell you the truth," replied Jesus, "that no one can enter the Kingdom of God unless he is born of water and the Spirit. A man is born physically of human parents, but he is born spiritually of the Spirit. Do not be surprised because I tell you, 'You must all be born again.' The wind blows wherever it wishes; you hear the sound it makes, but you do not know where it comes from or where it is going. It is the same way with everyone who is born of the Spirit."

"How can this be?" asked Nicodemus.

Jesus answered, "You are a great teacher of Israel, and you don't know this? I tell you the truth: we speak of what we know, and tell what we have seen, yet none of you is willing to accept our message. You do not believe me when I tell you about the things of this world; how will you ever believe me, then, when I tell you about the things of heaven? And no one has ever gone up to heaven except the Son of Man, who came down from heaven."

As Moses lifted up the bronze snake on a pole in the desert, in the same way the Son of Man must be lifted up, so that everyone who believes in him may have eternal life. For God loved the world so much that he gave his only Son, so that everyone who believes in him may not die but have eternal life. For God did not send his Son into the world to be its Judge, but to be its Saviour.

Jesus and the Woman of Samaria

Jesus came to a town in Samaria named Sychar, which was not far from the field that Jacob had given to his son Joseph. Jacob's well was there, and Jesus, tired out by the journey, sat down by the well. It was about noon.

A Samaritan woman came to draw some water, and Jesus said to her, "Give me a drink of water." (His disciples had gone into town to buy food.)

The woman answered, "You are a Jew and I am a Samaritan — how can you ask me for a drink?" (Jews will not use the same dishes that Samaritans use.)

Jesus answered, "If you only knew what God gives, and who it is that is asking you for a drink, you would ask him and he would give you living water."

"Sir," the woman said, "you don't have a bucket and the well is deep. Where would you get living water? Our ancestor Jacob gave us this well; he, his sons, and his flocks all drank from it. You don't claim to be greater than Jacob, do you?"

Jesus answered, "Whoever drinks this water will get thirsty again, but whoever drinks the water that I will give him will never be thirsty again. The water that I will give him will become in him a spring which will provide him with living water, and give him eternal life."

"Sir," the woman said, "give me this water! Then I will never be thirsty again, nor will I have to come here and draw water."

"Go call your husband," Jesus told her, "and come back here."

"I haven't got a husband," the woman said.

Jesus replied, "You are right when you say you haven't got a husband. You have been married to five men, and the man you live with now is not really your husband. You have told me the truth."

"I see you are a prophet, sir," the woman said. "My Samaritan ancestors worshipped God on this mountain, but you Jews say that Jerusalem is the place where we should worship God."

Jesus said to her, "Believe me, woman, the time will come when men will not worship the Father either on this mountain or in Jerusalem. You Samaritans do not really know whom you worship; we Jews know whom we worship, because salvation comes from the Jews. But the time is coming, and is already here, when the real worshippers will worship the Father in spirit and in truth. These are the worshippers the Father wants to worship him. God is Spirit, and those who worship him must worship in spirit and in truth."

The woman said to him, "I know that the Messiah, called Christ, will come. When he comes he will tell us everything."

Jesus answered, "I am he, I who am talking with you."

Jesus Heals an Official's Son

So Jesus went back to Cana of Galilee, where he had turned the water into wine. There was a government official there whose son in Capernaum was sick. When he heard that Jesus had come from Judea to Galilee, he went to him and asked him to go to Capernaum and heal his son, who was about to die. Jesus said to him, "None of you will ever believe unless you see great and wonderful works."

"Sir" replied the official, "come with me before my child dies."

Jesus said to him, "Go, your son will live!"

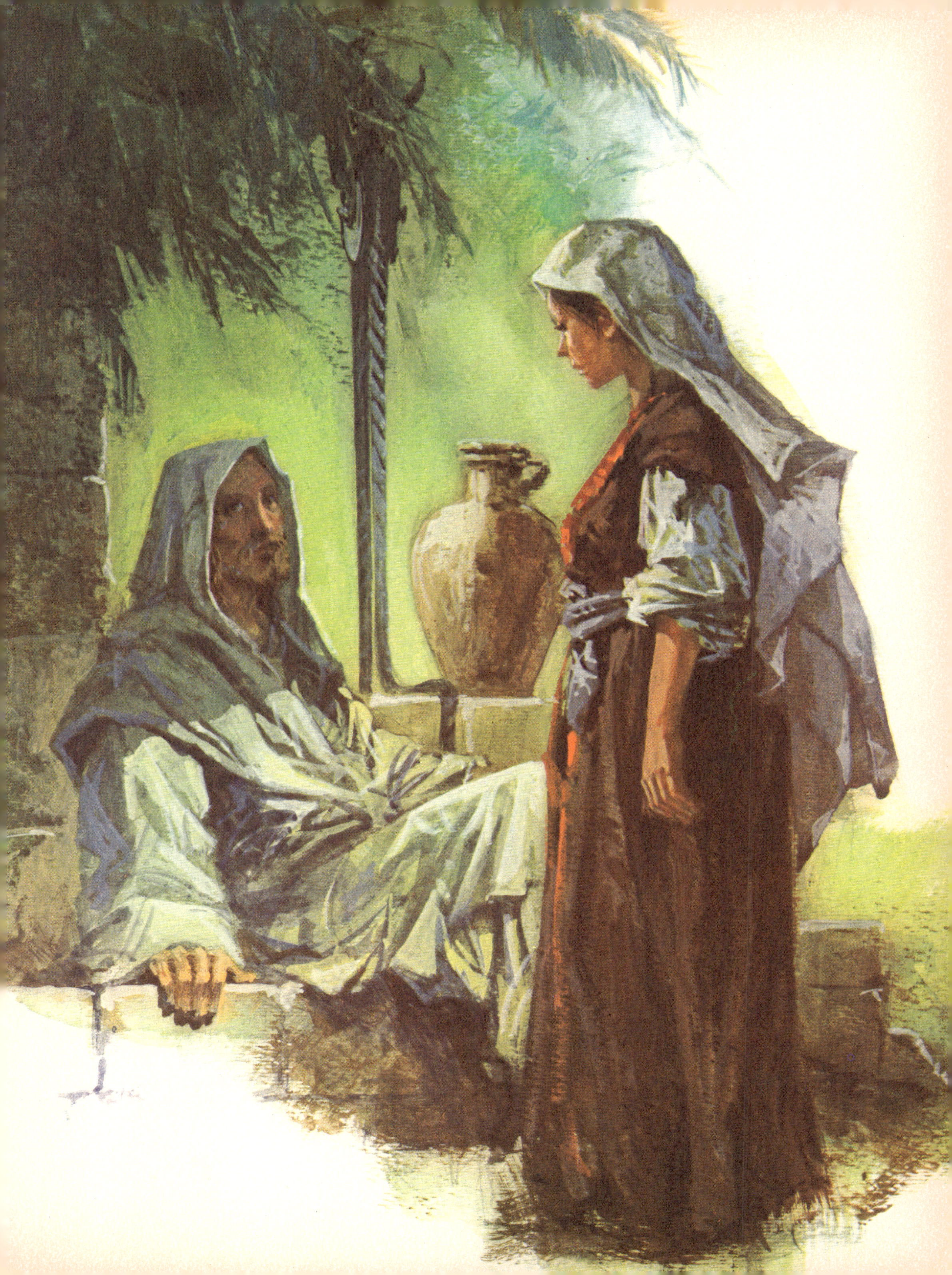

The man believed Jesus' words and went. On his way home his servants met him with the news, "Your boy is going to live!"

He asked them what time it was when his son got better, and they said, "It was one o'clock yesterday afternoon when the fever left him." The father remembered, then, that it was at that very hour when Jesus had told him, "Your son will live." So he and all his family believed.

Jesus the Bread of Life

"I am the bread of life," Jesus told them. "He who comes to me will never be hungry; he who believes in me will never be thirsty. Now, I told you that you have seen me but will not believe. Everyone whom my Father gives me will come to me. I will never turn away anyone who comes to me, because I have come down from heaven to do the will of him who sent me, not my own will. He who sent me wants me to do this: that I should not lose any of all those he has given me, but that I should raise them all to life on the last day. For what my Father wants is this: that all who see the Son and believe in him should have eternal life; and I will raise them to life on the last day."

Jesus Forgives a Woman in Jerusalem

Early next morning he went back to the temple. The whole crowd gathered round him, and he sat down and began to teach them. The teachers of the Law and the Pharisees brought in a woman who had been caught committing adultery, and made her stand before them all. "Teacher," they said to Jesus, "this woman was caught in the very act of committing adultery. In our Law Moses gave a commandment that such a woman must be stoned to death. Now, what do you say?" They said this to trap him, so they could accuse him. But Jesus bent over and wrote on the ground with his finger. As they stood there asking him questions, he straightened up and said to them, "Whichever one of you has committed no sin may throw the first stone at her." Then he bent over again and wrote on the ground. When they heard this they all left, one by one, the older ones first. Jesus was left alone, with the woman still standing there. He straightened up and said to her, "Where are they, woman? Is there no one left to condemn you?"

"No one, sir", she answered.

"Well, then," Jesus said, "I do not condemn you either. Go, but do not sin again."

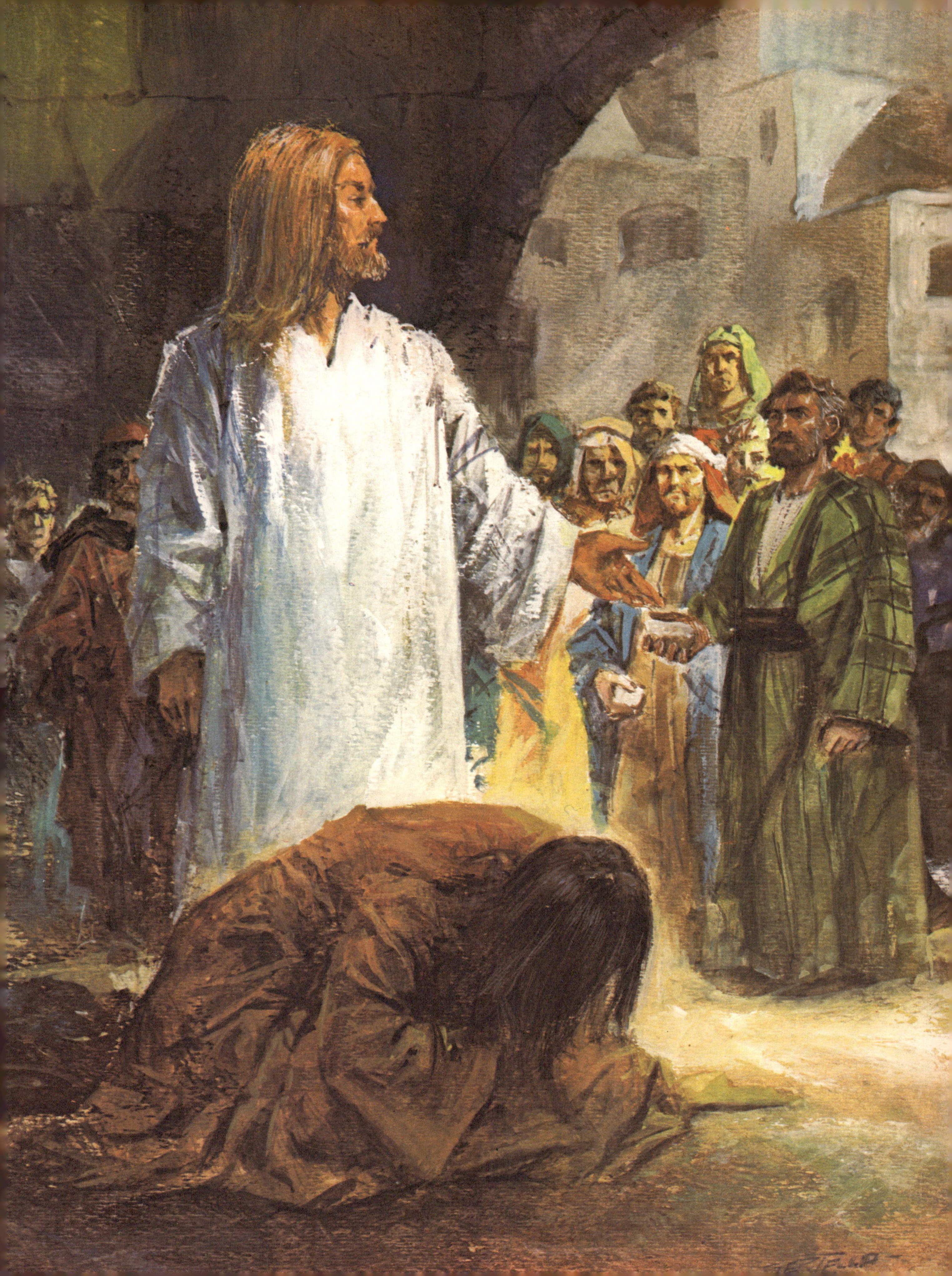

Jesus the Resurrection and the Life

One of the great signs of the power of Jesus is given in John's gospel when Jesus raises Lazarus from the dead. Jesus explains this to Martha, the sister of Lazarus.

Jesus said to her, "I am the resurrection and the life. Whoever believes in me will live, even though he dies; and whoever lives and believes in me will never die."

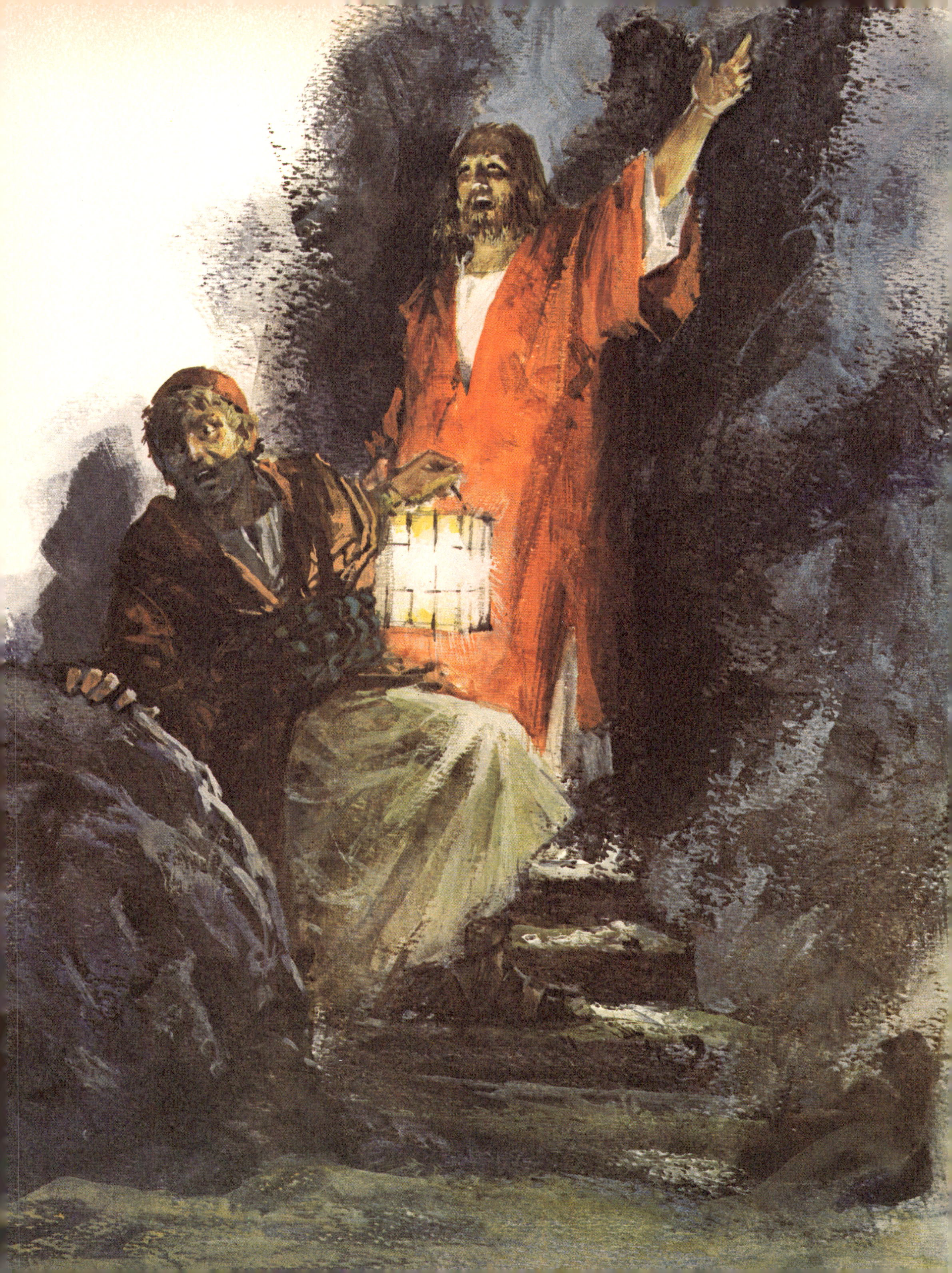

Jesus the Light of the World

Jesus spoke to them again, "I am the light of the world. Whoever follows me will have the light of life and will never walk in the darkness."

Jesus Heals a Man Born Blind

As Jesus walked along he saw a man who had been born blind. His disciples asked him, "Teacher, whose sin was it that caused him to be born blind? His own or his parents' sin?"

Jesus answered, "His blindness has nothing to do with his sins or his parents' sins. He is blind so that God's power might be seen at work in him. We must keep on doing the works of him who sent me, as long as it is day; the night is coming, when no one can work. While I am in the world I am the light for the world."

After he said this, Jesus spat on the ground and made some mud with the spittle; he rubbed the mud on the man's eyes, and told him, "Go wash your face in the Pool of Siloam." (This name means "Sent"). So the man went, washed his face, and came back seeing.

His neighbours, then, and the people who had seen him begging before this, asked, "Isn't this the man who used to sit and beg?"

Some said, "He is the one," but others said, "No he isn't, he just looks like him."

So the man himself said, "I am the man."

"How were your eyes opened?" they asked him.

He answered, "The man named Jesus made some mud, rubbed it on my eyes, and told me, 'Go to Siloam and wash your face.' So I went, and as soon as I washed I could see."

The Parable of the Sheepfold

Jesus said, "I tell you the truth: the man who does not enter the sheepfold by the door, but climbs in some other way, is a thief and a robber. The man who goes in by the door is the shepherd of the sheep. The gatekeeper opens the gate for him: the sheep hear his voice as he calls his own sheep by name, and he leads them out. When he has brought them out, he goes ahead of them, and the sheep follow him, because they know his voice. They will not follow someone else; instead, they will run away from him, because they do not know his voice."

Jesus told them this parable, but they did not understand what he was telling them.

Jesus the Good Shepherd

So Jesus said again, "I tell you the truth: I am the door for the sheep. All others who came before me are thieves and robbers; but the sheep did not listen to them. I am the door. Whoever comes in by me will be saved; he will come in and go out, and find pasture. The thief comes only in order to steal, kill, and destroy. I have come in order that they might have life, life in all its fulness.

"I am the good shepherd. The good shepherd is willing to die for the sheep. The hired man, who is not a shepherd and does not own the sheep, leaves them and runs away when he sees a wolf coming; so the wolf snatches the sheep and scatters them. The hired man runs away because he is only a hired man and does not care for the sheep. I am the good shepherd. As the Father knows me and I know the Father, in the same way I know my sheep and they know me. And I am willing to die for them. There are other sheep that belong to me that are not in this sheepfold. I must bring them, too; they will listen to my voice, and they will become one flock with one shepherd.

"The Father loves me because I am willing to give up my life, in order that I may receive it back again. No one takes my life away from me. I give it up of my own free will. I have the right to give it, and I have the right to take it back. This is what my Father has commanded me to do."

Jesus Washes his Disciples' Feet

It was now the day before the Feast of Passover. Jesus knew that his hour had come for him to leave this world and go to the Father. He had always loved those who were his own in the world, and he loved them to the very end.

Jesus and his disciples were at supper. The Devil had already decided that Judas, the son of Simon Iscariot, would betray Jesus. Jesus knew that the Father had given him complete power; he knew that he had come from God and was going to God. So Jesus rose from the table, took off his outer garment, and tied a towel round his waist. Then he poured some water into a washbasin and began to wash the disciples' feet and dry them with the towel round his waist. He came to Simon Peter, who said to him, "Are you going to wash my feet, Lord?"

Jesus answered him, "You do not know now what I am doing, but you will know later."

Peter declared, "You will never, at any time, wash my feet!"

"If I do not wash your feet," Jesus answered, "you will no longer be my disciple."

Simon Peter answered, "Lord, do not wash only my feet, then! Wash my hands and head, too!"

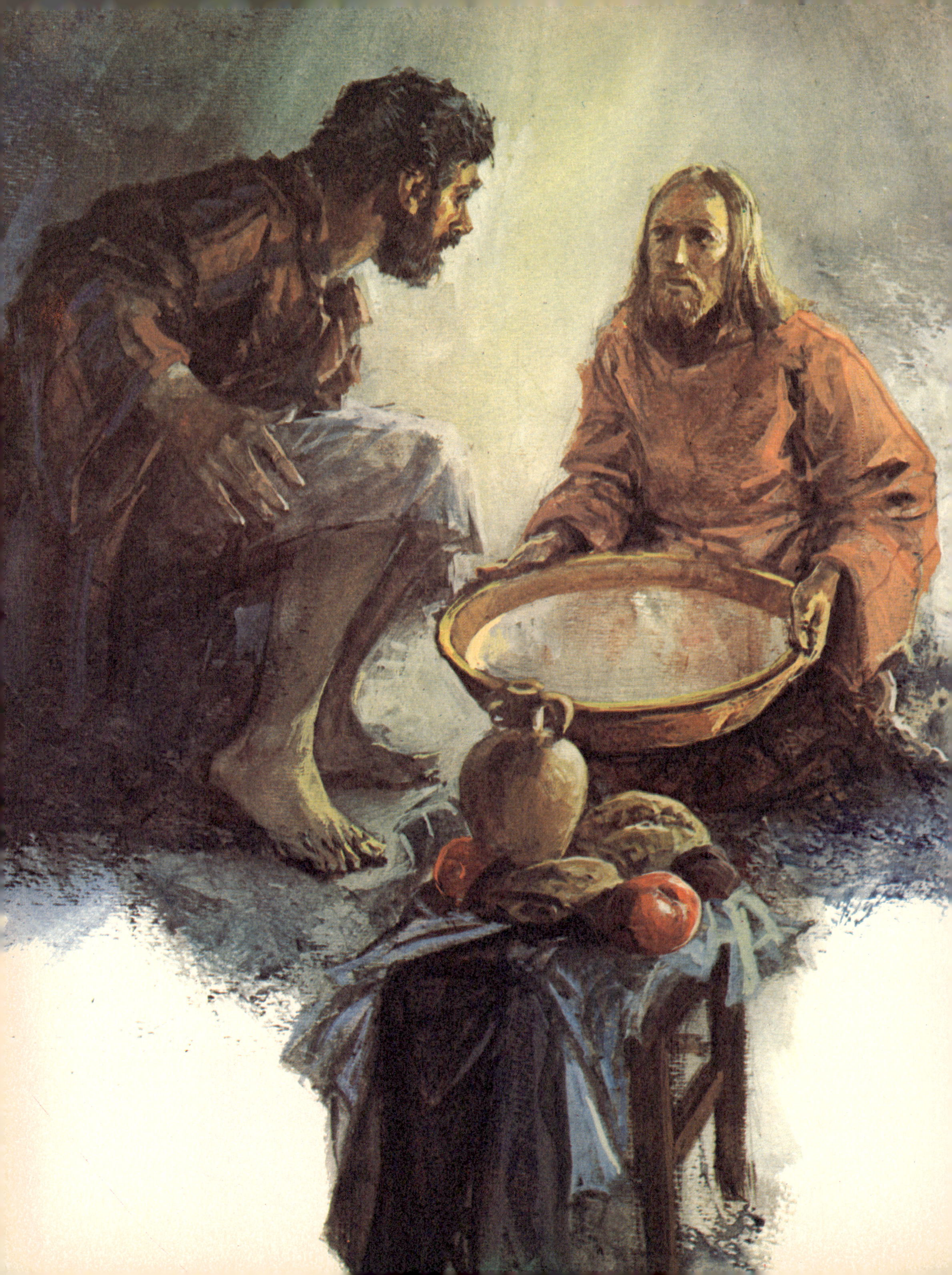

Jesus said, "Whoever has taken a bath is completely clean and does not have to wash himself, except for his feet. All of you are clean — all except one." (Jesus already knew who was going to betray him; that is why he said, "All of you, except one, are clean.")

After he had washed their feet, Jesus put his outer garment back on and returned to his place at the table. "Do you understand what I have just done to you?" he asked. "You call me Teacher and Lord, and it is right that you do so, because I am. I am your Lord and Teacher, and I have just washed your feet. You, then, should wash each other's feet. I have set an example for you, so that you will do just what I have done for you. I tell you the truth: no slave is greater than his master; no messenger is greater than the one who sent him. Now you know this truth; how happy you will be if you put it into practice!"

Jesus Speaks to his Friends at the Last Supper

Jesus the Way to the Father

"Do not be worried and upset," Jesus told them. "Believe in God, and believe also in me. There are many rooms in my Father's house, and I am going to prepare a place for you. I would not tell you this if it were not so. And after I go and prepare a place for you, I will come back and take you to myself, so that you will be where I am. You know how to get to the place where I am going."

Thomas said to him, "Lord, we do not know where you are going; how can we know the way to get there?"

Jesus answered him, "I am the way, the truth, and the life; no one goes to the Father except by me. Now that you have known me," he said to them, "you will know my Father also; and from now on you do know him, and you have seen him."

Philip said to him, "Lord, show us the Father; that is all we need."

Jesus answered, "For a long time I have been with you all; yet you do not know me, Philip? Whoever has seen me has seen the Father. Why, then, do you say, 'Show us the Father'? Do you not believe, Philip, that I am in the Father and the Father is in me? The words that I have spoken to you," Jesus said to his disciples, "do not come from me. The Father, who remains in me, does his own works. Believe me that I am in the Father and the Father is in me. If not, believe because of these works. I tell you the truth: whoever believes in me will do the works I do — yes, he will do even greater ones, because I am going to the Father. And I will do whatever you ask for in my name, so that the Father's glory will be shown through the Son. If you ask me for anything in my name, I will do it."

The Promise of the Holy Spirit

"If you love me, you will obey my commandments. I will ask the Father, and he will give you another Helper, the Spirit of truth, to stay with you forever. The world cannot receive him, because it cannot see him or know him. But you know him, because he remains with you and lives in you.

"I will not leave you alone; I will come back to you. In a little while the world will see me no more, but you will see me; and because I live, you also will live. When that day comes, you will know that I am in my Father, and that you are in me, just as I am in you.

"Whoever accepts my commandments and obeys them, he is the one who loves me. My Father will love him who loves me; I too will love him and reveal myself to him."

Judas (not Judas Iscariot) said, "Lord, how can it be that you will reveal yourself to us and not to the world?"

Jesus answered him, "Whoever loves me will obey my message. My Father will love him, and my Father and I will come to him and live with him. Whoever does not love me does not obey my words. The message you have heard is not mine, but comes from the Father, who sent me.

"I have told you this while I am still with you. The Helper, the Holy Spirit whom the Father will send in my name, will teach you everything, and make you remember all that I have told you.

"Peace I leave with you; my own peace I give you. I do not give it to you as the world does. Do not be worried and upset; do not be afraid. You heard me say to you, 'I am leaving, but I will come back to you.' If you loved me, you would be glad that I am going to the Father, because he is greater than I. I have told you this now, before it all happens, so that when it does happen you will believe. I cannot talk with you much longer, because the ruler of this world is coming. He has no power over me, but the world must know that I love the Father; that is why I do everything as he commands me."

Jesus the Real Vine

"I am the real vine, and my Father is the gardener. He breaks off every branch in me that does not bear fruit, and prunes every branch that does bear fruit, so that it will be clean and bear more fruit. You have been made clean already by the message I have spoken to you. Remain united to me, and I will remain united to you. A branch cannot bear fruit by itself; it can do so only if it remains in the vine. In the same way you cannot bear fruit unless you remain in me.

"I am the vine, you are the branches. Whoever remains in me, and I in him, will bear much fruit; for you can do nothing without me. Whoever does not remain in me is thrown out, like a branch, and dries up; such branches are gathered up and thrown into the fire, where they are burned. If you remain in me, and my words remain in you, then you will ask for anything you wish, and you shall have it. This is how my Father's glory is shown: by your bearing much fruit; and in this way you become my disciples. I love you just as the Father loves me; remain in my love. If you obey my commands, you will remain in my love, just as I have obeyed my Father's commands and remain in his love.

"I have told you this so that my joy may be in you, and that your joy may be complete. My commandment is this: love one another, just as I love you. The greatest love a man can have for his friends is to give his life for them. And you are my friends, if you do what I command you. I do not call you servants any longer, because a servant does not know what his master is doing. Instead, I call you friends, because I have told you everything I heard from my Father. You did not choose me; I chose you, and appointed you to go and bear much fruit, the kind of fruit that endures. And so the Father will give you whatever you ask of him in my name. This, then, is what I command you: love one another."

The World's Hatred

"If the world hates you, you must remember that it has hated me first. If you belonged to the world, then the world would love you as its own. But I chose you from this world, and you do not belong to it; this is why the world hates you. Remember what I told you; 'No slave is greater than his master.' If they persecuted me, they will persecute you too; if they obeyed my message, they will obey yours too. But they will do all this to you because you are mine; for they do not know him who sent me. They would not have been guilty of sin if I had not come and spoken to them; as it is, they no longer have any excuse for their sin. Whoever hates me hates my Father also. They would not have been guilty of sin if I had not done the works among them that no one else ever did; as it is, they have seen what I did and they hate both me and my Father. This must be, however, so that what is written in their Law may come true, 'They hated me for no reason at all.'

"The Helper will come — the Spirit of truth, who comes from the Father. I will send him to you from the Father, and he will speak about me. And you, too, will speak about me, because you have been with me from the very beginning.

"I have told you this so that you will not fall away. They will put you out of their synagogues. And the time will come when anyone who kills you will think that by doing this he is serving God. They will do these things to you because they have not known either the Father or me. But I have told you this, so that when the time comes for them to do these things, you will remember that I told you."

The Work of the Holy Spirit

"I did not tell you these things at the beginning, because I was with you. But now I am going to him who sent me; yet none of you asks me, 'Where are you going?' And now that I have told you, sadness has filled your hearts. But I tell you the truth: it is better for you that I go away, because if I do not go, the Helper will not come to you. But if I do go away, then I will send him to you. And when he comes he will prove to the people of the world that they are wrong about sin, and about what is right, and about God's judgment. They are wrong about sin, because they do not believe in me; about what is right, because I am going to the Father and you will not see me any more; about judgment, because the ruler of this world has already been judged.

"I have much more to tell you, but now it would be too much for you to bear. But when the Spirit of truth comes, he will lead you into all the truth. He will not speak on his own, but he will speak of what he hears and tell you of things to come. He will give me glory, because he will take what I have to say and tell it to you. All that my Father has is mine; that is why I said that the Spirit will take what I give him and tell it to you."

Sadness and Gladness

"In a little while you will not see me any more; and then a little while later you will see me."

Some of his disciples said to the others, "What does this mean? He tells us, 'In a little while you will not see me, and then a little while later you will see me'; and he also says, 'It is because I am going to the Father.' What does this 'a little while' mean?" they asked. "We do not know what he is talking about!"

Jesus knew that they wanted to ask him, so he said to them, "I said, 'In a little while you will not see me, and then a little while later you will see me.' Is this what you are asking about among yourselves? I tell you the truth: you will cry and weep, but the world will be glad; you will be sad, but your sadness will turn into gladness. When a woman is about to give birth to a child she is sad, because her hour of suffering has come; but when the child is born she forgets her suffering, because she is happy that a baby has been born into the world. That is the way it is with you: now you are sad, but I will see you again, and your hearts will be filled with gladness, the kind of gladness that no one can take away from you.

"When that day comes you will not ask me for anything. I tell you the truth: the Father will give you whatever you ask of him in my name. Until now you have not asked for anything in my name; ask and you will receive, so that your happiness may be complete."

Victory over the World

"I have told you these things by means of parables. But the time will come when I will use parables no more, but I will speak to you in plain words about the Father. When that day comes you will ask him in my name; and I do not say that I will ask him on your behalf, because the Father himself loves you. He loves you because you love me and have believed that I came from God. I did come from the Father and I came into the world; and now I am leaving the world and going to the Father."

Then his disciples said to him, "Look, you are speaking very plainly now, without using parables. We know now that you know everything; you do not need someone to ask you questions. This makes us believe that you came from God."

Jesus answered them, "Do you believe now? The time is coming, and is already here, when all of you will be scattered, each one to his own home, and I will be left all alone. But I am not really alone, because the Father is with me. I have told you this so that you will have peace by being united to me. The world will make you suffer. But be brave! I have defeated the world!"

Jesus Prays for his Friends before his Death

After Jesus finished saying this, he looked up to heaven and said, "Father, the hour has come. Give glory to your Son, that the Son may give glory to you. For you gave him authority over all men, so that he might give eternal life to all those you gave him. And this is eternal life: for men to know you, the only true God, and to know Jesus Christ, whom you sent. I showed your glory on earth; I finished the work you gave me to do. Father! Give me glory in your presence now, the same glory I had with you before the world was made.

"I have made you known to the men you gave me out of the world. They belonged to you, and you gave them to me. They have obeyed your word, and now they know that everything you gave me comes from you. I gave them the message that you gave me, and they received it; they know that it is true that I came from you, and they believe that you sent me.

"I pray for them. I do not pray for the world, but for the men you gave me, because they belong to you. All I have is yours, and all you have is mine; and my glory is shown through them. And now I am coming to you; I am no longer in the world, but they are in the world. Holy Father! Keep them safe by the power of your name, the name you gave me, so they may be one just as you and I are one. While I was with them I kept them safe by the power of your name, the name you gave me. I protected them, and not one of them was lost, except the man who was bound to be lost — that the scripture might come true. And now I am coming to you, and I say these things in the world so that they might have my joy in their hearts, in all its fulness. I gave them your message and the world hated them, because they do not belong to the world, just as I do not belong to the world. I do not ask you to take them out of the world, but I do ask you to keep them safe from the Evil One. Just as I do not belong to the world, they do not belong to the world. Dedicate them to yourself, by means of the truth; your word is truth. I sent them into the world just as you sent me into the world. And for their sake I dedicate myself to you, in order that they, too, may be truly dedicated to you.

"I do not pray only for them, but also for those who believe in me because of their message. I pray that they may all be one. Father! May they be in us, just as you are in me and I am in you. May they be one, so that the world will believe that you sent me. I gave them the same glory you gave me, so that they may be one, just as you and I are one: I in them and you in me, so that they may be completely one, in order that the world may know that you sent me and that you love them as you love me.

"Father! You have given them to me, and I want them to be with me where I am, so that they may see my glory, the glory you gave me, because you loved me before the world was made. Righteous Father! The world does not know you, but I know you, and these know that you sent me. I made you known to them and I will continue to do so, in order that the love you have for me may be in them, and I also may be in them."

Conclusion

Now, there are many other things that Jesus did. If they were all written down one by one, I suppose that the whole world could not hold the books that would be written.

9
How to Follow Jesus

Luke wrote a second book after his gospel: The Acts of the Apostles. He told how Christianity spread from Jerusalem to Rome because it was filled with the power of God, the Holy Spirit.

Some letters of John have survived, and they show the love and the hope which gave such joy to Christian life.

Some of Paul's letters were also treasured, and they help us to understand that this love and hope can still produce great joy, whenever anyone learns from Jesus what love means.

Why the Apostles Acted

Luke writes

Jesus Is Taken up to Heaven

When the apostles met together with Jesus they asked him, "Lord, will you at this time give the Kingdom back to Israel?"

Jesus said to them, "The times and occasions are set by my Father's own authority, and it is not for you to know when they will be. But you will be filled with power when the Holy Spirit comes on you, and you will be witnesses for me in Jerusalem, in all of Judea and Samaria, and to the ends of the earth." After saying this, he was taken up to heaven as they watched him; and a cloud hid him from their sight.

They still had their eyes fixed on the sky as he went away, when two men dressed in white suddenly stood beside them. "Men of Galilee," they said, "why do you stand there looking up at the sky? This Jesus, who was taken up from you into heaven, will come back in the same way that you saw him go to heaven."

Then the apostles went back to Jerusalem from the Mount of Olives, which is about half a mile away from the city. They entered Jerusalem and went up to the room where they were staying: Peter, John, James and Andrew, Philip and Thomas, Bartholomew and Matthew, James, the son of Alphaeus, Simon the Patriot, and Judas, the son of James. They gathered frequently to pray as a group, together with the women, and with Mary the mother of Jesus, and his brothers.

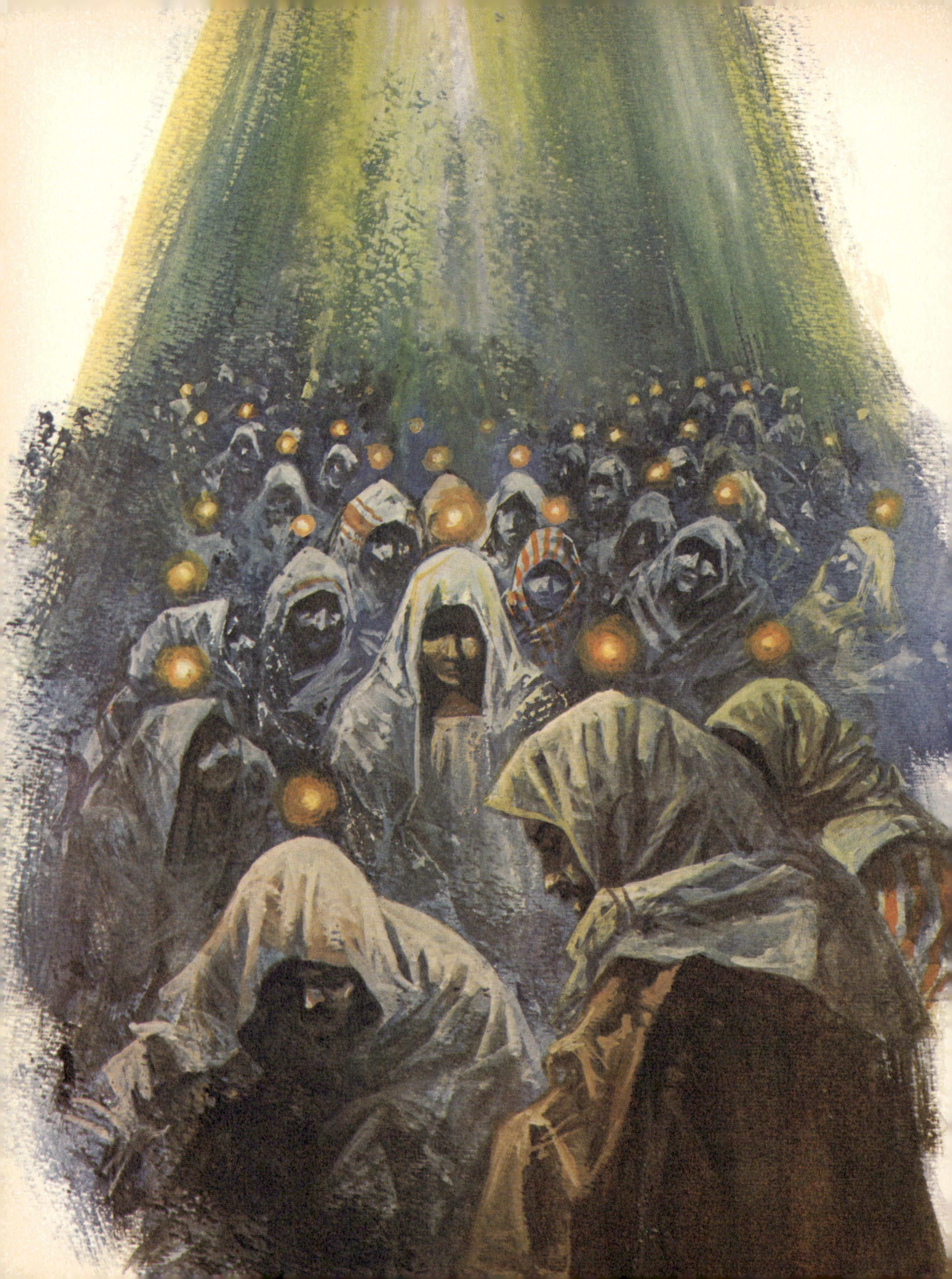

The Coming of the Holy Spirit

When the day of Pentecost arrived, all the believers were gathered together in one place. Suddenly there was a noise from the sky which sounded like a strong wind blowing, and it filled the whole house where they were sitting. Then they saw what looked like tongues of fire spreading out; and each person there was touched by a tongue. They were all filled with the Holy Spirit and began to talk in other languages, as the Spirit enabled them to speak.

There were Jews living in Jerusalem, religious men who had come from every country in the world. When they heard this noise, a large crowd gathered. They were all excited, because each one of them heard the believers talking in his own language. In amazement and wonder they exclaimed, "These men who are talking like this — they are all Galileans! How is it, then, that all of us hear them speaking in our own native language? We are from Parthia, Media, and Elam; from Mesopotamia, Judea, and Cappadocia; from Pontus and Asia, from Phrygia and Pamphylia, from Egypt and the regions of Libya near Cyrene; some of us are from Rome, both Jews and Gentiles converted to Judaism; and some of us are from Crete and Arabia — yet all of us hear them speaking in our own languages of the great things that God has done!" Amazed and confused they all kept asking each other, "What does this mean?"

But others made fun of the believers, saying, "These men are drunk!"

Peter's Message

Then Peter stood up with the other eleven apostles, and in a loud voice began to speak to the crowd, "Fellow Jews, and all of you who live in Jerusalem, listen to me and let me tell you what this means. These men are not drunk, as you suppose; it is only nine o'clock in the morning. Rather, this is what the prophet Joel spoke about.

'This is what I will do in the last days, God says:
    I will pour out my Spirit upon all men.
Your sons and your daughters will prophesy;
        your young men will see visions,
        and your old men will dream dreams.' "

Peter made his appeal to them and with many other words he urged them, saying, "Save yourselves from the punishment coming to this wicked people!" Many of them believed his message, and were baptized; about three thousand people were added to the group that day. They spent their time in learning from the apostles, taking part in the fellowship, and sharing in the fellowship meals and the prayers.

Life among the Believers

Many miracles and wonders were done through the apostles, and this caused everyone to be filled with awe. All the believers continued together in close fellowship and shared their belongings with one another. They would sell their property and possessions and distribute the money among all, according to what each one needed. Every day they continued to meet as a group in the temple, and they had their meals together in their homes, eating the food with glad and humble hearts, praising God and enjoying the good will of all the people. And every day the Lord added to their group those who were being saved.

John Writes about God's Love

Children of God

See how much the Father has loved us! His love is so great that we are called God's children — and so, in fact, we are. This is why the world does not know us: it has not known God. My dear friends, we are now God's children, but it is not yet clear what we shall become. But we know that when Christ appears, we shall become like him, because we shall see him as he really is. Everyone who has this hope in Christ keeps himself pure, just as Christ is pure.

Whoever sins is guilty of breaking God's law; because sin is a breaking of the law. You know that Christ appeared in order to take away men's sins, and that there is no sin in him. So everyone who lives in Christ does not continue to sin; but whoever continues to sin has never seen him or known him.

Let no one deceive you, children! Whoever does what is right is righteous, just as Christ is righteous. Whoever continues to sin belongs to the Devil, because the Devil has sinned from the very beginning. The Son of God appeared for this very reason, to destroy the Devil's works.

Whoever is a child of God does not continue to sin, because God's very nature is in him; and because God is his Father, he cannot continue to sin. Here is the clear difference between God's children and the Devil's children: anyone who does not do what is right, or does not love his brother, is not God's child.

God Is Love

Dear friends! Let us love one another, because love comes from God. Whoever loves is a child of God and knows God. Whoever does not love does not know God, because God is love. This is how God showed his love for us: he sent his only Son into the world that we might have life through him. This is what love is: it is not that we have loved God, but that he loved us and sent his Son to be the means by which our sins are forgiven.

Dear friends, if this is how God loved us, then we should love one another. No one has ever seen God; if we love one another, God lives in us and his love is made perfect in us.

This is how we are sure that we live in God and he lives in us: he has given us his Spirit. And we have seen and tell others that the Father sent his Son to be the Saviour of the world. Whoever declares that Jesus is the Son of God, God lives in him, and he lives in God. And we ourselves know and believe the love which God has for us.

God is love, and whoever lives in love lives in God and God lives in him. The purpose of love being made perfect in us is that we may have courage on Judgment Day; and we will have it because our life in this world is the same as Christ's. There is no fear in love; perfect love drives out all fear. So then, love has not been made perfect in the one who fears, because fear has to do with punishment.

We love because God first loved us. If someone says, "I love God," but hates his brother, he is a liar. For he cannot love God, whom he has not seen, if he does not love his brother, whom he has seen. This, then, is the command that Christ gave us: he who loves God must love his brother also.

A Prayer in the Letter to the Ephesians

For this reason, then, I fall on my knees before the Father, from whom every family in heaven and on earth receives its true name. I ask God, from the wealth of his glory, to give you power through his Spirit to be strong in your inner selves, and that Christ will make his home in your hearts, through faith. I pray that you may have your roots and foundations in love, so that you, together with all God's people, may have the power to understand how broad and long and high and deep is Christ's love. Yes, may you come to know his love — although it can never be fully known — and so be completely filled with the perfect fulness of God.

To him who is able to do so much more than we can ever ask for, or even think of, by means of the power working in us: to God be the glory in the church and in Christ Jesus, for all time, forever and ever! Amen.

Unity and Love: Paul Writes to the Corinthians

One Body with Many Parts

Christ is like a single body, which has many parts; it is still one body, even though it is made up of different parts. In the same way, all of us, Jews and Gentiles, slaves and free men, have been baptized into the one body by the same Spirit, and we have all been given the one Spirit to drink.

For the body itself is not made up of only one part, but of many parts. If the foot were to say, "Because I am not a hand, I don't belong to the body," that would not make it stop being a part of the body. And if the ear were to say, "Because I am not an eye, I don't belong to the body," that would not make it stop being a part of the body. If the whole body were just an eye, how could it hear? And if it were only an ear, how could it smell? As it is, however, God put every different part in the body just as he wished. There would not be a body if it were all only one part! As it is, there are many parts, and one body.

So then, the eye cannot say to the hand, "I don't need you!" Nor can the head say to the feet, "Well, I don't need you!" On the contrary, we cannot do without the parts of the body that seem to be weaker; and those parts that we think aren't worth very much are the ones which we treat with greater care; while the parts of the body which don't look very nice receive special attention, which the more beautiful parts of our body do not need. God himself has put the body together in such a way as to give greater honour to those parts that lack it. And so there is no division in the body, but all its different parts have the same concern for one another. If one part of the body suffers, all the other parts suffer with it; if one part is praised, all the other parts share its happiness.

All of you, then, are Christ's body, and each one is a part of it. In the church, then, God has put all in place: in the first place, apostles, in the the second place, prophets, and in the third place, teachers; then those who perform miracles, followed by those who are given the power to heal, or to help others, or to direct them, or to speak in strange tongues. They are not all apostles, or prophets, or teachers. Not all have the power to work miracles, or to heal diseases, or to speak in strange tongues, or to explain what is said. Set your hearts, then, on the more important gifts.

Best of all, however, is the following way.

Love

I may be able to speak the languages of men and even of angels, but if I have not love, my speech is no more than a noisy gong or a clanging bell. I may have the gift of inspired preaching; I may have all knowledge and understand all secrets; I may have all the faith needed to move mountains

— but if I have not love, I am nothing. I may give away everything I have, and even give up my body to be burned — but if I have not love, it does me no good.

Love is patient and kind; love is not jealous, or conceited, or proud; love is not ill-mannered, or selfish, or irritable; love does not keep a record of wrongs; love is not happy with evil, but is happy with the truth. Love never gives up: its faith, hope, and patience never fail.

Love is eternal. There are inspired messages, but they are temporary; there are gifts of speaking in strange tongues, but they will cease; there is knowledge, but it will pass. For our gifts of knowledge and of inspired messages are only partial; but when what is perfect comes, then what is partial will disappear.

When I was a child, my speech, feelings, and thinking were all those of a child; now that I am a man, I have no more use for childish ways. What we see now is like the dim image in a mirror; then we shall see face to face. What I know now is only partial; then it will be complete, as complete as God's knowledge of me.

Meanwhile these three remain: faith, hope, and love; and the greatest of these is love.

Paul's Prayer

The grace of the Lord Jesus Christ, the love of God, and the fellowship of the Holy Spirit be with you all.

The Christian Life in Paul's Letters

Father, my Father!

To show that you are his sons, God sent the Spirit of his Son into our hearts, the Spirit who cries, "Father, my Father." So then, you are no longer a slave, but a son. And since you are his son, God will give you all he has for his sons.

The Spirit and Human Nature

What I say is this: let the Spirit direct your lives, and do not satisfy the desires of the human nature. For what our human nature wants is opposed to what the Spirit wants, and what the Spirit wants is opposed to what human nature wants. The two are enemies, and this means that you cannot do what you want to do. If the Spirit leads you, then you are not subject to the Law.

What human nature does is quite plain. It shows itself in immoral, filthy, and indecent actions; in worship of idols and witchcraft. People become enemies, they fight, become jealous, angry, and ambitious. They separate into parties and groups; they are envious, get drunk, have orgies, and do other things like these. I warn you now as I have before: those who do these things will not receive the Kingdom of God.

But the Spirit produces love, joy, peace, patience, kindness, goodness, faithfulness, humility, and self-control. There is no law against such things as these. And those who belong to Christ Jesus have put to death their human nature, with all its passions and desires. The Spirit has given us life; he must also control our lives. We must not be proud, or irritate one another, or be jealous of one another.

The Power of the Gospel

I have complete confidence in the gospel; it is God's power to save all who believe, first the Jews and also the Gentiles. For the gospel reveals how God puts men right with himself: it is through faith, from beginning to end. As the scripture says, "He who is put right with God through faith shall live."

The Whole Armour of God

Build up your strength in union with the Lord, and by means of his mighty power. Put on all the armour that God gives you, so that you will stand up against the Devil's evil tricks. For we are not fighting against human beings, but against the wicked spiritual forces in the heavenly world, the rulers, authorities, and cosmic powers of this dark age. So take up God's armour now! Then when the evil day comes, you will be able to resist the enemy's attacks, and after fighting to the end, you will still hold your ground.

So stand ready: have truth for a belt tight round your waist; put on righteousness for your breastplate, and the readiness to announce the Good News of peace as shoes for your feet. At all times carry faith as a shield; with it you will be able to put out all the burning arrows shot by the Evil One. And accept salvation for a helmet, and the word of God as the sword that the Spirit gives you. Do all this in prayer, asking for God's help. Pray on every occasion, as the Spirit leads. For this reason keep alert and never give up; pray always for all God's people. And pray also for me, that God will give me a message, when I am ready to speak, that I may speak boldly and make known the gospel's secret. For the sake of this gospel I am an ambassador, though now I am in prison. Pray that I may be bold in speaking of it, as I should.

To Live Is Christ

I want you to know, my brothers, that the things that have happened to me have really helped the progress of the gospel. As a result, the whole palace guard and all the others here know that I am in prison because I am a servant of Christ. And my being in prison has given most of the brothers more confidence in the Lord, so that they grow bolder all the time in preaching the message without fear.

Of course some of them preach Christ because they are jealous and quarrelsome, but others preach him with all good will. These do so from love, because they know that God has given me the work of defending the gospel. The others do not proclaim Christ sincerely, but from a spirit of selfish ambition; they think that they will make more trouble for me while I am in prison.

It does not matter! I am happy about it — just so Christ is preached in every way possible, whether from wrong or right motives. And I will continue to be happy, because I know that by means of your prayers and the help which comes from the Spirit of Jesus Christ, I shall be set free. My deep desire and hope is that I shall never fail my duty, but that at all times, and especially right now, I shall be full of courage, so that with my whole being I shall bring honour to Christ, whether I live or die. For what is life? To me, it is Christ. Death, then, will bring more. But if by living on I can do more worthwhile work, then I am not sure which I should choose. I am caught from both sides. I want very much to leave this life and be with Christ, which is a far better thing; but it is much more important, for your sake, that I remain alive. I am sure of this, and so I know that I will stay. I will stay on with you all, to add to your progress and joy in the faith. So when I am with you again you will have even more reason to be proud of me, in your life in Christ Jesus.

Now, the important thing is that your manner of life be as the gospel of Christ requires, so that, whether or not I am able to go to see you, I will hear that you stand firm with one common purpose, and fight together, with only one wish, for the faith of the gospel. Don't be afraid of your enemies; always be courageous, and this will prove to them that they will lose, and that you will win, because it is God who gives you the victory. For you have been given the privilege of serving Christ, not only by believing in him, but also by suffering for him. Now you can take part with me in the fight. It is the same one you saw me fighting in the past and the same one I am still fighting, as you hear.

Christian Joy and Peace

May you always be joyful in your life in the Lord. I say it again: rejoice!

Show a gentle attitude towards all. The Lord is coming soon. Don't worry about anything, but in all your prayers ask God for what you need, always asking him with a thankful heart. And God's peace, which is far beyond human understanding, will keep your hearts and minds safe, in union with Christ Jesus.

In conclusion, my brothers, fill your minds with those things that are good and deserve praise: things that are true, noble, right, pure, lovely, and honourable. Put into practice what you learned and received from me, both from my words and from my deeds. And the God who gives us peace will be with you.

Running towards the Goal

I do not claim that I have already succeeded or have already become perfect. I keep going on to try to win the prize for which Christ Jesus has already won me to himself. Of course, brothers, I really do not think that I have already won it; the one thing I do, however, is to forget what is behind me and do my best to reach what is ahead. So I run straight towards the goal in order to win the prize, which is God's call through Christ Jesus to the life above.

Paul's Farewell

As for me, the hour has come for me to be sacrificed; the time is here for me to leave this life. I have done my best in the race, I have run the full distance, I have kept the faith. And now the prize of victory is waiting for me, the crown of righteousness which the Lord, the righteous Judge, will give me on that Day — and not only to me, but to all those who wait with love for him to appear.